Disorders of the Self

PERSONALITY-GUIDED PSYCHOLOGY BOOK SERIES

THEODORE MILLON, SERIES EDITOR

Personality-Guided Therapy for Posttraumatic Stress Disorder
George Everly Jr. and Jeffrey M. Lating
Personality-Guided Therapy in Behavioral Medicine
Robert G. Harper
Personality-Guided Forensic Psychology
Robert J. Craig
Personality-Guided Relational Psychotherapy
Jeffrey J. Magnavita
Personality-Guided Cognitive–Behavioral Therapy
Paul R. Rasmussen
Personality-Guided Behavior Therapy
Richard F. Farmer and Rosemery O. Nelson-Grey
Personality-Guided Therapy for Depression
Neil R. Bockian
Disorders of the Self: A Personality-Guided Approach
Marshall L. Silverstein

Disorders of the Self

A PERSONALITY-GUIDED APPROACH

Marshall L. Silverstein

Series Editor Theodore Millon

AMERICAN PSYCHOLOGICAL ASSOCIATION

WASHINGTON, DC

KH

Published by
American Psychological Association
750 First Street, NE
Washington, DC 20002
www.apa.org

To order
APA Order Department
P.O. Box 92984
Washington, DC 20090-2984
Tel: (800) 374-2721; Direct: (202) 336-5510
Fax: (202) 336-5502; TDD/TTY: (202) 336-6123
Online: www.apa.org/books/
E-mail: order@apa.org

In the U.K., Europe, Africa, and the Middle East, copies may be ordered from
American Psychological Association
3 Henrietta Street
Covent Garden, London
WC2E 8LU England

Typeset in Goudy by Stephen McDougal, Mechanicsville, MD

Printer: United Book Press, Baltimore, MD
Cover Designer: Berg Design, Albany, NY
Technical/Production Editor: Harriet Kaplan

The opinions and statements published are the responsibility of the authors, and such opinions and statements do not necessarily represent the policies of the American Psychological Association.

Library of Congress Cataloging-in-Publication Data

Silverstein, Marshall L.
  Disorders of the self : a personality-guided approach / by Marshall L. Silverstein. — 1st ed.
    p. cm. — (Personality-guided psychology series)
  Includes bibliographical references and indexes.
  ISBN-13: 978-1-59147-430-2
  ISBN-10: 1-59147-430-2
  1. Personality disorders. 2. Separation-individuation. 3. Self psychology. I. Title.
II. Series: Personality-guided psychology.

  RC554.S55 2006
  616.85'81—dc22   2006000975

British Library Cataloguing-in-Publication Data
A CIP record is available from the British Library.

Printed in the United States of America
First Edition

2/7/08

CONTENTS

Series Foreword . . . .   *vii*

Acknowledgments . . . .   *ix*

Introduction   3

I. **Theoretical Foundations . . . .**   **9**

   Chapter 1.   Theoretical Introduction   11

   Chapter 2.   Narcissistic Personality Disorder   27

II. **Devitalization: The Unmirrored Self (Schizoid, Schizotypal, and Avoidant Personality Disorders) . . . .**   **59**

   Chapter 3.   Descriptive Psychopathology and Theoretical
                 Viewpoints: Schizoid, Schizotypal, and
                 Avoidant Personality Disorders   61

   Chapter 4.   A Self Psychological Viewpoint: Schizoid,
                 Schizotypal, and Avoidant Personality
                 Disorders   73

III. **Forestalling Fragmentation (Paranoid, Obsessive–
      Compulsive, and Borderline Personality Disorders) . . . .**   **95**

   Chapter 5.   Descriptive Psychopathology and Theoretical
                 Viewpoints: Paranoid, Obsessive–Compulsive,
                 and Borderline Personality Disorders   97

Chapter 6.   A Self Psychological Viewpoint: Paranoid,
              Obsessive–Compulsive, and Borderline
              Personality Disorders   115

IV. Alternative Pathways for Preserving a Cohesive Self
    (Dependent, Histrionic, and Antisocial Personality
    Disorders)   143

     Chapter 7.   Descriptive Psychopathology and Theoretical
                   Viewpoints: Dependent, Histrionic, and
                   Antisocial Personality Disorders   145

     Chapter 8.   A Self Psychological Viewpoint: Dependent,
                   Histrionic, and Antisocial Personality
                   Disorders   171

 V. Other Disorders of the Self (Depressive Personality
    Disorder, Disorders of the Self and Somatic Reactivity,
    and Disavowal and the Vertical Split)   203

     Chapter 9.   Depressive Personality Disorder   205

     Chapter 10.   Disorders of the Self and Somatic Reactivity . .   233

     Chapter 11.   Disavowal: The Vertical Split   249

Afterword   263

References   273

Author Index   299

Subject Index   305

About the Author   315

SERIES FOREWORD

The turn of the 20th century saw the emergence of psychological interest in the concept of individual differences, the recognition that the many realms of scientific study then in vogue displayed considerable variability among "laboratory subjects." Sir Francis Galton in Great Britain and many of his disciples, notably Charles Spearman in England, Alfred Binet in France, and James McKeen Cattell in the United States, laid the groundwork for recognizing that intelligence was a major element of import in what came to be called *differential psychology*. Largely through the influence of psychoanalytic thought, and then only indirectly, did this new field expand the topic of individual differences in the direction of character and personality.

And so here we are at the dawn of the 21st century, ready to focus our attentions ever more seriously on the subject of personality trait differences and their impact on a wide variety of psychological subjects—how they impinge on behavioral medicine outcomes, alter gerontological and adolescent treatment, regulate residential care programs, affect the management of depressive and PTSD patients, transform the style of cognitive–behavioral and interpersonal therapies, guide sophisticated forensic and correctional assessments—a whole bevy of important themes that typify where psychologists center their scientific and applied efforts today.

It is toward the end of alerting psychologists who work in diverse areas of study and practice that the present series, entitled *Personality-Guided Psychology*, has been developed for publication by the American Psychological Association. The originating concept underlying the series may be traced to Henry Murray's seminal proposal in his 1938 volume, *Explorations in Personality*, in which he advanced a new field of study termed *personology*. It took its contemporary form in a work of mine, published in 1999 under the title *Personality-Guided Therapy*.

The utility and relevance of personality as a variable is spreading in all directions, and the series sets out to illustrate where things stand today. As will be evident as the series' publication progresses, the most prominent work at present is found with creative thinkers whose efforts are directed toward enhancing a more efficacious treatment of patients. We hope to demonstrate, further, some of the newer realms of application and research that lie just at the edge of scientific advances in our field. Thus, we trust that the volumes included in this series will help us look beyond the threshold of the present and toward the vast horizon that represents all of psychology. Fortunately, there is a growing awareness that personality variables can be a guiding factor in all spheres of study. We trust the series will provide a map of an open country that encourages innovative ventures and provides a foundation for investigators who wish to locate directions in which they themselves can assume leading roles.

Theodore Millon, PhD, DSc
Series Editor

ACKNOWLEDGMENTS

I am grateful to Theodore Millon for his invitation to take on the problem of conceptualizing personality disorders from a self psychological perspective. Millon has long been one of the most scholarly and influential thinkers about personality and its disorders, and his interest in self psychology has added an important voice in support of its value as a personality theory. I also appreciate the support of Long Island University for granting me a sabbatical leave to complete this book. I thank Raina Kirshy and David D'Alessio for their able assistance in compiling references. I value the keen eyes of Sara Chilton, Edward Friedel, Geoff Goodman, and Robert Keisner, who read and commented on earlier versions of sections of the manuscript. As always, I am especially indebted to Joanne Marengo, Michael Simon, and Marian Tolpin for their sustaining support.

Disorders of the Self

INTRODUCTION

There are many concepts of personality and many theories about its disturbances. Psychoanalysis was the predominant viewpoint for thinking about personality disorders during much of the last century, but its theories have become less influential as interest has recently shifted toward delineating a reliable system for the classification of these disorders. Benefiting from the multiaxial approach to diagnosis that has influenced the past three editions of the *Diagnostic and Statistical Manual of Mental Disorders* (DSM; American Psychiatric Association, 1980, 1987, 1994), the fields of psychiatry and psychology now strive to achieve a better understanding about the domain of personality disorders (Axis II of the *DSM*).

As personality disorder theorists moved toward emphasizing nosology and refining reliable instruments for clinical assessment, psychoanalysis focused its attention elsewhere, attempting to reconcile its newer viewpoints with Freud's classical drive theory and ego psychology. One of these newer theories was the psychology of the self, or *self psychology*, which Heinz Kohut introduced at first as a theory of narcissism (Kohut, 1959, 1966, 1971). As his work progressed, Kohut (1977, 1984) broadened its purview to represent a formulation of personality centering on the self as a fulcrum for understanding many forms of psychopathology. As a result, self psychology's emphasis on disorders of the self was concerned more with differentiating its concepts from mainstream psychoanalysis than with diagnosis, including that of narcissistic personality disorder. Self psychology began reconceptualizing neuroses and personality disorders as disturbances of self-cohesion. Moreover, other psychoanalytic perspectives began to emerge. Some—like intersubjectivity theory—were closely allied with self psychology, whereas others—like relational psychoanalysis—evolved from a different tradition.

One implication of these developments has been a widening gulf between the foci of interest within psychoanalysis (including self psychology) and contemporary personality disorder theory and research. Where psychoanalysis has struggled with a conflict-versus-deficit model of psychopathology, the field of personality disorders has been primarily concerned with redefining what constitutes personality disorders and how they should be assessed.

Against this backdrop, my purpose in this book is to extend a self psychological viewpoint to understanding personality disorders as they are currently designated on Axis II. Self psychology's concepts about the cohesiveness of the self and means of sustaining its viability, which have not previously been considered in this way, add another perspective on reconsidering the life struggles and affective states of patients with personality disorders. Thus, I will discuss an approach in which the disorders on Axis II are recast as disorders of the self, centering on combating devitalization, forestalling fragmentation, and seeking alternative pathways to a cohesive self. This way of conceptualizing Axis II is intended to complement a descriptive psychopathology of Axis II disorders without regard to the differential merits of categorical and dimensional approaches—one of the issues that at present occupies considerable interest in the area of diagnostic nosology. I do not intend to suggest that these life struggles with self-cohesion should be construed as potential dimensions for classification, but neither do I wish to imply that I am championing a categorical approach by organizing my discussion around discrete Axis II disorders as they are presently defined. Although I appreciate the importance of achieving a satisfactory framework for classifying personality disorders, I will say only that the case for an optimal or superior conceptual approach will need to be decided in another way. My goal in this volume is to demonstrate how self psychological views may potentially add to and deepen an understanding of the disorders as they are presently denoted on Axis II.

To say that this book is about self psychology is itself too broad a characterization. To be precise, this is a book about a particular school of psychoanalytic self psychology—Kohut's original (1959, 1966, 1971) and subsequently expanded (1977, 1984, 1996) views—with only passing mention of other developments within self psychology. Thus, my focus rests with Kohut's formulation, which is sometimes referred to as *traditional* or *classical* self psychology. Though I will briefly mention other contemporary self psychological views, my main emphasis will be on Kohut's framework and that of colleagues working closely with him. I will suggest that a cautious reintegration of a psychoanalytic formulation such as Kohut's self psychology can add a deeper layer of understanding to the framework built on descriptive symptoms such as those of the *DSM* or the *International Classification of Diseases* (World Health Organization, 1992). However, it is always useful to remember that such descriptive approaches were never intended to explain etiologies or ways of conceptualizing personality disorders.

In chapter 1, I establish a frame of reference for the self psychological perspective I propose by discussing several issues concerning what remains unsettled about the definition of personality disorders. I briefly describe several recent important developments in personality disorder research—such as uniform diagnostic criteria and assessment—and some of the dilemmas surrounding them. I also briefly comment on some related issues, such as continuity between normal personality development and psychopathology, comorbidity, and Axis II disorders as spectrumlike variants of Axis I disorders.

I also consider in chapter 1 differences between the conflict model of psychopathology, in classical drive theory and psychoanalytic ego psychology, and the deficit model of psychopathology, such as that represented by self psychology. I describe how self psychology developed as a reaction to mainstream psychoanalysis and originated with its theory of narcissistic personality disorder—the disorder that self psychology first addressed.

In chapter 2, I address important self psychological concepts in the context of a discussion of narcissistic personality disorder. I include Kohut's original ideas about the self and its disorders as well as ideas that began with Kohut's (1996) previously unpublished lectures originally delivered between 1972 and 1974, crystallizing with *The Restoration of the Self* (Kohut, 1977) and the posthumously published *How Does Analysis Cure?* (Kohut, 1984). I then present the reformulation I am suggesting for the other Axis II personality disorders. This formulation recharacterizes how the various stylistic behavior and symptom patterns of personality disorders represent deficits in self-cohesion. These three self-cohesion deficit patterns impede life functioning by interfering with patients' attempts to

1. sustain self-esteem in the face of devitalization or depletion (chaps. 3 and 4),
2. maintain self-cohesion when the self is threatened by fragmentation (chaps. 5 and 6), and
3. preserve a buoyant self by developing partially successful compensatory structures (chaps. 7 and 8).

Selfobjects strengthen the self by fostering self-cohesion. Self-selfobject functions characterize the relationships between the self and its selfobjects. The first pattern or organization of self–selfobject functions occurs when self states are predominantly characterized by *devitalization*, representing deficient mirroring. This constellation appears most clearly in schizoid, schizotypal, and avoidant personality disorders. After outlining in chapter 3 their descriptive psychopathology and several important theoretical viewpoints concerning these Axis II disorders, I present a self psychological reformulation in chapter 4. The central problem of the unmirrored self is that of maintaining its vitality when needs for affirmation or admiration have been ignored or are insufficient. (The mirroring, idealization, and twinship selfobject functions are described in detail in chap. 2.) What becomes undermined in this group of Axis II disorders is the securing of an engaged, enthusiastic response to mirroring selfobject needs. Thus, distanced withdrawal or aversiveness become entrenched as the prevailing ways such patients react to people around them, who fail to sustain the patient's vigorous or cohesive self. Accordingly, schizoid, schizotypal, and avoidant patients conduct their lives by removing themselves from the painful rebuffs resulting from chronically ignored needs for admiration.

The second self-cohesion deficit pattern represents attempts to *forestall fragmentation* when the self is threatened by destabilization. This pattern is prominent in paranoid, obsessive–compulsive, and borderline personality disorders, and I discuss these disorders' psychopathology and their theoretical understanding in chapter 5; chapter 6 presents a self psychological reformulation. Such patients fear that the fragile self-cohesion they manage to sustain is brittle and may easily come apart. Their lives are built around safeguarding themselves against threats to their intactness, threats that reexpose them to fragmentation or breakup of the self.

The third pattern is concerned with *alternative paths for preserving a cohesive self*, in which compensatory structures, such as those seen in dependent, histrionic, and antisocial personality disorders, develop to repair chronically injured self-cohesion deficits. I begin in chapter 7 by surveying these disorders' descriptive psychopathology and other theoretical explanatory approaches before presenting a self psychological approach for understanding compensatory structures in chapter 8.

I also consider disturbances that are not presently considered personality disorders in the nomenclature of the fourth edition of the *DSM* (*DSM–IV*; American Psychiatric Association, 1994). One is under consideration for possible inclusion in a future version—depressive personality disorder (chap. 9). Two other conditions described, though not presently considered personality disorders in the *DSM*, nevertheless represent mental disorders whose characteristics are consistent with the general definition of *personality disorder* as a pattern of deviant inner experience and behavior that is enduring, inflexible, and pervasive and that produces clinical impairment (i.e., harmful dysfunction). Chapter 10 describes a personality pattern that either aggravates or minimizes somatic reactivity, a pattern I consider to be substantially independent of Axis I somatoform disorders. Chapter 11 describes a personality pattern or organization that Kohut (1971) and Goldberg (1999) designated the *vertical split*. My purpose in describing these three disorders is not to suggest their consideration as formally recognized Axis II disorders, but rather to characterize these interesting disturbances as chronic, ingrained (enduring) personality patterns that are readily amenable to explanation from a self psychological framework; indeed, self psychologists have considerable experience working with such disturbances.

This general overview of the organization of the chapters that follow provides a roadmap of my specific subgoals. The guiding principle is first and foremost my attempt to comprehend how undermined self-cohesion compromises the functioning of patients with personality disorders in their struggles with living. Self psychology has not previously applied its theoretical framework to this broad group of disorders in a systematic way. These formulations stand apart from concerns about an optimal classification framework—be it categorical, dimensional, or a hybrid of the two. Rather, I attempt to introduce a way of regarding disturbances of self-cohesion that should be considered in any rubric for meaningfully conceptualizing disorders of personality. My proposal for this reorganization is centered on already existing categories, in spite of the unsettled matter of categorical and dimensional models and the problem of substantial comorbidity among Axis II disorders. My plan for reorganizing the categorical disorders of Axis II according to major premises of self psychology accepts the *DSM–IV* classification as a conventional standard; this plan is not intended to represent a solution to the categorical–dimensional model dilemma. Consequently, I will not be suggesting a reformulation of Axis II disorders as a classificatory scheme. I will thus present a recharacterization intended to survive any possible reorganizations of Axis II based on dimensional traits, because dimensions themselves represent descriptions of phenomena that remain open to various ways of being theoretically understood. At present, however, it seems unlikely that self psychological concepts can be expressed satisfactorily as dimensional traits.

Though I will be reconsidering the 10 personality disorders as they presently exist in the *DSM–IV*, I do not propose this approach as a superior or even as an alternative rubric for classification. Moreover, my recharacterization of Axis II disorders is not intended to suggest a need to modify the existing odd–eccentric, dramatic–disorganized, and anxious–fearful clusters, which are themselves a subject of some dispute.

I

THEORETICAL FOUNDATIONS

1

THEORETICAL INTRODUCTION

If one wishes to extend the propositions of any theory of personality, including those of self psychology, to explain personality disorders, one must consider as well the broader context of contemporary personality disorder theory and research. Consequently, it is important to know what remains unsettled about the definition of personality disorders to know where a viewpoint such as self psychology might contribute something new and, one hopes, illuminating. Before discussing how self psychology provides a unique perspective on personality disorders, in this chapter I describe several recent developments and dilemmas in personality disorder research involving uniform diagnostic criteria and assessment and continuity between normal personality development and psychopathology, classification, and comorbidity.

I also discuss in this chapter the relationship between self psychology and psychoanalytic theory, particularly classical drive theory and ego psychological views, to show why self psychology emerged initially to address a clinical problem—the treatment of narcissism. I emphasize how self psychology represented a reaction to psychoanalytic concepts that had seemed limited, particularly in their explanations of severe personality (character) pathology such as narcissistic and borderline personality disorders. I frame this discussion around the evolution of self psychology as a deficit model of psychopathology, representing a reformulation of the conflict model of earlier psychoanalytic formulations. I also show how self psychology's concepts extended to mental disorders beyond narcissism as well as to normal development.

CURRENT ISSUES CONCERNING PERSONALITY DISORDERS

Although the literature on personality disorders has been dominated in recent years by concerns about classification of these conditions, the field also has been struggling to better delineate well-defined diagnostic criteria for disorders of personality and how to differentiate disturbances from normal personality features. I consider several of these issues below.

Diagnostic Criteria and Assessment

Attempts to define personality and related concepts of character and temperament have long histories, yet a coherent point of view acceptable to most personality theorists remains elusive. There can be little doubt that the neo-Kraepelinian tradition in modern descriptive psychiatry as well as trait theories' influence on factor analytic psychometric models contributed to greater clinical and scientific precision. Nevertheless, the largely observational reports of the first half of the 20th century and even some pre-20th-century observations have never been surpassed for the richness and perceptiveness of their insights.

As with the many theories of personality that exist, classifications of personality disorders have also failed to meet with uniform agreement over many decades. Different terms have been used at different points in time to denote such disorders (e.g., passive–dependent vs. dependent personality), and differing points of view have prevailed regarding whether certain disorders should even be designated as disorders of personality (e.g., depressive personality). What has remained generally constant, however, is the syndrome approach to defining such disorders, more recently containing inclusion and sometimes exclusion criteria. This is the long-standing categorical approach to classification, but even it has been seriously questioned in recent years, specifically in terms of its adequacy to cogently explain enough of the variability among disorders of personality (Livesley, 1995). A persuasive case has been argued for a shift from the categorical approach to either a dimensional approach or an undetermined hybrid of the categorical and dimensional models. Consequently, it remains uncertain whether an optimal classification of personality disorders should continue to use discrete categories or some as yet unknown combination of traits or dimensions. Furthermore, influenced by spectrum concepts of psychopathology, some have suggested that several Axis II disturbances (e.g., obsessive–compulsive or depressive personality disorders) may not represent discrete entities as much as variants of Axis I disorders (Siever & Davis, 1991).

One impetus for establishing reliable diagnostic definitions of the personality disorders originated with the problem of the diagnostic definition of schizophrenia. As recently as 30 years ago, progress in understanding basic mechanisms and core deficits in schizophrenia was hampered by different diagnostic definitions. These definitions ranged from the broad, inclusive U.S. definition emphasizing Bleuler's (1911/1950) primary symptoms to a far narrower definition favored in European psychiatry of a nuclear syndrome based on Kraepelin's (1919) emphasis on a progressive, deteriorating course or Schneider's (1959) first-rank symptoms. It was only with the introduction of the third edition of the *Diagnostic and Statistical Manual of Mental Disorders* (*DSM–III*; American Psychiatric Association, 1980) and its important forerunners—Feighner et al.'s (1972) criteria and the Research Diagnostic Criteria (Spitzer, Endicott, & Robins, 1978)—that the U.S. definition became relatively standardized and corresponded more closely to most international criteria represented by the *International Classification of Diseases* (ICD; World Health Organization, 1992).

Until the *DSM–III* was introduced, clinical definitions of personality disorders and delineations of their dominant features were even more imprecise than were those of schizophrenia. Improvement in defining schizophrenia with the *DSM–III* led to better diagnostic differentiation between it and affective disorders, particularly bipolar I and bipolar II disorders and, later, schizoaffective disorder. The diagnostic criteria of the *DSM–III* and its successive editions also achieved greater precision in defining other Axis I disorders and paved the way for improving the clarity of personality disorder descriptions. With this, personality disorders achieved greater distinctiveness as discrete disorders, and more careful studies of diagnostic overlap (comorbidity) became possible, both among the Axis II disorders and between Axis II and Axis I disorders. Although the problem of comorbidity among personality disorders remains unsettled, relatively clear-cut criteria for identifying personality disorders facilitates their scientific study.

Accordingly, as Axis II conditions became progressively operationalized, there emerged new instruments to assess the presence and relative prominence of personality disorder features. Personality disorder scales became increasingly sophisticated, with interview-based instruments benefiting from the precision of measurement achieved on inventories such as the Present State Examination (Wing, Cooper, & Sartorius, 1974) and the Schedule for Affective Disorders and Schizophrenia (Spitzer & Endicott, 1978). Self-report scales benefited from greater attention to psychometric properties such as item analysis, scale construction, and diagnostic efficiency statistics. Some of these interview-based or self-report inventories were theory-based instruments like the Millon Clinical Multiaxial Inventory (Millon, Davis, & Millon, 1994) and the Schedule for Nonadaptive and Adaptive Personality (Clark, 1993). Other instruments included the relatively atheoretical Structured Clinical Interview for the *DSM–IV* Axis II Personality Disorders (First, Gibbon, Spitzer, Williams, & Benjamin, 1997), the International Personality Disorder Examination (Loranger, 1999), and the Personality Disorder Interview (Widiger, Mangine, Corbitt, Ellis, & Thomas, 1995). Still other instruments were tailored for particular conditions, such as the Diagnostic Interview for Borderlines (Zanarini, Gunderson, Frankenburg, & Chauncey, 1989) and the Psychopathy Checklist (Hare, 1991), or for examining theoretical formulations, such as the Temperament and Character Inventory (Cloninger, Przybeck, Svrakic, & Wetzel, 1994). The Shedler–Westen Assessment Procedure (SWAP–200; Westen & Shedler, 1999a, 1999b) was designed to jointly assess elements of categorical and dimensional approaches.

Normal Personality Development and Psychopathology

Despite their unquestionable importance, delineating standardized criterion sets and ensuring their reliable assessment have not solved a number of theoretical problems regarding personality disorders. Nor has refined assessment of personality features brought greater clarity to theories of normal personality and its development, such as idiographic versus nomothetic bases for understanding personality; differential influences of genetic and environmental determinants; nonindependence among normal temperament, character dispositions, and pathological variants of such patterns or traits; consistency of personality or degree of resistance to change; and longitudinal course and outcome of personality disorders.

Even defining what is meant by *normal personality* is unresolved, including differentiating personality from concepts such as character and temperament. Rutter (1987) differentiated temperament from personality by describing personality as a broader range of attributes than temperamental traits. Thus, personality and its disorders were seen in part as outgrowths of temperament. Cloninger, Svrakic, and Przybeck (1993) identified three components of character (self-directedness, cooperativeness, and self-transcendence), regarding them as learning- or experience-influenced dimensions. Cloninger et al. further distinguished character from heritable temperament dimensions.

Concepts of character, personality, and temperament also have different meanings in personality theory. Rutter (1987), for example, commented that most definitions of temperament incorporate varying combinations of emotionality, activity level, and sociability. Although researchers may disagree about properties thought to constitute temperament, it is generally understood that individual differences in temperament are measurable phenomena that show good predictability in both normal and pathological populations.

Because temperament has neurobiological and genetic correlates, it affects risk for psychopathology. Rutter (1987) regarded temperamental dimensions as characteristics that appear early in childhood and remain stable over time. Millon (1996) described various temperament theorists' viewpoints, among which W. McDougall's (1932) was noteworthy for taking into account the dimensions of intensity, persistence, and affectivity. Cloninger et al.'s (1993) identification of four temperament dimensions in adulthood (novelty seeking, harm avoidance, reward dependence, and persistence) was also important in differentiating between temperament and character dimensions and in extending these dimensions to the study of personality disorders.

Another unresolved issue in personality disorder research concerns the matter of normality and psychopathology as points on a continuum. There seems to be reasonably good agreement that dimensional factor structures are comparable in normal and abnormal populations. Nevertheless, it is still unsettled whether personality traits are different in kind when they occur in personality disorders or whether personality disorders represent exacerbations of personality traits. For example, in Siever and Davis's (1991) model of biological influences on personality, dimensions such as affective instability and anxiety/inhibition can range from normal levels to pathological manifestations. Dimensions such as affective instability intersect with both Axis I and Axis II disorders; however, the reliability of assessment of such dimensions on Axis I and Axis II may not be comparable.

Classification and Comorbidity

Perhaps the most crucial contemporary theoretical concern in personality disorder research is the controversy between advocates of retaining the traditional categorical model for Axis II and advocates of a dimensional model based on traits such as the so-called Big Five personality factors (Costa & Widiger, 1994). The arguments surrounding this issue are more complex than this summary will show. However, a succinct statement of the problem concerns the matter of an optimal classification strategy—whether this should be the categorical approach in current use that is based on neo-Kraepelinian concepts or whether the current approach should be replaced by a dimensional approach representing patients' relative positions on some unspecified number of continuous distributions of traits. A dimensional model has also been suggested as one potential resolution of the comorbidity problem plaguing current categorical definitions of personality disorders. The problem of comorbidity and the matter of personality disorders as normal variants of personality traits also disposed Widiger (1993), Shea (1995), and Clark (1999) to favor some form of a dimensional model.

Critics of categorical models have also pointed out that poor validity of the Axis II–defined categories may be attributable to dichotomizing continuous variables to determine presence or absence of diagnostic criteria. Problematic concerns about validity are further complicated by poor reliability of diagnoses over time, thus calling into question the stability of categorically based definitions. Moreover, the clinical utility of several Axis II categories, including dependent and avoidant personality disorders, has been questioned, insofar as differentiating among some personality disorders is frequently inconsequential for treatment or prognosis. In addition, Jang and Vernon (2001) and Kilzieh and Cloninger (1993) pointed out that overlapping and inconsistent categories of Axis II disorders lead to unsuitable phenotypes for studying genetic influences on personality disorders.

Proponents of the categorical model have called attention to a need to balance the worthwhile benefits of a dimensional approach against the problem of fractionating personality into some number of scalable dimensions or configurations. One prominent example of dimension-based approaches is the five-factor model, based on a concept first proposed by Fiske (1949). Now best known as the Big Five (Costa & McCrae, 1992), its factors are Neuroticism, Extraversion, Openness to Experience, Conscientiousness, and Agreeableness. Other important dimensional models include Eysenck's (1987) three personality dimensions and Cloninger et al.'s (1993) seven factors comprising four temperament and three character dimensions. Criticisms of dimensional models (Kernberg, 1996; McAdams, 1992; Millon, 1991) have questioned the clinical sense inherent in dimensional approaches. For example, Kernberg (1996) doubted whether such factors adequately described normal personality in sufficient depth. He also questioned their clinical utility, at least from the viewpoint of psychoanalytic theory. Kernberg further questioned the clinical reality behind the notion of equivalence of dimensions derived from factor analysis, particularly concerning the psychopathology of personality disorders. On a similar note, McAdams (1992) referred to the five-factor model as a "psychology of the stranger" (p. 348), characterizing its traitlike structure as being insufficiently complete and integrative to explain the contextual and conditional influences on personality.

Frances, Pincus, Widiger, Davis, and First (1990) and Millon (1991) observed that no classification system to date has managed to capture faithfully the clinical realities of psychopathology—whether categorical or dimensional in type—and that the goal of classification should be to provide anchors for furthering understanding. However, Millon also noted that dimensional models preserve more clinical diagnostic information than categorical models, which tend to overemphasize one or two attributes, sometimes to the exclusion of others. Further, dimensional models usually take account of poorly understood (and thus frequently ignored) mixed or atypical syndromes and ill-fitting cases more effectively than categorical models.

R. D. Davis and Millon (1993) pointed out the tendency for scale configurations to become reified into categories in dimensional models. Dimensions may ultimately become oversimplified "so that we are left with essentially the same problems we have today" (p. 107). This observation is not unfamiliar in diagnostic nosology. For example, with the *DSM–III*, narrowing the broad U.S. definition of schizophrenia meant that many formerly diagnosed schizophrenics would subsequently receive diagnoses of ill-defined or atypical affective disorders. Thus, reducing the noise inherent in a broad definition of one disorder may not resolve but merely shift the diagnostic problems to another category of disorders. A similar problem may thus be created by shifting from a categorical model to a dimensional model for classifying the personality disorders on Axis II.

Other heuristic approaches have been suggested in which flexible, hybrid prototype models could combine elements of both categorical and dimensional approaches. One approach relies on philosophy of science considerations to generate theory-guided explanations. For example, R. D. Davis and Millon (1993) argued that a prototypical approach could use conceptually grounded ideas to organize empirically established facts. Westen and Shedler (1999a, 1999b) suggested a second viewpoint, echoing Meehl (1954); Meehl commented that clinicians and statistical approaches both perform well but for different functions. Westen and Shedler used a prototype-matching approach based on a Q-sort method to obtain clinicians' sortings of statements about patients' personality traits and symptoms (SWAP–200). These statements were then submitted to a factor analysis to aggregate statements into clusters (Q factors) that Westen and Shedler defined as templates of seven theoretically consistent categories of personality disorder. A matrix of correlations among the seven Q factors generated a profile of personality disorder scores for each patient, thus providing a dimensional basis for diagnosis in addition to a categorical classification. The categorical classification was based on threshold cutpoints derived from levels of certainty about the closeness of matching Q factors and Axis II categories. A third approach to create a hybrid blending of categorical and dimensional approaches is the multistage prototype approach recommended by Livesley (1987, 1995). Yet a fourth approach is one that Blashfield and McElroy (1995) termed *hierarchical*. They suggested that categorical and dimensional models need not be thought of as antithetical but rather as complementary. According to this view, dimensions may be nested within categories, but certain categories would take on greater salience than others in assigning diagnoses and understanding mechanisms of personality and personality disorder.

Widiger (1992) criticized prototype solutions for not offering a better alternative for achieving reliable diagnoses. He argued that clinicians invariably apply different thresholds to criteria for inclusion or exclusion, despite generally improved specification of these criteria (criterion sets). Widiger also argued that too often, categorical models force diagnostic decisions to be reduced to arbitrary dichotomizations, consequently lowering their reliability because quantitative information about clinical dimensions is sacrificed. In addition, there is a problem of *information variance*, which Endicott and Spitzer (1978) described as differences in diagnostic data or information obtained from clinicians' ratings of patients' self-reports. Nearly all classification approaches are plagued by compromised validity because of patients' diminished self-awareness, which may influence patients' capacity to differentiate between shallow emotions and accurate affect states of clinical magnitude. This problem is particularly relevant to variation among patients' numerous subtle judgments about themselves that determine threshold levels of presence or absence of symptoms and signs. Westen and Shedler (2000) and Millon (1996) also considered the present version of Axis II to be insufficiently comprehensive, particularly because it does not adequately account for important dysphoric or depressive phenomena and provides only an appendix containing criterion sets proposed for consideration in later revisions of the *DSM*.

Personality disorder theorists often refer to Plato's discussion of the problem of "carving nature at its joints" (Hempel, 1965, p. 147) with respect to discovering regularities of nature. Nevertheless, dilemmas such as those outlined in this section require approaches that are independent of specific theories. Resolving the complex issues of classification of personality disorders will ultimately require a meaningful theoretical proposition to synthesize the observable phenotypes with various latent taxa that have been proposed as better solutions, be they mathematical (psychometric), genetic, or evolutionary in nature (Millon, 1990, 1991).

PSYCHOANALYTIC VIEWPOINTS ABOUT PERSONALITY DISORDERS: CONFLICT AND DEFICIT MODELS

As the study of personality disorders evolved in the directions outlined in the preceding sections, psychoanalysis has generated a less formative influence on personality disorder theory and research. In consideration of developments in thinking about nosology and their influence on the *DSM* and *ICD*, a declining interest in psychoanalysis was perhaps inevitable, particularly given its imprecise concepts such as psychoneurosis and neurotic character. At the same time, however, there has been considerable interest in narcissistic and borderline personality disorders. Views concerning these disorders were substantially influenced by psychoanalytic ideas, and these disorders were thought to properly belong with the group of Axis II personality disorders.

Although precision in diagnostic nosology unquestionably represents an important advance, at the same time it must necessarily be limited in conceptual breadth to achieve a degree of etiologic neutrality acceptable to multiple theoretical points of view. But the relative neglect of efforts to develop a meaningful way to understand in depth the experiences that precipitate or sustain chronic disturbances like personality disorders exacts a toll. Notable exceptions are broadly integrative conceptualizations such as those advanced by Millon (1996), Cloninger and colleagues (Cloninger, Bayon, & Svrakic, 1998; Cloninger et al., 1993), Westen and Shedler (1999a, 1999b), and Schore (2003a, 2003b). Nevertheless, psychoanalysis and other personality theories provide important perspectives for understanding the phenomenological experience and inner lives of patients with personality disorders. The diminished influence of these theories constrains this level of understanding, regardless of how the problem of categorical and dimensional classification models will ultimately be resolved. Bornstein (2005), however, recently proposed a way to integrate psychoanalytic theory with Millon's (1990, 1996) integrative personological framework.

Recent developments in psychoanalytic theory have taken a different direction than those of contemporary personality disorder theorists. The more influential insights of psychoanalytic theory should not be discarded, however, even though vestiges of psychoanalytic formulations contributed their share to the problems of validity and reliability of personality disorder syndromes that still plague the field today. Psychoanalysis remains particularly important for understanding subtle overtones of characterologically ingrained personality disturbances.

Hardly any of the unsettled matters outlined in the previous section were considered problematic when psychoanalysis first emerged as a theory of mental functioning and as a technique of treatment. Its most active development occurred at a time when understanding of psychiatric disorders was far more limited than it is today. Indeed, except for the psychoses and psychiatric aspects of neurological diseases, the psychopathologic conditions that were recognized early in the past century were primarily limited to the psychoneuroses such as hysteria, obsessional neurosis, and phobias. Freud (1914/ 1957b) and Abraham (1911/1927b) typically considered the psychoses to fall outside the reach of clinical psychoanalysis, which was the predominant treatment option available at that time. A general, though not well understood, recognition of character neuroses was that they were asymptomatic manifestations of the psychoneuroses. It was not until W. Reich (1933/1949) extended psychoanalytic theory and technique to these conditions that attention to character pathology took hold.

For the most part, contemporary psychoanalysis has not addressed personality disorders with any particular interest, although developments in psychoanalysis have occurred in other theoretical areas. I discuss in the following section psychoanalytic views that may be particularly useful for understanding personality disorders. In emphasizing etiologic views of personality formation or structure, I reserve the term *character* (based on Freud's, Fenichel's, and Reich's use of the term) to denote personality and the term *character disorder* to denote psychopathology of personality or personality disorder.

Early Psychoanalytic Formulations: A Conflict Model

Freud's early writings (1908/1959a, 1915/1957c, 1916/1957d) on character formation emphasized fixations at or regressions to the psychosexual developmental stages; thus, he described oral, anal, phallic, and genital characters. This work was influenced largely by his early attention to problems of the anal character type that emerged from his analysis of the Rat Man (Freud, 1909/1955). Fenichel's (1945) preference was to classify character disorders according to their more apparent manifestations, in which he identified phobic, obsessional, and hysteroid types. Freud (1915/1957c, 1916/1957d) observed that certain reactions to conflict did not produce symptom neuroses. Although such asymptomatic reaction formations were different from the psychoneuroses in their clinical presentation, their dynamic underpinnings were indistinguishable from the symptomatic forms from which they were derived. Thus, Freud understood character formation predominantly as an asymptomatic form of conflict. It represented an adaptation to obtain disguised gratification while forestalling anxiety, and thus it was ego syntonic. Baudry (1983) pointed out that Freud's early writings on the subject of character also seemed to imply the possibility that character formation could resemble a relatively healthy development not unlike sublimation.

Interest in character formation increased after Freud (1923/1961a, 1926/1959b) formulated the tripartite model that became the structural theory, leading to greater understanding of superego influences, masochism and aggression, and an increasing emphasis on analysis of resistance. But it was not until W. Reich's (1933/1949) technical contributions to psychoanalytic treatment that the systematic confrontation of resistances was advocated as the method of choice to analyze the nearly impenetrable defenses of a so-called character armor.

Anchored by the structural theory, Hartmann (1939) developed influential views of character formation as an adaptive pattern insofar as it becomes relatively autonomous or independent from its origins in conflict. The compromised but subtle disturbances in relationships, work accomplishment, and productivity or creativity ultimately become patients' chief complaints. Though patients are often spared the distress of a symptomatic neurosis, the absence of symptomatic psychopathology frequently comes at the price of chronic loneliness, isolation, or distrust. This typically interferes with intimacy in friendships or love relationships and with work or realizing life goals (Lax, 1989). Pathological exaggerations of character traits such as haughtiness, shyness, self-righteousness, politeness, or generosity thus become inflexible characterological manifestations of the personality, manifestations that are typically nonresponsive to environmental events. Many such patients report at most a general malaise or ennui as they dutifully go through the motions of living, all the while feeling that something is missing in their lives. A subclinical yet prolonged sense of emptiness or disaffection thus pervades their experiences of themselves and their relationships.

Self Psychology: A Deficit Model

Psychoanalytic views of character and its pathology link maladaptations in life to their roots in conflict in accord with drive or ego psychological theory. When Kohut (1966, 1971) introduced self psychology, his formulation of psychopathology from the outset attributed disturbances of personality and behavior to deficit states rather than to conflict. Kohut's early formulations centered on the narcissistic personality and behavior disorders, which had not previously been conceptualized satisfactorily in drive theory or ego psychological frameworks. Moreover, the narcissistic character had not proved amenable to psychoanalytic treatment informed by mainstream theoretical viewpoints. Kohut articulated a view of the self as a central agency of mental life, which differed from the prevailing formulation emphasizing drives seeking discharge and counterforces built up to modulate libidinal and aggressive impulses. Although Kohut did not reject this formulation, he called attention to the self as a center of experience or agency of the mind with its own line of development.

Kohut (1966, 1971) clearly regarded his concept of the self as an expansion of the structural theory of psychoanalysis. Though he considered self-cohesion to be more crucial than drives as a central fulcrum of the total personality, Kohut did not discard the conflict model as one of the fundamental principles of psychoanalytic theory. Kohut considered the self and drives as alternating between foreground and background in importance in a way that resembled Pine's (1988) view of four major theoretical concepts in psychoanalysis (drive, ego, object relations, and self). Pine considered these essential concepts as offering different foci of emphasis to guide thinking at various stages of the clinical process. In advocating that each of these reference points deserves a place in clinicians' minds, Pine likened these four psychologies of psychoanalysis to a set of tools that might be used flexibly to construct a house—his metaphor for the total functioning personality. Kohut, too, considered the self and its selfobject functions as a complementary view rather than as a view in opposition to mainstream psychoanalysis. Nevertheless, he frequently considered a deficit model to offer more efficacious explanations and treatment indications than a conflict model.

Kohut (1966, 1968, 1971) contended that psychopathology resulted from the chronic or pronounced failure of caregivers to provide sufficiently attuned responsiveness to sustain self-cohesion. Thus, failed empathic responsiveness from persons who were needed to provide what Kohut called *selfobject functions* led to deficits of self-cohesion. A selfobject is an internalized experience that functions to invigorate or strengthen the self, both in normal development as a legitimate need for sustaining self-cohesion, and in states of distress when its purpose is to restore or repair an injury to the self. *Self-selfobject* functions refer to the relationship between the constituents of the self—for example, its cohesiveness and vitality—and ways other people or ideals and values serve to shore up the self. Selfobject functions of mirroring, idealization, and twinship—which are described in greater detail in chapter 2—firm up or strengthen the cohesiveness of the developing self. Self psychology regards such selfobject deficits as frequently being more etiologically influential in causing psychopathology than intrapsychic conflict. For this reason, self psychology was an important development within psychoanalysis, because it expanded—and challenged—the prevailing ego psychological viewpoint. Moreover, its introduction of newly identified selfobject transferences substantially influenced technical approaches to treatment.

Although at first proposed as a theory of narcissism, Kohut's (1977, 1984) psychology of the self subsequently developed in such a way that it embraced much of psychopathology. With *The Restoration of the Self* (Kohut, 1977), Kohut expanded his clinical theory into a viewpoint that could no longer be regarded only as an important addition to mainstream psychoanalysis. In this work, Kohut denoted the self as the major fulcrum of psychological regulation. As the center of psychological existence, the self was considered to be more crucial than the ego of the structural theory of psychoanalysis. Self psychology's articulation of the self's predominant constituents became the focal point for understanding personality and its disorders, particularly how selfobject functions become important for sustaining and thus regulating self-cohesion.

Kohut (1977, 1984) continued to emphasize the developmental importance of empathic attunement for achieving self-cohesion. He pointed out that chronic experiences of selfobject failures produced an empty quality of depression, leaving some people feeling underpowered or devitalized. Affect states associated with depletion include feelings of being adrift in life; a lack of purpose or goals; and infrequent feelings of enthusiasm about oneself, one's work, or other people. Other patients perpetually seek out intensely held idealizing selfobject relationships, subsequently feeling let down and dropped when their need to perceive greatness or vigor is met with the disappointments that inevitably ensue. Kohut considered such phenomena to represent deficit states reflecting weakened cohesiveness of the self rather than products of conflict between drives and their counterforces (defenses).

In addition to the forms of narcissistic personality disorder Kohut (1968, 1971) first described, he noted that the same psychological dynamics of selfobject failures could also produce what he called *narcissistic behavior disorders*. The symptomatic manifestations of these disorders are often characterized by *disintegration products*—the clinical manifestations of sequelae of selfobject failures or disturbances of self-cohesion, such as addiction, a propensity for intense outbursts of helpless anger (narcissistic rage), or the sexualization of painful affect states (e.g., perversions, sexual masochism or sadism, promiscuity, and voyeuristic or exhibitionistic acts). Through addiction or sexualization, the patient attempts to achieve a momentary soothing to replace the developmentally expectable internalization of a self-soothing capacity that failed to develop. In contrast, a selfobject environment that welcomes and is empathically attuned to selfobject needs permits the patient to tolerate the inevitable disappointment of discovering the shortcomings of idealized or mirroring selfobjects. I will describe in greater detail in chapter 2 the selfobject functions and Kohut's description of the constituents of the self.

Some clinicians and investigators may not be aware of developments in self psychology beyond Kohut's (1971) early contributions. They may thus mistakenly assume that his subsequent work represented further articulation of concepts about narcissism. However, Kohut's work in the decade before his death in 1981 broadened his view of the self. In his later writings (Kohut, 1977, 1984), Kohut articulated how his viewpoints were both related to and different from Freud's major formulations. For example, he deemphasized oedipal conflict in personality formation, considering it to represent a normal display of vigor and excitement that becomes pathological only when the child is not responded to with welcoming enthusiasm (Kohut, 1984). Kohut thus reserved the term *oedipal complex* for the pathological disturbances arising from parents' misattuned reactions to their children's need for selfobject responsiveness during this period of development. For this reason, Kohut did not consider oedipal dynamics to be the central issue around which personality is built. He therefore did not regard its resolution during the course of an analysis to be necessary or essential. This view differed considerably from that of mainstream psychoanalysis at that time.

Related but still independent self psychological viewpoints about the self were also starting to appear, such as the intersubjectivity theory of mutual influence in dyads (Stolorow & Atwood, 1992; Stolorow, Brandchaft, & Atwood, 1987), motivational systems (Lichtenberg, 1989), attachment theory (Lichtenberg, 1983; Shane, Shane, & Gales, 1998), and observations of mother–infant interactions (Beebe & Lachmann, 2002; D. N. Stern, 1985). These emerging perspectives represented somewhat different approaches to understanding the self and its development than Kohut's and were formulated outside the scope of research and contemporary thinking about personality disorders. In addition, the authors of recently proposed views of relational psychoanalysis were in varying degrees influenced by Kohut's writings while striving to build a point of view and a hegemony of their own (Aron, 1996; Hoffmann, 1992; Mitchell, 1988). These authors considered the traditional self psychology of Kohut, even in its broadened view (Kohut, 1977, 1984), as being too theoretically linked with drive theory and ego psychology.

Fosshage (1992) commented that Kohut never satisfactorily resolved the matter of the independence of the self, as a center of initiative having its own line of development, from drives or the ego as the focus of psychological development and motivation. Fosshage claimed that the distinction was blurred between a so-called one-person psychology (such as ego psychology or object relations theory) and a two-person psychology (such as intersubjectivity theory, motivational systems theory, or relational psychoanalysis). Thus, it leaves unanswered the question whether self psychology should be considered a theory of intrapsychic processes (Wolf, 1988), an object relations theory (Bacal & Newman, 1990), or a theory of interpersonal interactions rather than the subjective or intrapsychic experience of interpersonal events.

From another perspective, Kernberg (1975) extended his views of borderline personality organization to encompass narcissistic personality disorder, considering both conditions as showing several essential dynamic features and ego weaknesses in common. Contemporaneously with Kohut's early development of self psychology in the middle 1960s and early 1970s, Kernberg's view remained anchored in ego psychology and object relations theory. It also did not pose the kind of revisionist challenge to mainstream psychoanalysis that self psychology represented. Moreover, Kohut (1971, 1977), unlike Kernberg (1975), was for the most part unconcerned with problems of comorbidity, differential diagnosis, and refining precise diagnostic criteria to differentiate among various personality disorders. Nonetheless, self psychology was interested in reconceptualizing as self disorders conditions such as addictions, eating disorders, psychotic states, antisocial or sociopathic personality, and some adolescent and child disturbances.

The influence of Kernberg's (1975) view of borderline personality organization was more familiar to many personality theorists and clinicians and to the developers of DSM–IV than was self psychological theory, particularly its broadened scope (Kohut, 1977, 1984). But as psychoanalytic theory became less influential on further refinements of Axis II, there was less interest in the explanatory potential of psychoanalytic formulations of either borderline or narcissistic personality disorders. Accordingly, the differential diagnostic significance of narcissistic and borderline disorders, including their relationship to affective disorders, became more important than their theoretical underpinnings as framed by either Kernberg or Kohut.

Even within the framework of what could be called a traditional (Kohutian) formulation of self psychology, views about the self—such as those of optimal responsiveness versus optimal frustration (Bacal, 1985; Bacal & Herzog, 2003), the vertical split (Goldberg, 1999, 2000), an expanded view of selfobject transferences (Wolf, 1988), and forward edge strivings (M. Tolpin, 2002)—all contributed in important ways to an understanding of the role of the self in normal development as well as in psychopathology. These developing and still emerging ideas have not been examined systematically within the framework of the psychopathology of personality disorders or in the diagnostic nomenclature represented by the DSM Axis II.

This brief description represents only a sketch of how the widened scope of self psychology has extended beyond problems of narcissism. Following chapter 2, which discusses narcissistic personality disorder based largely on Kohut's (1966, 1971, 1977) seminal contributions, the remaining chapters offer a way of understanding and conceptualizing personality disorders from a self psychological perspective in which I suggest that personality disorders can be viewed as disturbances of self-cohesion using Kohut's framework.

CONCLUSION

Attempts to define and explain personality have long histories, yet a coherent point of view acceptable to most personality theorists remains elusive. Psychoanalysis dominated psychiatric thinking during the first half of the 20th century. However, psychoanalytic theory developed independently of the descriptive tradition in psychiatry championed by Kraepelin (1923) and Bleuler (1911/1950) and the phenomenological tradition of Jaspers (1948) and Schneider (1959). There was little interface among these conceptual approaches.

This chapter has summarized independent developments in psychoanalysis and advances during recent decades in personality disorder research as the gulf between these fields widened. I began by considering prominent issues of concern for contemporary personality disorder theory and research, including the overriding question of whether personality disorders are better viewed as categorical entities or as dimensions. I then presented a general introduction to a psychoanalytic viewpoint of personality disorders framed around a conflict model of psychopathology. I discussed the origin of self psychology first as a theory of narcissism and subsequently as a broader theory of disorders of the self—a deficit model of psychopathology. Finally, to establish a basic working premise for the remainder of this book, I suggested that deficits in self-cohesion may be reconceptualized as personality disorders.

2

NARCISSISTIC PERSONALITY DISORDER

The problem of understanding narcissism holds considerable interest, particularly in psychoanalysis, although increasingly so in the field of personality disorder theory and research. It is a condition that Sigmund Freud struggled with and rethought at several stages of his career (Baudry, 1983). Like other psychoanalytic explanations of personality disorders, a complete understanding of narcissistic personality disorder remains unsettled, despite Kohut's (1971, 1977) and Kernberg's (1975) systematic formulations of narcissism. It is also a condition plagued by imprecise terminology, perhaps more so than other personality disorders.

I have reserved narcissistic personality disorder for a chapter by itself, not because it should be considered the paradigmatic or signature disorder of Kohut's self psychology, but rather because narcissistic personality disorder provides the clearest illustration of the fundamental premises of Kohut's ideas about the self. Consequently, this chapter serves both to introduce Kohut's concepts of the self and to apply these concepts to an understanding of narcissistic personality disorder.

As I will do for each of the Axis II disorders in forthcoming chapters, I begin by examining the current status of this disorder with respect to its diagnostic validity, clinical phenomenology, and relationships with other personality disorders. I summarize personality theory viewpoints about narcissism and then psychoanalytic perspectives emphasizing developmental and object relations views. Next, I present an overview of narcissistic personality disorder and the main tenets of Kohut's self psychology. I will emphasize in this context an important though sometimes overlooked point: Kohut's viewpoint began as an attempt to understand narcissistic personality disorder as an expansion of drive theory and psychoanalytic ego psychological premises. An idea introduced in chapter 1 bears repeating: As Kohut extended his theory about narcissism to what was to become a broader psychology of the self, his observations and theories were no longer confined to this particular disorder. Indeed, it is the main purpose of this book to demonstrate how the broad scope of self psychological ideas may add to an understanding of the personality disorders of Axis II. I also include a discussion of related self psychological viewpoints (primarily intersubjectivity theory) that were influenced by Kohut's self psychology. Finally, I conclude (as I will in the chapters on other disorders) with a comprehensive discussion of a clinical case illustrating a self psychological approach to understanding narcissistic personality disorder.

CLINICAL CHARACTERISTICS AND PHENOMENOLOGY: DESCRIPTIVE PSYCHOPATHOLOGY

From a descriptive viewpoint, narcissistic personality disorder has a relatively low prevalence rate (Mattia & Zimmerman, 2001); however, its diagnostic overlap with other Axis II disorders is high, cutting across all three clusters described in the fourth edition of the *Diagnostic and Statistical Manual of Mental Disorders* (*DSM–IV*; American Psychiatric Association, 1994). Because diagnostic overlap varies considerably across studies, Gunderson, Ronningstam, and Smith (1995) suggested that idiosyncrasies of diagnostic criteria and their assessment may partially explain why narcissistic personality disorder is particularly difficult to define, sampling variations across studies notwithstanding. For example, problems concerning definitions of empathic failure and the nonspecificity of "excessive envy" are notable. However, grandiosity has been one of the better criteria for isolating narcissistic personality disorder. Paris (1995) observed that part of the difficulty results from having to rely on a substantial capacity for introspection on the part of patients. Diagnostic inconsistency also arises from variation in clinicians' judgments about the boundaries between normal and pathological dimensions (e.g., grandiosity, empathy, and hypersensitivity) on the one hand and boundaries between observable (behavioral) and nonobservable (inferred internal dynamics) characteristics on the other.

Gunderson, Ronningstam, and Smith (1995) also pointed out that validation studies are lacking or insufficient; thus, "the value of including this diagnosis in *DSM* rests solely upon the attributions of clinical utility from a widely recognized, psychodynamically informed clinical literature and tradition" (p. 209). This statement about narcissistic personality disorder, a disturbance primarily of outpatients, raises a question about the validity of this condition, a question that is raised less often about other personality disorders: It suggests that narcissistic personality disorder is an important clinical entity for psychoanalytic clinicians but that it is of uncertain significance for nonpsychoanalytic clinicians, at least as a condition in its own right.

The concept of narcissism and its clinical variants has also been considered from nonpsychoanalytic frameworks. Bursten (1973) described four types of narcissistic disorders (craving, paranoid, manipulative, and phallic), which resemble a broad range of personality disorders similar to those described in the *DSM–IV* as dependent/histrionic, paranoid, antisocial, and narcissistic. Previously, Leary (1957), an early social–interpersonal theorist, described two broad forms of narcissism—one characterized by a cold exterior, interpersonal aversiveness, and heightened independence resulting from fearfulness of dependency and a second type characterized by depression, hypersensitivity, and preoccupation with diminished self-esteem. Beck and Freeman's (1990) cognitive viewpoint emphasized schemas directed toward perpetuating an aggrandized self-image coupled with disregard for others, leading to insensitivity to normal cooperativeness or reciprocity in social interactions. These characteristics described by Beck and Freeman predated Costa and Widiger's (1994) suggestion that narcissistic personality disorder patients are characterized chiefly by low agreeableness on the five-factor model.

Millon's (1969) biopsychosocial approach originally emphasized the grandiose, overvalued aspect of narcissistic personality disorder, noting its origins in an unsustainable parental aggrandizement of a child's qualities or abilities. His more recent emphasis on an evolutionary perspective (Millon, 1996) devoted attention to a passive pattern of accommodation in narcissism, where narcissistic individuals seek to have others acquiesce to their wishes. Millon also stressed such patients' self-interest orientation, characterized by diminished or indifferent interest in others. These patterns of individuation in such patients' adaptive styles could account for their arrogant or haughty demeanor, exploitative behavior, and expansive thinking patterns. Millon also observed that these patients' overconfidence can give way to depression and feelings of emptiness when defenses fail, causing them to turn to an inner life of rationalizations to satisfy needs external reality no longer can provide.

Millon (1996) described various prominent clinical manifestations, including an exaggerated exploitative nature centering exclusively on patients' needs. This form overlaps with several key features associated with antisocial personality behavior. Another manifestation is a seductive Don Juanism dominated by patients' grandiose fantasies about their abilities accompanied by indifference to their targeted objects' needs. A less overt aggrandized clinical presentation is characterized chiefly by attempts to compensate for deficiencies by ever-constant aspirations for superior achievements; patients engage in an elitist way of life centered on markedly overvalued self-images and self-promoting behavior.

Millon (1996) attributed the development of narcissistic personality disorder to parental overindulgence, whereby parents imparted a sense of specialness that gave way to excessive expectations of praise or subservience from others. People who are raised with such expectations typically do not learn to consider the needs of other people; thus, they acquire a limited sense of interpersonal responsibility and poorly developed skills for reciprocal social interaction. Such individuals feel entitled to have their own needs recognized as the most important ones and think that nothing is wrong with exploiting others to get what they want. Once patterns like these are set in motion, a pathogenic character style is perpetuated, resulting in the relatively inflexible constellation of personality characteristics of most clinical definitions of narcissistic personality disorder. Turning inward for gratification, narcissistic (as well as antisocial) personality disorder patients strive more to enhance how they see themselves than to influence what others think of them, in part out of a fear of losing self-determination. Because they often devalue other people's points of view, narcissistic patients are more arrogant and entitled than antisocial patients, who are generally inclined to be more distrustful.

PSYCHOANALYTIC VIEWPOINTS

Freud (1910/1957e) considered narcissism to be a stage of development that led eventually to libidinal involvement (cathexis) of others and object love. He considered psychoanalysis to be unsuitable as a treatment method for narcissism for the same reason it was unsuitable for the psychoses—there was a failure in both kinds of patients to develop an object (libidinal) transference. Regarding narcissism at times as a perversion and at other times as a form of severe psychopathology, Freud returned at various times to the problem without reaching a satisfactory resolution. His writings on the subject addressed the matter of narcissism as a developmental process (primary narcissism) progressing to object love (Freud, 1910/1957e) and at other times as a withdrawal of narcissistic libido from object cathexes back into the ego (secondary narcissism; Freud, 1914/1957b). This conceptualization of narcissism became the basis for the ego ideal, which Freud recognized as the repository of remnants of infantile narcissism. Freud's (1931/1961c) evolving ideas about narcissism continued with his later description of a narcissistic libidinal type characterized by self-confidence and, at an extreme, grandiosity. Narcissistic libido thus became the foundation of self-esteem. Freud's (1914/1957b) recognition of this connection influenced

Kohut's (1966, 1968, 1971) early formulation of narcissism and later views about the self as well.

Freud's contributions to understanding narcissism thus were an important starting point for Kohut's viewpoint. It was through Freud's recognition of the relationship between the ego and external objects that he introduced the concept of the ego ideal and its self-observing capacity (Freud, 1914/1957b). In this respect, the ego ideal became the forerunner of the superego.

W. Reich (1933/1949), in his expansion of psychoanalysis beyond symptom neuroses to characterology, continued Freud's (1914/1957b) and Andreas-Salome's (1921) attempts to understand the balance between narcissism as a normal developmental pattern and as a pathological disorder. Reich likened the developmental level of such patients to character formations based on erogenous zones. Thus, Reich's description of the narcissistic character was referred to as *phallic narcissism*; for the same reason, he characterized oral–dependent and anal–compulsive character types. Fenichel (1945) was one of the earliest analytic writers to emphasize prominent feelings of emptiness or diminishment in patients with narcissistic disorders, in contrast to the over-valuing of the self and disdain for others Reich and Freud had previously emphasized.

Other psychoanalytic thinkers called attention to various associated qualities such as exhibitionism as a defense against inferiority (A. Reich, 1960) and self-idealization and omnipotent denial (Rosenfeld, 1964). Hartmann (1964) proposed a formulation of narcissism as a hypercathexis of self rather than as ego representations. Jacobson (1964) added an emphasis on superego functions in narcissism to explanations of identity development and self-esteem regulation. She also viewed psychosis largely as a product of narcissistic identifications, representing the breakdown or dedifferentiation of internalizations of ego and superego identifications.

The sections that follow provide an overview of subsequent psychoanalytic viewpoints about narcissism, some of which were formulated specifically as theories of narcissistic pathology and some of which represented developments in ego psychology or object relations theory. My discussion of these views will center on their similarities to and differences from Kohut's self psychology.

Developmental Viewpoints

Spitz (1965) and Mahler, Pine, and Bergman (1975) contributed a developmental perspective on narcissism, emphasizing good and bad representations of the self and objects. They considered magical omnipotence, mastery, and self-love to represent steps toward the development of the self and the attainment of self-esteem. Interruptions or arrests of normal narcissism in the developmental progression to object love set the stage for various forms of narcissistic pathology. Remaining within an ego psychological framework in which the object world was made up of good and bad part objects, "Mahler's baby" (M. Tolpin, 1980) was continually trapped in intrapsychic conflict where individuation requires renunciation of objects.

Psychoanalytic views of early infant development began to shift, however, from an emphasis on conflict toward an emphasis on deficiency (Kohut, 1971; M. Tolpin & Kohut, 1980) as a more important influence on narcissism. Taking a different view from Mahler et al. (1975), M. Tolpin (1980) referred to "Kohut's baby" as "a baby which 'every mother knows' although heretofore this baby has not been integrated into a tenable clinical theory" (p. 54). M. Tolpin emphasized how young children's early development is characterized less by splitting defenses and curbing aggressive drives—which are among the fundamental dynamics of classical drive theory in psychoanalysis—than by vigorous, developmentally in-phase needs that lead to competence and pride in their attainments. Normal development, therefore, involves a progressive unfolding of infants' pride and vitality "to announce his legitimate developmental needs" (p. 55). For this and other reasons, D. N. Stern's (1985) detailed videotaped recordings of mothers interacting with their infants, and more recently Beebe and Lachmann's (2002) extension of infant–mother observation to adult treatment, may also be thought of as important self psychologically informed reformulations of the conflict model of psychoanalytic ego psychology. Further, Teicholz's (1999, p. 172) reconciliation of Kohut's views with ego psychological and postmodern viewpoints considered D. N. Stern's observations of infants as "a meeting place" for these and similar views.

In considering the matter of development of the self as terminating in a state of individuation, as Mahler et al. (1975) maintained, Kohut (1977, 1984) instead considered needs for self-cohesion as continuing throughout life. Thus, for example, the need for cohesiveness of the self does not disappear; ongoing sources of responsiveness or vitalization are required for shoring up the self. Although he noted differences between his ideas and Mahler et al.'s, Kohut (1980) also saw similarities, commenting in a letter to Mahler that he believed they "were digging tunnels from different directions into the same area of the mountain" (p. 477).

Kernberg's Viewpoint

Kernberg (1975) proposed a view of narcissistic psychopathology that represented aspects of both ego psychology and object relations theory. His clearly specified descriptions of narcissistic personalities were important for establishing the clinical criteria of recent editions of the *Diagnostic and Statistical Manual of Mental Disorders* (American Psychiatric Association, 1980, 1987, 1994). Kernberg highlighted the clinical importance of narcissistic patients' unusual degree of self-reference, noting also the contradiction between their inflated self-image and their heightened needs for love and admiration. He called attention to frequently associated features, such as their shallow emotional lives, diminished empathy, and limited enjoyment of life beyond narcissistic gratifications. He described how narcissistic patients

> feel restless and bored when external glitter wears off and no new sources feed their self-regard. They envy others, tend to idealize some people from whom they expect narcissistic supplies and to depreciate and treat with contempt those from whom they do not expect anything (often their former idols). (p. 228)

Kernberg (1975) went on to describe narcissistic patients' undifferentiated affect states and their frequent emotional flare-ups. Such patients lack genuine feelings of sadness, despite their propensity for depressive reactions, which he explained as the resentful sadness of feeling abandoned or disappointed rather than the sorrow of mournful longing. Kernberg considered the essential psychological structure of narcissism to closely parallel that of borderline personality organization. Thus, he regarded narcissistic patients' smooth social capacities coexisting with omnipotence and grandiosity as surface manifestations of pronounced ego and superego defects. Consequently, Kernberg considered narcissism to be characterized by defenses of splitting, projective identification, and primitive idealization in a personality structure otherwise prone to intense oral–aggressive conflicts, not unlike those seen in borderline personality organization.

Kernberg (1975) observed that narcissistic patients often fail to develop a capacity to depend on and trust others, despite overt indications of dependency. If rejected, these patients feel hate as they drop and devalue their former idols. They may also lose interest in people who looked up to them, even becoming offended if people who no longer interest them move on to develop other interests or sources of admiration. Thus, the essential nature of their object relationships is narcissistic exploitation based on the need to be admired. They are also prone to experience emptiness as a defensive minimization of the anger or envy that Kernberg regarded as regularly associated with object relationships.

Narcissistic patients may have better impulse control and social functioning (which Kernberg [1975] termed *pseudosublimatory potential*) than patients with borderline personality organization. Narcissistic personalities may therefore be seen as leaders in their work and professional activities or in creative fields, although

> careful observation . . . of their productivity over a long period of time will give evidence of superficiality and flightiness in their work, of a lack of depth which eventually reveals the emptiness behind the glitter. Quite frequently, these are the "promising geniuses" who then surprise other people by the banality of their development. (Kernberg, 1975, pp. 229–230)

Kernberg (1975) observed that such patients often had mothers who exploited special qualities in them while simultaneously showing callous indifference and spiteful aggression. This pattern exposed such children to revengeful envy or hatred by others. A cold rather than a comforting maternal relationship would likely set in motion a search for compensatory admiration, although such children simultaneously developed a characterological devaluation of others. Kernberg considered his narcissistic patients to have more stable ego boundaries than did Jacobson (1964) and A. Reich (1960), who described their patients as being more vulnerable to ego regressions. Kernberg called attention to the pathological fusion among ideal self and object representations and actual self-images. He thought this interfered with normal differentiation of the superego, leading to primitive and aggressive superego pathology. As Kernberg (1975) wrote, "It is the image of a hungry, enraged, empty self, full of impotent anger at being frustrated, and fearful of a world which seems as hateful and revengeful as the patient himself" (p. 233). Narcissistic patients' defensive organization, like that of borderline patients, is dominated by splitting or primitive dissociation of split-off ego states. This personality organization can account for the coexistence of grandiosity and inferiority, not unlike the vertical split Kohut (1971) proposed to describe how contradictory self states might appear simultaneously as conscious phenomena.

Kernberg (1975) considered his view of the pathological structural deficit in narcissistic personality disorder to be fundamentally different than Kohut's (1971), which I will describe more fully in a separate section. Kernberg placed particular emphasis on rage and the relationship between libidinal and aggressive drives. He regarded this dynamic feature to be a fundamental one, whereas Kohut viewed narcissistic pathology as an interruption of the development of a normal albeit archaic self. Kernberg's position did not emphasize a continuity between normal and pathological narcissism.

Their theoretical differences may reflect differences in the types of patients Kernberg and Kohut saw in treatment while formulating their views. For example, Kernberg (1975) recognized that narcissistic patients often functioned in life at a higher level of competence than did borderline patients, at least when judged by overt indications. But as Kernberg came to understand narcissistic patients in greater depth, their structural deficits and degree of pathology became more apparent, and they began to resemble patients with borderline personality disorder.

Kohut (1966, 1968, 1971), however, formulated his ideas by studying patients in psychoanalytic treatment who did not necessarily show the propensity for regression, splitting, and archaic pathology resulting from poorly integrated rage of the type Kernberg treated and thus emphasized. Kohut considered the patients he treated to have achieved a more stable, intact degree of self-cohesion than those with borderline disorders, despite their propensity for self-esteem dysregulation producing excessive grandiosity or inferiority and vulnerability to disappointment. Kohut also called attention to such patients' depletion depression or anxiety, diminished zest or enthusiasm, and in some cases hypochondriacal preoccupations.

Whereas Kernberg (1975) conceptualized narcissism from the framework of pathological internalized object relations, Kohut's (1966, 1971) approach was derived from his discovery of specific transferences. Kohut did not, however, delineate clinical characteristics of narcissism as clearly as Kernberg did. Kohut also regarded narcissism as a line of normal development much like but different from object love. He thus considered pathological narcissism to be a derailment of normal narcissism, whereas Kernberg emphasized its inherently pathological structure and regarded it as being clearly different from normal narcissism. Thus, Kernberg saw a closer relationship between narcissistic and borderline personality disorders than Kohut did.

Other Object Relations Viewpoints

Kernberg's (1975) integration of ego psychology and object relations theory was influenced in part by M. Klein's (1930, 1935) view of narcissism as a defense against envy. The so-called middle or independent school of object relations also proposed views about narcissism and the self that were influenced by Klein, though these views departed from some of Klein's more extreme views. Whereas Kernberg proposed a view of narcissism, object relations theories such as Winnicott's (1965) and Fairbairn's (1954) were about the self and its development.

Winnicott (1965) in particular considered early development largely as an existence in which a "good enough" mother provides a holding environment that facilitates infants' and young children's growth and development. His concept of a maternal *subjective object* comprises the nearly indivisible unit formed by mother and infant that gave rise to his well-known comment, "There is no such thing as a baby" (p. 39), by which he meant that infants could not be understood in the absence of mothers' maternal care. This concept has a close but not identical correspondence with Kohut's (1977, 1984) concept of selfobject functions and the self–selfobject unit described later in this section. However, Bacal (1989) regarded Winnicott's concept of a subjective object as being nearly synonymous with Kohut's original idea of the selfobject operating as an extension of the self—that is, the psychological or internal experience of an object that provides functions that sustain and strengthen the self. Notwithstanding this similarity, Winnicott's (1971) reference to the mirroring function of a mother's face, for example, does not indicate that Kohut borrowed Winnicott's idea of mirroring to express Kohut's own concept of mirroring; Kohut's concept of the mirroring selfobject function is more nuanced than Winnicott's use of the idea of a mirror, which Winnicott intended mostly as an analogy.

Winnicott (1965) also distinguished between true and false selves; the false self is a defensive presentation patients use to protect themselves from an authentic but fragile true self. Consequently, the authentic or true self becomes undermined by the absence of a sufficiently caring holding environment, resulting in the prominent appearance of a false self. Winnicott's true self and Kohut's (1971) cohesive self are similar in that they both represent favorable outcomes of maternal responsiveness in normal development. Winnicott's false self parallels Kohut's (1971) vertical split (described in chap. 11), in which pseudo-omnipotent grandiosity conceals a simultaneously experienced but split-off enfeebled self.

Although Bacal (1989) understood Kohut (1971) to intend mirroring to refer to archaic grandiosity, Kohut, like Winnicott (1965, 1971), had in mind the idea that mirroring represented confirmation of one's unique or creative capacities. Bacal also pointed out that both Winnicott and Kohut commented on the capacity to be alone. For Winnicott, this represented an internalized psychological experience of an adequate holding environment; for Kohut, it represented the psychological experience of a cohesive self derived from the experienced sense of there being available a sustaining selfobject surround.

Bacal and Newman (1990) and Summers (1994) considered that Fairbairn (1954), Winnicott (1965), Balint (1968), and Guntrip (1969, 1971) developed object relations formulations of several phenomena Kohut (1971) would later emphasize, anticipating positions that Kohut brought together in a more crystallized form. For this reason, Bacal and Newman (1990) and Summers (1994) regarded Kohut's self psychology as a further step within object relations theory rather than as the paradigmatic advance that Kohut and several of his followers considered it to be. In any case, Kohut, as well as all of these object relations theorists, had in mind a concept of infants as engaging in object seeking from birth or shortly thereafter. *Selfobject* was Kohut's particular term for denoting the idea of the self's object.

Although Fairbairn (1954) and Guntrip (1969, 1971) used the term *ego* much as Kohut used the term *self*, their concepts of the object differed from the drive theory and ego psychological views of an object as an embodiment of libidinal or aggressive drives. All three theorists considered libidinal and aggressive experiences as being satisfying when early relationships were adequate. They spoke of libidinal and aggressive experiences as representing drive discharges or pathological breakdowns when early relationships were frustrating. Moreover, Fairbairn's view of the outcome of successful development was a mature dependence on objects based on differentiation between self and object. Fairbairn's and Guntrip's views were considerably different from Kohut's emphasis on the predominant role of empathic failures in self–selfobject relationships. Fairbairn and Guntrip emphasized instead the ever-constant struggles between the longing to be in relationships and the fearful distrust that intimacy leads to feeling devoured.

A SELF PSYCHOLOGICAL VIEWPOINT

The Self and Its Basic Constituents

Kohut's (1966, 1968, 1971) seminal works on narcissistic personality disorder opened up a new period of psychoanalytic theory formation. They represented a different way for clinicians to understand and treat a type of patient that stymied them by defying treatment attempts based on classical drive theory and ego psychology. As I noted earlier in this chapter, narcissism had presented an explanatory problem for Freud and for psychoanalysis since its beginnings. Although Kohut has been criticized for seeming to ignore important views in psychoanalysis that could legitimately be seen as forerunners of his own viewpoint (Bacal & Newman, 1990; Summers, 1994), the innovations he introduced nevertheless formed the basis for a new psychoanalytic view of psychopathology, one that despite criticism called for a substantial revision of psychoanalytic theory and treatment.

Although Kohut distinguished between narcissistic personality disorders and narcissistic behavior disorders, he sometimes used these terms interchangeably because their main dynamics were similar. *Narcissistic personality disorder* encompassed disturbances where the primary symptomatic presentation included depression, purposelessness, chronic boredom or disappointment, or related aspects of depletion and generalized experiences of diminished self-esteem. The *narcissistic behavior disorders* were disturbances in which most of these same phenomena were manifested as behavior disorders rather than as psychological experiences. Such behavior disorders included sexualizations (e.g., perversions), addictions, or delinquent (antisocial) acts.

Kohut (1959, 1966, 1971) identified empathy as a primary method of clinical investigation. Empathic listening was a way of understanding patients' verbalized and nonverbalized experiences and their clinical histories. Understanding such experiences and what gave rise to them thus enables clinicians to reconstruct patients' lives as their struggles to sustain self-esteem and cohesiveness of the self. Considered in this way, empathy has little (if anything) to do with sympathetic expressions of understanding or tenderheartedness. It is instead the way a clinician gathers information and then attempts to comprehend clinical data.

Kohut (1971, 1977) also introduced the term *selfobject* to refer to the internal psychological experience of an object that provides functions necessary for self-regulation. In self psychology, as in psychoanalysis more generally, the term *object* often refers to an actual person (such as a mother or other person sought for his or her maternal functions). Its accurate definition is the psychological function such a person has come to provide or represent (mental representation). Thus, a mother or a maternal object in the sense of an object relation is really that person's maternal capacity. From the self psychological viewpoint, therefore, a selfobject is an object needed by the self for its cohesion or vitalization. That is, the meaning of a person as a selfobject is understood from the vantage point of how that person promotes (or fails to promote) self-cohesion. Further, selfobjects need not be persons; they may be ideals or values, such as political or philosophical beliefs that are bound up with the core of a person's existence. As such, abstract representations would have to be sufficiently embedded in a person's psychological structure that it could be said that they provide important self-regulatory functions.

Self psychology stresses that it is the self, an agency of mental life, and not drives or the ego that is the fundamental clinical problem in narcissistic disorders. Ornstein (1978, p. 98) observed that Kohut (1971) initially regarded the self as an "adjacent territory"—that is, as an extension of drive theory and ego psychology. However, Kohut never clearly articulated what he meant by the self as clearly as the concepts of drives and ego had been defined. Kohut referred to the self in an ill-defined, vague way as a content of mental life or experience; he did not consider the self to be a mental structure like the ego or superego. Although this description of the self remained unacceptably nonspecific, Kohut did specify its attributes as providing cohesion, vigor, and harmony. Many of the central concepts of Kohut's self psychology emerged from a further delineation of these attributes of the self.

The attribute Kohut (1971) characterized as *cohesion* refers to experiencing the self as either intact or fragmented. Self-cohesion is the relatively enduring experience of the self either as integrated when it is intact or as breaking apart when it is vulnerable to fragmentation. The *vigor* or vitality of the self is an attribute best described as one's feeling of being assured or strong, not necessarily in the sense of confidence about one's abilities but rather of a firmed-up capacity to stand up to the world without sinking or caving in. Finally, *harmony of the self* is the way Kohut referred to a capacity for feeling calmed or soothed, a quality that is itself related to how cohesive or invigorated people experience themselves to be.

These constituents of inner experience were what Kohut (1966, 1971) emphasized in attempting to understand narcissism. It was as close as he came to providing a definition of the self. Narcissistic personality disorder was thus in his view a disturbance of the regulation of self-experience rather than an imbalance among the structures of id, ego, and superego (Freud, 1926/1959b). Its symptoms or clinical manifestations might take the form of grandiosity or an exaggerated sense of one's importance, self-centeredness to the extent that other people's needs barely exist or matter, pronounced entitlement, or envy. These, of course, are the familiar manifestations that form the basis of most diagnostic criterion sets. But Kohut, like Fenichel (1945) before him, observed that narcissistic personality disorders may also assume a form in which the opposites to grandiosity or entitlement are seen. These include, for example, self-depreciation, denigration of one's abilities, excessive shame or modesty, or deep-rooted feelings of not belonging or of not being able to hold one's own, sometimes masquerading as excessive shyness or unassertiveness. Paradoxical reactions such as these may comprise the main clinical presentation for some patients, or these reactions may first emerge after an initial burst of superficial, grandiose bravado gives way and a fundamentally injured self appears. The most crucial considerations in Kohut's understanding of narcissistic personality disorders were the characteristic deficiencies in cohesion, vitality, or harmony of the self.

Selfobject Functions

Kohut's (1966, 1971) early descriptions of narcissistic personality disorder emphasized how the three attributes of the self—cohesion, vigor, and harmony—operate to produce the clinical forms of the disorder. He explained that the self requires attuned responsiveness from the external world to sustain its cohesiveness. By *attuned responsiveness* Kohut meant empathic selfobject experience. (As I noted earlier in this chapter, clinicians apprehend the psychological significance of attuned or failed selfobject experience through empathy as a mode of investigation.) Kohut at first identified two primary kinds of selfobject experience—mirroring and idealization, representing sectors or poles of a bipolar self (Kohut, 1971, 1977). He later added a third, twinship, which previously was included in mirroring and was subsequently differentiated as a selfobject function in its own right (Kohut, 1984).

Mirroring

Mirroring is the "echoing presence" Kohut regarded as the means by which others' affirming responsiveness strengthens the self. It is one route for firming up a sense of being valued. Mirroring is built up from experiences in normal development in which young children expect that their accomplishments will be recognized and met with prideful satisfaction. Kohut (1971) conceptualized mirroring needs as arising from what he termed the *grandiose–exhibitionistic self*, comprising three forms. The most psychologically archaic form is a fusion of self and other (the self and its selfobjects), which is detected in treatment by a merger transference. A second, healthier manifestation is, as Kohut phrased it, a *mirror transference* in the narrow sense, which is the familiar seeking of an affirming or admiring presence without compromising the boundary between self and mirroring selfobject. The third form of mirroring is the *twinship* or *alter ego transference*, representing a need for another to be a faithful replica of the patient. Kohut (1984) subsequently reformulated the twinship transference as a distinct selfobject function, one that was separate from mirroring, which I discuss in a separate section.

As Kohut (1977, 1984) further developed the psychology of the self, he de-emphasized the idea of a grandiose–exhibitionistic sector of the self as a pathological formation. He shifted his emphasis, therefore, from a theory of psychopathology to a view of infants' and young children's exhibitionistic displays of their abilities—exaggerated and overestimated though they may be—as normal developmental strivings. Consequently, the appropriate parental response to mirroring needs (and their grandiose–exhibitionistic manifestations) is simply an admiring recognition of this aspect of children's experience in a timely, developmentally in-phase way. This type of acknowledgement serves to instill normal pride and feelings of well-being. It becomes the echoing presence of empathic attunement to young children's native talents and skills that emerge normally during development. Thus, Kohut no longer regarded this prideful boasting as pathologically grandiose or exhibitionistic strivings. Rather, he understood it as a product of vitality resulting from caregivers' empathic responsiveness to their accomplishments in the form of proud encouragement.

Idealization

Before Kohut (1984) differentiated twinship from mirroring as a distinct selfobject function, he described another sector (pole) of the self (Kohut, 1966, 1971)—the *idealized parental imago*. Idealization as a selfobject function is mobilized when a sustained impetus emerges in young children to turn to others as all-powerful in order to feel calmed by their strong or steadying presence; in this way, the others become idealized selfobjects. Like mirroring and twinship, idealization is a product of a normal developmental thrust. It becomes apparent when children experience their caregivers as providing a soothing function when their own capacity to calm themselves is incompletely strengthened from within, thus compromising self-cohesion. Children idealize selfobjects whom they can look up to in this way for their all-knowing or all-powerful vigor. Children's longings to merge with idealized selfobjects' strength foster the restoration of equilibrium when the self is experienced as weakened. Bacal and Newman (1990) aptly expressed this idea in their description of the self as "walking proudly in the shadow" (p. 232) of its admired object; they thus captured the essential quality of the idealization selfobject experience as consolidating self-cohesion.

Selfobject failures may occur when idealized selfobjects no longer can provide this function. Idealized selfobjects may lose interest or prematurely withdraw their availability and in so doing interrupt a normal, developmentally in-phase process. A child or a patient with a prominent idealization selfobject need may experience such disruptions as abandonment if they occur before the person has internalized enough of what he or she needs to sustain self-cohesion.

Idealization selfobject disturbances may compel the patient to perpetually seek perfection in selfobjects who offer the promise of fulfilling his or her thwarted idealization longings. Patients with such idealization needs may thus attempt to merge with omnipotent selfobjects, sometimes successfully revitalizing self-esteem. However, such mergers are often short-lived and thus futile, because they typically do not lead to a dependable structure that strengthens self-cohesion. Many patients with such thwarted idealization longings are frequently left feeling disappointed in once-idealized selfobjects. Attempts to secure self-cohesion through repeated idealizations often fail to restart a developmental process of internalizing self-cohesion that had been interrupted. Kohut (1971) referred to this developmental process as *transmuting internalization*. In its absence, chronically disappointing or unavailable idealized selfobjects reexpose such patients to injuries that can overwhelm an infirm self (M. Tolpin, 1971).

Relatively healthy sublimations may also occur, such as the acquisition of deeply felt convictions or principles. In general, though, many patients with idealization deficits remain vulnerable to feeling disappointed in idealized selfobjects. They are frequently unable to gradually let go of their need for omnipotence in idealized selfobjects. Others cling to idealized selfobjects long past the point when holding onto this possibility is viable. Further, it is not uncommon to reconstruct histories of parents' failures to recognize their children's idealization needs or of a parent, uncomfortable being idealized, who unwittingly fails to welcome or prematurely dismisses the child's normal idealized selfobject longings. Such parents may seem surprised to find that their children feel rejected by them, having misinterpreted their children's need for idealizing selfobject functions as clinging dependency. Deficits arising from rebuffed idealization needs may also result in the child's inability to calm or soothe him- or herself.

Idealization may represent another opportunity in early development to repair the injuries to the self if mirroring needs were thwarted. A sufficiently robust idealization selfobject relationship that solidifies self-cohesion in the face of mirroring deficiencies can provide a compensatory structure (Kohut, 1977; M. Tolpin, 1997). In this way, if mirroring has been irreparably damaged as an avenue for strengthening the self, it may be possible to achieve a reasonably robust and enduring degree of self-cohesion if another route (such as idealization or twinship) is available to sustain a damaged self. A compensatory structure established in this manner may permit development to proceed on course instead of leading to an inevitable state of chronic devitalization from which recovery cannot be expected.

Twinship

The third primary selfobject function Kohut identified was the twinship or alter ego transference. He originally identified this selfobject function as a manifestation of mirroring (Kohut, 1971), but he later became convinced of its significance as an independent selfobject function (Kohut, 1984). Like mirroring and idealization selfobject needs, twinship also represents a normal developmental striving. Kohut (1984) characterized it as a longing for an intimate experience in which a selfobject is perceived as a faithful replica of oneself, capable of matching one's psychological states as if self and selfobject were one and the same. It is not a merger, in which the sense of an autonomous self is submerged, although in archaic forms it may manifest in this way. More typically, twinship selfobject needs spur people to turn to their selfobjects and experience them as a part of the self. The twinship or alter ego selfobject function, like those of mirroring and idealization, exists to provide calming of a vulnerable self. It operates as a silent presence to keep one company when self-cohesion requires bolstering. Corresponding in some ways to the colloquial term *soulmate*, the twinship selfobject function refers to the experience of a companionate presence that feels and thinks just like oneself. It is akin to the feeling of a special connection with someone who uncannily finishes one's sentences, although this sense of connection goes far deeper to sustain self-cohesion when the self is experienced as being devitalized.

Disorders of the Self: Narcissistic Personality and Behavior Disorders

As noted earlier in this chapter, the symptomatic manifestations of self disorders centering on mirroring, idealization, or twinship selfobject failures are often indistinguishable on clinical presentation. Therefore, one must determine the predominant selfobject disruption that is compromising self-cohesion. Moreover, admixtures of selfobject deficits are not uncommon. Selfobject needs may also shift in prominence as a result of time, stressors, and progress of treatment and over the course of life. Although the narcissistic personality and behavior disorders need not reflect one selfobject deficit alone (indeed, manifestations of more than one selfobject failure may very likely appear), one sector of the self is usually more prominently injured. Compensatory structures (Kohut, 1977; M. Tolpin, 1997) may sometimes become established and relatively firmed up as reparative—although still imperfect—attempts to substitute one selfobject function (typically idealization) for another (usually mirroring).

Finally, the selfobject functions of mirroring, idealization, and twinship may not represent a complete complement of such functions; these are only the ones Kohut himself addressed. Kohut and Wolf (1978) and Wolf (1988) outlined other possibilities, such as adversarial and efficacy selfobject functions; however, these and other potential selfobject functions have not been sufficiently studied.

Experiences of empty depression and lack of purpose or enthusiasm may ensue when normal mirroring, idealization, or twinship selfobject needs become mobilized and then are thwarted. Empathic failures of normal selfobject responsiveness typically imply that a caregiver providing selfobject functions failed to recognize and appreciate that a normal need had emerged, one that could not be overlooked or ignored but that instead needed to be accepted enthusiastically (M. Tolpin, 1978; M. Tolpin & Kohut, 1980). Frequently, narcissistic manifestations (as well as self disorders in general) become expressed as depletion or fragmentation phenomena accompanied by tension states that are incompletely relieved and chronic affect experiences of being adrift in life or lacking purpose or goals. Some people feel chronically under-powered or devitalized. Others perpetually seek out intense idealization selfobject relationships and often feel let down or dropped when their need to perceive greatness or vigor in such selfobjects is met with the disappoint-ments that inevitably ensue. Such patients struggle hard to feel enthusiastic about themselves, the people they love, their work, and the people or values that would normally enhance self-esteem and make them feel their lives are worthwhile.

Regardless of how prominently the surface manifestations of grandios-ity or entitlement may initially appear in narcissistic personality disorders, eventually weaknesses or deficits such as those just described will become evident, especially in treatment. Just as therapists need to recognize such patients' defensive bravado and loud, angry clamorings as their way of pro-tecting themselves, they must understand the depression, ennui, and dimin-ished zest that emerge alongside such defenses as the outcome of devitalized strivings to sustain a robust, assured self.

Selfobject deficits may be noted clinically as chronic empty depression or as a cold or arrogant demeanor. Manifestations such as these indicate that the patient is defensively sequestering feelings of shame and self-depreciation that are not far from the surface presentation. Heightened sensitivity to slights and criticisms also is common. Rageful reactions (narcissistic rage) are often apparent that represent the anger resulting from rebuffed expectations of affirming selfobject responsiveness from others. Narcissistic rage, if pro-nounced and widespread, may signal fragmenting self-cohesion, here under-stood as the breakdown (disintegration products) of a devitalized, underpow-ered self. Disintegration products may also take the form of addictions or perversions, which function to momentarily shore up the self.

When insufficient mirroring is prolonged during early development, the ensuing injuries to young children's normal prideful strivings derail their hopes for themselves, frequently leading to devitalization. In adult treatment, establishing empathic therapeutic understanding requires the therapist to reconstruct how his or her own misunderstandings from time to time repeat caregivers' chronic empathic failures. The diminished self-esteem that en-sues in treatment is thus a repetition of childhood reactions to thwarted needs for selfobject responsiveness. By understanding how therapy reexposes pa-tients to caregivers' empathic breaches, the psychotherapist is able to see how deficient mirroring responsiveness created the condition for a core ex-perience to take root in which the patient came to perceive him- or herself as inadequate or devalued, concealed though it may be behind a veneer of de-fensive bravado. This veneer of grandiosity or exhibitionism may recede when patients come up against uncertainty about their abilities. They come to feel that their accomplishments do not matter, predisposing them to feelings of empty depression, disappointment in themselves as well as others, and a gen-eralized sense of ennui about their lives.

Thus, narcissistic personality disorder typically results from failures of the echoing, affirming responsiveness of mirroring selfobjects or from failures of potentially idealizable selfobjects to provide a dependably sustaining presence. Sometimes both mirroring and idealization selfobject failures may be detected, particularly when a stable compensatory structure could not be established. So injured as young children, patients with a disorder of the self move into adolescence and then adulthood, repeatedly failing to realize their goals. They frequently achieve far less in life than the promise they once may have shown. Ambition is often stifled; initiative is manifested clinically as lethargic indifference associated with depression, affective constriction, or blunting. Hypochondriacal concerns may occur, in which somatization overlies an ever-present sense of a weakened, devitalized self. A propensity to shame is also common, coexisting with rage reactions when shortcomings are exposed.

Such disturbances do not preclude other forms of psychopathology, including comorbid Axis I syndromes and Axis II personality disorders. Comorbid disorders may represent depressive, anxious, impulsive, aggressive, or other symptomatic perturbations of an underlying self disorder. The narcissistic behavior disorders in particular may resemble Axis I and Axis II disorders characterized by perversions (sexualizations) of painful affect states, addictions, delinquency, or propensity for intense outbursts of helpless anger (narcissistic rage). These behavioral dysfunctions typically achieve only momentary soothing; they replace the internalizations of selfobject functions that failed to develop, thus impeding a capacity to calm or soothe the self.

Maturation of Narcissism in Normal Development With Treatment

Kohut (1966, 1977, 1984) frequently observed that there is no self without a selfobject, which was how he expressed the idea that throughout life the self requires persons, ideals, or sustaining goals from which it can derive vitality and cohesion. Selfobjects never become completely unnecessary; instead, they always remain important to fuel or sustain self-cohesion, which Kohut likened to a kind of psychological oxygen. A selfobject surround may consist of parents or other caregivers (including grandparents, other close relatives, or sometimes beloved nannies); love objects; intimate friends; teachers, mentors, or similar admired or beloved figures; or even profoundly meaningful values, principles, or institutions. The selfobject environment functions to affirm one's attributes or qualities to ensure a sense of initiative, efficacy, and well-being. Selfobject needs in normal development, therefore, are not thought of as inherently pathological; rather, they represent a baseline of legitimate expectations. One turns to the people or other selfobjects who are important in one's life, it is hoped with confidence, expecting to be responded to in a way that invigorates the self.

Cohesiveness of the self comes about through internalization, which is how selfobject functions become firmed up as a mental structure. In keeping with drive theory, Kohut (1971) regarded frustration to be the basis for strengthening the self, but only if frustration was optimal (i.e., not prolonged or intense). Optimal frustration strengthens self-cohesion by firming up the self as a stable mental structure. Kohut's term for this process of gradual strengthening of self-cohesion was *transmuting internalization*. This concept of Kohut's may be considered a specific form of internalization, which is it-self a broad concept in psychoanalysis. For example, internalization has been described as a defense whose distortions influence various forms of psychopathology. Internalization is also the mechanism by which psychological growth achieved through treatment becomes consolidated. It is in this latter sense that transmuting internalization is thought to promote cohesiveness of the self. However, Kohut believed that growth-fostering internalizations occurred mainly as a result of optimal frustration.

Failures of internalization lead to disorders of the self. A chronically unresponsive selfobject environment that produces mirroring or idealization failures creates frustration, but not of the kind that promotes internalization and self-cohesion. Transmuting internalizations during normal development may be impeded by untimely interruptions such as early parental loss or ill-ness or a pronounced and abrupt (i.e., traumatic) withdrawal of responsive-ness from needed selfobjects. Several of Kohut's followers objected to his insistence that frustration was necessary to establish internalizations of selfobject experience to build self-cohesion. Bacal (1985) and Terman (1988) considered optimal responsiveness, rather than optimal frustration, to be a more decisive influence for promoting self-cohesion.

Kohut (1971) thus did not view selfobject needs as drive states that required being rechanneled as sublimations; instead, he viewed deficits of selfobject functions as representing derailments of normal development. In self psychologically informed treatment, the therapist understands patients' clamoring for attention or their angry disillusionment not primarily as de-rivatives of drives but rather as rebuffed legitimate needs for selfobject re-sponsiveness. The therapist sees ignored selfobject needs as reactivations of empathic selfobject failures to meet normal developmental needs. Thus, self psychology provides a way of viewing and successfully treating patients' prob-lems that previously were subject to long, unproductive treatments. In many such instances, treatment remained at an impasse because legitimate needs for selfobject responsiveness were misinterpreted as drive states in traditional psychoanalytic treatment.

Kohut (1971, 1977) stressed not only the importance of interpreting defenses, which occupies the typical ongoing work in treatment, but also the need to interpret them as expressions of thwarted but still hoped-for strivings for empathic selfobject responsiveness. Kohut considered such strivings to be the leading edge of treatment, which he contrasted with a so-called "trailing edge" (Miller, 1985) of conflicts, defenses, and symptoms. M. Tolpin (2002) recently revived this concept, which Kohut spoke about informally (Miller, 1985) but did not write about. Tolpin described "forward edge" transferences that coexist with a self disorder; these transferences frequently are silent and difficult to recognize because they may be deeply submerged. Nonetheless, searching for and integrating forward edge transferences can represent an important mutative factor, because such transferences reach the potentially revivable tendrils of selfobject longings that have been driven underground. The remobilization of such buried (but not entirely abandoned) efforts may allow previously interrupted development to continue, thus restarting a process of securing more advantageous empathic selfobject responsiveness. These transferences represent patients' hopeful anticipation that something that had gone awry in their development will be recognized and responded to as a reasonable, normal need rather than as a pathological need state.

Thus, Kohut and his colleagues considered the emergence in treatment of patients' mirroring, idealization, and twinship selfobject needs as both reactivations of earlier injuries and as attempts to convey to others what they require to promote repair of the self. This understanding of selfobject transferences was not technically different from the way other transferences were approached in treatment. Thus, selfobject transferences were amenable to interpretation using essentially the same technical approach as that of other well-understood transference configurations. Further, Kohut did not discard drives as important psychological mechanisms, but he increasingly regarded them as requiring a different way of being understood without delegating them to a position of secondary importance (Kohut, 1977, 1984). He understood sexual and aggressive drives as vitalizing functions to enhance well-being and self-cohesion (M. Tolpin, 1986). This understanding of drives became a part of how self psychologically informed treatment facilitated reviving patients' initiative to pursue goals with enthusiasm and to take pride in their abilities and accomplishments.

Kohut (1971, 1977) also was not convinced of the primacy of an aggressive drive, certainly not in the way Kernberg (1975) and other followers of Melanie Klein's (1935) work had emphasized. Kohut considered Klein's "essential attitude that the baby is evil" and "a powder keg of envy, rage, and destructiveness" (Kohut, 1996, p. 104) to be misguided. Kohut (1972) instead considered narcissistic rage reactions to arise from selfobject failures when caregivers did not respond to phase-appropriate needs—the relatively normal, expectable developmental needs of childhood. He explained narcissistic rage as excessive or severe frustration and not as primary or archaic residuals of an aggressive drive. Though Kohut considered frustration to be optimal when it promoted firmed-up self-cohesion through internalization, he regarded excessive frustration as producing a breakup or fragmentation of self experience. Kohut called fragmentations of the self *disintegration products*, and narcissistic rage is one example. Kohut (1996) also observed in this context that "the baby cries, and then the baby cries *angrily* when whatever needs to be done is not done immediately. But there is no original need to destroy; the original need is to establish an equilibrium" (p. 199).

Other Self Psychological Viewpoints

Although I have emphasized Kohut's psychology of the self, other self psychological perspectives also exist that were influenced by and extend Kohut's views. These viewpoints were not concerned specifically with narcissism, and even Kohut's later formulations emphasized self disorders rather than narcissistic disorders. Nonetheless, the other self psychological views I outline in this section all have implications for understanding narcissistic personality disorder.

Stolorow and his colleagues' intersubjectivity theory was one of the earliest to have evolved (Stolorow & Atwood, 1992; Stolorow, Brandchaft, & Atwood, 1987). Lichtenberg's (1989) concept of motivational systems and Shane, Shane, and Gales's (1998) integrative viewpoint based on Thelen and Smith's (1994) nonlinear dynamic systems theory are also closely allied with psychoanalytic approaches to disorders of the self. Lichtenberg's and Shane et al.'s emphases on development and the self incorporated aspects of attachment theory as well.

Intersubjectivity Theory

Stolorow and Atwood (1992) considered their intersubjective viewpoint to be closely allied with Kohut's self psychology insofar as both viewpoints regarded selfobject experience as a primary aspect of mental life. Like Kohut, intersubjectivity theorists emphasized empathic understanding as a method for therapists to use in obtaining the subjective data needed to apprehend patients' experience of the self and its constituents. Stolorow and colleagues' (Stolorow & Atwood, 1992; Stolorow et al., 1987) intersubjective viewpoint is perhaps more closely related to (but not necessarily derived from) Kohut's concept of the self and selfobject functions than are other viewpoints based on intersubjectivity, such as Ogden's (1994). Stolorow and Atwood commented that they arrived at their point of view independently of Kohut and that their view emerged from a different frame of reference, one that was influenced appreciably by Tomkins's (1963) theory of affect regulation. Further, intersubjectivity theory expanded self psychology's understanding of borderline and psychotic disorders (Brandchaft & Stolorow, 1984; Stolorow et al., 1987).

Stolorow and his colleagues (Stolorow & Atwood, 1992; Stolorow et al., 1987) stressed the primary importance of *intersubjective contexts*, which they defined as an intersection of two subjectively true realities, such as that between a child and its caregivers or that between a patient and his or her therapist. This intersection is thought to construct (their term for this, like that of many relational theorists, is *coconstruct*) a new or different reality than that of either party alone. By contrast, Kohut and his colleagues regarded others as independent persons who provide selfobject functions to shore up the self. Intersubjectivity theory advocates that psychological experience cannot be understood without considering the intersubjective field. Thus, other persons' motivations and perceptions (i.e., subjectivities) are believed to equally influence the perception of one's own sense of psychological reality. The perceptions and beliefs resulting from such a newly created intersubjectivity, whether accurate or faulty, represent what Stolorow and his colleagues termed *invariant organizing principles*. Their view has been criticized, however, for conflating experience with social determinism (Summers, 1994), perhaps even with an extreme form of it.

A crucial concept in intersubjectivity theory concerns the central role of affects rather than drives as primary organizers of experience. Affect states that are inevitably embedded in intersubjective fields are themselves regulated by the reciprocal influence that occurs in dyads. Psychopathology, therefore, represents failures to integrate affective experience (Socarides & Stolorow, 1984–1985) because the early child–caregiver system of reciprocal mutual influence that normally promotes affective integration has broken down. Under more optimal conditions, the child–caregiver mutual influence system ensures that affect states become integrated with ongoing experience. Affects can thus be tolerated and differentiated to signal what people experience at any given moment. Disturbed affect articulation results therefore from intersubjective contexts in early development where affects were walled off or inhibited, usually because caregivers remained unattuned to their children's affect states.

The intersubjectivity perspective is integrally anchored in the self psychological point of view in which the self is the center of psychological experience. Stolorow and colleagues (Stolorow & Atwood, 1992; Stolorow et al., 1987) have consistently stressed the importance of affects as organizers of the experience of the self. They also emphasized the mutual (bidirectional) influence of dyads as the basis for self regulation and selfobject experience. This emphasis is congruent with studies of observations of infants and mothers in interaction (Beebe & Lachmann, 2002; D. N. Stern, 1985); these studies also highlight the importance of the mother–infant dyad as a mutually influencing system that is important for self regulation. In recent years, Stolorow and colleagues have increasingly taken the position that Kohut's so-called traditional self psychology remained too wedded to the one-person psychology of drive theory and ego psychology. Consequently, intersubjectivity theorists have criticized important self psychological concepts such as transmuting internalization, because they consider its view of selfobject experience to be too closely anchored in a Cartesian isolated-mind tradition of conceptualizing internal experience. These theorists have argued that self psychology does not sufficiently emphasize what Stolorow and Atwood (1992) considered to be of crucial importance—dyadic systems and the intersubjective context. However, self psychologists consider Stolorow and colleagues' distinction to be of limited importance. They instead have emphasized that the central feature of both views—one that differentiates them from early psychoanalytic positions—is a fundamental concern about the interdependency between self and others, regardless of whether this is conceptualized as selfobject experience or as an intersubjective field.

Motivational Systems and Development

Lichtenberg's (1989) view of the self is derived partly from Kohut's emphasis on the self–selfobject unit and partly from assumptions of intersubjectivity theory and the mother–infant observation literature. His particular emphasis rests on motivational systems that underlie self-regulation, a concept Lichtenberg introduced to expand the scope of self psychology beyond the empathically observed data of clinical psychoanalysis. His is a theory of the self, because it considers experiences of optimally attuned selfobjects to be affectively invigorating when needs are met, thus strengthening the self. (Lichtenberg's term *self-righting* approximates Kohut's concept of repair or restoration of the self.) The motivational systems Lichtenberg outlined included a description of their precursors in infancy based on attachment patterns. Thus, he linked motivation with development as crucial influences on self-integration. Lichtenberg also attempted to integrate intersubjectivity theory's emphasis on child–caregiver interactions as serving mutually affect-regulating functions for both children and their caregivers. His concept of the self emphasizes motivation more as a sense of initiative than as drive states. Motivations thus serve to organize and integrate experience, specifically selfobject experiences, which Lichtenberg defined as the mutual or reciprocal regulatory relationship of the self and its objects.

Like Lichtenberg, Shane et al. (1998) also integrated a literature beyond the data of the consulting room, building on Kohut's views by incorporating recent knowledge from contemporary attachment theory, mother–infant observation research, developmental psychology, neurobiology, and studies of trauma. Their integration of these areas with self psychology formed the basis for what they termed *nonlinear dynamic systems*, based on a perspective first proposed by Thelen and Smith (1994). According to Shane et al.'s adaptation of this model, development represents a consolidation of the self and of the self with the world outside it. They viewed trauma as interfering with consolidation of the self, broadly defining it as including neglect and loss in addition to overt abuse. Such disruptions of normal development lead to self-protective coping mechanisms that do not promote consolidation of the self. Shane et al. did not consider these self-protective adaptations to be fundamentally pathological defenses, but rather survival strategies of vulnerable children. They also considered this view from an attachment theory perspective, observing that such adaptations attempted to preserve an attachment to needed others.

Like Kohut (1971, 1977), Shane et al. (1998) considered that treatment could possibly mobilize a reactivation of normal developmental strivings that had been interrupted. Treatment should be conducted with the goal of fostering consolidation of the self, which is the same process Kohut called *self-cohesion*. Shane et al. regarded the work of repair in treatment as *self-with-other consolidation*, in which patients turn to others for security and self-regulation. They considered this concept to be one that was implied but not specifically articulated by Kohut's concept of selfobject functions. Shane et al. thus reformulated Kohut's view of selfobjects as relational configurations for promoting a new experience of the "self-transforming other." Shane et al. discussed several specific configurations representing trajectories of developmental progressions to achieve the self and self-with-other consolidations they emphasized.

Current Status of Self Psychological Viewpoints

As I noted earlier in this chapter, these and other theories recently allied with a self psychological viewpoint do not explicitly formulate views about narcissism or narcissistic personality disorder. They can, however, readily be applied to an understanding of narcissism. My main intent in including other self psychological theories in this discussion of Kohut's self psychology is not to argue for their specific relevance to narcissism but rather to show how they have provided a context for understanding ongoing developments in the psychology of the self since Kohut formulated his ideas.

I will not characterize most of these views or their differences from Kohut's self psychology beyond the general descriptions presented in the preceding sections, although readers should note that good comparative reviews of the various self psychologies are available by Goldberg (1998), Shane and Shane (1993), and Wallerstein (1983). In this and succeeding chapters, I make note of complementary or alternative viewpoints such as those outlined above alongside Kohut's when such concepts offer related perspectives for understanding a self psychological point of view. In regard to whether one or several self psychologies may be said to have existed since Kohut's formulations, suffice it to say that Goldberg regarded the primary concepts that Kohut first articulated as having led to "separate tributaries, each of which lays some claim to serve as the major voice in the field" (p. 254). Shane and Shane considered Kohut to have "clearly shaped the advances in self psychology" during his lifetime; however, further developments, although "dedicated to his vision," also were "not limited by it" (p. 779).

CLINICAL ILLUSTRATION

The clinical history and course of treatment presented in this section illustrate a self psychological approach to conceptualizing narcissistic personality disorder. The patient, Mr. A., presented with a mixed anxiety–depressive syndrome with features of hypomania and somatic symptoms. My discussion will demonstrate how these comorbid conditions may be conceptualized within a self psychological framework. This case is of interest because the characteristic Axis II narcissistic personality disorder features of grandiosity and entitlement were not initially prominent, although they became more apparent in his treatment with me shortly after he was clinically stabilized.

Mr. A. was a 27-year-old single White man, a college graduate who worked as an occupational therapist. He was admitted by his internist to a general hospital with a specialized medical service for treating illnesses with a prominent psychiatric overlay or medical management problems. Mr. A. had developed chest pains and dizziness complicated by an 8-month period of heavy drinking that he had terminated on his own before admission. Medical workups were negative. He presented with depression and agitation, and he showed a histrionic preoccupation with somatic functions and was fearful that he was dying. His history revealed that he had had a similar but less severe and protracted reaction at age 18, during his 1st year at college. Mr. A.'s current somatic complaints had begun about 1 year before the episode under discussion, and he had attempted to subdue them with alcohol use. His somatic symptoms had intensified during the 3 months preceding admission, perhaps associated with his self-imposed termination of alcohol abuse.

Several events during the previous year contributed appreciably to the onset of the present illness. First, Mr. A.'s father, who had a 20-year history of heart disease, had suffered another heart attack 18 months previously, and he had died 9 months before the patient's hospital admission. The patient felt that his father was particularly weakened several months before he died, but Mr. A. had little overt emotional reaction to his father's decline and eventual death. However, once he had begun treatment in the hospital, Mr. A. became more overtly depressed and agitated, mainly out of concern for himself and how he would manage without his father.

For 4 years, Mr. A. had been living in an apartment in the home of married friends. He felt needed there, because this married couple argued frequently, and he had become a source of emotional support for both of them, sometimes acting as a go-between. About 1 year previously, he had moved out of this apartment, even though he did not feel secure enough to live alone. His decision to try living on his own coincided with his father's weakening condition and Mr. A.'s feeling that his father would soon die. His chest pains began around that time. The patient ended up sharing an apartment with a friend he knew casually. Mr. A. was unhappy in this situation; he felt that his roommate was irresponsible and worried that his new living arrangement was unstable, a worry that coincided with his worsening somatic symptoms and the onset of alcohol abuse.

Mr. A. became increasingly worried about his chest pains and drinking, and he attempted to contact his long-time, admired family doctor. He was devastated to learn that the doctor had himself recently suffered a heart attack, and Mr. A. feared that the doctor "wasn't there to lead me in the right direction." Mr. A. did stop drinking on his own, and he was soon able to see the doctor when the latter returned to his practice. Mr. A. felt sustained by the support of the benevolent family physician, who managed his somatic problems, arranged for diagnostic tests, and eventually admitted Mr. A. to the hospital. Throughout this period, and for 1 or 2 years previously, Mr. A. was also struggling with homosexual longings, which he came to terms with shortly after beginning treatment.

Mr. A. was the only child of parents who were highly dependent on each other and were rarely apart. He described a close relationship with his mother, who had been a clerk for the same company for 40 years. Although Mr. A. said that she was loving toward him and unselfish, he added that she had waited on his father hand and foot. He also complained that while she visited him in the hospital, she often talked with other patients when he thought her complete attention should have been directed to him. Mr. A. commented on his mother's steadying presence in the home, but he also felt she was "a little dumb," by which he meant that she seemed satisfied with nondemanding work and her role as wife and mother.

Mr. A. was often ill with colds or respiratory infections as a child. He realized that he had dramatized his distress to induce his mother to stay home with him, and she complied readily. As he entered high school, however, his mother no longer indulged Mr. A.'s dramatizing his illnesses, and she no longer was willing to stay home with him. He began to cultivate a relationship with the family physician (the same doctor who had admitted him to the hospital), who seemed to assume the comforting maternal functions he felt his mother no longer provided.

Mr. A. felt that his father was the weaker parent and needed both his wife and his son to be accepting of him and to look up to him. Mr. A. usually complied willingly with his father's wishes; he enjoyed how his father planned everything in advance, and he let his father take care of many things that the patient would otherwise have had to worry about. He also described his father as the "social director of the block." Mr. A. noted that although his mother ceased being overprotective when he was in high school, his father never stopped. He experienced his father's protectiveness at times as overcontrolling and thus unwelcome, although he believed that his father's intentions were benevolent. For example, Mr. A. was not allowed to have driving lessons at the age other adolescents were getting learners' permits. Mr. A.'s father also wanted him to attend a college 200 miles away that the father preferred, but Mr. A. failed the first quarter because he felt unready to leave home and therefore, as he said, "punished both of us in the process." At the time of this failure at college, Mr. A. had had an episode of agitated depression with chest pains, an episode that remitted when he returned home and finished college locally.

During adolescence, Mr. A. began arguing with his father, feeling that he could never make his father understand what he needed and that his father was too judgmental and insistent on being right. Mr. A. felt that he usually gave in to his father's insistence, which he experienced as his father making him feel inferior. Nevertheless, Mr. A.'s anger provoked his father to tears. It seemed that the father worried that Mr. A. would break away psychologically and cease to provide what the father needed from his son.

Mr. A. felt that he could not manage on his own and that even more than his father, he needed to remain physically near people from whom he found it hard to separate. An early memory was his telephoning his parents when he was left with a babysitter, asking them to return home. On one occasion, around age 8, Mr. A. became so distressed when his parents were away on a trip that they cut their vacation short to return home. He was enuretic until age 8 and described himself in childhood as "nervous," which I understood in part to indicate his difficulty feeling soothed or calmed. He alternated between struggling to forestall separations and achieving a measure of autonomy.

Mr. A. had a dramatic, histrionic clinical presentation while in the hospital. In contrast to his labile affect concerning fears for his health, this patient seemed unconcerned about other patients' problems. He was overly attuned to bodily reactions and medication side effects. Mr. A. sought frequent attention from the nursing staff to his needs of the moment, despite their reassurances that they had not forgotten about him while they attended to other responsibilities. He could initially appear demanding, but he could also settle down quickly once his exaggerated affective expressions of fearfulness were simply acknowledged.

Mr. A.'s expectation that he should be listened to at any given moment was sometimes conveyed with petulant entitlement or haughtiness, but this demandingness could be understood as a momentary fragmentation when he felt lapses of the responsiveness he needed to ensure self-cohesion. Thus, his need was not as much for attention as it was for securing the selfobject function of a calming presence. Self psychologists often regard what appears as angry demandingness or arrogance as disintegration products or depletion anxiety. Similarly, Mr. A.'s apparent grandiosity regarding his distress as being more important than that of others need not be understood mainly as a dislikable quality of entitlement or specialness but rather as the desperate expression of someone who feels he cannot hold himself together.

Once I explained the overt grandiosity and entitlement to Mr. A. in this way, with interpretations of selfobject needs and empathic failures, the humiliation underlying his exaggerated dramatic protests became more evident. It exposed how diminished or underpowered he could feel when his selfobject environment seemed undependable. The loss of his father as a protective anchor and the illness of his admired doctor devastated Mr. A., because both represented the danger of a fragmenting self in the absence of these needed selfobjects.

During the early period of treatment following discharge, Mr. A. described situations in which he would make himself useful so other people would need him, like his father used to do, and he derived satisfaction from the appreciation he thus received. He made several job moves, typically motivated by the desire for more gratitude for what he had to offer when he felt insufficiently appreciated at the job he was preparing to leave. Several of his short-lived relationships with men were characterized by fast involvements in which he attempted to fill all of their needs; he enjoyed being told how indispensable he was.

In therapy, he would alternate between a dramatic, agitated appearance and verbal affirmations about how well he was feeling. These frequent shifts eventually revealed his need to have me nearby. He appeared distressed enough to keep me interested in him, like he did as a child with his mother, while simultaneously wanting to assure me that he was getting better and becoming independent. He also felt he had to placate me and to persuade me that I was the reason he felt better, much like he had had to reassure his father of the father's importance to him. When he was feeling on an even keel, Mr. A.'s restored equilibrium did not provide an enjoyable sense of autonomy, because he feared it would not last. Being in treatment represented a constant reminder of his dependency. He once said, as I returned after canceling two sessions, "You're unimportant to me as a person, but what you say is important." On another occasion, after I cancelled a session, Mr. A. reported a dream about a person falling out of a shiny, silver-colored car. The play on my name seemed to represent the danger of depending on idealized selfobjects.

It appeared, therefore, that the transference remobilized both mirroring and idealization. He seemed to need me to provide mirroring selfobject functions and to proudly admire his accomplishments. However, Mr. A. also warily defended himself against equally vital idealization needs. Although he needed idealized selfobjects as a lifeline to bolster his self-cohesion, Mr. A. simultaneously feared its dissolution. He was afraid that he could not manage on his own without the strength or calming function provided by idealized selfobjects. Thus, Mr. A. attempted to keep people in his corner by trying to meet all their needs or by letting them know how much he needed them. He simultaneously minimized their importance to protect himself from the vestiges of his father's overcontrol. I thus began to understand why he minimized feeling dependent on the protective, steadying function he craved from his father and doctor.

Mr. A. was often vague in providing details about precipitants of his agitated states and came to quick explanations on his own. This lack of detail appeared to represent his need to block my seeing matters differently from him, thus allowing him to feel in control of his emotional states. He was not very interested in understanding the meanings of his reactions to events in his life, saying at one point, "I'm afraid to be devastated by all kinds of problems and conflicts right now. I feel like I'm walking on thin ice, although it's getting thicker, and I'll let you know when I'm ready to look at problems." For Mr. A., as with many patients with self disorders (not only those with primarily narcissistic presentations), interpretations of content and meanings sometimes count for relatively little. What may be more therapeutic than interpreting dynamics for these patients is to reestablish narcissistic equilibrium by permitting a silent development of an idealization transference. Premature interpretation of this transference risks diminishing its importance for such patients' psychological stabilization. Thus, pointing out selfobject needs too soon might be construed as a criticism exposing a deficiency. The therapist walks a fine line between conveying that the patient has a problem and providing a greater therapeutic benefit of permitting a developmental process to proceed. In Mr. A.'s case, he was settling into an idealizing selfobject transference while still immunizing himself from becoming destabilized when he felt I let him down. For example, when I forgot things Mr. A. told me, he felt angry or disappointed, because he was reexposed to feeling the imperfection of people he relied on. He tried to minimize his dependence on treatment to protect himself against becoming undermined by anything I might say that could threaten his growing but still vulnerable self-cohesion.

But he also came to see that constantly appeasing others wore them down and sometimes made them indifferent to him. He would then either cool his involvements and move on—for example, in his work and relationships—or he would turn to others for strength or calming when he felt rebuffed. This mechanism was also reminiscent of his turning to the family doctor as a young adolescent to provide continued calming reassurance, a need his mother seemed not to recognize that he still had. When Mr. A. described his mother as "dumb," referring to her readily accepting a limiting role in her work and in relation to her husband, I began to understand that this assertion represented his hurt anger at her not being as attuned to his brittle self-cohesion as he needed her to be. She mistook his entering adolescence as a time of greater self-reliance than he felt prepared to assume.

Mr. A. attempted to find a balance between mirroring and idealization selfobject needs for shoring up the self, much as he had tried as an adolescent to hold onto his father while simultaneously breaking away from his father's infantilizing. At the same time, Mr. A. could not afford to become dependent on or to be in awe of others, because he perceived disappointment in weaknesses of potential idealized selfobjects as inevitable. Thus, he became either panic-stricken (e.g., on discovering his admired doctor's illness) or indifferent (e.g., by minimizing his idealizing transference if he felt that it was too risky to place so much trust in my hands). This patient was similarly indecisive in life, vacillating between appearing self-reliant while concealing how much he needed to lean on others. Mr. A. wanted other people to make decisions for him, and he would try to control their influence through his expressions of tearful neediness when he felt they were not sufficiently sympathetic to him. He thus felt vulnerable underneath an appearance of acting accomplished.

Over time, Mr. A. settled into a pattern of coming into sessions feeling distressed and quickly feeling relieved, though he provided few details about the precipitants of these mental states. It seemed that Mr. A. was forming an idealizing transference in which he expressed confidence in me for something I did not in fact say or do to make him feel better. He could thus imagine the calming strength of an idealizing transference without actually experiencing that need. He once responded angrily, when I asked him for details about what sounded like a precipitating event for feeling anxious, "Whenever you ask me that, it's like a veil or block comes in front of my eyes." I began to see that his anger at me was caused by my not being responsive to his need to be taken care of by removing an unhappy or distressed state. Sometimes, pointing out this dynamic was not therapeutic. Instead, continuing to accept the silent idealization—without interfering by interpreting it—was necessary for building up the self-cohesion Mr. A. needed to secure.

His image of me as a "fix-it person" whom he needed when in distress alternated with an image of me as someone he neither needed nor was curious about when he felt well. I became a selfobject who was there not as a person in his own right but instead as someone who provided a needed function only when the self was in danger of fragmentation. Mr. A. preferred to think of therapy as a chore or imposition on his time unless he was thrown into a self state of feeling destabilized. During untroubled moments, he thought about me as a reminder of his vulnerability to not feeling in omnipotent control, which made him feel dependent or flawed. He would also at times show anger—for example, when my vacations or other absences interrupted the regularity of his sessions or when I forgot things. This reexposed him to feeling the imperfection of idealized selfobjects.

When he felt that psychotherapy was an imposition, Mr. A. was reminded of how angry he had felt when his father belittled him into doing what his father wanted, barely letting Mr. A. feel he had a life of his own. He felt this way when I expected him to come for treatment sessions on a regular basis even when he did not wish to do so. This expectation revived his father's overcontrol, reexposing him to the narcissistic rage he felt about being belittled. Feeling controlled and intimidated, Mr. A. could not risk standing up to an adversarial selfobject to build up the kind of confident autonomy that develops from a vigorous self. Instead, he feared alienating and thus losing the person on whom he depended for idealizing selfobject functions and for restoring calm when he felt endangered by an enfeebled self.

Mr. A.'s relationship with a boyfriend of a few months began to unravel as the boyfriend increasingly disliked Mr. A.'s constant checking in with him. Mr. A. thought this objection meant that his boyfriend did not care very much about him. Mr. A. in turn became less interested in his boyfriend. He commented that he always used to get what he wanted from his parents and in effect controlled their lives by his needy states of distress. In contrast, his boyfriend only withdrew more when Mr. A. acted fearful, and Mr. A. thus felt rebuffed.

Mr. A. was also angry at his mother's stoic reactions to how life had changed after his father's death. He resented her denial of her loneliness while he still experienced a desperate longing for his father. This realization led to a productive period in which I came to understand Mr. A.'s sense of loss and anger at his mother for what he experienced as her turning away from him as he entered adolescence, when she saw him as more autonomous than he felt. Mr. A. was not ready to do things on his own, and he had turned to his father out of a need for the father's protective overcontrol, despite his unsuccessful struggles with his father. Mr. A.'s admiring relationship with the family doctor also represented his attempt to secure a protectively calming assurance that he would be all right (i.e., that self-cohesion remained intact) when he felt his mother was "too dumb" (by which I think he meant too empathically misattuned) to discern how vulnerable he still felt.

Over time, Mr. A.'s fragmentation became less prominent as his self-cohesion became better cemented. It was replaced by depression as his main reaction to the empathic failures of an unreliable or imperfect idealization selfobject environment, both in the transference and in his expectations of the people in his life. In small increments over time, the internalizations afforded by a stable idealization selfobject transference provided enough self-cohesion to secure a more durable repair of a fragmentation-prone self. Gradually, Mr. A. better tolerated the disappointments of the moment-to-moment empathic failures and flaws of his selfobject world. Ultimately, the cohesion-fostering internalizations that took hold substantially relieved his depression. Thus feeling a more securely strengthened sense of self-cohesion, Mr. A. was able to terminate treatment to move to a part of the country where he wished to live because he enjoyed its warm weather. He had always feared moving there after college because he did not feel he could hold himself together sufficiently, but he now felt able to take this step on his own. I received a note from Mr. A. 6 months after his move indicating that despite moments of uncertainty about steadying himself, he was starting to establish a satisfying life.

CONCLUSION

In this chapter, devoted to narcissistic personality disorder, I surveyed this disturbance from the vantage points of descriptive psychopathology and the contemporary personality disorder theory and research literature, the classical drive theory and ego psychology tradition in psychoanalytic theory, and Kohut's self psychology. Kohut's views about the self began with his identification of selfobject transferences (mirroring, idealization, and twinship), a discovery that enabled psychoanalytic examination of disorders of self-cohesion. Kohut's views, particularly on selfobject transferences, represented an important breakthrough not only for understanding narcissistic personality disorder but also for better understanding a broad range of other forms of psychopathology. This chapter therefore addressed Kohut's early views and his later perspective on the psychology of the self as it continued to evolve. The expanded view of disorders of the self and of deficient self-cohesion forms the basis of discussion not only of narcissistic personality disorder, which is outlined in this chapter, but also of the personality disorders that I discuss throughout the remainder of this book.

II

DEVITALIZATION: THE UNMIRRORED SELF (SCHIZOID, SCHIZOTYPAL, AND AVOIDANT PERSONALITY DISORDERS)

3

DESCRIPTIVE PSYCHOPATHOLOGY AND THEORETICAL VIEWPOINTS: SCHIZOID, SCHIZOTYPAL, AND AVOIDANT PERSONALITY DISORDERS

Schizoid and schizotypal disorders have an established tradition in clinical psychopathology, particularly in their relationship to concepts of schizophrenia. Avoidant personality disorder is a relative newcomer to psychopathology, having been reformulated as a personality disorder by Millon (1969), who was mindful of its historical association with anxiety disorders and its relation to his biopsychosocial theory. Schizoid phenomena have also occupied an important position in British object relations theory.

In this chapter, I will examine several of these viewpoints, emphasizing clinical phenomenology and descriptive psychopathology as well as personality theories. This exposition will serve as a point of reference for chapter 4, in which I will consider schizoid, schizotypal, and avoidant personality disorders within the framework of Kohut's psychology of the self and subsequent developments in self psychology.

SCHIZOID PERSONALITY DISORDER

A close correspondence exists between schizophrenia on Axis I and schizoid and schizotypal personality disorders on Axis II. Consequently, an understanding of these two personality disorders is inextricably linked with contemporary conceptualizations of schizophrenia. Despite their genetic, biological, and phenomenological interrelationships, both schizoid and schizotypal conditions have largely been removed from diagnostic definitions of schizophrenia, and their relationship to schizophrenia remains uncertain.

For most of the 20th century, there were distinctive differences between European and American concepts of schizophrenia, with little agreement about its prominent symptoms. Even its essential features as a syndrome were in question, and there was little consensus about its related forms or variants. European concepts remained generally faithful to Kraepelin's (1919) view, in which a chronic, nonremitting, and progressively deteriorating course primarily defined the illness. This was the so-called *nuclear syndrome* definition, which American psychiatrists regarded as the *process* or *poor-prognosis* form. The continental viewpoint also incorporated ideas from the German school of phenomenological psychiatry, particularly Schneider's (1959) view about symptoms of first-rank importance.

In contrast, American psychiatry subscribed to a broader view influenced by Bleuler's (1911/1950) emphasis on primary symptoms on the one hand and by psychoanalysis on the other. What are now considered schizoid and schizotypal personality disorders would have been classified as schizophrenia in the broad American conceptualization before the introduction of the third edition of the *Diagnostic and Statistical Manual of Mental Disorders* (*DSM–III*; American Psychiatric Association, 1980). This view stressed Bleuler's primary symptoms, such as flat affect and loose associations, more than the secondary symptoms, such as delusions or hallucinations. It also incorporated conditions variously described as *schizophreniform* (Langfeldt, 1971), *reactive* or *acute* (Arieti, 1974), and *schizophrenia of good prognosis* (Stephens, 1978; Vaillant, 1964) or *with good premorbid adjustment* (Cromwell, 1975; Strauss, Klorman, & Kokes, 1977). Bleuler's view incorporated even nonpsychotic forms, denoted *simple*, *latent*, or *residual* schizophrenia, and disorders variously described as *borderline schizophrenia* or *pseudoneurotic schizophrenia*, a forerunner of borderline personality disorder (Knight, 1953). In this way, the broad American view included conditions considered to represent genetic variants of schizophrenia, variants that Kety, Rosenthal, Wender, and Schulsinger (1968) denoted the *schizophrenia spectrum*.

To rectify this fundamental conceptual and clinical discrepancy, Feighner et al. (1972) introduced criteria to provide clearly specified, reliable diagnostic guidelines to narrow the overly broad American diagnostic practice. Indeed, the Feighner et al. criteria became the forerunner of the

Research Diagnostic Criteria (Spitzer, Endicott, & Robins, 1978) and subsequently the *DSM–III*, the revised third edition (*DSM–III–R*), and the fourth edition (*DSM–IV*; American Psychiatric Association, 1980, 1987, 1994). Thus, schizophrenia as it is currently defined remains closer to the European concept of the nuclear syndrome. The broader reactive or good prognosis forms—which European psychiatry never considered to be true schizophrenia—ultimately were encompassed in the schizoid and schizotypal personality disorders on Axis II. Schizoaffective disorders, poor prognosis bipolar or mixed schizophrenic–affective syndromes, and atypical but nonremitting psychoses remained as Axis I disorders, but such hybrid forms were generally no longer regarded as schizophrenia per se. Their clinical course and outcome as well as family history of psychopathology are generally intermediate between those of schizophrenia and those of affective disorders, which may explain the greater comorbidity and familial risk for major depression and schizophrenia in schizotypal personality disorder.

Further, the problem of a close correspondence between schizoid personality disorder and the prodromal phase of schizophrenia has not been resolved satisfactorily. As a result, the familial and genetic links between these disorders remain speculative. There also are biological markers associated with schizophrenia in schizotypal personality disorder, such as impaired saccadic eye-tracking movements (Siever et al., 1987), attentional deficits (Braff, 1986), and ventricular enlargement on computed tomography (Siever et al., 1987). Premorbid schizoid personality traits are frequently found in studies of the childhood precursors of schizophrenia and across various methods of study, including parents' retrospective recollections, examination of childhood records, and high-risk study designs. However, it remains uncertain whether premorbid schizoid personality features are risk factors predisposing to clinical schizophrenia in adulthood. Premorbid schizoid features also may represent early manifestations of a neurodegenerative disorder that is itself a precursor of adult-onset schizophrenic psychosis.

Torgerson (1995) suggested that the modifications of the *DSM–IV* criteria for schizoid personality disorder inadvertently created two disorders instead of a single condition—an affect-constricted disorder resembling schizotypal personality disorder and a seclusive disorder closely resembling avoidant personality disorder. Though schizoid and schizotypal personality disorders are classified in *DSM–IV* as personality disorders (Axis II), these disorders, together with paranoid personality disorder, form a cluster characterized by odd or eccentric behavior (Cluster A). However, it is generally recognized that there exists little agreed-on empirical justification for the cluster distinctions within Axis II.

Kalus, Bernstein, and Siever (1995) reported a median prevalence rate of schizoid personality in several studies as 8.5%. However, most schizoid patients live complacent and largely asymptomatic lives, unsatisfying though they may be, and such patients infrequently present for treatment or clinical evaluation, suggesting that the true prevalence may be higher than that reported in the literature.

In renaming Kraepelin's (1919) dementia praecox syndrome *schizophrenia*, Bleuler (1911/1950) emphasized a division or splitting of the core cognitive and affective areas of experience and deemphasized the central importance of the inevitable deteriorating course Kraepelin considered crucial. In favoring splitting among the primary symptoms, Bleuler may have been particularly influenced by Kraepelin's description of autistic personality, a mild personality defect closely resembling the contemporary definition of schizoid personality disorder. Autistic personality showed a stable, nondeteriorating course, and Kraepelin regarded it as a less severe variant of dementia praecox. Bleuler's focus on this prepsychotic variant, a focus that coincided with the emergence of psychoanalysis, was particularly influential in the United States. Consequently, the emphasis on splitting and a preoccupation with internal life became essential criteria for the diagnosis and clinical understanding of schizophrenia and schizoid conditions.

The schizoid type is regarded sometimes as a premorbid form of clinical schizophrenia and sometimes as a severe but stable personality disorder. It is highlighted more by constriction and avolition than by overt psychosis. Because it compromises social and vocational functioning, schizoid disorder resembles a mental state that J. Hughlings Jackson (1887) first identified as *negative symptoms*; this was later reconceptualized as a *negative symptom syndrome* (Andreasen, 1982; Crow, 1980) or *deficit syndrome* (Carpenter, Heinrichs, & Wagman, 1985).

Bleuler's (1911/1950) view of schizophrenia, particularly its nonpsychotic forms, closely paralleled W. Reich's (1933/1949) expansion of psychoanalysis to consider character disorders as asymptomatic forms of psychoneuroses. Thus, a psychoanalytic understanding of personality disorders was facilitated by a changed emphasis from symptom neuroses to the character neuroses, now typically termed *character disorders* (W. Reich, 1933/1949). A shift in focus occurred from circumscribed symptomatic clinical complaints to vaguely articulated dissatisfactions with life, inhibitions, diminished accomplishments, and the inability to experience vitality or to sustain interests. W. Reich remained committed to drive theory in psychoanalysis, which emphasized the view that symptom formation resulted from conflict between drives and their counterforces (defenses). However, he also allowed for the possibility that the marked preference for isolation associated with schizoid patients, often disposing them to depersonalization and derealization, could represent a characterological disturbance resulting from a profound sense of inner deadness.

Some schools of psychoanalytic thinking moved increasingly toward models that regarded drives and conflict in different ways. For example, British object relations theories, beginning with Melanie Klein's work (1930, 1935), considered schizoid mechanisms as a split between persecutory and idealized objects. Klein referred to this developmentally primitive split as the *paranoid–schizoid position*. She considered splitting to be a defense to preserve psychological intactness. This view established a basis for Fairbairn's (1954) and Guntrip's (1969) subsequent work describing schizoid phenomena centering on isolation as a self-protective mechanism. Although it was protective, prominent isolation also required the patient to be on guard against potential danger. Kernberg (1967) emphasized a splitting mechanism as well, but his viewpoint located the split between that of contradictory shameful and exalted self-representations. M. Klein and Kernberg both stressed the importance of aggression in the pathogenesis of severe psychopathology, including but not limited to schizoid personality.

Fairbairn (1954) formulated the problem of schizoid states differently. He considered isolation and detachment as hallmarks of such patients' sense of the self and of the external world. An artificial way of relating to others—as if behind plate glass—became such persons' predominant experience, an experience produced by a phenomenological sense that loving, closeness, or intimacy of any sort would lead only to danger. Originating from pronounced maternal deficits in conveying affection, schizoid patients' experiences or fantasies about intimacy and its ensuing threats dominate their inner lives. Loving therefore cannot be trusted, because the internal mental representations of patients' object worlds are characterized by prominent fantasies of malevolence. This perceived menace necessitates keeping people at a great distance. Depersonalization also markedly diminishes the emotional value of objects. Guntrip (1969, 1971) extended Fairbairn's views by noting that the quality of schizoid depersonalization is not that of a sense of unreality but rather that of feelings of not belonging or of being profoundly out of touch with the world. Consequently, such patients experience themselves as deeply isolated and cut off from others. Though typically nonpsychotic, schizoid patients characteristically feel disconnected from other people and are largely incapable of involved, intimate human relationships.

Thus, Fairbairn (1954) and Guntrip (1969, 1971), although influenced in part by M. Klein (1930, 1935) but disinclined to follow her controversial views about aggression, emphasized the central problem of schizoid patients as being unable to feel close intimacy. The danger of close intimacy is that, out of a sense of deep distrust, such patients' needs for contact and intimacy are so submerged that relationships with others become emotionally dessicated. Needs for love are experienced as intense object hunger, which Guntrip (1969) called "love made hungry" (p. 24). Thus, such patients fail to develop attachments because the voraciousness of their needs for affection runs the risk of becoming uncontrollable. As a result, schizoid patients back away from affectional needs, remaining withdrawn and self-sufficient. It is not a problem of inability to form or even to maintain relationships. Rather, the problem is being able to be in a relationship without constantly experiencing a compelling need to remain apart from it. Winnicott (1965) described the same phenomenon and spoke of a false self that covers up and protects a submerged true self. The false self does not experience life in any real or genuine affective way; it represents an outward presentation of a deceptive false sense of integration. Winnicott regarded the socially conforming veneer of the false self as protectively concealing an emergence of the true self. It was Winnicott's view that such patients defensively put the true self into a kind of cold storage when they perceive the object world to be either malevolent or insufficiently sustaining. This view is similar to that of Guntrip's (1971) "regressed ego . . . in which the infant found his world so intolerable that the sensitive heart of him fled into himself" (p. 152). Josephs (1992) also called attention to a split between public and private aspects of self experience, in which aloof superiority occurs alongside feelings of being rejected. Josephs emphasized such patients' surface presentation of defensive detachment while they privately await recognition of their special but unrecognized attributes.

Other approaches to understanding schizoid personality disorder have grappled with conceptual problems associated with differences between categorical and dimensional models. One approach combining elements of both is Cloninger's (1987) psychobiological model. Using three temperament dimensions, Cloninger characterized patients with schizoid personality disorder as showing low levels of novelty seeking, harm avoidance, and reward dependence. In his original view, this accounted for their characteristic inflexible resistance to change and disinterest in novel stimuli, ease in adjusting to unfamiliar situations (despite a preference for sameness and a disinclination to seek novelty), and indifference to social–interpersonal motivation. A subsequent examination of Cloninger's temperament dimensions confirmed the low levels of novelty seeking and reward dependence but did not demonstrate a distinctively low level of harm avoidance (Battaglia, Przybeck, Bellodi, & Cloninger, 1996).

Westen and Shedler (1999a, 1999b) also proposed a model of personality disorders that incorporated dimensional aspects while preserving a categorical approach, and they identified a schizoid factor using Q-sort analysis. Their description of the schizoid factor resembles salient customary diagnostic criteria such as limited intimate relationships and affective constriction. It is also broader in scope, incorporating characteristics that often have been implied but infrequently delineated in the nomenclature of resources such as the DSM or the International Classification of Diseases (World Health Organization, 1992). Thus, other characteristics Westen and Shedler identified included difficulty expressing wishes or interests, problems interpreting others' behavior, shallow insight into self and others' motives or psychological states, and concrete thinking.

Millon's (1969) earlier work emphasized a passive–detached prototype in schizoid personality disorder, defined in part by diminished or bland affectivity and indifferent interpersonal relations. This prototype was also characterized by a complacent self-image, sometimes accompanied by deviant but not grossly disordered cognitive functions. Millon's (1996) more recent reconceptualization expanded his prototype view, incorporating evolutionary (adaptive) considerations superimposed on the basic schizoid personality prototype.

SCHIZOTYPAL PERSONALITY DISORDER

Most clinical descriptions of schizotypal personality disorder emphasize its chief features as odd or eccentric behavior and thinking distortions, like magical thinking or circumstantial speech, but without formal thought disorder. Other common features include referential ideas; suspicious, secretive, or paranoid ideation; and unusual perceptual aberrations such as somatic illusions. Schizotypal clinical features usually fall short of delusional intensity and thus represent subthreshold psychotic phenomena. Constricted but not overtly flat affect and social–interpersonal deficits complete the clinical picture.

Rado (1956) introduced the term *schizotypal* to describe a condition he considered a phenotypical variant of schizophrenia. In this conceptualization of the schizotypal condition based on its genetic relationship to schizophrenia, Rado emphasized two central deficits. The first was a pronounced pleasure deficiency (anhedonia), a concept that subsequently became part of both Meehl's (1962) and Chapman, Chapman, and Raulin's (1976) thinking about schizophrenia. The second fundamental deficit was a disturbance of the proprioceptive sense, interfering with muscle and joint feedback about bodily orientation (Ritzler & Rosenbaum, 1974). Rado believed that these two deficits compromised what he described as an *action self* necessary to forestall psychological disintegration. Rado's viewpoint also influenced Meehl's view concerning the importance of a core neural integrative defect in schizotypy and schizophrenia, a view also represented in Fish's (1977) concept of pandevelopmental regression and, more recently, in R. M. Murray, O'Callaghan, Castle, and Lewis's (1992) neurodevelopmental view. Recognizing that some schizotypal patients progress to develop clinical schizophrenia, Meehl postulated that constitutional, biochemical, and environmental vulnerabilities, alone or in combination, represented major etiologic factors in producing an overt schizophrenic illness. His concept of the taxon identified the schizotaxic diathesis as a probable genetic basis for the stable, compensated schizotype. Rado's and Meehl's views also influenced the concept of a schizophrenia spectrum (Kety et al., 1968)—a range of genetically related conditions differing predominantly in clinical phenotypes that reflect varying degrees of genetic penetrance. Thus, schizotypal personality disorder might represent one such disorder; it also could be considered a stable, ingrained taxon with its "relatively enduring templates . . . serving as the underlying architecture of the mind" (Millon, 1996, p. 609).

Apart from the British object relations theorists' views about schizoid mechanisms and Rado's (1956) emphasis on anhedonia, a well-defined body of psychoanalytic literature about schizotypal personality does not exist. In general, psychoanalysis was considered an inadvisable treatment for schizophrenia-like conditions, possibly including schizotypal personality disorder, because of Freud's (1924/1961d) distinction between transference neuroses that were analyzable and narcissistic neuroses that were not (which included most psychoses). This classical drive theory formulation regarded schizophrenics as unsuitable for psychoanalysis because they were unable to establish a workable transference; consequently, they would fail to cathect the analyst as a transference object. Nevertheless, some of Freud's followers attempted to treat schizophrenics analytically. Abraham (1916/1927a) attempted to do so but eventually abandoned this effort; Federn (1953) later may have achieved some success in it.

Interest in schizophrenia within psychoanalysis remained generally limited relative to the field's interest in severe character pathology. As a result, theoretical advances within psychoanalysis were influenced more through work with nonpsychotic conditions than through the treatment of the psychoses. Besides Federn (1953), however, some psychoanalytic theorists did take on the problem of schizophrenia—primarily Sullivan (1947), Fromm-Reichmann (1950), Searles (1965), and Arieti (1974). Despite these few but notable exceptions, psychodynamic theories of schizophrenia lagged behind theoretical interest in borderline and schizoid conditions. Moreover, views about variants, subtypes, or related schizophrenia-like conditions did not attract prominent attention apart from formulations about schizoid personality disorder.

Notwithstanding psychoanalytic theory's limited interest in such conditions, the predominant psychodynamic perspective placed particular emphasis on compromised maternal adequacy, including hostile criticism or remote detachment in early development. Arieti (1974) identified four fundamental negative maternal characteristics (anxiety, hostility, detachment, and unpredictability) as the most salient qualities influencing preschizophrenic children, resulting in an internalization of the mother as malevolent. Arieti also commented that this malevolent introjection extended as well to the father. Together, these developmental failures impaired formation of "the other important inner object—the self-image" (p. 92). Thus encumbered, such patients exhibit pronounced disturbances of reality testing, thought disorder, an impaired sense of identity, and body image distortions. These coalesce to form the central premorbid or prodromal abnormalities of schizophrenia: withdrawal, estrangement from social or conventional reality, and preoccupation with internal fantasies of rage or disintegration.

Psychoanalytic formulations of schizophrenia did not require a new or different psychodynamic proposition to explain schizophrenia and its variants. Thus, schizophrenia was regarded as different in degree but not in kind from analyzable nonpsychotic (neurotic) disorders. As a result, it mainly represented a more severe form of psychopathology. Some formulations emphasized projection as a principal defense. Freud's (1924/1961d) view was that disavowal of external reality was a specific restitutive defense in schizophrenia. Jacobson (1967) emphasized exaggerated pseudoautonomy from the environment, and Federn (1953) stressed prominent boundary disturbances. M. Klein (1935) differentiated the primitive part object relationships of paranoid and schizoid phenomena from the more developmentally mature whole object relationships of a depressive position. Despite these different formulations, most conceptualizations of schizophrenia and related conditions such as schizotypal personality disorder subscribed in part to a view of the disorder as a new organization built up from primitive and concrete integrations of external reality.

Approaching the interrelationships among various disorders from a different perspective, Westen and Shedler (1999b) reported that patients with clinical diagnoses of schizoid, schizotypal, and avoidant personality disorder all showed a distinctive clustering on the Q sort–identified schizoid factor, suggesting that these personality disorder syndromes might not be empirically distinct. Millon (1996) considered schizotypal personality disorder to be a more severe, structurally defective clinical manifestation of a pleasure-deficient subgroup of personality disorders. He regarded schizotypal personality disorder as being similar conceptually to schizoid and avoidant personality disorders and differentiated two subtypes representing perturbations of schizoid or avoidant phenomena. For schizoid personality disorder, a breakdown into a more severe degree of personality decompensation might assume the form of schizotypal personality disorder. A still further breakdown might result in what Millon called a *terminal personality*, which would be clinical schizophrenia in the case of the schizoid and schizotypal personality disorders. Spitzer, Endicott, and Gibbon (1979) emphasized the importance of differentiating schizotypal phenomena from borderline personality disorder, with schizotypal disorder being dominated by chronic psychosis-like features and borderline disorder being dominated by affective instability and impulsivity. As might be expected, the problem of comorbidity with other Axis II disorders and with Axis I syndromes cannot be overlooked.

Despite their substantial overlap in the *DSM–IV* with Axis I conditions (schizophrenia primarily, but sometimes also major depression), schizotypal, schizoid, and paranoid personality disorders are grouped together, constituting a cluster of disorders typically characterized as having odd or eccentric clinical presentations (Cluster A). There are also patterns of comorbid relationships among these three personality disorders, as well as reported comorbidity among schizotypal personality disorder and Cluster C conditions representing anxious/fearful detachment, such as avoidant and obsessive–compulsive personality disorders.

AVOIDANT PERSONALITY DISORDER

Although avoidant personality disorder may show less overlap with schizophrenia than schizoid and schizotypal personality disorders, it was Millon (1969) who first recognized the similarities between schizoid and avoidant typologies. However, in his view, these conditions represented more than variations of a single diagnostic entity. Millon's thinking was influenced by his distinction between passive and active forms of detachment, representing an intersection between the pleasure–pain and active–passive polarities (dimensions) that are central to his biopsychosocial framework. Thus, Millon was able to incorporate what Bleuler (1911/1950) and Kretschmer (1925) considered to be variants of a preschizophrenic disposition by differentiating these two predominant modes of organization of behavior and experience.

The chief clinical characteristics of the avoidant personality disorder are interpersonal aversiveness (avoidance) and social inhibition, sometimes manifested as clinically overt social phobia or as a milder, subclinical variant. A prominent relationship between this disorder and phobic disorder suggests that habitual avoidance may achieve anxiety reduction. In addition, important associated characteristics include hypersensitivity to criticism, rejection, or shame—features that also are prominent in narcissistic personality disorder. Appreciable concern about inadequacy is also typically present, accompanied by behavior intended to conceal its appearance. Millon (1969) elaborated on these core features, emphasizing avoidant patients' hyperalertness to signs of potential negative appraisal, affective–cognitive distortions, and interpersonal distrust. Avoidant personality disorder shows prominent comorbidity with schizoid personality disorder on Axis II and phobic disorder on Axis I, which is not surprising, as the main defining features and theoretical underpinnings of all three disorders are interrelated.

The similarity between avoidant and schizoid personality disorders understandably led some to regard avoidant personality as a variant of schizoid personality disorder (Livesley & West, 1986). Other clinical observers regarded it to be a phenomenologically related but nevertheless independent personality configuration. In the latter view, although it may resemble schizoid personality, avoidant personality disorder is nonetheless different enough to be regarded as a conceptually and perhaps etiologically distinct condition (Millon & Martinez, 1995). Still another approach has emphasized the similarity between avoidant personality disorder and a spectrum of anxiety–phobic conditions (Siever & Davis, 1991).

Although Bleuler (1911/1950) and Schneider (1959) described features generally resembling what Millon would later term *avoidant* (Millon, 1996), it was largely Kretschmer's (1925) earlier clinical description of a hyperaesthetic subtype of the schizoid temperament that influenced Millon's formulation. For Kretschmer, the hyperaesthetic solution was one of minimizing outward stimulation by avoidance, because it had become too difficult for such patients to tolerate the chronic turmoil they felt most of the time about their relationship to the external world. The avoidant patient is thus considered hypersensitive rather than indifferent to others.

Psychoanalytic conceptualizations about avoidant personality disorder were closely linked to formulations about symptom disturbances such as obsessive–compulsive or phobic neurosis, despite the relative absence or diminished prominence of anxiety in its overt clinical presentation. Avoidant personality disorder may therefore be viewed as a characterologically ingrained pattern of avoidance in the interest of minimizing anxiety. Psychoanalytic views also regarded avoidance not as representing disinterest, as with schizoid detachment, but rather as representing a fear of rejection or criticism despite a desire for approval. Horney's (1945) detached personality type was similarly conceptualized as typically fearing rejection or criticism. W. Reich's (1933/1949) and Rado's (1969) attention to character pathology also emphasized how stable ego-syntonic adaptations such as pronounced avoidance contained anxiety associated with instinctual gratification while providing a concealed means of satisfying drives.

Millon (1996) differentiated what he referred to as the "hard protective wall" of the avoidant personality from the indifferent, disinterested schizoid patient who appears not to need others. He regarded avoidant personality disorder patients as only appearing outwardly disinterested because they feared showing how much they craved contact with others. Millon also considered Menninger's (1930) description of "isolated personalities" who withhold themselves from social contacts as being closer to contemporary views of avoidant personality disorder. Menninger differentiated such isolated personalities from schizoid patients, noting the hypersensitivity and pervasive discouragement of the former and the asocial nature of the latter.

An adaptation centered on isolation or withholding gives rise to the interpersonal difficulties characteristically seen in patients with avoidant personality disorder. Thus, fearful distrust of people, typified by both wanting intensely and fearing rejection or derision, leads to the interpersonal aversiveness or pananxiety that forecloses intimacy in all but the most secure of relationships. Such patients make other people uncomfortable in their presence because of their intense social distress and what others perceived as an ever-constant yet needless "testing the waters" with the people around them. Avoidant patients also invite alienation because of the uncomfortable distance they create, thereby relegating themselves to a position of isolation. Consequently, their being on the fringes of involvements with people creates perches from which they can observe people or situations around them with a sharp eye, appraising how safe from potential criticism or humiliation they seem to be. Shame fuels their hypervigilance, which differs from the quality of hypervigilance seen in paranoid patients, for whom protecting themselves from a malevolent world filled with danger becomes the overriding concern.

Millon also commented on avoidant patients' fragile personality organization, speculating that their hyperarousal derived in part from a biological predisposition to sensory irritability or from a constitutionally anxious temperament. He regarded this disposition as stemming from a heightened sensitivity in infancy to tension states associated with overwhelming sensory stimuli. Millon's view is consistent with Siever and Davis's (1991) view that a genetic or psychobiological vulnerability underlies social aversiveness found in various disturbances, including avoidant personality disorder. Siever and Davis's model suggests that an anxiety–inhibition dimension involved in sympathetic nervous system and adrenocortical hyper-responsivity may account for such patients' shyness and interpersonal apprehensiveness. These models are also consistent with Schore's (2003a) proposition that affect regulation, including a capacity to modulate anxiety, is impeded during development by maternal aversiveness or disinterest. This kind of mother–child interaction pattern might give rise to an insecure, avoidant attachment pattern that Schore postulated could foster faulty affective regulation. This would in turn influence autonomic nervous system reactivity and in the process modify developing orbitofrontal neural pathways.

CONCLUSION

This chapter reviewed several viewpoints about schizoid, schizotypal, and avoidant personality disorders, emphasizing contributions from descriptive psychopathology and the literature on contemporary theories of personality. Schizoid and schizotypal personality disorders were discussed in relation to schizophrenia, focusing particularly on the evolving breadth of diagnostic definitions of schizophrenia. Further, I considered schizoid and schizotypal conditions as clinically distinct but also genetically related variants. Other views of these conditions were discussed, particularly those influenced by the British object relations school of psychoanalysis and more recent formulations proposed by Cloninger (1987), Westen and Shedler (1999a, 1999b), and Millon (1996). Current concepts of avoidant personality disorder also were reviewed, taking into account its origins in Kretschmer's (1925) and Menninger's (1930) formulations, and more recent views in descriptive psychopathology.

4

A SELF PSYCHOLOGICAL VIEWPOINT: SCHIZOID, SCHIZOTYPAL, AND AVOIDANT PERSONALITY DISORDERS

In chapter 3, I outlined clinical characteristics and several important psychoanalytic and personality theory viewpoints on schizoid, schizotypal, and avoidant personality disorders. In this chapter I consider these disorders from a self psychological vantage point emphasizing a primary deficiency in the mirroring sector of the self. According to this view, deficient mirroring produces varying configurations of distancing that characterize the clinical presentations of these three personality disorders. I will argue that a chronic, prolonged mirroring defect presages an organization of the self that is fundamentally characterized by devitalization. Thus, experiences of depletion become the predominant experiences of such persons' lives. The theoretical discussion of each of these personality disorders concludes with a case study to illustrate how devitalization may be conceptualized.

Kohut (1971, 1977, 1984) did not specifically address schizoid, schizotypal, and avoidant personality disorders except in passing; however, his expanded view of the self permits generalization of its concepts to characterize these personality disorders. As I explain in this chapter, Kohut's ideas provide a way to understand how merging with the mirroring functions of caretaking selfobjects solidifies self-cohesion. I will argue that schizoid, schizotypal, and avoidant personality disorder patients' mirroring selfobjects are too unstable or frightening to permit such a merger to proceed comfortably. Thus, the central problem for these patients is an unmirrored self, resulting in an insufficient capacity to maintain vitality or buoyancy of the self when it is injured.

These self disorders become ingrained as personality disturbances when needs for affirmation or admiration are met with prolonged empathic selfobject failures. Such patients' efforts to secure an engaged, enthusiastic response to mirroring selfobject needs is undermined. Although devitalization may result from other selfobject deficiencies, such as idealization and twinship, it is often most evident when a mirroring disturbance is the prominent source of selfobject failure. Moreover, devitalization is not unique to schizoid, schizotypal, and avoidant personality disorders. It may characterize other disorders, including other personality disorders and asymptomatic adaptational disturbances. My point is that devitalization as a predominant self experience is a primary feature of these personality disorders.

Selfobject failures, including those of the mirroring sector of the self, are frequently ascertained in treatment when patients' sense of confidence in their abilities is diminished or when they find it hard to respond with enthusiasm to things that matter in their lives. Goals or ambitions may no longer be compelling; indeed, for some people, a sense of purpose never really developed in the first place. Such people lack the vitality that often comes from having burning desires or feeling passionate about their interests. They often experience chronic boredom, and they feel as if they drift through life without purpose or direction. A sense of buoyancy is replaced by a feeling of depletion. They repeatedly experience the kind of mirroring selfobject responsiveness that fails to instill a firmed-up sense of believing oneself to be worthwhile or deserving of admiration. Such patients experience mirroring selfobjects as having psychologically forgotten about or ignored them; thus, devitalized, they often feel psychologically invisible.[1]

Manifestations of devitalization may resemble depressive states, particularly subsyndromal depressions. Indeed, mirroring deficiencies are often prominent in self states of chronic depressions such as depressive personality disorder, which I will discuss in detail in chapter 9. Devitalization, however, is not synonymous with depression, because the predominant experience of a self disorder is depletion that interferes with self-cohesion. The devitalization

---

[1] A particularly vivid example is the character Amos's song, "Mister Cellophane," from the musical play *Chicago* (Ebb & Fosse, 1976). The lyric uses the metaphor of cellophane paper to convey how this character feels himself to be transparent rather than translucent. Amos describes people who see beyond or through him but do not psychologically "see" him. One part of the song describes how, as a small boy, his parents moved and forgot to take him along (Ebb & Fosse, 1976, p. 63). I have previously cited this example (Silverstein, 2001) to differentiate between abandonment and being chronically forgotten psychologically.

of the self is manifested in chronic depressions by depressive affect; devitalization is manifested in schizoid, schizotypal, and avoidant personality disorders by withdrawal or aversion. The distanced withdrawal or aversiveness that typifies these conditions, even in the more severe schizotypal manifestation, may be reconceptualized as steps taken to prevent further injury to an already depleted self. Withdrawal closes off possibilities for alternative paths to revitalize an unmirrored self, such as attempting to secure idealization or twinship selfobject responsiveness.

In the following discussion of mirroring deficiencies, I will also incorporate elements of intersubjectivity theory. Intersubjectivity theory represents a further extension of self psychology that stresses a two-person interactive context. As I noted in chapter 2, it emphasizes the importance of the affect-laden interactions between caregivers and infants and the ways such interactions mutually influence these parties, thus creating an intersubjective field or context. Human interactions—what Stolorow and Atwood (1992) described as an intersection of individual subjectivities—contain the selfobject meanings people look for in one another. An intersubjective context also encompasses the ways individuals serve mutually regulating functions for each other's experiences of affect states.

SCHIZOID PERSONALITY DISORDER

Like any theory of personality and development, a self psychological understanding of mirroring deficits in schizoid personality disorder must take into account the effects of genetic or family history predisposition, particularly because these effects may influence empathic functions. For example, the deficiencies of caregivers—usually mothers—who themselves suffer from an illness of any severity within the schizophrenic spectrum will very likely compromise their empathic capacity. Such deficits can include diminished affective responsiveness and defective capacity for empathic resonance, both necessary for ensuring important caregiving functions. In other cases, caregivers who are relatively free of overt illness may be confronted with an infant showing manifestations of a schizophrenia spectrum condition. This kind of child requires an extraordinary level of selfobject attunement that could challenge even the most empathically capable of caregivers, particularly mothers who are themselves compromised by a genetic predisposition likely to interfere with normal empathic function.

Faulty empathic responsiveness diminishes a caregiver's capacity to notice and then respond accurately to a child's moment-to-moment fluctuations in self states. If a caregiver's diminished attunement is prominent, or if his or her impaired capacity for empathic responsiveness becomes prolonged or chronic, then a mirroring deficiency is created. This defect interferes with a developing child's reasonable expectations for being understood or responded to accurately. Empathic failures leave such children feeling forgotten about and psychologically dropped. Thus, children's needs to feel affirmed fail to develop normally, and this unmet need then becomes the prominent characteristic of a severe mirroring disturbance. They withdraw from the unresponsive caregiver, acquiring as a result an aloof, precocious self-sufficiency that becomes their predominant reaction to empathic unresponsiveness. Efforts to secure an engaged, enthusiastic response to mirroring selfobject needs are undermined. A child so affected becomes unable to sustain vitality or buoyancy. Detachment and affective constriction become self-protective defense operations. This response may occur particularly if an alternative pathway to solidify self-cohesion through idealization or twinship does not develop into a sufficiently robust compensatory structure.

In this way, a mirroring deficit can become so pronounced that the cementing of self-cohesion through transmuting internalizations (defined in chap. 2) does not take hold. An internal capacity to regulate intense affect states does not develop because an internal structure is not formed. Turning their backs on a disappointing selfobject environment, such patients ultimately feel lifeless or alienated. Patients sometimes describe this self state using imagery such as paranoid fantasies about robots or other manifestations of a mechanical existence dominated by a lack of warmth or human sentiments.

Thus, schizoid patients typically reveal histories of an absent or minimal sense of feeling valued. As children, the grandiose strivings that are part of normal development were ignored or thwarted. Interfering with the precursors of a robust self, this deficit impedes their acquiring a healthy sense of feeling proud and desired. Normal grandiose strivings are not meant to connote grandiosity in the sense of hypomanic omnipotence or delusional thinking. Rather, they refer to the sense of imagining oneself as special—and thus vibrant—as a mother's adored child. A genetically vulnerable child who fails to evoke "the gleam in the mother's eye," as Kohut often phrased it, feels unresponded to when his or her selfobject environment cannot detect this selfobject need for mirroring. In many self disorders, the stirrings of a prideful sense of accomplishment are compromised, resulting in diminished self-esteem, depression, chronic boredom, or ambitionless life goals that are sometimes concealed behind a veneer of defensive grandiosity. For the schizoid patient, however, a mirroring deficiency may lead in a more ominous direction: Believing that anything he or she might do would lead nowhere, this kind of child disappears psychologically into a type of existence that foreshadows the schizoid adaptation to a life of feeling unimportant or unrecognized.

Young children normally turn to what they expect should be a reasonably empathic selfobject environment, in effect saying, "Look at me," or "Notice that I'm here [or smiling, or unhappy] and that I want to interact with you." Their expectation is that such motivations will be welcomed, but their requests may fall on deaf (i.e., empathically unresponsive) ears. The problem is not one of abandonment, yet children growing up in an insufficiently responsive selfobject environment end up seeming to take care of themselves. They react to their primary caregivers mechanically and in emotionally distant ways. Their caregivers do not seem to decipher cues beyond the basic caretaking functions of responding to biological needs for feeding, warmth, or cleaning. They seem either to lack the empathic wherewithal or to have given up on the struggle to grasp their charges' unspoken and sometimes veiled selfobject needs (similar to Fonagy et al.'s [1996] concept, in a different but not unrelated context, of reflective function). Moreover, genetically vulnerable children may not be able to signal very well what they need, not because they do not need selfobject responsiveness, but because their selfobject surround has not responded in a way that encourages them to display what normal children or infants manage to convey spontaneously.

Therefore, children who eventually develop the hallmark signs of schizoid personality disorder do not acquire a sense of invigoration of the self. A sustained sense of joyful admiration emanating from an appropriately mirroring caregiver has become chronically interrupted. The infant research literature on normal development is replete with examples of the subtle moment-to-moment, mutually interacting communications between mothers and their infants that promote the development of self-cohesion (Beebe & Lachmann, 2002; Lichtenberg, 1983). Children whose unsuccessful efforts to evoke the engagement of a responsive, psychologically alive selfobject environment ultimately experience their lives as profoundly disengaged from others. The ensuing withdrawal emerges increasingly over time, ushering in what will coalesce as a schizoid personality adaptation. Mirroring needs do not disappear as children mature; indeed, normal mirroring longings continue, although they may be displayed oddly, making it even more difficult for the children's caregivers to comprehend their needs, especially those who are unable to grasp a reasonably normal display of mirroring longings.

Expecting little from the world, such children retreat entirely into themselves to gratify needs. This view closely resembles Winnicott's (1965) concept of the false self or Guntrip's (1969) view of the schizoid problem. However, a self psychological formulation places less emphasis on an inner pseudoexperience of life than it does on a failure to feel enough of a sense of inner buoyancy or vitality. In Kohut's view, a sufficiently mirrored self produces an emotionally enlivened sense of being in resonant contact with an affirming world of selfobjects. Such a person can rely on his or her selfobject environment and turn to it with the expectation of finding attuned sustenance. A self psychological view of psychopathology thus places unique emphasis on an impoverished or unavailable selfobject milieu that cannot respond enthusiastically to normal mirroring longings.

Consequently, schizoid patients get by in life through their emotionally dampened-down withdrawal and empty interpersonal involvements, which represent their characteristically severely limited capacity for intimacy. Their isolation serves to protect them from threats to self-cohesion offered by a world that has come to feel unrewarding in its neglect of and unresponsiveness to normal mirroring needs. These patients have a preponderance of defensive rather than compensatory structures. What little closeness or companionship they may find is often seen on closer analysis to emanate from other kindred spirits or "lost souls." Such relationships may be formed from twinship selfobject experiences that provide some measure of emotional connection with someone else just like themselves. If they are durable and of sufficient depth, twinship selfobjects may be sustaining enough to consolidate a compensatory structure, thus enabling the patient to secure a reasonably robust degree of self-cohesion (M. Tolpin, 1997). However, fleeting instances of twinship experiences do not establish a stable compensatory structure; relationships based on mutual feelings of being "damaged goods," although they provide a modicum of feeling that one is not alone in the world, cannot securely take hold and solidify the self.

Early origins of schizoid personality disorder may also be considered from the vantage point of the intersubjectivity branch of psychoanalytic self psychology. According to this view, when mothers' faulty affect attunements are ongoing and of sufficient magnitude, the infant–caregiver system becomes destabilized. Intersubjectivists regard this form of developmental trauma as a profound disruption of the reciprocal affect-regulating homeostasis between caregivers and their infants. This disruption is not necessarily one of object loss or abandonment; it represents a perturbation of a mutual regulation bond that had existed previously or that never developed well enough in the first place. The disruption of the mother–infant mutual affect-regulating intersubjective field is the model for poorly integrated affect states; it is the foundation for experiences that predominate in the detached, affectively flattened relatedness of schizoid patients. Affective misattunement may originate with a constitutionally disposed infant, an affectively impaired mother, or both. In any case, the intersubjective field is disturbed by the failure of one or both parties to function adequately as reciprocal influences for regulating each other's affective states.

The expectation of misattuned responsiveness from others who are needed to help regulate one's affect states may produce the schizoid adaptation of withdrawal and affective flattening. This expectation becomes a predominant organizing principle of such patients' experience (Stolorow, Atwood, & Brandchaft, 1987). For the schizoid patient, the primary organizing principle is the expectation of confused or inconsistent cues about affective reality. The expectation leads the patient to seek the safety of withdrawal from interpersonal contact to preserve reality testing, albeit at the cost of constricted emotionality and isolation. Thus, such patients see others' emotional reactions as being too asynchronous with their own affective states to be experienced as rewarding, and as a result they consider relationships to be best avoided. The expectation that misattuned, asynchronous interactions will be repetitive and regularly occurring is similar to Millon's (1996) concept of "preformed inclinations."

Clinical Illustration of Schizoid Personality Disorder

The clinical history described in this section illustrates a self psychological understanding of a patient who presented with a compensated schizoid adaptation. Ms. B. was a 48-year-old White married woman with no prior treatment history who worked in a kennel providing general care and training of animals. Her clinical presentation was characterized by a bland and limited range of affect, inarticulateness concerning what she was feeling, and a disconnected (but not disorganized) way of describing events in her life. She displayed a degree of affective constriction and lack of reflectiveness about her life that made it difficult for me to feel engaged with or curious about her internal psychological existence.

Ms. B. sought treatment because she had recently been feeling angry with her boss's children, who had begun working in the kennel, upsetting her routines and making fun of her behind her back. The precipitant for seeking treatment was an upsurge of anger, which confused her and which she did not know how to manage. Her opening remark in the initial diagnostic session was, "I don't like children. I get angry a lot." She felt that she was being increasingly shut out of work duties, and she was having trouble understanding why she felt so marginalized in her job. Ms. B. also had several pets of her own at home, and her favorite dog had been put to sleep recently after it had attacked another dog. As she described this event, introducing it out of nowhere in particular, she seemed sad, although her words gave little real clue as to what she was feeling.

Ms. B. had held the job at the kennel for 15 years; the job required that she come in every day of the week, sometimes for long hours. As a result, Ms. B. saw her husband of 24 years very little. He spent most of his time with his own friends, and Ms. B. spent much of her time at the kennel. They had no children, which was her own preference, because, as she said, "The world sucks, and I didn't want to bring a child into this dog-eat-dog world." Ms. B. expressed no regrets about her decision, nor did she complain about her long work hours or the fact that she spent relatively little time with her husband. She described her marriage as "staying together out of force of habit; we're not passionate." Ms. B. had met her husband when she was 17 years old, and although she had not previously dated because she was shy, she said that her future husband was the only person who had paid attention to her: "I thought if I didn't marry him, I'd never get married. I don't know what he liked about me. He's not very open about his likes and dislikes." Although Ms. B. described her marriage as cordial, she was also able to say that she always wanted more in the relationship, but that "there's nothing to do about it, that's the way it is."

Ms. B.'s descriptions of her parents centered on recollections of limited contact, about which she showed little insight. For example, she said that her father was doting and devoted to the family, but her memories of him were vague, except that he worked long hours and was tired much of the time when he was at home. She characterized her mother in vague platitudes, such as, "She made friends easily," unlike Ms. B. herself, who was painfully shy and not popular. She recalled that her mother recognized but was unsympathetic to Ms. B.'s shyness. She felt that her mother could not understand why Ms. B. was unpopular and that her mother could not help her. Ms. B. described how her mother was absorbed with the many animals she kept around the house, including a horse and several dogs and cats. Her mother devoted much of her energy to controlling the behavior of her dogs and spent much of her time training and disciplining them. Ms. B. seemed not to make any connection between her own work and her mother's interest.

Ms. B. presented a history that seemed incongruent with her description of her "normal home," suggesting that *normal* may have represented *depleted* or *understimulated*. Nothing much happened in her affective experiences, and her memories were empty rather than vivid. Ms. B.'s description of her mother as gregarious seemed to cover an apparently neglectful, empathically unattuned maternal relationship. In Ms. B.'s narrative, her mother came across as relatively uninterested in or insensitive to Ms. B.'s painful problems with shyness, showing instead a more enthusiastic interest in controlling the various pets with which she surrounded herself. She may have cultivated a particular quality of empathy attuned to certain kinds of responses in animals but not her capacity for empathic understanding of persons. It is possible to regard Ms. B.'s interest in animal care as an attempt to vicariously create an empathic bond she might have sensed was possible from observations of her mother. It suggests as well that the primary deficit was in the mirroring sector of the self, influencing the schizoid adaptation that apparently characterized Ms. B.'s life. Her capacity to turn to her father for the kind of interested responsivity that she must have needed seemed limited, because although she described her father as doting, what she recalled was his being tired and absent.

Ms. B. probably felt ignored, although there is no reason to believe that she was overtly neglected. She could not consolidate a cohesive sense of self to sustain feelings of being worthwhile or lovable. Her marital choice was based largely on the fact that someone took notice of her, which surprised her, because she felt that she was hardly the apple of anyone's eye. The affective blandness of her childhood was thus recreated in her long but joyless marriage.

Considered from the intersubjective viewpoint in self psychology, the parental unresponsiveness that typified this schizoid patient's early development may have interfered with her acquiring the capacity to differentiate her own and others' affect states (Krystal, 1975; Socarides & Stolorow, 1984–1985). An impaired capacity to use affects as internal signals for articulating self states and attachment motivational needs (Lichtenberg, 1989) emerged from the intersubjective context of Ms. B.'s relationship with her mother. The mother made light of Ms. B.'s painful shyness and could not understand how she could feel so ignored and unhappy. Thus, unable to make satisfying emotional contact with her mother to feel understood, Ms. B. withdrew from her mother's empathic failures. She submerged her distress behind an affectively flattened schizoid veneer so as not to lose her mother's affection, despite her awareness that her mother's affection went largely to her pets. Ms. B.'s sense of "normal"—which to me sounded more like "forgotten about" or "not being taken seriously"—may have represented the selfobject failures of both parents to respond affectively to her. Such failures would interfere with this patient's affect life becoming integrated with an articulated sense of the self (Kohut, 1977; Socarides & Stolorow, 1984–1985; M. Tolpin, 1971). The vitalization of Ms. B.'s affects to promote efficacious attachment patterns was also compromised (Lichtenberg, 1983). Instead, Ms. B.'s shut-down of affective experiences resulted from a depleted, unresponsive selfobject environment.

The precipitating complaint that led Ms. B. to seek treatment was a (for her) uncharacteristic eruption of anger that she could not submerge to maintain her more typical joyless, flattened existence. Stimulated in part by her boss's children doing what adolescent children frequently do, her complaint about their getting in her way and interfering with her routines was disregarded by her boss. This slight perhaps reexposed Ms. B. to her own longings to be responded to by a mother who only had eyes and ears for the pets she was so intent on keeping in their place. Moreover, echoing Ms. B.'s disinclination to have children of her own in a "dog-eat-dog world," the liveliness or demandingness of children might have represented the revival of affects she could not understand because of an unresponsive selfobject milieu.

As a result, Ms. B. spent much of her life keeping unarticulated and thus confusing self states dampened down. She preferred to deal with her emotional life as her mother did, by focusing on the animals she spent most of her time managing. Ms. B. also lost the company of one of her own pet dogs, who attacked another dog and thus had to be sacrificed, providing another example of what can happen when one's anger gets out of control in a dog-eat-dog world. Ms. B. re-created in her marriage the experience of a father who was too psychologically distant to be able to help her secure selfobject responsiveness in the form of a compensatory structure (Kohut, 1977; M. Tolpin, 1997). Her complaints about the boss's children's intrusion appeared to be motivated not by competition for attention but rather by the desire to be left alone to her monotonous routines and to keep emotions in relationships turned on low volume in her schizoid existence of joyless, deadened relationships.

Ms. B. decided after a short while that she no longer wanted to work at the kennel, and she left to start a new job as an inventory clerk on the graveyard shift at a department store. In this way, the patient reconstituted her schizoid existence based on repetitive monotony and limited interpersonal contact with others. She restored a comfortingly familiar and safe existence where people left her alone or were, like her father, present but psychologically asleep. She could again abandon normal-enough strivings to meet mirroring needs to be apprehended and responded to adequately. In so doing, Ms. B. managed to reconstitute a self she could live with, notwithstanding its limitations, which were of little concern to her. Ms. B. thus resolved the threat to self-cohesion and terminated her treatment.

SCHIZOTYPAL PERSONALITY DISORDER

By virtue of family history or genetic predisposition, patients with schizotypal personality disorder were typically exposed in childhood to the influence of at least one parent with clinical schizophrenia or a schizophrenia-like illness. Consequently, their biological vulnerability is compounded by growing up in a disorganized environment, further undermining their efforts to develop cognitive and social skills. Their early experiences were likely compromised by an environment dominated by pathological communications that would seriously confuse a young child seeking constancy and reliability. The development of many such people is handicapped by being cared for by one or more primary caregivers who were themselves vulnerable to decompensation. A parent or caregiver so affected typically is too affectively preoccupied or uncomprehending of a child's emotional needs to respond with empathically accurate attunement. A disorganized or disengaged parental environment does not readily promote consolidation of robust self-cohesion. Parents who fail to appreciate a young child's normal desire to be seen as desirable or welcomed provide instead a selfobject environment in which their children feel rebuffed rather than valued. They feel unimportant and at the periphery of their selfobject environment. Dependent on an uncomprehending and possibly thought-disordered or delusional parent, such children cannot easily establish a vigorous, vitalized self.

When a parent is seriously distressed or withdrawn and the rest of the family system is similarly impaired, the child's selfobject surround can be considerably impoverished. *Assortative mating*, or the inclination for affected persons to seek out similarly ill partners, increases the likelihood that both parents are psychiatrically impaired, adding to the type and degree of psychopathology to which their children are exposed. The presence of illnesses in siblings or other first-degree relatives may further compromise the family's ability to assist or stabilize an impaired caregiver. Multiple illnesses in the family system also increase the psychological barriers to development by reducing the child's possibilities of turning to another family member to acquire self-sustaining capacities in the face of primary mirroring deficits. Such children have less of a protective buffer to confer immunity and less opportunity to find another route to secure the necessary selfobject functions to foster self-cohesion. The possibilities for forming compensatory structures (Kohut, 1977; M. Tolpin, 1997) are correspondingly limited, and children in such families come to feel there is nowhere to turn to relieve a devitalized, affectively barren existence.

A selfobject environment compromised by a family system with multiple ill members is certainly not unique to patients whose psychopathology takes the form of a schizotypal personality disorder. Patients with other personality disorders—particularly schizoid and borderline conditions—and, of course, those who go on to develop clinical schizophrenia—all have been exposed to pathogenic parental and familial disorganization. One difference, however, may be a greater tendency for schizotypal patients compared with schizoid personality disorder patients to have an overtly schizophrenic mother. A related difference may be that schizotypal patients' prominent symptoms, such as eccentric behavior, disordered thinking, and perceptual anomalies, might represent greater genetic vulnerability to the core schizophrenic syndrome.

Caregivers' empathic inconstancy and failures of attunement to developmental needs also lead to vulnerabilities to disturbances that Wolf (1994) described as occurring during a preemergent phase in the development of the self. Preemergent phase disorders of the self constitute severe forms of psychopathology, including the psychoses, borderline states, and severe personality disorders. Disruptions during the preemergent phase may produce the primary disturbances of the self—the narcissistic personality and behavior disorders—that Kohut (1971) and Kohut and Wolf (1978) identified. Because of their early appearance, which Wolf assumed to occur before 18 months of age (Kohut himself did not specify developmental stages in this way), such disturbances may damage the self, particularly in the mirroring sector. Patients who are exposed to a traumatically vulnerable selfobject environment during this stage of development of the self are, later in life, prone to resort to addictions or perversions in the absence of internalized self-soothing capacities. They also may be disposed to depersonalization or derealization phenomena.

As I noted in chapter 2, intersubjectivity theorists consider invariant organizing principles (the repetitive dimension) as being different from the selfobject dimension Kohut emphasized. Human experience therefore consists of both dimensions. With regard to a condition such as schizotypal personality disorder, self experience may be regarded as being influenced by defective mirroring selfobject responsiveness such as that outlined in this section (the selfobject dimension) and by a strongly embedded organizing principle based on expectations that one's needs will go unrecognized and may be chaotically responded to (the repetitive dimension). This predominant organizing principle, experienced time and again in schizotypal patients' lives, represents an embedded set of expectations that their selfobject environment will be undependable and untrustworthy.

Clinical Illustration of Schizotypal Personality Disorder

Mr. C., a 31-year-old single White man, was a college graduate who had held several jobs as a factory worker and was currently employed as a clerk. He reported chronic anxiety and a troubling sense that he might not live much longer, although he could not articulate his fear of dying more clearly. Although he denied suicidal ideation, Mr. C. reported that he sometimes had thoughts about walking in front of cars. He stated that he needed a wife to love him, but he also disliked having to depend on people. He described himself as becoming jealous easily, feeling used, and not getting what he deserved in life. Mr. C. felt that society was "brainwashing" him to be more like most people, which made him angry, and he reported vague feelings that situations were set up to "get at me." He reported having no close friends and spending most of his time alone feeling anxious or depressed. He worried that people were putting drugs in his food, and he wondered whether people could control his body and mind. These ideas of reference fell short of delusional conviction, however. His affect was generally blunted.

This patient was seen in consultation for psychodiagnostic evaluation. On the Rorschach test, the Comprehensive System approach (Exner, 2003) findings included an elevated Coping Deficit Index ($CDI = 4$) coupled with diminished organized or resourceful adaptive resiliencies (Experience Actual [EA] = 4). The depression and suicide constellations were not of significant concern. The Perceptual–Thinking index ($PTI = 1$) was unremarkable, although the cognitive special scores indicative of disordered thinking or ideation were elevated ($WSum6 = 28$). Nevertheless, accuracy of form perception remained generally within normal limits ($XA\% = .86$, $WDA\% = .92$, $X+\% = .50$). Among Mr. C.'s three human movement responses, none was of poor form quality ($M- = 0$).

Despite a paucity of ego resources for effective adjustment, this patient seemed to manage a degree of functional equilibrium by minimizing psychological stressors in his life. However, this appearance of stability belied Mr. C.'s vulnerability to becoming destabilized as stressful demands increased and as he felt uncomfortable tolerating life's ambiguities. He seemed particularly inclined to avoid affective arousal. To keep affective stimulation at manageable levels, Mr. C. kept his life simple and predictable, withdrawing from interpersonal contacts when these became too much for him to handle comfortably.

This patient also managed to distance himself from feeling hopeless about his lot in life. He felt comfortable when estranged from conventional social reality, but this preference also contributed to his difficulty sustaining a stable pattern of identifications. Although he might behave appropriately in a number of social situations, Mr. C. showed fundamental flaws in his understanding of interpersonal interactions. Furthermore, some degree of social ineptness could provoke embarrassment about social failure, disposing him to feel ignored and shunted to the side by people who might well regard Mr. C. as too aloof.

Despite Mr. C.'s highly idiosyncratic though generally intact reality testing, he was inclined to reach decisions casually and without sufficient forethought. The marginal quality of this patient's thinking revealed how he could withdraw into his imagination when distressed by affects or need states he could not manage well. He was also plagued by intrusive thoughts that could interfere with his otherwise flexible ability to see different courses of action. Such a pattern is frequently useful for differentiating a schizotypal personality disorder like Mr. C.'s from schizoid personality disorder.

I undertook a thematic content analysis to augment the formal Comprehensive System interpretation of Mr. C.'s Rorschach protocol (Silverstein, 1999). Although both of these interpretive approaches were consistent with an impression of schizotypal personality disorder, the content analysis more clearly revealed the predominant self states accounting for this young man's vulnerable self-cohesion. For example, despite the conventional percept of a bat on Card I, Mr. C. elaborated that the bat preys on lower forms of life. He proceeded to describe figures moving freely and easily so they never get close to one another, which was followed by a description of a wounded creature defined just by a combination of its bodily organs. He commented that Card II "scares me" and then described creatures communicating through "the warmth of their blood . . . feeling each other out." He elaborated on this response by referring to the creatures' need for protection because they "don't want to show their realness—they're scared of being rejected."

Although the form quality of these percepts remained uncompromised, Mr. C.'s descriptions emphasized his estrangement from intimate connections in order to protect his vulnerable sense of the danger that getting close can engender. In particular, his unusual reference to communicating by sensing the warmth of blood conveyed a psychologically visceral quality of merging with an object to secure a selfobject function. But for Mr. C., his selfobject world was depersonalized. Thus, making contact would call for merging with an oddly remote selfobject; that was as close as he dared get to what he needed. He also could proudly imagine being able to do without the closeness of contact, though at the cost of experiencing the self and its selfobjects in a depersonalized way—as being little more than a collection of organs. Mr. C. was understandably "scared" of Card II and the limited options it afforded him for meeting his needs as he attempted to secure selfobject functions from psychologically desiccated sources. A pattern of test performance such as this—more characteristic of a schizotypal rather than a schizoid personality disorder—also suggests that Mr. C. seemed unsteady in an existence that he could not manage to sustain for very long without "psychological oxygen"—an expression Kohut was known to favor—to invigorate the self.

Notwithstanding an oblique reference to a textural quality when he mentioned the creatures communicating by the warmth of their blood to feel each other, a careful inquiry failed to reveal the necessary shading requirement to capture the texture code on formal Comprehensive System scoring. However, the nature of his verbalization conveyed a remote yet still strangely intimate quality of a need for contact. Mr. C.'s percept of a wounded creature defined by its bodily organs added to my impression that he inhabited a mechanical, minimally subsistent inner world. Thus, by representing an existence in which he felt injured and without an integrated center to hold himself together, this sequence of responses in a schizotypal patient shows how a devitalized self state might appear on projective tests. It also reveals how this patient sought self-cohesion through the reanimation that in-depth contact sometimes affords. However, emotional depth was defensively denied; it was walled off behind images of a selfobject world peopled by unreal, fantastic specimens whose lives (and liveliness) existed in unreal bodies with hard-to-imagine forms of connection. This patient was left craving a greater affective connection but wound up depleted instead, unable to secure the crucial selfobject functions he needed to survive.

Much of the remainder of Mr. C.'s Rorschach protocol consisted of responses about animals or creatures he described as "something alive, or it used to be" (Card III); "I figure it's just got the main stuff that living creatures have . . . just all the junk that we have" (Card IV); or "It's got all the basic components for a living organism, but now it's dead" (Card VI). Several of these were depreciated or cynically disposed of—for example, "Now they're useless because man killed them for commercial purposes" (Card IV); "Their life is not meaningful" (Card III); or "They're two old grandmas rocking on rocking chairs, getting old and ready to die, they're worthless . . . a reunion of the grandmas . . . this picture bores me" (Card VII). On several of the blots, Mr. C. became absorbed in trying to decide whether figures were dying off or were being reborn as new forms of life. For example, on Card X, he described a monster that "represents hope that after we're all dead, something else will survive again; we just have to be patient."

Thus, Mr. C. felt surrounded by selfobjects with little more than the "basic components of living things" and with uncertain or ambivalent value, offering him little. The only human figures he reported—grandmothers on rocking chairs—were also spurned; these grandmothers evoked cynical and perhaps bitter disparagement of their capacity to be of meaningful use and perhaps also to provide comfort. It is but a short step to empathically grasp the kind of early mirroring responsiveness Mr. C. must have experienced. Whether he was a constitutionally difficult infant to warm up to or whether his mother's capacity for responsive mirroring was insufficiently robust, this patient did not feel buoyed enough to acquire a sense of himself as valued or affirmed. He was left without a psychological connection with a selfobject surround that could find him lovable.

Considered alongside the Rorschach, Mr. C.'s Thematic Apperception Test (TAT; H. A. Murray, 1943) responses provided further indications of his feeling devalued and inconsequential. He began on Card 1 by describing the boy as having ambitions to play the violin well "to feel proud about himself." Although Mr. C. described an outcome of failing, it was nevertheless the first indication of a self that was not experienced as diminished. Thus, Mr. C. showed some possible interest in restoring a prideful self despite caving in to failure.

On TAT Card 2, Mr. C. described a man struggling to sustain a farm to keep his family alive, and on Card 3BM, he told a story about a woman dying ("the world is letting her die") but displaying her sickness "as a protest," leading to someone rescuing and taking care of her. As on Card 1, he revealed some capacity to imagine revitalization—once again, in a way that was barely suggested on the Rorschach. Although he evidenced the deleterious effect of deficient mirroring, Mr. C. retained a capacity to envision what he might need to overcome an injured self. These responses also helped me understand his preoccupation with illness and dying: Using sickness as his "protest" was the way he strove to keep himself afloat. Together with the ambitiousness suggested on Card 1 and the struggle indicated on Card 2, Card 3BM continued the theme of attempting to secure what little he could manage to preserve an injured self.

When Mr. C. reached Card 6BM, he provided for the first time a story representing a relationship with a mother. He related how the young man in the picture needed money from his mother to sustain his life. Mr. C.'s story gave no indication of any response from the mother, or even her awareness of his plight. The man in the story took the money he needed from the mother, noting that the mother was getting older and that he might die before her. This story was not as logically coherent as his earlier TAT stories; this incoherence was perhaps triggered by confusion surrounding his understanding of affects associated with a problematic relationship involving a mother. Nevertheless, the theme of dying prematurely suggested that empathic unresponsiveness to his states of distress resulted from deficient mirroring. For Mr. C., defective mirroring responsiveness perturbed self-cohesion, which in turn represented an experience of a kind of psychological death—more accurately, the depletion or devitalization of an unmirrored self.

AVOIDANT PERSONALITY DISORDER

Although self psychology has not specifically addressed avoidant personality disorder, this condition is easily characterized as a self disorder. Withdrawing from emotionally engaging involvement with others may be one adaptation to faulty mirroring selfobject responsiveness. Such individuals cannot turn to the world in expectation of being admired. They anticipate derision or chronic empathic failures because they cannot count on the assurance of a selfobject environment that is on their side. Thus, avoidance may represent not so much anxious withdrawal as it does a self-protective turning inward to the safety of isolation as a place to assuage the injuries to self-esteem that lead to a devitalized self.

Considered in this way, avoidance does not result from anxiety dysregulation. Rather, it is an understandable reaction to a faulty mirroring selfobject environment that cannot sustain or invigorate a buoyant self. One cornerstone of Kohut's self psychology centered on the self's exquisite vulnerability to rejection, particularly to empathic failures to grasp the person's needs for affirmation necessary to promote enlivening of the self. Whereas schizoid patients respond to deficient mirroring by affectively closing down an expectation of responsive mirroring, avoidant patients do not isolate themselves from their selfobjects. They instead maintain the expectation that mirroring might be possible, but they cautiously insulate themselves from the painful rejection of empathic failure by keeping an affective distance, resembling one or more subclassifications of a preoccupied attachment style (Main & Goldwyn, 1994). Although hesitant to approach the selfobject surround out of fear that occasional indications of mirroring may be untrustworthy, avoidant patients remain vigilantly engaged with their selfobjects. Although from a distance, they watchfully wait for signs, not so much that the coast is clear but rather that their selfobjects will be empathically responsive to their mirroring strivings.

Kohut (1971) described an aspect of mirroring selfobject functions that emphasized the importance of merging with a calming mirroring selfobject to dissipate diffuse tension states. However, avoidant personality disorder patients more typically vacillate between positions of merger longings and the self-protective distance of an unmirrored self. Kohut (1996) provided the following example to show how conflicted longings concerning merging with a soothing selfobject may originate in development:

> A mother who says, "Oh, for goodness sake, don't cry, there's nothing to be anxious about," does not allow this particular kind of merger and does not help the child. She rejects and pushes the child away. A mother who goes to pieces over the child's anxieties also doesn't encourage the merger. Why? Because why do you want to merge into something that is as anxious as you yourself are, or even more so? A mother who misunderstands the child and thinks that he's anxious when he's in pain or in pain when he's anxious is also no good. (p. 7)

Early mirroring failures may therefore interfere with the capacity to merge with a calming selfobject. This in turn may lead to a search for indications about whether the selfobject surround is dependable or responsive. Looked at in this way, hypersensitivity to rejection may be better comprehended as a hypersensitivity to mirroring responsiveness. Rejection may thus precipitate avoidant distancing in response to an unreliable selfobject environment. However, the vulnerability may consist not as much of a fear of repudiation as of reexposure to a more fundamental injury. The potential injury is that needs for mirroring or merging with a calming selfobject will be ignored or will go unnoticed. Moreover, self-contemptuous feelings of unworthiness are understood as secondary reactions to selfobject nonresponsiveness.

From an intersubjectivity perspective, which stresses the mutually regulating affective system between caregiver and infant, an empathically misattuned caregiver would drive a child away from close involvement. In contrast, a child who develops the withdrawn indifference of the schizoid patient, for example, closes off his or her needs and resorts to an interpersonally diminished search for intimacy. Such children cultivate a walled-off self-sufficiency, barely even realizing how lonely an existence they have created for themselves by their schizoid adaptation. Although their avoidant solution preserves some degree of need for closeness, avoidant patients react to the empathic failures of their caregivers by keeping a safe distance. Caregivers may thus be uncertain how to respond to their children's distanced avoidance, not knowing whether to interpret avoidance as shyness, disinterest, or inability to warm up to them. This degree of ambiguity can accentuate the trouble empathically unresponsive caregivers have deciphering their children's motivations and need states. Beebe and Lachmann (2002) described what they called a "chase-and-dodge protocol" from the mother–infant interaction literature illustrating how maternal reactions may lead to infants' aversive withdrawal.

Clinical Illustration of Avoidant Personality Disorder

Mr. D. was a 42-year-old single Black man who worked in the engineering services industry. He had had several depressive episodes in his adult life and had obtained little relief or recovery from several courses of antidepressant therapy. The patient lived a particularly isolated life, feeling that people held little interest for him other than to help him fill his time. Mr. D. derived little pleasure from being with others. However, he was unhappy that he could not derive greater enjoyment being with other people. He had also abandoned dating because he found women uninteresting to talk to beyond simple companionship. Mr. D. desired a wife or girlfriend but had never found a woman he felt to be interesting enough to become involved with emotionally.

This patient felt that he wanted more satisfying relationships in his isolated, pleasureless existence. Although he could not understand why he found people uninteresting, Mr. D. was not overtly critical of others, nor was he particularly fearful of criticism. He also felt that he was a failure in life, which contributed to his disinclination to be around people he imagined as being more accomplished than himself. The incongruity between his defensive indifference and what had emerged as a craving for closeness suggested an avoidant pattern of detachment.

When he began treatment, Mr. D. was working in a marketing division, and he could set his own hours. He was paid only for the hours he worked in addition to commissions from selling advertising space. However, Mr. D. could rarely manage to arrive at the office before midafternoon on most days, despite the fact that he had little money and was barely meeting his expenses. Mr. D. would stay up late in his cluttered apartment, which was filled with books and magazines that he could not discard—sometimes for years—until he had looked at each item. According to his report, his piles of clutter made it difficult to walk from room to room.

He also maintained a cluttered array of computers to build communicating networks he could never manage to connect. Mr. D. also accumulated piles of unwashed plastic plates and utensils in the kitchen sink, which he did not intend to throw away in case he might need them in the future. He was ashamed of his apartment and of how uninhabitable it had become; it resembled a storage area more than a space for living. Moreover, Mr. D. owned a van that also was cluttered with overflow from his apartment, and he carried in this vehicle everything he thought he might require should he encounter trouble on the road. Gradually, it became clear to Mr. D. that his collection of outdated, often useless material served a purpose besides that of compulsive collecting: The obsessive–compulsive behavior reflected his need to hold onto everything he could acquire so he would never be without something should a need arise.

One of the closest attachments he had developed was to a horse he once owned. Mr. D. rode his horse on weekends, and he felt that his horse was undemanding and required little effort. Mr. D. did develop some casual friendships on his riding weekends, although these relationships did not last after his horse became ill and died. He dated some of the women who were his riding companions, but they, like others he had dated throughout his life, wanted greater involvement from him. He would eventually tire of what he saw as their neediness, not comprehending why the women he met wanted increasingly more involvement from him whereas his horse had seemed content with the status quo. Mr. D. discontinued riding after his horse died.

During childhood, Mr. D.'s mother was minimally involved with him. He enjoyed the fact that she seemed to magically appear to cater to his every need, such as laying out his clothing and bringing things to him, without apparently expecting Mr. D. to learn to do much for himself. According to the patient's recollection, his mother did not explain much about everyday life situations, such as how to coordinate his clothing or what to wear depending on seasonal changes. He seemed to experience his mother as distant and emotionally aloof, as though she functioned as a valet for him. His recollections of times spent with her lacked detail or emotional vividness. This patient's limited recollections about his mother, the times they spent together, and what her personality was like suggested an affectively dulled relationship that was neither overtly neglectful nor richly interactive. Her empathic responsiveness sounded mechanical rather than emotionally nuanced. Indeed, Mr. D. seemed most comfortable understanding relationships with women that were characterized by a compliantly responsive, chambermaid-like caring for his needs. His mother may have been limited in her capacity to anticipate and mirror Mr. D.'s needs to feel valued as a buoyant child with an active imagination.

Although Mr. D.'s relationship with his father was also sparsely detailed, he remembered more compared with his "amnesia" (as he described it) concerning his mother. Mr. D.'s father, however, was also distant, a man who preferred to be by himself rather than interact with his wife and children. Mr. D. recalled trying to talk with or get close to his father, who would be reading the newspaper while listening to music. Although his father did not overtly push Mr. D. away, neither did he stop what he was doing to make time for his son or to give him undivided attention. Mr. D. also recalled going places with his father, who often was more animated with other people, usually in a boastful way, and Mr. D. was left feeling that he was not as interesting to his father as other people were. He hardly ever felt that he was the object of his father's interest or pride.

Mr. D. had memories of attempting to look up to his father, but his idealizing longings were frustrated because his father seemed to have little interest in his son beyond his serving as an audience or cheering section for the father's boastfulness. Mr. D. was also embarrassed by his father's buffoonlike manner in public. He eventually pulled away from his father, unable to turn to him in the hope of securing what was already lacking in his mother's diminished empathic mirroring responsiveness. Neither parent seemed able to notice what Mr. D. needed as a child, either in the form of invigorating mirroring to bolster self-cohesion or a fostering of his drawing close for merging to calm distressed self states. Unable as well to develop an idealizing transference to his father as a possible compensatory structure to revitalize an unmirrored self, Mr. D. seemed to have no other route to fortify himself.

At age 8, Mr. D. was "dispossessed" of his bedroom, as the only son, to give his larger room to his younger sisters. He virtually walled off his new, smaller room as an "inner sanctum." He later commandeered an area of the basement as a workshop, collecting capacitors and large numbers of small parts, so that he had on hand whatever he might need to repair the model boats and equipment he enjoyed working with. Pushed out of his original room, he psychologically barricaded himself in his fortresslike new room and basement workshop. Here he pursued his solitary interests of acquiring numerous objects he imagined potentially needing, even though he could not really specify why he might need many of them. It was as if Mr. D. were fortifying himself for a long siege or a period of anticipated deprivation.

I considered his collecting to represent an attempt to protect himself against any need state. Thus fortified and ready for any shortage, I imagined how Mr. D. prepared to fend for himself if his parents were not there for him or if they failed to notice how alone he felt. Concealing a brittle sense of self-cohesion, Mr. D. shunned intimacy with others and took solace in collecting phonograph records and stockpiling parts and supplies. His collections would have to suffice to convince him that he had available whatever he might potentially need. This effort seemed to take the place of a robust, vigorous self to help him remain psychologically afloat.

Unlike the detachment of patients with schizoid personality disorder, Mr. D. did not disavow his desire for responsive mirroring by turning it off through self-sufficient indifference. Rather, his disengagement represented an attempt to find a way to keep self-cohesion intact in light of his parents' unawareness that he wanted to feel treasured in their eyes. Mr. D.'s avoidant retreat was to an activity that he attempted to use to salvage and stimulate an uninvigorated self in a self-protective flight from chronically deficient mirroring. In my reconstruction, he submerged his normal longings for the selfobject responsiveness that would permit him to feel like a valued person rather than a prop for his father's conceit or someone to be serviced in his mother's eyes. Mr. D.'s depression can also be understood as a result of chronic injuries to an unmirrored, depleted self.

It became easier for me to differentiate the safe but still involved distance of an avoidant personality disorder from the indifferent, self-sufficient existence of a schizoid adaptation because Mr. D.'s treatment centered on his developing relationship with a new employer. He started working for a highly accomplished and successful boss who appeared quite impressed with himself. Admiring this man's abilities and success, Mr. D. hoped to learn from him to advance his own prospects. However, his new employer frequently ignored Mr. D.'s desire to understand how the boss figured out business problems, expecting Mr. D. to absorb what the boss knew by simply observing. The boss imposed his own overdemanding standards on Mr. D., expecting Mr. D. to keep the same hypomanic schedule. This boss, like Mr. D.'s father, frequently boasted of his Herculean accomplishments in a tone that seemed to say, "Can you top this?" Indeed, many of the employer's accomplishments sounded larger than life.

Nevertheless, my patient was proud of his boss's abilities, remobilizing an idealizing selfobject need he had long submerged because of the injury to self-esteem he experienced when his self-absorbed father seemed not to notice his son's longings. Mr. D. welcomed the revival of a selfobject relationship with his boss. He became affectively reawakened as he basked in his employer's accomplishments, and he hoped that his boss would notice and appreciate Mr. D.'s own abilities and take him under his wing. He felt excited as he proudly described his boss's accomplishments to others. Also during this period, Mr. D. reported experiencing pleasure on hearing a friend proudly relate one of his own son's accomplishments. Mr. D. began feeling energetic and enthusiastic about removing some of the clutter in his apartment. He also spoke about how tearfully happy he felt reciting responsively with the rest of the congregation while attending Easter services with a cousin's family. The powerful affect that came over him reminded Mr. D. of how in elementary school he felt an equally strong surge of emotion when the class would recite in unison, for example, the Pledge of Allegiance. Thus, Mr. D. was becoming increasingly aware of feeling more affectively invigorated as he saw himself involved with other people in a way that made him feel a part of their emotional lives. He began to feel connected in a psychologically involving way with people instead of being fearfully distanced from friends and family. He felt less inclined to resort to his customary lonely activities surrounded by all his clutter, trying to make disconnected things work right or assembling collections of objects to feel internally prepared for any emergency.

As time went on, the patient became increasingly worried that he could never meet his boss's standards. He was disappointed that he could not manage to get his boss to listen to him or to respond vigorously enough to his idealizing longings. In fact, his employer seemed uninterested in teaching his field to Mr. D., who came to see the more critical, narcissistic side of his employer. Mr. D.'s turning away from his idealization longings reactivated his more familiar depletion and the deadened affect associated with feeling ignored. Mr. D. feared asking his boss questions about work because he worried that he would be dismissively criticized, evoking his feelings as a child when his father acted more animatedly with other people while seeming uninterested in Mr. D. He also felt unable to measure up to what the boss thought Mr. D. should have absorbed after a short time. If Mr. D. suspected that his employer was preoccupied and not interested in conversing, he would sit on the steps in front of the office building for several minutes before entering each morning, worrying whether his boss would greet or even notice him that day. On the one hand, Mr. D. hoped his boss would invite him to work alongside him, but on the other hand, Mr. D. was afraid to try to engage his boss by asking him what he was working on or whether he could help.

Mr. D. took refuge once again in the isolation of his cluttered apartment, in the company of his collections of objects that were useless save for their function of shoring up a devitalized self. Retreating in disappointment thus revived for Mr. D. the injury to an uninvigorated self that sought revitalization. He felt relegated to being a dispensable prop, just as he had with his father. He felt psychologically dropped and resorted to what he knew best to assuage the injury—retreating to the avoidant solution of his inner sanctum. Mr. D. thus withdrew again into the caved-in depletion depression that was all too familiar to him.

He turned away from friends again and became more erratic in attending treatment sessions. Mr. D. worried that he would no longer be interesting to me in his depressed, uninvigorated state, despite the fact that his treatment was perhaps the only place, besides the company of a supportive cousin, where Mr. D. felt understood and not disparaged. In this context, Millon's (1996) description of the self-deserting avoidant subtype is especially apt. Millon's description exquisitely captures how avoidant personality disorder patients who turn inward to escape the despair of the external world come to discover that their inner life is equally empty. Thus, an avoidant solution exposes such patients to an "emotional numbness in which they become completely disconnected from themselves" (p. 271).

From an intersubjective viewpoint, Mr. D.'s falling back on an organizing principle of keeping his distance to avoid injury represented his way of managing a lifetime of experiences of affect misattunements. Superimposing Lichtenberg's (1983) view of thwarted attachment or exploratory-assertiveness motivations on the intersubjective viewpoint, Mr. D.'s disinclination to see friends or to seek relationships could be regarded as shutting off need states because the selfobject environment had become disappointing and unstimulating. The intersubjective context thus became one in which Mr. D.'s need states could not be conveyed to or discerned by his employer, just as they also had not been discerned by his parents. The patient responded to the diminished affective responsiveness of his selfobject surround with avoidance as his main affect-dissociating defensive operation to assuage an unmirrored self.

CONCLUSION

This chapter reconsidered schizoid, schizotypal, and avoidant personality disorders from the framework of self psychology. The disorders were cast as maladaptive solutions to chronic, prolonged mirroring selfobject failures that produce the predominant experiences of devitalization in such patients' lives. Their central problem is that of an experience of the self characterized chiefly by vulnerability to depletion. Consequently, such patients have a diminished capacity to sustain self-cohesion when needs are triggered for admiration to invigorate goals or ambitions. The remote withdrawal of a schizoid adaptation and the odd or idiosyncratic thinking and perception of the schizotypal personality were discussed from the standpoint of expected deficient mirroring responsiveness when a heritable schizophrenia spectrum illness perturbs the selfobject environment during early development. Avoidant personality disorder was considered as a self-protective turning inward to insulate patients from their hypersensitivity to rebuffs when mirroring deficits compromise self-cohesion.

III

FORESTALLING FRAGMENTATION (PARANOID, OBSESSIVE–COMPULSIVE, AND BORDERLINE PERSONALITY DISORDERS)

5

DESCRIPTIVE PSYCHOPATHOLOGY AND THEORETICAL VIEWPOINTS: PARANOID, OBSESSIVE–COMPULSIVE, AND BORDERLINE PERSONALITY DISORDERS

In the previous chapter, I considered schizoid, schizotypal, and avoidant personality disorders from a self psychological perspective based on the idea that they reflected a prominent mirroring disturbance disposing affected persons to a devitalized self. The present chapter provides a general overview of paranoid, obsessive–compulsive, and borderline personality disorders, which will be discussed from a self psychological perspective in chapter 6. I have grouped these disorders in a different way than they are designated in the fourth edition of the *Diagnostic and Statistical Manual of Mental Disorders* (*DSM–IV*; American Psychiatric Association, 1994); paranoid, obsessive–compulsive, and borderline personality disorders are represented on Axis II in the odd/eccentric (Cluster A), anxious/fearful (Cluster C), and histrionic/dramatic (Cluster B) clusters, respectively. The self psychological reconceptualization I propose assumes that a struggle to preserve self-cohesion cuts across the symptom-based rationale of the *DSM–IV* cluster groupings.

I consider these three disorders together because they reflect a similar need to forestall fragmentation of the self. It is not difficult to see that borderline and paranoid personality disorders can represent fragile conditions. Indeed, Millon (1996) designated them as structurally defective personalities. However, I also include obsessive–compulsive personality disorder as one of the fragmentation-prone disturbances, because I consider its fundamental problem to be holding together an intact psychological structure. Viewed from a self psychological framework, therefore, I suggest that all three of these disorders are predominantly characterized by vulnerability to self-cohesion ruptures, potentiating fragmentation.

I will begin, as I did in chapter 3, with an overview of these disorders that considers descriptive psychopathology and contemporary personality disorder theory and research. I discuss several psychoanalytic viewpoints, particularly classical drive theory or ego psychology and object relations formulations. In chapter 6, I will consider these three disorders from a self psychological viewpoint as manifestations of a need to forestall fragmentation.

PARANOID PERSONALITY DISORDER

There is a distinctive quality of brittleness in paranoid personality disorder; its prominent characteristics in clinical presentation are hypersensitivity to potential slights and suspicious, hypervigilant orientation to the world. These patients' brittleness underlies their persistently rigid scanning for signs of potential danger. Perhaps because they rarely relax their tenacious guardedness, such patients go through life with a serious, joyless demeanor that frequently turns into surliness. They are difficult to like, and their company is nearly impossible to tolerate, let alone enjoy. They have difficulty comprehending the loneliness they may feel because their serious, hostile guardedness causes others to retreat from even the most casual involvement. Patients with paranoid personalities also alienate others by misinterpreting others' intentions and by suspecting other people of undermining their autonomy. Paranoid personality disorder patients also often harbor feelings of envy, and they are quick to find and haughtily point out the faults of others. These feelings of envy underlie the touchiness they bring to most situations and their tendency to externalize blame for their own failures or weaknesses. They self-protectively find reasons why problems are characteristically provoked by others and never by themselves.

The psychotic variant of paranoia was first recognized by Kahlbaum (cited in Kolb, 1968); Kraepelin (1919) subsequently included it as a prominent symptom of dementia praecox. Distinctions among frank delusions, delusional ideation, and delusion-like phenomena often can be difficult to discern. More so than for other personality disorders, there exists uncertainty about the relationship between the prominent clinical features of paranoid personality disorder and related Axis I conditions such as schizophrenia and delusional disorder. Thus, for example, paranoid personality disorder falls on the relatively milder side of a continuum of disorders included in schizophrenia spectrum illnesses (Kety, Rosenthal, Wender, & Schulsinger, 1968; Siever & Davis, 1991). Further, Vaillant (1964) and Stephens (1978) both regarded paranoid features as a favorable prognostic indicator in schizophrenia. Paranoid personality features have sometimes been viewed as a precursor of paranoid schizophrenia, appearing clinically—though subtly—during the prodrome of middle or late adolescence, or even in nascent form during the still earlier premorbid period preceding onset of the initial psychotic episode. The precise relationship of paranoid personality disorder to delusional disorder is unknown, although the presence of delusional ideation characterizes both disorders. Furthermore, Kendler, Masterson, and Davis (1985) reported a higher morbid risk for paranoid personality disorder in first-degree relatives of delusional disorder patients compared to those of schizophrenic patients.

Paranoid personality disorder shows substantial overlap with other Axis II disorders, including narcissistic, antisocial, avoidant, obsessive–compulsive, borderline, and particularly schizotypal personality disorders. Despite the comorbidity between paranoid and schizotypal personality disorders, Bernstein, Useda, and Siever (1995) did not regard the evidence sufficiently compelling to consider these conditions as the same disorder. They also thought that paranoid personality disorder resembled delusional disorder more closely than it resembled schizophrenia spectrum disorders.

Psychoanalytic interest in paranoia originated with one of Freud's infrequent case reports. In his analysis of Schreber, a judge who developed a paranoid psychosis, Freud (1911/1958) emphasized the role of repressed homosexual impulses in giving rise to paranoia, which is a view that has not been uncritically accepted by most analytic theorists. In constructing this formulation, Freud called attention to the importance of denial and projection, which continued to be regarded as central dynamics of paranoid ideation (Fenichel, 1945). Although Freud did not further examine paranoia, Abraham (1921/1927c) stressed the importance of anal–sadistic incorporation in paranoid fantasies, thus establishing a relationship between obsessional neurosis and paranoia that remained prominent in drive theory for several decades. W. Reich's (1933/1949) approach to asymptomatic forms of character pathology influenced the concept of a psychotic character (Frosch, 1988). However, Grinker, Werble, and Drye (1968) and Kernberg (1975) considered Frosch's description of the psychotic character to resemble borderline syndrome more closely than paranoia.

Shapiro (1965) described an ego psychological approach to what he called a *paranoid style*. Richly capturing the phenomenological experience of paranoid ideation and reality orientation, Shapiro emphasized the suspiciousness that permeates almost all areas of psychological experience among such patients. He suggested that their pervasive mistrust disposes such patients to scan their surroundings with unrelenting intensity until they have found what they expect to find, thus confirming their suspicions of external malevolence. Shapiro described paranoid patients as being unpersuaded by rational arguments contrary to beliefs they consider unequivocally true. The vigor of their hyperscanning is purposive; they are driven to find what they are unshakably convinced is there to be found. Shapiro (1965, p. 59) contrasted this "rigidly intentional" manner of scanning with the careful, measured processing characteristic of obsessive–compulsive patients and the casual quality of attention seen in hysterical personalities.

Patients with the paranoid style avoid the surprise of the unfamiliar. They cannot tolerate surprise, because they cannot easily relax their constant vigilant attentiveness. Shapiro (1965) suggested that the overly rigid thinking of obsessive–compulsive patients is narrowed, whereas paranoid patients cannot afford to focus narrowly but must instead scan broadly and vigorously. The paranoid patient is always alert to potential harm or ill will and "avoids surprise by virtually anticipating it" (Shapiro, 1965, p. 62). Such patients become intensely preoccupied by whatever does not fit their rigid expectations, whereas obsessive–compulsive personalities are inclined to ignore whatever does not fit their rigid expectations.

Shapiro (1965) also noted the diminished spontaneity and consequent constriction of patients with paranoid personality. Because paranoid patients focus their attention intently on predetermined meanings they seek to confirm, attention deployment is narrowed by their penetrating examination of inconsequential but exaggerated matters. Paradoxically, however, their attentional focus is at the same time exceedingly broad. It is broad because paranoid patients need to detect the malevolent intentions they expect lurk everywhere, in every gesture, statement, and event. These broad and narrow aspects of attention to the outside world leave little room for spontaneity, including in their affective experience, which is characteristically rigid and serious. Tightly guarded constriction, therefore, is a by-product of both broad paranoid hypervigilance and narrowed scanning.

M. Klein's (1930, 1935) views about primitive mental contents initiated an influential movement in psychoanalytic theory based on theories of object relations. She proposed a view of paranoid psychopathology that stressed developmentally primitive defenses. M. Klein regarded projection as externalized aggression to protect infants and their primitive capacities for ego integration from being destroyed. In M. Klein's view, projected or externalized destructiveness created a part object relationship, in which maternal objects were split rather than integrated. This proposition—which M. Klein called the *paranoid–schizoid position*—underlay her concept of the part object, in which all-bad objects were split off from all-good (idealized) objects. In her view, an all-bad object (the attacking, destructive breast as it is experienced in primitive fashion by infants) became the basis for paranoia. She contended that infants' rageful fantasies sustained the split between all-good and all-bad objects, which at this primitive, preambivalent stage of development, were not whole, fully realized objects.

M. Klein (1930, 1935) speculated that in normal development, the paranoid–schizoid position matures to allow a more reality-oriented, ambivalently perceived (and thus not split) maternal object—the *depressive position*. When this developmental step fails to occur, the paranoid–schizoid position prevails as the predominant organization of the object world, thus disposing to persecutory (paranoid) anxiety stemming from projection of aggression. M. Klein considered the fundamental dynamic of the paranoid–schizoid position to be that of an internalized good object needing to protect itself from potential attack by a persecutory object that has been externalized.

Millon (1996) viewed paranoid personality disorder as a structurally defective and therefore more severe form of personality disorder. He differentiated five variants of paranoid personality disorder, several of which represented decompensated breakdowns of the personality:

1. The *fanatic paranoid* variant is the subtype most similar to narcissistic personality disorder because of the prominence in these patients of haughty pretentiousness and an inclination to deprecate others, having been overindulged by parents who instilled a sense of inflated self-worth. Consequently, when confronted with the realities of life and their inability to maintain relationships requiring consideration of others' needs, such patients resort to illusions of omnipotent greatness when the outside world does not provide their parents' boundless indulgence.

2. The *malignant paranoid* is a decompensated variant of sadistic personality disorder, characterized largely by resentful mistrust; envy; and a belligerent, intimidating manner.

3. Millon's (1996) structurally defective variant of the obsessive–compulsive personality disorder is represented by the *obdurate paranoid* subtype, characterized by rigid obedience to rules and a grim and humorless manner. Their paranoid decompensation from an otherwise obsessive–compulsive personality style results from externalization; such patients project hostile wishes and consequently feel persecuted by others.

4. The *querulous paranoid* is a subtype characterized chiefly by a stubborn negativism that makes these patients seem obstructive at every turn. Typically discontented, such patients feel sullen resentment over being misunderstood.

5. Finally, the *insular paranoid* subtype represents a decompensated, reclusive variant of avoidant personality disorder. Such patients overinterpret others' perceived hurtful or malevolent

intentions. This variant is the least successful of Millon's subtypes in maintaining a projective defense position. Such patients turn away from other people when their rage becomes dysregulated, provoking self-depreciation and sometimes suicidal impulses.

Cloninger, Svrakic, and Przybeck (1993) referred to a *fanatic character*, which is their term for Kraepelin's (1919, 1923) clinical description of paranoid character. In Cloninger et al.'s personality typology based on temperament and character dimensions, the fanatic/paranoid is regarded as showing a high degree of self-directedness and self-transcendence but a low degree of cooperativeness. The multidimensional personality configuration of the fanatic character consists of a creative or hyperthymic character potentiated by appreciable hostility. Finally, Westen and Shedler (2000) described a paranoid Q factor characterized by grudges, feelings of being misunderstood or maltreated, and anger or criticism of others.

OBSESSIVE–COMPULSIVE PERSONALITY DISORDER

Obsessive–compulsive personality disorder requires for its diagnosis, just as in all personality disorders, a sufficient degree of compromised functioning, regardless of level of experienced distress. It is an Axis II disturbance that may contain adaptive features, particularly in its relatively mild manifestations; thus, it is also a condition that may easily be overlooked. However, clinicians attuned to subtle clinical manifestations of obsessive–compulsive personality disorder can usually agree that its nuances may interfere with adjustment or the quality of interpersonal relationships, especially intimate relationships.

One distinctive feature concerns such patients' dogged persistence, a quality that extends beyond thorough attention to detail. Overly thorough attention to detail can easily become transformed into unresourceful ruminative thinking that sidetracks patients from their goals. Characteristically seeing trees more than the forest, obsessive–compulsive personalities are disposed to indecisiveness, inaction, and procrastination. The people in their lives—partners in intimate relationships, colleagues at the workplace, or casual friends—often react by withdrawing, giving up in frustration over the impossibility of feeling close to or collegial with them.

Obsessive–compulsive personality disorder remains an uncertain clinical entity, despite the long history of attention devoted to its conceptualization by psychoanalytic theorists of various persuasions. Although it is frequently regarded as a variation of obsessional or compulsive neurosis described in Freud's (1908/1959a) early formulations, obsessive–compulsive personality appeared in the 10th edition of the *International Classification of Diseases*

(World Health Organization, 1992) in connection with Schneider's (1950) term—*anankastic personality*. Both Schneider's description of an "insecure" type and Kretschmer's description of a "sensitive" type (cited in Millon, 1996) represented attempts to isolate its singular characteristics of affective constriction leading to pedantic indecisiveness, insecurity, and shame.

The classical drive theory formulation of psychoanalytic theory suggests a commonality between obsessive–compulsive and paranoid personality disorders, in which paranoid disorder represents a decompensation from a faltering obsessive–compulsive personality structure. The compulsive character neurosis predominantly consists of overmeticulousness in manner or dress, frequently accompanied by preoccupation with dirt or cleanliness; rigid moral standards accompanied by a stern, cold demeanor; pronounced indecisiveness; preoccupation with trivialities; superstitiousness; and an obstinate, unyielding manner in personal relationships. Like paranoid personality, though less prominently so, patients with obsessive–compulsive personality disorder show a heightened but inflexible oversensitivity to moral standards, rigid adherence to duty, and marked indecisiveness or ambivalence (Shapiro, 1965).

After his initial studies of hysterical neurosis and phobias, Freud (1908/1959a) turned his attention to the obsessional and compulsion neuroses, which he considered compromise formations between instinctual gratification and guilt. This view was consistent with his theoretical departure from his original "hydraulic" model of anxiety. Freud's studies of obsessions and compulsions served as one impetus for his revised theory of anxiety and symptom formation emphasizing the structural theory of mental operations. However, the character traits Freud initially identified—and that Abraham (1921/1927c) and W. Reich (1933/1949) developed further—represent the major clinical characteristics of the current conceptualization of obsessive–compulsive personality disorder.

Baudry (1983) and Lax (1989) delineated two trends in psychoanalytic viewpoints of character formation. The first trend derived from Freud's (1908/1959a) description of the libidinal stages of development. Obsession–compulsion psychoneurosis and character was for him the anal stage of psychosexual development. His formulation was based on his analysis of the Rat Man (Freud, 1909/1955), whose central conflict Freud regarded as that between obedience and defiance. A second trend was Fenichel's (1945) classification of character pathology according to the similarity between symptomatic and characterological forms. In obsessive–compulsive neurosis, Fenichel's approach in particular stressed how reaction formation protects against the danger of the emergence of instinctual urges. Fenichel's view was more in keeping with the emphasis on the tripartite model and the structural theory in psychoanalysis, which stressed the nonconflictual (ego-syntonic) and sometimes adaptive aspects of character traits, particularly as ego psychology became preeminent. Hartmann (1939) emphasized character traits originating as defensive operations that become autonomous personality characteristics, which he called *apparatuses of secondary autonomy*. Examples of such characteristics in obsessive–compulsive character disorder include orderliness, attention to detail, and frugality. Freud (1908/1959a) himself commented on the characterological significance of anal traits such as these, but as Baudry (1983) and Liebert (1988) observed, Freud's own writings on character pathology were not extensive. It was largely Abraham (1921/1927c) and especially W. Reich (1933/1949) who were responsible for extending this aspect of Freud's views.

Traits such as extreme frugality and obstinate refusal to give up objects that are no longer needed form part of Freud's and Abraham's formulations of the anal character, typified by possessiveness and withholding. Frugality reflects one's inability to separate from what belongs to oneself; objects or possessions must fervently be held onto, lest they be taken away. Classical analysis and ego psychology regarded characteristics such as these as constituting the central conflict in a struggle to maintain autonomy and control. Rado (1959) regarded this struggle as an obedience–defiance conflict with origins in parental demands concerning toilet training; for this reason, he referred to the struggle as "the battle of the chamber pot" (p. 330). Rado also considered what he called "rage abortion" to give rise to guilt, a precursor of superego development. Erikson (1950) reformulated this same conflict as one of autonomy versus shame and doubt.

Fromm (1947) characterized the conflict between obedience and defiance as a hoarding orientation toward the interpersonal world. Fromm, whose work predated the contemporary school of interpersonal psychoanalysis, further described obsessive–compulsive personalities as being insulated by fortifying themselves against external intrusions threatening to take from them what they must zealously keep protected. His neoanalytic viewpoint emphasized the social–interpersonal significance of drives and their derivatives more so than their inborn, instinctual character. Thus, his views emphasized how obsessive–compulsive preoccupation with orderliness, obstinacy, and cleanliness represented mastery of a potentially intrusive world seeking to control patients' lives. Fromm was not convinced that obsessive–compulsive personality represented defensive operations related to struggles surrounding toilet training and the ensuing conflict over control and guilt.

Other psychoanalytic theoreticians proposed modified views of obsessive–compulsive mechanisms, views that were influenced less by the primacy of drive theory's etiological view—based on psychosexual stages—than by the quality of engagement in relationships with parents or parental figures. Thus, for example, Gabbard (1994) emphasized the significance of extreme perfectionism in obsessive–compulsive character as an attempt to satisfy what was perceived as a demanding parental environment. Such viewpoints in psychoanalysis predate recent attempts to integrate drive theory with an interpersonal perspective (Aron, 1996; Mitchell, 1988). Other psychological formulations, influenced in varying degrees by psychoanalytic theory, have also stressed compliance with perfectionistic standards (Millon, 1969, 1996) and doubtful or anxious cautiousness inhibiting spontaneity (Salzman, 1985).

Shapiro (1965) called attention to the importance of guilt in the psychodynamic configuration of obsessive–compulsive character. Shapiro saw harsh superego demands as a central feature of these patients' psychological sense of themselves; relaxing their guard would be nearly unimaginable. Their deliberateness and tenacity become hypertrophied to minimize losing control. Decision making is often shrouded in agonizing internal struggles, culminating in abrupt choices when these patients have finally worn themselves out. The obsessive–compulsive character is also dominated by marked constriction of autonomy, in which overreliance on rules to guide decisions interferes with flexible spontaneity. Such patients also tend to disregard the emotional overtones of interactions with people, managing to filter affects out of their lived experience.

Obsessive–compulsive personality is also characterized by ritualistic procedures that constrain the vitality of emotional life. Such patients' lives seem to be dominated by imperatives that they "should" or "must" do, think, or feel certain ways. Consequently, they frequently substitute mechanistic modes of experience for what they actually experience. Shapiro (1965) compared this affectively remote quality of experiencing situations and people with that of a pilot flying a plane "as if he were seeing clearly, but nothing in his situation is experienced directly; only indicators are experienced, things that signify other things" (p. 50).

Shapiro (1965) also stressed that dogmatic convictions based on affectively narrowed experiences coexist with doubt, creating an attenuated sense of emotional reality. Constricted experience impedes "seeing things in their real proportions, apprehending the rich shadings, or recognizing the real substance of the world" (p. 52). Constriction also connotes how estranged obsessive–compulsive patients can become from their desires—for example, an obsessive–compulsive person who expresses an interest in reading a book is "actually interested only in having read it," or a person who seeks to act maturely or with propriety "imagines that he is mature when he is only stilted" (Shapiro, 1981, p. 83).

Other formulations about obsessive–compulsive character stressed conflict. Rado (1959) emphasized conflict between obedience and defiance. Millon (1996), though concurring with Rado's view of such patients as ambivalently conflicted, noted that outwardly compliant obsessive–compulsive traits actually keep antagonistic or oppositional impulses in check by concealing them. Shapiro (1965) was impressed by such patients' conflicted experiences between their dogmatic adherence to rules and their propensity for doubt. He regarded this as typifying his view that constricted autonomy is the central disturbance underlying obsessive–compulsive character style. Josephs (1992) also called attention to the importance of conflict in the obsessive–compulsive character, although he emphasized a split between the sense of indignant moral superiority and a more uncertain sense of self experience.

Cloninger (1987) described low novelty seeking and high harm avoidance as primary temperament dimensions in obsessional personality that predispose patients to this condition's characteristically rigid, rule-bound preoccupations and maintenance of self-control. He also differentiated two subtypes, one characterized by high reward dependence, which was passive–dependent and avoidant in nature, and a second in which low reward dependence produced an alienated disposition. He and his colleagues (Cloninger et al., 1993) subsequently abandoned framing personality disorders as categorical entities. Instead, Cloninger favored multidimensional temperament and character configurations representing interactions among temperaments, family environment, and individual life experiences. However, Cloninger and his colleagues did not again refer to obsessive–compulsive personality or its subtypes in later writings.

One early factor analytic study of obsessive–compulsive symptoms (Lazare, Klerman, & Armor, 1970) resulted in a factor solution that was consistent with psychodynamic formulations of obsessional traits. More recently, Westen and Shedler's (2000) Q-sort analysis also identified an obsessional cluster that resembled most extant descriptions of obsessive–compulsive personality disorder, though with an added emphasis on its adaptive as well as maladaptive components. In their analysis, conscientiousness and responsibility, articulateness, high moral standards, and productive use of talents and abilities were regarded as positive attributes. These coexisted with potentially maladaptive aspects such as being controlling, inhibited, and constricted. Millon (1996), Oldham and Morris (1990), and Pollak (1995) also noted adaptive variants of obsessive–compulsive personality disorder, commenting that conscientiousness—leading to diligent work standards—and conformity—giving rise to loyalty and conventionality—are both dominant personality characteristics that may exist independently of the inhibitions or severe constriction associated with the clinical disorder.

Millon's (1996) formulation in particular emphasized the conforming characteristic of obsessive–compulsive personality disorder, built on defensive operations such as reaction formation, isolation, and undoing. He considered such defenses as operating to compartmentalize or conceal aggression. Affective experience would thus be dominated by a characteristically grim or cheerless demeanor, accompanied by constriction. Such patients' overdisciplined conscientiousness and propriety thus influence their formal and sometimes ingratiating interpersonal style. Millon identified *conscientious, puritanical,* and *bureaucratic* subtypes in addition to a *parsimonious* subtype resembling Fromm's hoarding type and a *bedeviled* subtype representing an unresolved, ambivalent hybrid form alternating between obedient conforming and assertive oppositionality.

Recent studies of the prevalence of obsessive–compulsive personality disorder and its comorbidity with other disorders indicate that its overlap with other Axis II disorders is relatively variable (Millon, 1996; Pfohl & Blum, 1995). Moreover, it appears to show less overlap with obsessive–compulsive disorder on Axis I than it shows with anxiety–phobic and somatic conditions. Obsessive–compulsive disorder on Axis I also is no more likely to be comorbid with obsessive–compulsive personality disorder than other Axis II personality disorders (Pollak, 1987). Because obsessive–compulsive personality disorder has only recently begun to attract active interest from investigators in other areas of clinical psychopathology and neurobiology, it is not yet known how these fields of inquiry will influence the understanding of this condition, particularly its relationship with other Axis I and Axis II disorders.

BORDERLINE PERSONALITY DISORDER

The term *borderline* is now used to denote a distinct clinical entity that is neither predominantly psychotic nor nonpsychotic (neurotic), occupying an indistinct border between both. Although it shows important symptomatic features of both states, borderline disorder's clinical presentation is variable. This disorder, though more typically nonpsychotic, may sometimes show features of transient psychotic states, and it is characteristically unstable and variable in clinical severity. The disorder invariably produces seriously compromised functioning in most areas of life. Although its chronic, unstable course is consistent with most definitions of personality disorder, its status as a distinct clinical entity on Axis II has been challenged (Akiskal et al., 1985).

Borderline personality disorder was once viewed as a relatively mild prepsychotic or larval form of schizophrenia. Thus, what is currently considered borderline personality disorder was represented in the past by concepts such as latent (Bleuler, 1950), ambulatory (Zilboorg, 1941), and pseudoneurotic (Hoch & Polatin, 1949) schizophrenia. Borderline disorder was sometimes regarded as a relatively severe, intractable neurotic illness, albeit a disorder sometimes associated with transient psychotic-like decompensation. Although A. Stern (1938) introduced the term *borderline* to describe such disturbances, it was Knight's (1953) use of the term that attracted greater interest. The term *borderline* survived in the nomenclature, but not, as I describe in this section, without formidable misgivings (Frosch, 1988; Millon, 1996). Knight remained uncertain whether the condition was closer to schizophrenia or to psychoneurosis. Schmideberg (1959), however, considered this form of psychopathology to represent a stable but lifelong pattern of psychotic and psychopathic features interspersed with periods of normality.

Millon (1996) considered Kraepelin's (1921) excitable personality type, Schneider's (1923/1950) labile personality, and Kretschmer's (1925) cycloid–

schizoid temperament to be among the important precursors of contemporary views of borderline personality disorder. According to Schmideberg (1959), the symptomatic presentation was noncontributory for establishing a diagnosis of borderline disorder because its clinical differentiation from psychotic and nonpsychotic disorders relied more on the severity of the underlying personality disturbance. She emphasized in particular patients' propensity for hostile acting out, low frustration tolerance, and unstable living circumstances. Her generally accepted view was expanded to incorporate most aspects of life adjustment, thus presaging Modell's (1963) and Grinker et al.'s (1968) emphases on borderline patients' pervasive dysfunctions in work, intimate attachments and sexuality, affect, thinking, and reality appraisal.

Modell (1963) stressed subtle distortions of reality and regressive potential in borderline personality. He called attention in particular to an impaired sense of identity and dependence on omnipotent protectors alternating with intense fear of closeness. Grinker et al. (1968) identified a syndrome characterized by anger as the primary affect, impaired self-identity, depression characterized by pervasive loneliness, and limited intimacy in relationships. Grinker et al. delineated four subgroups of borderline patients, one of which they described as a core borderline subgroup characterized by inconsistent alternation between angry closeness and depressed isolation. Two other subgroups Grinker et al. identified represented relative positions on a psychosis–nonpsychosis continuum. One subgroup was characterized by severe distortions, including transient psychosis (the psychotic border), and the other was characterized chiefly by an empty quality of depression (the neurotic border). Grinker et al.'s fourth subgroup consisted of patients who showed a chameleon-like compliance dominated by a pervasive sense of feeling abandoned. These patients also showed diffused identity reminiscent of Deutsch's (1942) concept of the "as if" personality—a vacillating and thus unstable pattern of adapting identities in a facile way according to expectations of the moment. Grinker et al.'s subgroups represented one of the first systematic attempts to bring together a variety of regularly occurring clinical features as a single syndrome.

Frosch (1988), like Schmideberg (1959) and Grinker et al. (1968), also provided a psychoanalytic description of this disorder, which he designated *psychotic character*. He preferred this term because he considered it to provide a better description of the dynamic configuration of the personality and its pathology than the term *borderline*. Although Frosch argued for abandoning the term *borderline*—a position Millon (1996) also advocated—the term has remained in the nomenclature across the various iterations of the DSM. It survives in the psychoanalytic literature largely because of Kernberg's (1975) important influence on conceptualizing this disorder. Regardless of differences or overlap in terminology, all of these psychoanalytic theorists stressed that borderline personality disorder represents a condition in which unstable adjustment is discernible in almost every area of life. Moreover, it is a chronic disturbance that remains essentially unchanged throughout life. It is also a disorder that typically is clinically manageable rather than treatable in the sense of achieving substantial adaptational recovery.

Probably the most influential contemporary psychoanalytic formulation of borderline personality disorder is Kernberg's (1967, 1975) description of a stable but pathological ego structure. Although the disorder's clinical presentation can vary, primitive primary process thinking coexists with preserved reality testing, despite occasional psychotic lapses. Kernberg also called attention to a prominent identity disturbance accompanied by diminished understanding of the self and others. Like Grinker et al. (1968), Kernberg's view of identity diffusion took note of Deutsch's (1942) "as if" personality characterization; he also was influenced by Jacobson's (1953) views about affective instability and pathological internalized introjects. Kernberg's principal contribution was a description of the structural psychodynamic disturbance, which he referred to as "borderline personality organization." Its central psychopathology is a deficiency of ego structure resembling Knight's (1953) concept of ego weakness. It disposes patients to nonspecific disturbances such as impaired anxiety tolerance and impulse control and lack of a capacity for sublimation.

Kernberg (1967, 1975) also described primitive defenses, chiefly the splitting of all-good (libidinal) and all-bad (aggressive) object representations. This viewpoint was influenced by M. Klein's (1930, 1935) theorizing about object relations. Kernberg considered borderline personality organization to be characterized by the inability to integrate ambivalent (all-good and all-bad) object representations. Thus, love and hate are kept apart, largely through splitting as the primary defensive operation. Kernberg also identified several related defenses, such as omnipotence, devaluation, and primitive idealization, as attempts to preserve all-good object representations from contamination by patients' aggression. Projective identification was another defense Kernberg considered characteristic of borderline patients to assist them with managing their excessive aggression. Projective identification is based on the propensity to externalize aggressive self and object images, although at the cost of maintaining a substantial predominance of persecutory or retaliatory object images.

Although Kernberg's (1967, 1975) dynamic perspective seems to have predominated in the psychoanalytic literature on borderline states, his borderline personality organization construct remains broader in scope than the DSM–IV designation of borderline personality disorder. Looked at from a different perspective, it is reasonably clear that borderline personality is not a hybrid state that could be considered a genetically related or attenuated form of schizophrenia. Moreover, it has been questioned whether borderline personality disorder represents a distinct condition in its own right (Gunderson, 1977) or whether it should best be regarded as a variant of an affective disorder (Akiskal et al., 1985). For example, because of the disorder's often favorable response to antidepressant pharmacotherapy, its validity has been challenged in favor of a view regarding its clinical manifestations as a variant of a primary affective disorder (Akiskal, Djenderedjian, Rosenthal, & Khani, 1977; D. F. Klein, 1977). Despite persisting questions such as these, borderline personality disorder continues to be considered a disturbance in which a prominent characteristic is that functioning is fluid and usually seriously compromised.

Although their severity of dysfunction is variable, borderline patients reveal a clinical course and outcome that are not as prognostically unfavorable as schizophrenia, but their disease course cannot be considered benign. These patients are frequently difficult to treat, and some features of their illness are usually intractable. Moreover, borderline patients almost always show a chronic course with relatively stable functioning punctuated by periods of marked destabilization. Notwithstanding such deficits, patients who show specific talents are capable of productive or creative vocational accomplishments.

Certainly, unstable functioning and symptomatic regression remain among the most diagnostically significant features of borderline personality disorder. Borderline patients frequently alternate unpredictably between a relatively normal state and varying degrees of perturbations of distress, including mood fluctuations, anger or empty depression as predominant affect states, and self-destructive impulsivity. Identity diffusion or instability is nearly always ascertainable on clinical examination. Identity disturbance is, however, a particularly unreliable and nonspecific sign (Gunderson, Zanarini, & Kisiel, 1995); so, too, is chronic emptiness (S. Taylor, 1995). Imprecision in defining and specifying criteria for identity disturbance and chronic emptiness therefore adds to the problem of differential diagnosis among borderline, narcissistic, antisocial, and histrionic personality disorders, all of which show appreciable overlap.

Although borderline personality disorder is probably best classified as belonging on Axis II, Gunderson and Philips (1991) and Akiskal et al. (1985) stressed the importance of clearly distinguishing the boundary between borderline personality disorder and various forms of affective disorders. Their thinking was influenced by the observation that affective instability is a nonspecific sign that is clinically prevalent in several Axis II conditions, particularly schizotypal and histrionic personality disorders. In addition, Zanarini (1993) and Siever and Davis (1991) suggested that borderline pathology may be more usefully conceptualized clinically and etiologically as a disorder of impulsivity. Schore (2003a) hypothesized that borderline disorder, particularly when accompanied, as it often is, by histories of abuse, predisposes patients to a hyperaroused orbitofrontal corticolimbic system. He contrasted this neurobiological pattern with a different pattern characterized predominantly by hyperarousal; a good example of the latter is antisocial personality disorder, which is often accompanied by histories of early neglect.

There are other important conceptual and empirically based viewpoints about borderline personality disorder. In Millon's (1996) biopsychosocial–evolutionary model, the borderline (cycloid) prototype is characterized by conflictual patterns including each of the pleasure–pain, passive–active, and self–other polarities. Thus, although ambivalence and vacillation surround all areas of these patients' experiences, no single characteristic is predominant, because the fundamental nature of borderline disorder is its short-lived mood swings and largely unsuccessful efforts to manage anxiety. Mood states are labile, and behavior is characterized by impulsivity and inconsistent interpersonal relatedness. Millon acknowledged the importance of hostile affects, self-destructiveness, and self-denigration that many psychoanalytic theorists have noted. He also noted the central role of segmenting conflictual states, similar to Kernberg's emphasis on splitting as a primary defense. Millon further pointed out that an unstable self-image coupled with aimlessness or emptiness can dominate borderline patients' phenomenological experience. He identified four subtypes of borderline patients, each characterized by prominent patterns of discouragement, impulsivity, petulant anger, or self-destructiveness. Millon (2000) also emphasized the unique importance of sociocultural factors influencing the etiology and maintenance of borderline pathology, calling particular attention to the neglect of such influences in many psychoanalytic explanations of this disorder.

Cloninger (1987) compared borderline pathology with histrionic personality disorder in his model of temperaments, in which borderline disorder showed a pattern of high novelty seeking and reward dependence together with low harm avoidance. He noted the prominence of narcissistic, impulsive–aggressive, and dependent traits in borderline as well as histrionic patients, commenting that identity disturbance and emotional dependency were more prominent than narcissistic traits in borderline disorder patients. Cloninger did not propose a distinct typology specific to borderline pathology, acknowledging the uncertainty that exists in the literature concerning the clinical distinctiveness of borderline patients relative to those with other disorders (Cloninger, 1987; Cloninger et al., 1993). As Cloninger's thinking increasingly incorporated character as well as temperament dimensions, he seemed to regard borderline personality disorder features as similar to his description of explosive personality. Cloninger, Svrakic, and Svrakic (1997) characterized this condition as having a pattern of high novelty seeking and harm avoidance and low reward dependence. The explosive or borderline temperament, they believed, predisposes patients to underdeveloped self-directedness and cooperativeness, not unlike a similar pattern in antisocial and obsessional personalities. Cloninger and colleagues allowed, however, that social learning and random environmental events (or "luck," as they put it) also may moderate temperament structure.

Using an assessment instrument to chart the developmental trajectory of temperament influences on character patterns, Cloninger et al. (1997)

and Karasu (1994) located severe borderline pathology at an early stage of development, corresponding to psychoanalytic views of impaired sense of self, impaired mother–child relations, and separation–individuation problems. In Cloninger et al.'s typology, these disturbances are based on faulty developmental influences on trust and confidence, producing shame in the self-directedness character dimension, distrust in the cooperativeness character dimension, and a judgmental manner in the self-transcendence dimension of character. This pattern represents disturbances common to early-onset experiences of abuse associated with schizophrenic disorganization and sexual perversions.

Karasu (1994) further observed that mild borderline and narcissistic pathology conform to a pattern that Cloninger and colleagues considered to represent developmentally influenced character dimensions. This pattern is manifested by aimless rather than purposeful self-directedness, an unempathic quality in the cooperativeness dimension, and defiance typifying the character dimension of self-transcendence. Further, this developmental pattern predisposes patients to problems with impulse control, lowered capacity for intimacy, and difficulties with social commitment or internalization of values.

Westen and Shedler's (1999a, 1999b, 2000) Q sort–derived classification of Axis II disorders did not indicate a single distinctive factor representing borderline disorders. Most borderline patients were identified by a factor they termed *dysphoric: emotionally dysregulated*, representing patients with pronounced affective dyscontrol who engaged in self-injurious behavior or desperately sought others for soothing. Other borderline patients were represented in Westen and Shedler's *dysphoric: dependent–masochistic* or *histrionic* factors. The dysphoric: dependent–masochistic patients included borderline patients for whom states of distress were associated with intense neediness or dependency; such patients sometimes submit to abusive or rejection-prone relationships because of their propensity to form rapid attachments to unavailable people. Borderline patients who were identified by the histrionic factor showed an ego-syntonic quality of affective distress; consequently, they were cognizant of their distress. In contrast, borderline patients identified on both dysphoric factors were unaware of affective distress. The histrionic and dysphoric: dependent–masochistic factors were similar in that both were characterized by marked dependency or neediness and rapidly formed attachments. The histrionic factor, however, was further characterized by three features: (a) dramatic manifestations of needing people who were frequently idealized (to provide an affective regulatory or calming function), (b) requirements of excessive reassurance, and (c) hypersensitivity to rejection or abandonment.

Although borderline personality disorder was identified by all of these three factors (particularly the dysphoric: emotionally dysregulated factor), these factors are considered part of other personality disorders as well. Westen and Shedler (1999a, 1999b, 2000) considered these factors to represent ways in which patients experience distress (i.e., different sensitizing or precipitating situations) more than overt social or interpersonal dysfunction (i.e., different ways of regulating painful affects). Thus, Westen and Shedler regarded borderline, depressive, self-defeating, dependent, and avoidant personality disorders as relatively distinct clinical manifestations triggered by different pathological reactions or dispositions.

CONCLUSION

In this chapter, I traced the development of several viewpoints about paranoid, obsessive–compulsive, and borderline personality disorders. Emphasizing perspectives from psychoanalysis and descriptive psychopathology, this review suggests that views of obsessive–compulsive and borderline disorders have been predominantly influenced by psychoanalytic theories. In particular, ego psychology (in the case of obsessive–compulsive personality) and object relations theory (in the case of borderline personality disorder) have been the principal perspectives influencing theory about these disorders. Subclinical paranoia (paranoid personality disorder) has been viewed by psychoanalysis in relation to obsessive–compulsive disorder and by descriptive psychopathology in relation to schizophrenia. The following chapter will consider these personality disorders from the vantage point of self psychology, emphasizing a fundamental characteristic dominated by efforts to avert or forestall fragmentation of the self.

6

A SELF PSYCHOLOGICAL VIEWPOINT: PARANOID, OBSESSIVE–COMPULSIVE, AND BORDERLINE PERSONALITY DISORDERS

In the previous chapter, I summarized descriptive and psychoanalytic views of paranoid, obsessive–compulsive, and borderline personality disorders, which I will characterize in the present chapter as disorders of the self coalescing around fragmentation. It is important to keep in mind that *fragmentation of the self* does not necessarily refer to an emergent psychotic reaction or to the acute disruption of psychological functioning in the face of appreciable trauma. Fragmentation may indeed take such forms; borderline and paranoid personality disorders are good examples of conditions where reality testing, affective stabilization, and impulse control may become seriously undermined. Fragmentation of the self is here understood as denoting experiences portending a sense of dissolution, as if one were coming apart. As Wolf (1988) wrote, "The experience of a crumbling self is so unpleasant that people will do almost anything to escape the perceptions brought about by fragmentation" (p. 39). Kohut (1971) called such intense tension states *disintegration products.*

Fragmentation varies in severity, ranging from momentary disruptions of self-cohesion that reconstitute relatively quickly to prolonged states of disrupted self-cohesion that occur frequently or resolve slowly. Sufficiently prolonged or intense selfobject failures may precipitate phenomenological experiences characterized by a sense of crumbling within oneself. Either mild or severe fragmentation phenomena may produce frantic or hypomanic activity, substance abuse, delinquent actions, sexual acting out, or frank perversions—all of which may represent desperate attempts to subdue perturbations of immobilizing anxiety or depression. Phenomena such as these often represent patients' attempts to manage marked destabilization of self-cohesion, ranging in severity from diminished self-cohesion to pronounced disintegration of the self.

Fragmentation phenomena may be neither as destabilizing as a severe reality testing disturbance—such as psychotic decompensation—nor as frightening as the disinhibited impulsivity people experience if they feel they are falling apart because of a severe loss of control. Nevertheless, all of these forms of fragmentation may be understood as breakdowns of self-cohesion resulting from faulty responsiveness of the selfobject environment. Self disorders such as paranoid, obsessive–compulsive, and borderline personality disorders are described in this chapter predominantly as fragmentation-prone disorders, because the fundamental struggle of such patients' lives centers on ever-constant efforts to forestall fragmentation.

Aspects of self experience may become walled off in such a way that sectors of the self are not well integrated. A stable or cohesive structure that promotes self-regulation may fail to become securely established through *transmuting internalizations*, Kohut's (1971, 1977) term for incorporating selfobject functions in bit-by-bit fashion during normal development. Children of parents or caregivers who cannot provide the selfobject experiences of mirroring or idealization from which a firmed-up self coalesces lack the assurance that they will be able to tolerate ongoing tension states. Such children may become wary of signs of danger that they somehow recognize they cannot withstand because they have not been able to sufficiently internalize a self-calming capacity. Their early experience of a deficient selfobject environment could not help them assuage self states of unrelenting tension.

Paranoid hyperalertness and the chronic instability of borderline disorders are two outcomes for fragmentation-prone patients. Obsessive–compulsive personality disorder is perhaps a more benign form of a similar attempt to find a solution to the feeling of being chronically unanchored or adrift. Many patients describe such a self state as "feeling unglued."[1] In vary-

---

[1]Kohut (1996) regarded a need for "glue" as a legitimate, normal expectation in normal development, noting how it is "what holds us together, the unreserved responsiveness of those who surround us early in life" (p. 387). Unlike classical psychoanalytic theory, self psychology does not necessarily consider metaphors such as "glue" as simply representing palliative treatments. Kohut regarded as a more salient metaphor a favorite line of his from Eugene O'Neill's play *The Great God Brown* (1926/1941), in

ing degrees, all of these mental phenomena are characterized by rigid inhibition and the inability to relax tight overcontrol for fear of breaking apart. Considered from a self psychological vantage point, these personality disorders threaten to expose disintegration products such as narcissistic rage or internal states of depletion anxiety or depletion depression. The clinical manifestations of paranoid, obsessive–compulsive, and borderline personality disorders thus represent both the patient's vulnerability to fragmentation and his or her attempts to forestall its incursion on the cohesiveness of the self.

Considered from an intersubjective self psychological viewpoint, the fragmentation-prone disorders described in this chapter have in common a predominant organizing principle: to detect and counteract perceived threats by other people (Stolorow, Brandchaft, & Atwood, 1987). Preserving self-control or resiliency in the face of a brittle capacity to keep potential harm at bay is thus the principal organization of such patients' experiencing of the self and others (the selfobject dimension) and of their expectations of others' reactions or intentions (the repetitive dimension). Kohut (1977) regarded the capacity to acquire more satisfying or efficacious selfobjects to be the optimal signpost of repair. The intersubjectivity viewpoint, however, maintains that the selfobject dimension is not the only organizing principle or structure of subjective experience. Also central to the intersubjective position is its emphasis on affect regulation, through which a new organizing principle may emerge to effect repair of the self. For example, when a caregiver is able to calm a child's distressing affect state, the caregiver's own affect state is also regulated as he or she comes to feel competent in providing a calming function. In this way, the intersubjective context is important for ensuring mutual regulation of affects, but only if the child–caregiver dyad is affectively synchronized. That is, caregiver *availability* is not the same thing as *attunement*. For example, caregivers' diminished capacity to match and comprehend the needs or momentary distressing emotional states of their children may undermine mutual affect regulation for child and caregiver alike. Prolonged misattunement or asynchrony of this kind leads to faulty expectations (organizing principles) about other people's motivations, because the construal of others' intentions derives its meaning in an intersubjective context. Adult manifestations of fragmentation of the self thus develop out of such faulty mutual affect attunements.

A related self psychological formulation, by Lichtenberg, Lachmann, and Fosshage (1992), considered the importance of attuned selfobject responsiveness in vitalizing affects as well as in providing self-cohesion. Expanding on Kohut's understanding of selfobject functions to incorporate attunement to motivational states, Lichtenberg et al. suggested that compromised development leads to altered selfobject experiences that are not based

---

which Brown says, "Man is born broken. He lives by mending. The grace of God is glue" (p. 370). "Curing" in self psychology means fortifying or repairing the self.

on attuned (i.e., empathic) responsiveness to affect states. They distinguished between empathic failures of caregivers that lead to self disorders and empathic failures that create an expectation of nonresponsiveness. The latter condition creates an aversiveness to attachments, which patients perceive as depleting rather than vitalizing. Lichtenberg et al. described this distinction to explain why patients with the expectation of nonresponsiveness show a predilection for reexperiencing humiliations or hurtful relationships as familiar, albeit unsatisfying, forms of intimate relationships. The expectation of nonresponsiveness disposes patients to fragmentation phenomena such as angry rages, substance use, perversions, or sexualizations to assuage states of loneliness, boredom, or more general devitalization. Lichtenberg et al.'s view is similar to Kohut's (1971) description of disintegration anxiety and M. Tolpin's (1978) views about depletion anxiety and depletion depression.

According to the intersubjectivity view, the selfobject dimension is a background factor that contributes to the acquisition of new organizing principles. Intersubjectivists would consider repair by altering selfobject needs to be less crucial than mutual affect regulation, which is contrary to the traditional self psychological view. Thus, for example, Trop (1994) argued that selfobject transferences are predominantly byproducts of the disruption of older organizing principles (the repetitive dimension), although he recognized that the selfobject and repetitive dimensions occur simultaneously and are therefore virtually indivisible. The alteration of organizing principles that becomes reparative in treatment is thought to result from a balance between the intersubjective conjunctions and disjunctions that occur between patients' and clinicians' subjective understandings of events they both experience. A disjunction in treatment would occur when a disparity exists in this intersubjective context between clinicians' experiences or interpretations of events and patients' experiences, particularly when clinicians cannot assimilate their patients' experiences with their own. A therapist's recreation of misattunements similar to those of patients' caregivers in childhood may interfere with affect regulation, one consequence of which may be fragmentation phenomena.

PARANOID PERSONALITY DISORDER

In discussing paranoia, Kohut (1996) observed that "it is nothing but the traumatic state of a crumbling self that hypersensitively sees the whole world as an attacker. In other words, it feels itself breaking apart; it feels so fragile, so vulnerable, that everything becomes an attack" (p. 147). Further, Kohut observed, "Their dreams also indicate that things are falling apart. They are disorganized, chaotic, 'exploded' dreams. . . . They are more an expression of what the person feels about himself" (pp. 149–150). In addition, speaking of paranoid patients' hypersensitivity to sensory stimuli, Kohut added,

They smell the supposed mustiness of the office, or they have smelled a "peculiar, bitter smell" outside in the waiting room; and this also is the time when the slightest movement is a noise that becomes very, very annoying . . . and behind that is a self that at the present time is poorly put together, a self that has had some crushing defeat. (p. 149)

Statements such as these also reflect Kohut's recognition that a "crumbling self" is not unique to narcissistic personality disorders.

Paranoid personality disorder patients might thus develop wary suspiciousness to forestall the fragmentation of a self in constant threat of being undermined or attacked. Whether or not the fundamental mechanism of this Axis II disorder is a milder form of a pathological biological process, the early child–caregiver environment—in particular, the experience of one's existence as undependable—influences how the disorder develops. If such patients experience their world as unsafe as adults, it is because their nascent selves experienced the danger of falling apart. As children, they could not anticipate an engaging, vital selfobject environment to provide the mirroring responsiveness necessary to sustain a buoyant self.

Paranoid patients replace an enthusiastic welcoming of maternal involvement and the mirroring it provides with the expectation that their selfobject environment will fail to respond to their needs. Such patients as children were likely to have been exposed to uncomprehending mothers or caregivers and came to anticipate their primary caregivers' empathic failures. They could not feel assured of protective safekeeping that would provide even a temporary but reliable buffer to cement self-cohesion until they could firm up a robust self-cohesion on their own. Their mothers' pervasive empathic unresponsiveness would thus have fostered the experience of a fearful existence where vulnerability to fragmentation was ever present.

Such children's experiences of early maternal care left them frequently on the alert for signs of their mothers' capacity to comprehend when they were distressed. The initial disappointment of an unattuned mother's diminished or faulty selfobject responsiveness would give way over time to chronic hyperalertness to perceived dangers in a world they felt unprepared to understand. They experience the unfamiliar as threatening because they lack the sustaining buffer of an empathic selfobject environment. The selfobject environment failed to provide them with adequate reassurance that experiences of intense tension might eventually dissipate and be relieved.

Thus, feeling unprotected and vulnerable, such chronically unresponded-to children are not able to bolster the degree of self-cohesion people need to feel that their selfobject surround is on their side. They replace their disappointment in their caregivers with a prematurely acquired, hypervigilant attunement to protect their very survival. Like other precociously formed adaptations that become ingrained as a way of life, hypervigilance hypertrophies to become such patients' most workable mechanism to get by in life. Although they inhabit a world that is perhaps no more dangerous or malevolent than everyone else's, their early exposure to chronically uncomprehending, unattuned maternal failure disposes them to warily anticipate danger and to believe that the only source of help is someone who is present but cannot hear their pleas. Thus, a fearful, ever-present experience of weakened self-cohesion sets in, and guarding against danger becomes tantamount to guarding against fragmentation of the self. Vigilant watchfulness turns imperceptibly into an ingrained paranoid adaptation to a threatening world characterized by chronic selfobject failure and thus undermined self-cohesion.

Because they experience their existence in so fragile a way, patients with paranoid personality disorder are regularly exposed to potential fragmentation. Such patients' "exceedingly frail autonomy" (Shapiro, 1965, p. 80) results from an incapacity to relax or suspend the tight overcontrol they need. Paranoid personality disorder patients fail to experience the sense that they can will or control much of what happens in their lives. As I noted in chapter 5, Shapiro (1965) believed that these patients are constricted because their psychological resources are so extensively devoted to securing self-preservation. Consequently, there is no room in their existence for playful or relaxed abandon or for letting down their rigidly maintained guard. Shapiro (1965, 1981) regarded impaired volition as one of the chief hallmarks of the rigid autonomy that permeates the paranoid orientation to the world.

These patients' weakened sense of autonomy leads to their defensive rigidity. Paranoid personalities cannot easily experience intentionality that feels assuredly their own. Shapiro's (1965) insightful observations may be reconsidered as describing the experience of a self that is underpowered or devitalized. Moreover, a sense of flexible freedom of action is covered over by a defensive arrogance or obstinate negativism that conceals devalued self-esteem. Such patients also may feel ashamed that they cannot feel free or proud because they feel diminished.

Kohut (1977) regarded both paranoid and schizoid personality disorders as conditions in which distancing mechanisms serve to defensively forestall the potential for enfeeblement or breakup of the self. For Kohut, the main difference between these disorders is their symptomatic manifestations, which for paranoid patients takes the form of hostility and suspiciousness and for schizoid patients, emotional coldness or shallowness. I suggest another difference as well: Whereas schizoid patients' withdrawal or coldness represents mirroring deficiencies, paranoid patients' hypervigilant hostility represents the forestalling of potentially destabilizing fragmentation.

In some patients, the danger of fragmentation of the self becomes infused with projected aggression, leading to a sense of the self as endangered by a malevolent selfobject world. However, it is also conceivable that the angry resentment of paranoid patients does not emerge as directly from an aggressive drive as from a fragmentation-prone sense of reality. Thus, such patients' malevolent orientation to others and to the world in general would stem from failures leading to the disintegration products of a fragmentation-prone self, which may take the form of narcissistic rage. Thus, aggression in paranoid personality disorder may be understood as a threat of self-cohesion coming apart when the selfobject surround becomes undependable and thus frustrating.

An intersubjective view of paranoid personality disorder is that interactions with others are tinged with mistrust and peril. The intersubjective matrix of mutual regulation of affects is contaminated by paranoid patients' sense of others' malevolent intentions toward them, resulting in a wary, uncomfortable style of interaction that elicits in others a corresponding sense of discomfort. However, other peoples' wary distancing is based not on malevolence, but rather on the difficulty of being in a relationship with a hypervigilant, critical, easily slighted individual. Consequently, paranoid patients' wariness is rarely assuaged by interactions with other people, who respond to paranoid suspiciousness with cautiousness and shy away from providing the very sentiments paranoid patients crave most. Thus, the self-protective aloofness of paranoid patients reinforces their perceptions that the intersubjective field so created is hostile or cold. Affective regulation may be too unstable to enable these patients to forestall the persistent sense of threat that pervades their lives.

The intersubjective field is threatening for both parties as a result, and the mutually influencing affect states remain tense and insufficiently regulated (except for withdrawal to safe distances for both parties, albeit for different reasons). Paranoid patients' selfobject needs thus remain unfulfilled. The ultimate result for these patients is a sense of self that remains deprived of just the kind of integration they require from the selfobject environment. They are unable to establish a capacity for self-regulation or to disengage their persistent fears of malevolent attack through their relationships with others. Therefore, altering paranoid patients' capacities to assimilate intersubjective disjunctions in treatment would be an important early step to modify an organizing principle formed around anticipating malevolence.

Stone (1993) also commented on paranoid patients' heightened sensitivity to aggression. He noted their fear of being influenced by others such that their ability to preserve a sense of self with firm boundaries may be compromised, which fosters their keeping emotional distance from people. Further, it was Stone's opinion that fear of dissolution of the self, representing loss of identity, contributed to these patients' grandiosity. This view is similar to what Millon (1996) called *attachment anxiety*, referring to sensitivity to loss of autonomy and control. Although Stone and Millon did not frame their views within a self psychological perspective, they provide explanations for paranoid patients' difficulty being dependent on others and their sensitivity to betrayal or to being manipulated. Millon also regarded grandiosity as replacing a diminished or undermined existence with a sense of self and of external reality that is more acceptable.

Clinical Illustration of Paranoid Personality Disorder

The case illustration in this section describes the projective testing protocol of a 35-year-old single Hispanic man, Mr. E., who became agitated following a fire in the building where he lived. Mr. E. was a devout and studious ex-seminarian; he abandoned seminary training after losing the confidence of the archdiocese, which had recommended him for a selective opportunity to study at the Vatican. Although Mr. E. was fearful of going overseas, he had been persuaded to accept the honor. He was unhappy there and experienced depression, agitation, and nightmares. He returned home unexpectedly, to the embarrassment of the archdiocese. He subsequently attended a seminary of another denomination from which he graduated, but he never accepted a pastoral assignment because he thought the work would be too stressful. Mr. E. completed two master's degrees and attempted doctoral study, but he refused to explain why he did not complete that degree. He had once enlisted in the military but was discharged shortly after enlisting because he "was too difficult to get along with." In recent years, Mr. E. had volunteered at a homeless shelter.

Mr. E. said that he had trouble getting along with people when he felt that he did not get the respect he deserved. He presented a demeanor of highly intellectualized arrogance and superiority. Mr. E. appeared emotionally constricted and distrustful of others, and he described what sounded like a vigilant, aloof distance from other people. He seemed to have alienated acquaintances and his family by flaunting his superior intellect and then reacting with a haughty sense of injury when he felt that they did not take him seriously.

There was no evidence of psychotic thinking or impaired reality testing in the testing material. However, I noted features of idiosyncratic but not overtly thought-disordered thinking. For example, when asked to explain the saying "One swallow doesn't make a summer," Mr. E. responded, "A swallow is usually a sign of summer. It's a complex thing. Things are complex." Disturbing thoughts would emerge sporadically and seem to frighten the patient, provoking renewed efforts from him to rigidly guard his inner life. For example, he would defiantly refuse to respond when I asked him to elaborate on certain responses, seeming to dig his heels in as if petulantly preparing to do battle. For example, when I asked him to describe his drawing of a human figure, Mr. E. mentioned that the figure was looking out into the future, fearing death. When I asked him to elaborate, he said, "Everyone's going to die, everything's useless. There's no point to anything." Asked about the figure's future, Mr. E. responded, "I don't know, I didn't ask him. It's just a flat surface, so I can't tell anything. I'm only doing this because the doctor forced me to do it." He angrily refused to say anything further about the drawing.

Later, when shown Card 2 of the Thematic Apperception Test (TAT; H. A. Murray, 1943), which depicts a farm scene with two women in the foreground and a shirtless man in the background, Mr. E. said, "I think it's an insult, it's an offense to my religion. It's sexual, and some of these are perverted." Looking offended, he stubbornly refused to tell a story. I thought he might feel more comfortable composing a story about Card 1, depicting a boy looking at a violin, which I considered to be a less provocative picture. Mr. E. said that that, too, was offensive, and he wanted to discontinue the TAT at that point. He was vague about why this card was offensive, saying only, in an arrogant tone of voice, that he knew the theory behind the test. These examples convey the quality of this patient's wary, guarded orientation to reality and provide a reasonably typical indication of how paranoid personality disorder may be discerned clinically on psychodiagnostic tests.

The sequence of five responses Mr. E. generated on Card I of the Rorschach (Exner, 2003) illustrates further his paranoid hypervigilance. Mr. E.'s first response, referring to a Peter Max painting of stars and an angel with wings, was delivered in a manner I took to convey his satisfaction at having supplied a clever, sophisticated response. When I asked him to describe the angel, Mr. E. said victoriously and with sarcasm, "Because of the wings, I told you that already." To my inquiry about the stars, the patient said, "You're getting very pedantic. I was just looking at the card, trying to respond to your question. There's no special interpretation here; most of it is trite." When inquired about his second response regarding a moth, Mr. E. said, "You're confusing this, I didn't see all this" and then proceeded calmly to describe the moth in a conventional manner. His third response to Card I described a woman standing in front of a mirror with "a reflection that isn't real, because you can fashion mirrors in such a way that they keep reflecting images ad infinitum." Mr. E. elaborated on his fourth response of "two people kissing— no, two angels" during the inquiry by saying, "I said all this about this one picture? Are you sure?" His final response described a squashed insect that was "damaged, stepped on, flattened."

When responding to the cards, Mr. E. displayed pleasure initially by proudly demonstrating his creative intellect, but he acted on inquiry as if I were challenging him with the intent of undermining him. His paranoid sensitivities were readily provoked when he felt disregarded or thought that I had not listened carefully (e.g., when I forgot that he had already mentioned the wings on the angel). His retaliation was quick and unforgiving—he would not indulge my error and simply repeat something that I could have overlooked. He was acutely sensitive to my wrongdoing and empathic ruptures and incisive in what I experienced as his punishing faultfinding. He thus revealed the diminished self-esteem of someone who was quick to feel misunderstood and slighted. I had become for him an inattentive, careless selfobject who failed to listen to his every word, thus jeopardizing the perfectly attuned responsiveness he seemed to insist on commanding. And this was just the first response—there were nine cards to go!

As the Rorschach continued, Mr. E. continued to complain about the pedantic inquiry and trite blots, externalizing in this way his feeling of being belittled or attacked. He appeared to feel insulted as he realized that calling me to task for not listening carefully enough did not deter my effort to continue the inquiry. Thus, braced to do battle, Mr. E. struck back harder. However, he also may have sensed the brittleness of his capacity to sustain a flagging self under the continuing "attack" of the Rorschach inquiry. In describing the patient–examiner relationship during a Rorschach inquiry, Schachtel (1966) observed the following:

> No matter how convincingly the tester may try to explain to them that he is interested in their responses and he wishes they would tell him some more about them, they will interpret it, unconsciously if not consciously, that now they have to justify what they have seen. . . . So the tester must have found something the matter with their responses. . . . And the countless people with an always ready reservoir of guilt and inferiority feelings may now feel embarrassed or ashamed. . . . Sometimes this change in attitude is so great that people really do not recognize any more what they have seen before. . . . The general effect of the defensively experienced inquiry will be restrictive . . . along the lines of having to be more careful and accurate, of having to defend or better one's "record." (pp. 313–314)

Schachtel's (1966) comments also anticipated an intersubjective sensibility in which patients and clinicians influence each other, just as children or infants and their caregivers also form a mutually self-regulating dyad. In considering Mr. E.'s response to Card I, I could well imagine how others might find Mr. E. difficult to interact with ("a piece of work," to use the current vernacular). I could also imagine how he might have worn out his mother, much as he did me. Schachtel's observation illustrates how an intersubjective context may be present in psychodiagnostic assessment, an area of clinical activity not always fully appreciated as an influence on test findings. Mr. E.'s test protocols amply demonstrate both an intersubjective context in the course of a psychodiagnostic examination and the particular flavor of a fully engaged paranoid personality organization in the dynamic interplay between patients and examiners. Schachtel's observations and this patient's quality of engagement demonstrate as well his desperate struggle to forestall fragmentation and thus preserve self-cohesion.

After he had criticized my pedantic questions and what he experienced as an attempt to trip him up, Mr. E. recovered enough to let go of his paranoid intensity to proceed normally in describing the determinants of the moth percept. But his apparent recovery did not last long; his next response regarding a reflection in a mirror intimated that the mirror was set up or "fashioned" to distort reality. Mr. E.'s fragmenting self-cohesion reemerged as he lapsed into confusing verbiage while seeming to struggle with the idea of an image in a mirror that did not reflect objects veridically.

Mr. E. did not go anywhere near the intimacy or tenderness of the need state he seemed to hint at in his next response about angels or people kissing. In fact, he was at first caught off guard by my reiteration of his response ("I said all this?") and then became distrustful and externalizing ("Are you sure?"). In his final response that Card I depicted a squashed insect, Mr. E. seemed to have lost the battle he himself started, ending up with an evocative depiction of a "damaged, stepped-on" sense of the self and its vulnerability to being unprotected.

As Mr. E. proceeded through Card I, he had increasing difficulty containing a potential for fragmentation and ultimately resorted to blaming me for his own confusion by attributing malevolent intentions to me and denying what he had said earlier about his percepts. His responses suggested the helpless anger of someone trying to prevent fragmentation—in this case, the evocation of narcissistic rage about feeling trapped or humiliated when confronted with his own compromised self-cohesion.

And so it went throughout this patient's protocol. I felt as though I had been "put through the wringer" even at this point. I considered the possibility that his being Hispanic and my being White may have influenced the testing situation. I concluded that the nature of the psychopathology far outweighed any potential influence of a patient–examiner ethnic difference; moreover, the quality of our interaction was unlike that of nearly all other psychodiagnostic evaluations I have conducted with non-White patients.

In summary, Mr. E. revealed the tenuous self-cohesion of a fragmentation-prone paranoid adaptation. He struggled to conceal it but ultimately could not manage to do so in a sufficiently robust or vigorous manner. The paranoid effort to invigorate a devalued, underpowered self was his best effort to keep a brittle self afloat, but it faltered as the selfobject functions he needed to sustain self-cohesion failed to become viable possibilities. This patient resorted to keeping me at a safe distance through his retaliations and accusations, but his efforts to forestall fragmentation weakened. He experienced his existence as untrustworthy, requiring him to be on the lookout for events going against him; evidence of this vigilance included his accusations that I was planting his responses rather than reflecting what he had said, that I was not listening carefully enough, or that I was confusing him by putting words in his mouth. This patient also expressed the feeling that one could be tricked by distorting situations, such as mirrors that should accurately reflect what is before them but that can be fashioned to do otherwise. Mr. E. perceived the inquiry sometimes as an affront and sometimes as a challenge against which he had to defend himself. As the examiner, I was a transference object representing a malevolent, adversarial selfobject threatening to undermine Mr. E.'s vulnerable self-cohesion. The slights and empathic misattunements of the selfobject environment alert patients such as Mr. E. to the importance of being on guard against setups intended to trick them.

OBSESSIVE–COMPULSIVE PERSONALITY DISORDER

As with most forms of psychopathology, Kohut (1971, 1977, 1996) considered obsessive–compulsive disturbances to be disorders in which the self and its cohesiveness are the primary phenomena to be understood and treated. He also regarded obsessions and compulsions as symptoms representing disintegration products. Kohut minimized (but did not ignore) the two traditions in psychoanalysis regarding obsessive–compulsive syndromes—the developmental viewpoint, emphasizing anal stage regression, and the structural theory, emphasizing defensive operations to protect against emergence of aggression.

Kohut (1971, 1977, 1996) considered a mistake the central importance attributed to aggression in drive theory as an explanation of the irresistible urges of obsessive–compulsive behavior. He also proposed that a hypercathexis of thinking does not represent defensive undoing as much as it is "meant to do away with a defect in the self, to cover it, or to fill it via frantic, forever repeated activity" (M. Tolpin & Kohut, 1980, p. 439). M. Tolpin (1978) also noted that a neurotic-like superstructure overlying a "deficiency illness" frequently expressed "pathologically intensified, persisting needs for new versions of the self-objects which originally failed in their functions of adequately acting in place of inner firming, confirming, and guiding" (p. 178). Anticipating what she would later call a *forward edge transference* M. Tolpin (2002) emphasized how the presenting symptom picture both contains and self-protectively conceals expressions of what patients need to revitalize an injured self, taking note of Greenacre's (1971) differentiation between a progressive growth force and an aggressive drive.

Kohut (1996) provided an example of his reformulated viewpoint in his discussion of a patient who began obsessionally describing the contents of his pockets during a therapy session, which Kohut at first thought represented the patient's anger after Kohut announced an upcoming absence. He thus regarded the patient's anger as being transformed into a repetitive description of the patient's pocket contents. Kohut came to realize, however, that the patient's boring recitation was reminiscent of an important aspect of the patient's childhood in which he was left alone for long stretches of time. To calm or reassure himself, he would collect his possessions into a small pile, count them, and become obsessionally involved with these items, thus holding himself together until someone returned. Thus, Kohut came to consider the patient's obsessional description of his pocket contents not as a struggle against hostility triggered by his therapist's upcoming absence but rather as a response to reexposure to the experience of being unable to master a situation outside his control. It was an attempt to hold together for himself "one tiny bit in the world, at least that pocket . . . to be certain about at least something in an otherwise uncontrollable world" (Kohut, 1996, p. 171).

This kind of formulation of an obsessive–compulsive activity is in keeping with Kohut's emphasis on self psychology as an expansion of, rather than a departure from, classical psychoanalytic theory. Thus, Kohut did not abandon the importance of conflict and defense in psychopathology. Kohut (1996) commented, for example, that "when we talk about a drive versus a defense, we are really talking about a driven self versus a defending or defensive self" (p. 389). Rubovits-Seitz (1999), a collaborator and coteacher with Kohut during the 1960s, noted that although Kohut thought of conflicts as integral events in life, he did not consider their influence to be as decisive as classical theory suggested. Rather, Kohut argued that the self and its cohesiveness influenced how successfully people managed intrapsychic conflicts. Kohut thus regarded the self as a superordinate entity of mental life, which did not mean that mental structures such as id, ego, and superego were no longer important. Rather, their properties and functions were filtered through the self. Like Freud, Kohut regarded defenses as protective; however, whereas Freud stressed the protection of the ego and its resiliency, Kohut increasingly emphasized protection of the self and its cohesion.

Kohut (1971, 1977) distinguished between patients with a relatively cohesive self, for whom signal anxiety represents conflict, and other patients with damaged self-cohesion, for whom anxiety represents the threat of fragmentation. Thus, disintegration anxiety represents selfobject failure, producing the "anticipation of the breakup of the self" (Kohut, 1977, p. 104). Sufficiently restored selfobject functions (whether by mirroring, idealization, or twinship) form the crucial basis for repairing the fragmentation threatening self-cohesion. Thus, it is essential to understand the salience for preserving self-cohesion of obsessive–compulsive personality features like orderliness, excessive preoccupation with detail, and rigid tenacity.

From an intersubjectivity theory formulation of self psychology, obsessive–compulsive personality can be understood as resulting from patients' expectation that important selfobjects will not comprehend their affects or be able to calm them. Such patients expect others to misunderstand what they need or to fail to comprehend their wishes. They become increasingly distanced from their internal states as they get lost in the obsessive preoccupations or compulsive pulls representing the perpetuation of unrelieved distress. Thus, slavish or inflexible preoccupations with control, obedience, propriety, or rules and procedures, for example, may be understood as patients' attempts to steady themselves when they cannot count on the reliable presence of caregivers to understand their deepest concerns.

Patients with obsessive–compulsive personality disorder may become preoccupied with holding themselves intact when they feel ignored or unsupported. Adherence to a formula that never varies, rigid compliance with dogma, or proscriptive, forced thinking and action that tightly limits behavior are all ways of narrowing self experience to contain fragmentation of the self. Patients may have experienced the kind of misattuned child–caregiver relationship that leads to faulty affect regulation (for both parties) when the intersubjective field so created fails to provide the calming reassurance an attuned psychological connection affords. An intersubjective matrix of faulty mutual affect regulation undermines a child's trust that an empathically attuned selfobject environment can contain the distressing affect states that come and go in normal development.

Clinical Illustration of Obsessive–Compulsive Personality Disorder

Mr. F. was a 36-year-old White married man who was employed as a manager of an accounting department. He had been having thoughts about having an extramarital affair for several years. The patient had begun three brief affairs in the 6 months before beginning treatment. The first two were short-lived relationships, but the third affair became more emotionally intimate because he enjoyed this woman's view of him as sophisticated and important to her. He became anxious about his deepening feelings and abruptly terminated the relationship. His anxiety had started to become immobilizing at home and especially at work, where his strict routines and attention to detail were slipping; he had made errors that drew the critical attention of his supervisor.

A few months after Mr. F. terminated the affair, the woman contacted him because she felt lost without him in her life. Although he felt guilty and uncertain about resuming the relationship, Mr. F. felt that he could not turn away from someone who desired him as much as this woman did, an experience that was new for him. On one occasion while he was with her, Mr. F. experienced a sudden anxiety attack, frightening him enough to go to a hospital emergency room. Shortly after the anxiety attack, he sought psychotherapy.

In treatment, his manner was businesslike and reserved; he characteristically shook hands at the beginning and end of most sessions. Although this represented a form of psychological connection, albeit stilted and remote, I began to wonder how lonely Mr. F. must have been despite his outwardly good-natured demeanor. I discovered that he had no close friendships at or outside of work. For many years, Mr. F. had experienced difficulties with coworkers, particularly those he supervised, who consistently found him bureaucratic though technically competent as an administrator and stiff in handling the interpersonal aspects of his job. His coworkers complained about his stern and aloof management style. He was slavishly devoted to his work and perfectionistic in what he expected of himself, sometimes unresourcefully devoting his efforts to overseeing how procedures were followed, which slowed his ability to finish important projects on time. My patient also found his position personally unsatisfying and felt that he was criticized for being caught up in small details rather than complimented for keeping on top of matters.

He also felt disappointed that the chief financial officer showed little interest when he proposed plans for streamlining office procedures. He had felt humiliated when his boss turned down a proposal he had submitted almost a year earlier. He felt that this further devalued his position with his coworkers and caused him to be more remote with them and exacting and inflexible in his attention to technical details. Shortly after this humiliation, Mr. F. began to act on his secret wish for an extramarital affair.

Mr. F. was the younger of two sons in a middle-class family with strong Baptist fundamentalist values. Both sons were required to attend a Baptist college. He recalled his father as an emotionally distant and strict man who was not close to either of his children. The father would frequently work on hobbies he cultivated by himself, discouraging either of his sons from observing or becoming involved with his interests. The patient's brother was more involved with church activities than was Mr. F., which Mr. F. thought made his father more interested in the brother than in himself. Mr. F. thought that his lack of interest in the church represented his defiance of his father's wishes, making him a disappointment to his father and creating friction in the family. Mr. F.'s brother continued to be religious, whereas the patient increasingly drifted away from the church during his college years, contributing further to the antagonism between the brothers. Mr. F. regarded his brother as moralistic, and the brother thought of Mr. F. as irreverent.

Mr. F. came to believe during adolescence that trying to become close to his father was fruitless, and he thought that his father drew increasingly distant from him. Mr. F. attempted to provoke his father in various ways, believing that defying him was the only way to have a relationship with him. Although his provocations often took the form of acting obstructive and contrary, he worried much of the time that he had gone too far in being what he considered rebellious but what sounded to me like willfully and unyieldingly obstinate. His father increasingly favored the brother, adding to the widening schism between the patient and his brother. He felt anxious when he thought he crossed a line that provoked his father's anger and subsequent prolonged silent treatment.

Mr. F. often had felt guilty and anxious while growing up, much like he felt when he became attached to the woman who admired him. In both situations, he felt that he had gone too far and had trouble maintaining the customary affective control that characterized his relationships with people. To make peace and avoid further alienation, Mr. F. gave in to his family's pressure to marry a devout Baptist woman he had met at college. Mr. F. realized he did not love his wife, but his father and brother had favored her because they considered her a good influence on him. They hoped he would return to the Baptist faith, a hope my patient never accepted or complied with. Throughout the 11 years of their marriage before he entered treatment, she had remained fervently religious and had raised their two children according to strict fundamentalist principles.

Mr. F.'s mother was a Sunday school teacher, and he had no vivid memories of her other than her being caring and available. When Mr. F. spoke about his mother, he sounded more respectful than affectionate, noting her emphasis on being tough and intolerant of weak will. He recalled how he had bought a Christmas present for her one year from his allowance and discovered some weeks later that she gave his present to a friend of hers. Mr. F. remembered feeling disappointed that his mother thought so little of his gift, but he feared complaining to her because she would see him as weak. He also recalled that he preferred spending time after school at the homes of neighbors rather than at his own home and that he would turn to other children's mothers for comfort and companionship, particularly when he was troubled by something that had happened at school. Mr. F. appeared to derive a sense of being understood more from other mothers in the neighborhood than from his own mother's matter-of-fact but unenthusiastic attentiveness to him.

His respectful depiction of his mother's remotely attuned responsiveness was echoed in his description of his marital life. Mr. F. acknowledged his wife's devotion and loyalty to their children, and although he did not seem to feel that she ignored him, her main interests were family life and religion. Feeling out of touch with his wife, he grew increasingly bored and uninterested. He also observed that he did not enjoy playing with his children and felt stilted around them. He seemed uncomfortable entering into their worlds, and it sounded as though his children acted stiff and distant around Mr. F. as well.

Mr. F.'s obsessive–compulsive personality and his vulnerable self-esteem dominated his tightly constricted affect life. Constriction became his way of containing anger at being ignored and dampening indulgent needs that he believed must be submerged. The experience of overt rebellion or joyful invigoration threatened his rigid, compliant adaptation. Consequently, upsurges of anxious guilt represented the potential fragmentation of a degree of self-cohesion Mr. F. had managed to sustain, albeit at the cost of an affectively diminished, depleted experience of the self. The effort required to avert compromised self-cohesion left him distanced from his needs to be responded to and to feel valued. Acting on his fantasy of an affair brought Mr. F. an outpouring of admiration that left him both guilty and stimulated. Feeling pushed aside in his home life and at the office, Mr. F. experienced the reawakened mirroring as too difficult to comfortably internalize.

Although he expressed guilt about the affair, I wondered about an alternative explanation for his distress. Indulging the gratification of disavowed needs for mirroring responsiveness that the affair brought him was probably too overstimulating to absorb, given this man's predominant adaptation to an affectively diminished existence. For Mr. F., affective flattening indicated a depleted self buried beneath the characterologically ingrained obsessive–compulsive structure he had developed. His narrow, affectively drained, joyless life—devoted to slavish attention to rules and minute details that no one around him cared about—represented the obsessive–compulsive character or personality that Shapiro (1965) so evocatively described. Consequently, the affect he experienced as an upsurge of anxious guilt may have resulted not so much from tasting the forbidden fruit as from feeling the danger of an overstimulated self on the verge of being flooded (Wolf, 1988). The tightly defended though uninvigorated degree of self-cohesion he had managed to secure threatened to come apart, producing the disintegration anxiety (Kohut, 1971) that presaged the fragmentation of a vulnerable self. Mr. F. was ill prepared to cope with the unfamiliar affects, normally submerged, that were now omnipresent and immobilizing.

Coming from a household characterized by emotional distance and stoic downplaying of affects, Mr. F. minimized mirroring longings by turning away from normal, expectable desires. He submerged affect states by disregarding them and sticking out hard times with a stiff upper lip. Compulsively and dutifully working hard became his way of getting on in the world. Although his mother was generally responsive to her children's needs, she rebuffed normal needs for mirroring that she probably considered too indulgent. Reconstructing Mr. F.'s memory of his mother's giving away his prized gift to her and his preference for the comfort of other neighborhood mothers evoked other recollections of ways his mother unwittingly undermined his self-esteem. The possibility of turning to his father to bolster self-cohesion through idealization was rebuffed; his father kept Mr. F. at a distance rather than making himself available. Mr. F. turned away in retaliative anger by rejecting the one potential route to becoming closer to his father—the Baptist faith. Thus, with his mirroring longings unrecognized by his mother and his idealization needs ignored by his father, Mr. F. looked to other mothers in the neighborhood for comfort when he felt vulnerable or injured.

Turning away from his father's insistent demands and his mother's hard-boiled pragmatism was Mr. F.'s reaction to the injury of both parents' selfobject failures to recognize what he needed from them. His quiet disappointment in this absence of attuned responsiveness became evident when he acted rebellious and obstructive but did not know why. His yearnings to be recognized and admired were driven underground, submerged behind either a respectful distance or a stubborn rejection of his parents' unyielding insistence that he accept Baptist values more completely. By becoming affectively constricted, he also became, in his own way, as rigid and emotionally unattuned as his parents.

By marrying a devout Baptist, Mr. F. rejected the option of alienating himself totally from his parents' wishes. However, he seemed to relive in his psychologically empty marriage the unresponsive attunement he had experienced in his relationship with both parents. He turned away from his sons, just as his own father had rebuffed Mr. F. as a small boy.

His attempts in his work to feel accomplished were met with the same lack of enthusiasm Mr. F.'s parents showed him. His boss's humiliating rebuff of a work proposal was the specific impetus for acting on what at first were vague thoughts about an affair. His emotional involvement in the affair offered the promise of an energetic responsiveness to a self that felt deadened—most recently by his boss's rebuff, but more generally by his wife's declining interest in him in favor of family duty and religion. Mr. F. also re-created in the affair his turning away from his mother toward other neighborhood mothers when he needed to revitalize a depleted self.

Responding with lively anticipation when his girlfriend wanted to resume their relationship, Mr. F. was understandably overstimulated by and unable to turn away from the possibility of finding himself desired and adored by someone. Feeling looked up to contrasted sharply with the image of the duty-bound provider he felt he had acquired at home, where even his children did what they could to avoid spending time with him. In contrast to his devalued status with his disengaged father and his unattuned mother's attention more to duty and values than to her son's self states, Mr. F. was now the apple of someone's eye. He felt himself to be appreciated and noticed; he was the proud, emotionally alive man he wanted to be. However, although he felt enlivened, his affect life, normally safely constricted, now frightened and overwhelmed him, because he had little basis for understanding what he was suddenly feeling. Throwing caution to the wind by trying to shed his obsessive–compulsive personality structure exposed Mr. F. to a degree of fragmentation he needed treatment to recover from. I also gained an understanding of his need to fortify himself against reexperiencing fragmentation, even if it meant stepping back from relaxing his obsessive–compulsive style, at whatever personal cost this might entail.

Mr. F. began psychotherapy with the same stiff, mechanically formal demeanor I imagined his office staff disliked about him. His shaking hands at the beginning and the end of sessions and tendency to talk about minor details left me with the impression that he approached each treatment session as if it were a business meeting. An important breakthrough occurred after I began noticing how regularly Mr. F. commented—in a veiled way, interspersed among trivial details—that some things can be expected to change only so much. I began to wonder whether this expectation (or organizing principle, as intersubjectivist theorists would describe it) signaled how much he had to deaden his hopes for being responded to with interest. Examining this dynamic in treatment opened a door to meaningful improvement.

Although his relationship with the other woman did not survive, he became somewhat more aware of his needs for affection and admiration. Mr. F. slowly began to express to his wife a side of himself she thought did not exist, and thus the foundation for a different relationship began to come into view. His 9-year-old son became more comfortable spending time with him, tentatively seeking out his father rather than trying to avoid him. Mr. F. was becoming, in his way, a bit more emotionally aware of people around him as he came to understand his submerged inner needs more clearly. Other people began to notice a little something different about him, although it seemed they did not quite know how to describe what was different. (No one beside his wife knew that he was in treatment.) Although Mr. F. never lost his compulsively technical approach to work, he slowly began to take more notice of the interpersonal dynamics of the office environment. He did not become especially skillful at managing his staff with ease, but he was at least more aware of what was going on with the people around him rather than burying obviously interpersonal problems in work tasks.

BORDERLINE PERSONALITY DISORDER

Kohut (1971, 1972, 1977, 1996) did not devote much attention to borderline personality disorder, generally discussing it together with the psychoses. However, he did not regard borderline pathology as a psychosis, despite his belief that a psychotic core was discernible when time-limited regressions occurred. Kohut considered borderline pathology to be a severe disturbance of the primary structures of the self and to represent a developmentally archaic form of psychopathology that Wolf (1994) would later characterize as "pre-emergent." Kohut regarded borderline personality disorder as a deficit state preceding the formation of a stable structure or rudimentary form of the self. Kohut also considered borderline pathology to be covered over by schizoid or paranoid defenses, among its other prominent clinical features, although he did not emphasize distinctions among borderline, schizoid, and paranoid disorders. He thought the borderline personality was best understood as a breakup of the nuclear self, oscillating between regressive fragmentation and a reconstituted narcissistic structure that was vulnerable and sometimes delusional. In contrast, he considered the narcissistic personality and behavior disorders to show only fleeting fragmentations representing momentarily enfeebled self states in a more cohesively stable personality structure. He believed that the narcissistic disorders rarely involved the degree or persistence of destabilization characteristic of borderline and psychotic disorders.

Kohut (1968, 1971) considered a trial period of treatment to assess the transferences that emerged to be a more crucial test for establishing the diagnosis than the presenting picture and clinical history. For diagnostic purposes, he also emphasized the importance of assessing a patient's capacity to contain reactions such as rage or regressive behavior when disappointed by a clinician's inevitably flawed early efforts at understanding (Goldberg, 1978; Kohut, 1971). Kohut regarded narcissistic rage to be particularly prominent in borderline personality disorders, although he noted that it occurs in nearly all self disorders. Because such rage reactions and the degree of regression their anger precipitates may undermine treatment, it becomes important to determine whether rage destabilizes self–selfobject ties and therefore leads to fragmentation of the basic constituents of the self. Kohut was not generally optimistic about the efficacy of intensive treatment of borderline disorders for this reason; he also cited the self-protective distancing from selfobjects that becomes evident when schizoid or paranoid features are also observed.

Kohut (1984) and P. Tolpin (1980, 1983) argued that borderline patients who had better histories of empathically responsive selfobject relationships were amenable to psychotherapeutic treatment, although typically not to psychoanalysis. Kohut thought that compensatory structures might be strengthened with treatment. He acknowledged, however, that his experience was confined principally to the treatment of patients with transient fragmentations. Kohut was more pessimistic about patients' prognosis when there was an appreciable threat of a breakup of self-cohesion such as that seen in borderline personality disorder. This distinction in prognosis, based on propensity for fragmentation, was one consideration in the self psychological approach to the differential diagnosis between borderline and narcissistic disorders.

Kohut (1996) postulated no specific pathway to borderline pathology other than a developmentally early deficit state and the consequences of such early impairments for destabilizing self-cohesion. He did not subscribe to Kernberg's (1975) position concerning aggression as a primary mechanism in borderline patients. He also did not accept the view that a primary aggressive drive underlies self disorders, including narcissistic personality disorder. Kohut regarded Klein's (1935) and Kernberg's (1975) emphasis on aggression to be overstated. Thus, he rejected Klein's "essential attitude . . . that the baby is evil and only gradually learns to be good" and that "the baby is a powder keg of envy, rage, and destructiveness," adding, "It's clear that this is not my attitude" (Kohut, 1996, p. 104). Instead, Kohut considered aggression to be a reaction to legitimate but unresponded-to strivings for selfobject functions, and he regarded narcissistic rage to emerge primarily when selfobjects were unavailable, disappointing, or frustrating. According to a self psychological viewpoint, the ubiquitous nature of aggression did not represent its primary importance in mental life. Aggression may trigger the ever-present danger of fragmentation of self-cohesion in borderline patients, but it was not usually so destabilizing for patients who presented with a better integrated personality structure.

Brandchaft and Stolorow (1988) emphasized an intersubjective view of borderline personality disorder in which the psychopathology was not conceptualized entirely as an internal deficit state. According to this position, the internal state of the self as precarious exists alongside a selfobject environment that is itself flawed. Brandchaft and Stolorow observed that the disorder is influenced jointly by patients' internal deficits and the failures of selfobjects to comprehend what such patients are experiencing. The selfobject environment or intersubjective surround thus fails to provide the kind of empathic response borderline patients need to assuage their distress. This failure can influence the intersubjective context of treatment as well. Taking care to point out that selfobject failures in treatment should not be regarded entirely as adverse iatrogenic influences, Brandchaft and Stolorow noted how difficult it can be for clinicians to understand such patients' compromised integration, given their propensity for brittleness and fragmentation. Thus, clinicians' confusion in treatment re-creates the selfobject failures of patients' childhood experiences, resulting in an intersubjective context that evokes their familiar disturbed self-regulatory functions, eroticization, narcissistic rage, and primitive defenses, all of which may compromise psychoanalytic treatment. Brandchaft and Stolorow suggested that treatment must emphasize interpreting such intersubjective distortions in addition to their representing repetitions of chronic selfobject empathic failures.

Like Kohut (1996), Brandchaft and Stolorow (1988) disagreed with the view that excessive primitive aggression resulting from dependency was at the root of borderline and narcissistic disorders. Brandchaft and Stolorow regarded patients' rage as an inevitable consequence of a therapeutic approach emphasizing interpretation of aggression such as that which Kernberg (1975) advocated repeatedly in his writings. They thought that patients with borderline personality disorder experienced such interpretations of their aggression as retraumatizing and thus injurious. Furthermore, they considered an emphasis on interpreting aggression to represent another kind of empathic failure, because it interferes with the revival of such patients' derailed developmental longings. Thus, a therapist's misconstrual of rage may iatrogenically perpetuate the patient's aggression as an understandable reaction to selfobjects who unempathically repeat earlier selfobject injuries in development rather than helping them understand their affects.

Kohut (1996) thought that the kinds of analytic patients he treated showed higher levels of ego resilience and self-cohesion than the disturbed patients M. Klein (1935), Kernberg (1975), and many other contemporary clinicians often saw in treatment. This may be one reason why Kohut's formulations were not prominently influenced by aggression. Indeed, Adler (1989) faulted Kohut's limited familiarity with borderline personality disorder compared with clinicians with extensive experience treating this condition, although he acknowledged Kohut's contributions to the concepts of selfobject transference and self-cohesion deficit in understanding borderline personality disorder. Adler particularly criticized what he considered to be Kohut's incomplete description of the internal world of borderline patients and self psychology's deemphasis of classical conflict theory, which Adler believed contributed to an insufficient account of the central importance of aggression and superego guilt. Adler further emphasized the importance of an impaired capacity for evoking images of good objects at moments of acute distress, an observation Giovacchini (1979) also noted.

Other views about the self have also been proposed in the psychoanalytic literature since borderline pathology began to prominently influence psychoanalytic thinking. For example, McGlashan (1983) proposed a concept that he termed the *we-self*, emphasizing borderline patients' fusion of self and object in an attempt to compensate for experiences of incompleteness. In his view, influenced in part by Meissner (1978), this fused amalgam would have adaptive value because it reconstructs for such patients a semblance of a sense of self when there has been a developmental failure to achieve self and object differentiation. Furthermore, the we-self permits some degree of self-organization to help manage the marked identity diffusion that most observers of borderline personality disorder have noted (Deutsch, 1942; Grinker, Werble, & Drye, 1968; Kernberg, 1975). Westen and Cohen (1993) criticized concepts of the self in relation to borderline personality disorder, however, particularly for their lack of theoretical clarity and unsubstantiated developmental propositions. Although some of these criticisms rightly faulted Kohut's (1971, 1984) reluctance to specify a sufficiently clear definition of the self, Westen and Cohen were critical of most psychoanalytic views about self pathology, including those of Kernberg (1975) and Masterson (1988).

Clinical Illustration of Borderline Personality Disorder

Ms. G., a 29-year-old single White woman, was admitted to the medical service of a general hospital complaining of persistent pain and complications from torn adhesions following a gastrectomy performed 1 year previously; she had been admitted 2 months earlier for the surgical repair of a hip fracture. This was her seventh medical admission during the previous 18 months, all at different hospitals and under the care of different attending physicians. This patient had a 4-year history of abuse of analgesics and narcotic compounds, which she initially used to manage pain but later increasingly relied on "in order to reach a point of not being there at all. I'd be apathetic and withdraw, but inside I'd hurt so bad." She had not worked since she had become ill almost 2 years previously, and she stayed at home alone most of the time, relatively isolated and abusing pain medications. Her substance abuse very likely accounted for the motor instability and falls that precipitated her recent hip fracture. She also experienced periodic derealization, but it was unclear whether these symptoms represented transient psychotic-like states or substance-induced mental states. Because Ms. G. was coherent and generally compliant, she initially managed to conceal from doctors and nurses the full extent of her substance abuse and the psychiatric overlay contributing to her medical illnesses. Once medical personnel began to suspect these problems (e.g., when it became evident that she was stockpiling pain medications), Ms. G. would withdraw from treatment or sign herself out of the hospital against medical advice.

Ms. G. lived with her mother, with whom she spent little time because her mother was too tired after returning from work to do much more than sleep or take care of minor chores. Ms. G. felt too weak to cook for herself, and her mother was too tired after work to cook for either of them, so Ms. G.'s nutrition was poor, and she looked undernourished. Her dental hygiene was also poor; she admitted, with considerable embarrassment, that she wore a denture.

During Ms. G.'s present hospitalization, her mother never visited or expressed interest in the unit staff's invitation to provide a history or attend meetings concerning Ms. G.'s treatment or discharge planning. Although Ms. G.'s mother complied with a request for an interview by telephone, it appeared that she felt that Ms. G.'s life was separate from her own and that she was tired of her daughter's substance abuse, lying, and what the mother regarded as attention-getting behavior and failure to progress in life. Ms. G.'s mother felt that she had done enough and that she could no longer continue coming to her daughter's rescue.

Ms. G. had first begun abusing drugs 8 years before seeking treatment during a time when she was active in political protests, an interest stimulated primarily by a boyfriend. Her 2-year relationship with this man, who was 20 years her senior, was based less on affection for him than on her admiration of his self-confidence and her dependence on his telling her what she should do and how she should think. Although she felt secure in depending on her boyfriend for direction, which she felt unable to provide for herself, Ms. G. also became angry at his overpowering control and his making her feel that she was wrong about everything. Her drug use accelerated as she became angrier and more disillusioned with this man; however, she remained dependent on what he did for her. She increasingly withdrew from him as her substance use kept her "functionally sedated." The boyfriend lost interest in her as she became unavailable, although they stayed in occasional contact by telephone. She had contacted him for advice during her recent illnesses and had asked him to tell her what he thought she should do.

Ms. G. had had a previous relationship with a physician at a hospital where she had once worked. The relationship with that man, who was also 25 years her senior, came to an abrupt end when she underwent a laparotomy for a tubal pregnancy. She saw him as weak, and she became angry at him for impregnating her. She was also disillusioned with him and discontinued the relationship because she felt ignored and unsustained by him.

Ms. G. had worked as a nurse's aide briefly and, most recently, as a library clerk for 5 years. As her drug use increased, she felt humiliated by her own uncontrollably odd behavior and left the library job. She then pursued a series of jobs that, according to her, she held briefly and soon quit. She also said that she had not worked for 2 years because of her illnesses and hospitalizations. Her mother, however, reported that Ms. G. had often been fired from her jobs, including her job at the public library, because she had failed to produce what was expected of her. Ms. G.'s mother also reported that Ms. G. had in fact not worked for 3 years and had stayed at home reading and watching television.

As an adolescent and young adult, Ms. G. had experienced pervasive anxiety, frequently anticipating that people would scream at her. This fear seemed to contribute to her interpersonal isolation and abuse of analgesics. She would often drive people away with her sarcasm, particularly potentially helpful people such as hospital staff. She described one counselor as "so kind, I liked him very much, and he helped me. I wanted him to put his arms around me and hold me, but because he couldn't, I cut him up and put him down." She had occasionally engaged in self-mutilation by cutting herself, beginning in high school and persisting until her analgesic abuse began.

Her mother worked as a bookkeeper at the YMCA, although she had a college degree in a prelaw curriculum. She had separated from her husband when Ms. G. was 8 years old, had never remarried, and did not socialize or leave her apartment unless she had to for errands. Ms. G. saw her mother as frustrated and unhappy and as having an angry temper. Nevertheless, she felt close to her mother, despite the many petty arguments they had. Ms. G. wanted to break away from her mother but feared any separation. Her father, a construction worker (who had also completed college and had once held a management position), had a history of alcohol abuse and mental illness with multiple psychiatric hospitalizations. Ms. G. saw her father occasionally after her mother told him to leave, but she had had no knowledge of his whereabouts for at least 10 years. Unlike her chronically angry, discontented mother, who cared for but was relatively uninvolved with Ms. G. and her older sister, Ms. G. remembered her father as fun to be around and as having taken the girls on outings. Ms. G. felt that her father had favored her over her sister, who appeared to have "a violent temper." The siblings fought frequently, and they never became close as adults. Ms. G. observed that her sister could "utterly annihilate me verbally" because the sister felt Ms. G. received more love from both parents. Ms. G. thought that her mother resented the sister as the "runt of the litter" because of the sister's juvenile diabetes and the care the sister required. Ms. G. felt that her mother was too angry to be closely involved with either one of them.

Ms. G. reported sucking her thumb until age 13, being agoraphobic, and being afraid during overnight Girl Scout outings that she would never get home again. As a prepubescent child, she had had friends with whom she played and had activities in common. During adolescence, however, Ms. G. began to dress unconventionally to draw attention to herself, which seemed to isolate her from school friends. Although she had previously received good grades and enjoyed school, Ms. G. felt indifferent about her academic performance during high school. She said that she knew more than she bothered to display in homework and examinations. Ms. G. disliked high school because it meant growing up; she preferred to be back in grammar school. She cut classes toward the end of school and eventually dropped out, but she received an equivalency diploma a few years later.

Ms. G.'s earliest memories were of her mother telling her she could not use diapers any longer because the family could not afford them and of her father giving her a nursing bottle. She reported a dream from childhood in which her house was flooded and was floating down the block, with her parents crying and panicking. She had daydreams about relocating her father, in which she would see him working and not drinking any longer, but she still expected to be disappointed by him. Fantasy material such as this, coupled with Ms. G.'s childhood and early adolescence behavior patterns, indicated the extent of Ms. G.'s regressive potential.

The symptomatic presentation and dynamics of borderline personality disorder appeared clear in this patient's presentation. Unstable interpersonal relationships alternating between rage and isolation characterized nearly all her friendships and intimate love interests. Ms. G. displayed chronic difficulty in establishing a stable pattern of functioning at work or school, despite normal or above average intelligence. A haphazard pattern of finding jobs on impulse was typical for her, but she was frequently dismissed because of her odd and distancing interpersonal style and irresponsible work behavior. She took on characteristics of the personalities of people with whom she became close but at the cost of submerging her own poorly articulated sense of who she was or what she wanted. Her history also included an uninvolved and chronically depressed mother; an unstable, alcoholic father; and a sibling who, like the patient, also showed considerable psychological maladaptation. Her more benevolent and psychologically engaging father served as a partial buffer; however, he was himself seriously handicapped by several psychiatric hospitalizations, chronic alcoholism, and marginal to poor vocational adjustment. Moreover, the father was not part of her life for most of her childhood.

Somewhat atypical but not inconsistent with borderline personality disorder dynamics were the type and extent of medical illness in this young woman. This case illustrates how Axis II psychopathology probably aggravated the progressive deterioration of a gastrointestinal illness, exacerbated by failure to seek and noncompliance with medical treatment, poor nutrition and self-care, and accelerating drug use. Moreover, although substance abuse is indeed common in patients with borderline personality disorder, undoubtedly her abuse of analgesic compounds—to subdue physical and mental distress—substantially contributed to her protracted recovery. Her fragile postsurgical course, already compromised by isolation and her mother's apparently limited support, created further medical problems, such as weakness and motor unsteadiness, leading to a hip fracture, which in turn compromised adequate nutrition, mobility, and self-care (including poor dental hygiene).

Ms. G. could not secure mirroring selfobject functions in any area of her life around which a vitalized or proud self might coalesce. A precariously balanced existence left her alternating between becoming involved with others and insulating herself from people who neglected, disappointed, or injured her. She experienced her mother as too embittered or detached to provide sensitive maternal care. Her perception of being "favored" must be considered in the context of either moderate neglect or of encouragement of premature self-reliance, given her mother's anger, chronic depression, and resentment about the burden of caring for Ms. G.'s diabetic sister. The mother seemed to turn her back on Ms. G., feeling too depleted and resentful to become psychologically involved with either Ms. G. or her sister. The mother apparently withdrew from her daughters' needs, leaving them when she could in the hands of their undependable father to entertain while he was there. However, the father could manage only erratic, intermittent support; whatever quality of psychological responsiveness he provided was curtailed after the mother ended the marriage. At that point, Ms. G.'s mother, with barely anything to sustain her own devitalized self, understandably retreated into herself. Sullen and withdrawn, Ms. G.'s mother seemed to psychologically abandon her combative daughters to their own devices. Ms. G. attempted to anesthetize herself from destabilizing affect states she could not otherwise manage, including the intense anger that threatened the fragmentation of her brittle self-cohesion. Because she could not afford to give up whatever selfobject responsiveness she could manage to secure, this patient held onto people who rebuffed her, trying to ignore how disillusioning or neglectful these relationships were in providing the selfobject functions she needed.

Ms. G. had thus spent the past several years preoccupied with illness, uncared for by her mother, befuddled by substance abuse, and too unable or indifferent to care for herself. She lacked friends to help her; she may have been shunned by companions or schoolmates during adolescence and early adulthood who found her too odd or nonconforming to befriend, and she also isolated herself from potentially helpful persons, becoming rageful when she felt overstimulated by the intensity of her needs. Her only friend was a man whom she really needed to take over her life; he provided some comfort when, feeling desperate, she would reluctantly contact him for advice, but he never called or visited her.

Despite her compromised judgment in seeking viable selfobject choices and confusion about being used versus feeling valued, Ms. G. managed to establish some relationships that offered promise for securing selfobject firming through idealization. However, the selfobjects she turned to were not stable or enduring enough to shore up the self. None came close to solidifying a compensatory structure to make up for the mirroring selfobject responsiveness she could not elicit from her depleted, withdrawn mother. Her mother could not tune in enough to recognize the patient's need for selfobject functions; probably preoccupied with her own psychological survival, Ms. G.'s mother dismissively criticized Ms. G.'s flawed attempts to preserve self-cohesion. Ms. G. became disillusioned with men, who seemed unable to provide the invigorating strength she sought to keep herself intact, and withdrew more and more into isolation and extended periods of substance use to numb the affective dysregulation of a fragmenting self. Her selfobject environment was incapable of providing the glue she required to repair the fragmented self.

Ms. G. sought out sympathetic or interested physicians and hospital staff, pastoral counselors, and therapeutic staff whom she thought of as strong or available. However, although she turned to such people with eager responsiveness, she would quickly become bitter or petulant when she sensed that they could not provide what she most needed. She would then typically frustrate their efforts to help her through her indifference to helping herself, just as she became indifferent as a child to her mother's neglect and her father's inconstant presence. Ms. G. managed to engender angry frustration in the therapeutic staff, reflecting her own sense of futility. Thus, Ms. G. repeatedly engaged in projective identification, devaluation, and splitting as she quickly turned all-good objects into all-bad objects. Such defenses may also reflect what happens after initial steps to secure selfobject responsiveness falter or when attempts to acquire compensatory structures fail to take hold: Narcissistic rage emerges as a breakdown product of a self unable to preserve its cohesion or to forestall unraveling or fragmenting. Thus, the self is not weakened and brittle because of rage, but rather diminished self-cohesion results in rage as a byproduct of a self that is fragile and vulnerable to fragmentation.

Feeling ambivalent and uncertain about her ability to comply with an outpatient treatment plan, Ms. G. became lost to follow-up attempts, which contributed to an unfavorable prognosis. Her mother was consistently unwilling or unable to intervene to secure continuing treatment for Ms. G. When I contacted Ms. G.'s mother by telephone 3 years after she terminated treatment to obtain follow-up information for a clinical presentation of this case, I found that Ms. G. had died at home at the age of 32 from complications secondary to an overdose of analgesics. She had thus continued the same course of isolation, neglectful self-care, and drug abuse.

CONCLUSION

In this chapter, I have considered paranoid, obsessive–compulsive, and borderline personality disorders as fragmentation-prone disturbances. These disorders show varying degrees of destabilized affect states and behavior organized around forestalling dissolution of self-cohesion. Fragmentation, a sense of crumbling or falling apart internally, may occur during brief periods of momentary disruptions, but it also may be prolonged or nearly constant. Hyperalertness to potential danger predominates in patients with paranoid personality disorder, who are on constant guard against the threat of injuries to the self. Borderline patients characteristically live with chronic instability punctuated by frequent, brief periods of fragmentation representing their failed adaptation as they anticipate threats to self-cohesion. Patients with obsessive–compulsive personality disorder may use a tightly inhibited, inflexible solution to hold on to a brittle sense of self-cohesion.

IV

ALTERNATIVE PATHWAYS FOR PRESERVING A COHESIVE SELF (DEPENDENT, HISTRIONIC, AND ANTISOCIAL PERSONALITY DISORDERS)

7

DESCRIPTIVE PSYCHOPATHOLOGY AND THEORETICAL VIEWPOINTS: DEPENDENT, HISTRIONIC, AND ANTISOCIAL PERSONALITY DISORDERS

In this chapter, I survey selected viewpoints on dependent, histrionic, and antisocial personality disorders, emphasizing how they are conceptualized from the clinical psychiatric, psychoanalytic, and contemporary personality disorder research perspectives. The current chapter serves as a preparation for my reformulation of these disorders in the next chapter as disorders of self-cohesion that potentially may be repaired by establishing an alternative pathway when selfobject failure in one sector of the self, usually mirroring, is closed off. Though the self remains injured and consequently weakened, it may not be permanently damaged. To achieve a restoration of self-cohesion, patients must form a compensatory structure (Kohut, 1977; M. Tolpin, 1997) through dependable idealizing or twinship selfobjects.

DEPENDENT PERSONALITY DISORDER

The most distinctive feature of patients with dependent personality disorder is their prominent externally oriented focus concerning need gratification. Such patients direct their thoughts and actions toward pleasing those persons on whom they rely for support. They are inclined to lean on others to run their lives, seeking out people who tell them what to do or how to think. Falling short of complete submissiveness, their extreme dependency leads them to act as if they had no autonomy or capacity to know how to conduct their lives without relying on other people whose direction they so intently need.

Such patients appear disinclined—or even unable—to draw on resources of their own to manage in life. This degree of dependence makes such patients vulnerable to feeling abandoned or to living in the shadow of feared abandonment by others, famously epitomized in Tennessee Williams's *A Streetcar Named Desire* (1947/2004) by Blanche Dubois's unraveling when her characteristic reliance on "the kindness of strangers" falters.[1] Dependent personality disorder patients become unduly subservient to those they rely on for sustenance. They are willing to do what they must to keep those they rely on in their corner. They generally do not risk initiating independent actions or thoughts, and they typically subordinate their own wishes to the people whose influence they need. One further consequence of such patients' nearly total subjugation of wishes and initiative is their proneness to be self-depreciating.

Dependency has been defined in most versions of the *Diagnostic and Statistical Manual of Mental Disorders* (*DSM*; American Psychiatric Association, 1980, 1987, 1994) as excessive passivity or submissiveness. Dependent personality disorder patients subjugate their needs to others who have become the objects of their dependency. Dependency often gives rise to anxiously clinging attachments based on perceived helplessness and consequent indecisiveness about making decisions. Such patients forgo responsibility for their own lives because they rely totally on others to make choices for them. They fear disagreement with those persons on whom they depend out of concern that they may alienate them. Such patients often have diminished confidence in their own abilities, which also limits independent initiatives, though this feature is not essential for establishing the diagnosis. Fear of being on their own, although usually present, is related more to an excessive need for support than to a fear of loneliness. Such patients are greatly fearful of abandonment by needed figures. When objects of these patients' dependency become unavailable, seeking replacement figures becomes an urgent concern. Such patients show associated characteristics of an overly trusting nature and hypersensitivity to criticism or slights, sometimes appearing touchy or

---

[1]The character of Blanche and her fragmentation may also be regarded as an illustration of other Axis II disorders—for example, borderline or narcissistic personality disorders—as well as being superimposed on Axis I psychopathology—for example, alcoholism or an impulse disorder. Alternatively, such symptoms or personality disorder patterns may be secondarily reactive to a more primary disturbance highlighted by pronounced dependency, particularly when the person's dependency fails to successfully contain destabilization. Thus, in literature as in life, comorbidity between dependent personality and other disorders may be discerned.

irritable (Bornstein, 1993; Lazare, Klerman, & Armor, 1970). Dependent patients' wariness about rejection or loss of support may incline them to be self-pitying.

Dependent personality disorder occurs infrequently in the absence of other Axis II diagnoses. Although dependent personality disorder overlaps most often with borderline and avoidant personality disorders, different clinical presentations typically represent varying emphases of underlying traits in such patients' lives. Thus, similar conflicts may be expressed outwardly in different ways. For example, patients with dependent and borderline personality disorders may be expected to show conflict surrounding abandonment, but the clinical manifestations likely take different forms: Borderline patients show a propensity to anger that is acted out as manipulative behavior, whereas dependent patients are more inclined to exacerbate clinging and submissive behaviors. Likewise, avoidant patients shy away from situations likely to provoke loss, whereas dependent patients react by increasing attachment and clinging behavior patterns (Hirschfeld, Shea, & Weise, 1995).

Although Kraepelin (1921) described disturbances of will, lability, and sensitivity to rejection as precursors of pathological dependency, psychoanalytic theorists such as Abraham (1924) and Fenichel (1945) emphasized the oral phase of libidinal development as the basis for dependency. The classical psychoanalytic formulation stressed overgratified maternal nurturance during infancy as an important etiologic factor, leading to preoccupation with feeding and the passive nature of being cared for. Dependency may be manifested in various ways, such as excessive clinging in an effort to forestall separation or passive compliance to retain attachment to a source of oral gratification (Bornstein, 1993). It may also appear in a conflicted form in which aggressive manifestations predominate or as an entitled orientation to objects who are expected to gratify wishes on demand. Even with the diminished emphasis on libidinal drives after Freud (1923/1961a, 1926/1959b) introduced the structural theory, the psychodynamic formulation of dependency as oral stage longings remained no less important as an etiologic influence on dependency behavior. Object relations theorists also subscribed to the role of orality in dependency, expressed particularly in Fairbairn's (1944) view that oral incorporation was a basis for identification with objects in a move from infantile dependence to mature dependence.

Several more recent psychoanalytic views of dependency were derived from the concept of oral libidinal longings; however, most of these did not rely very much on drive theory as a basis for their formulations. For example, Schachtel (1959) considered dependency to represent an example of what he termed an *autocentric perspective*, in which the patient views others narcissistically as being useful for what he or she needs them for rather than for who they are in a fuller dimension. Schachtel (1966) also regarded dependency as underlying conflicts surrounding independence from authority figures. Shapiro (1981) considered problems of autonomy to be embedded in conflict that was sometimes associated with dependency. Psychoanalytic theorists of a social–interpersonal orientation such as Horney (1945) and Sullivan (1947) also stressed views of dependency that emphasized passive helplessness or weak, clinging patterns of relationships. However, these theorists were less inclined to stress the libidinal focus on orality or oral character of classical analysts. Moreover, social learning and cognitive–interpersonal theorists, influenced by but largely independent of psychoanalytic viewpoints, also called attention to characteristics of dependency behavior such as passivity, helplessness, and subservience, although understandably their etiologic explanations were different.

Psychoanalytic ego psychology emphasized ego functions and their development, a perspective that was not centered on the predominant influences of drives (Hartmann, Kris, & Loewenstein, 1946). For example, Mahler (1968), influenced by the ego psychological tradition, proposed a stage theory of development anchored to a view of a normal progression in infant development from autism to symbiosis and then to separation and individuation. Based on observations of young infants (Mahler, Pine, & Bergmann, 1975), Mahler and colleagues suggested that the symbiotic phase represents interdependence, which for infants is initially a primitive, fused boundary between what could be a rudimentary idea of an independent self as a separate object from a mother. Gradual awareness of their physical separation comes with subsequent maturation. Thus, Mahler stressed the interdependence of the mother–infant symbiotic unit as an influence fostering a growing capacity to comprehend reality. This stage leads to the ensuing ego development that includes memory traces of need gratification and higher levels of object relations.

Mahler (1968) regarded failures of the symbiotic union to promote individuation as an explanation for childhood psychosis. Under optimal circumstances, a normal developmental progression unfolds toward separation and individuation, fostering young children's gradual awareness of their psychological separateness. Overindulging gratification by mothers too unable or unwilling to tolerate separation can thwart a normal progression of the developmental process toward separation and individuation, consequently fostering children's prolonged dependency. Precocious sensorimotor development or maturation might also promote a physical separation that arrives too prematurely for some mothers to tolerate. Mothers so disposed might attempt to inhibit a child's "hatching" (Mahler, 1968, p. 18), an incursion that Mahler considered particularly responsible for interfering with separation and individuation during the "practicing" subphase she identified. Alternatively, mothers who welcome the independence their children's curiosity and maturation affords them may remove themselves too prematurely from their children's psychological orbit before the children are sufficiently prepared to leave behind the safety of the mother's presence. Maternal distancing actions, if they occur during the "rapprochement" subphase, might threaten their children's security if the children have not yet confidently negotiated a transition from symbiosis through the various trial subphases of separation and individuation.

Clearly, there is a range of tolerance for the kinds of incursions that may be too much or too little and too early or too late. Mahler (1968) called attention to the importance of the timing of mothers' and their children's individual and joint readiness for progressing through the various sequences leading to the achievement of secure individuation, which Mahler considered the hallmark of development. One of the consequences of a failure in timing is a disturbance of the child's ability to manage dependency in relationships. However, Mahler did not regard dependency to be associated with specific disturbances.

Winnicott (1965) suggested that development progresses by degrees of independence; he thus identified "absolute" and "relative" dependence phases. Like Mahler (1968), Winnicott regarded the successful attainment of independence as crucial for forming an internal psychological structure. In Winnicott's view, a period of absolute dependence occurs outside infants' awareness, because self and other are not yet differentiated. Because of his emphasis on infant experience as closely linked with maternal experience, Winnicott stressed mothers' capacities to provide what he called the "holding environment" in this phase of absolute dependence. The holding environment functions to buffer moment-to-moment experiences of annihilation infants may be vulnerable to as a consequence of their total dependency and the impingements of external reality on this form of existence. This absolute dependency phase is followed by a phase of relative dependence, during which infants gradually differentiate themselves from objects and people outside themselves. In this phase, infants' awareness of their separation leads to an emergence of illusory thinking they manifest by the use of transitional objects. Transitional phenomena help infants manage the anxiety engendered by their sense of loss during temporary separations from those on whom they depend to meet their needs. Representations of maternal or need-gratifying objects are built up from the experiences of transitory separation followed by the reemergence of familiar, reassuring maternal functions.

Attachment theorists regard dependency in a different way, preferring to consider individuation and dependency needs as manifestations of established attachment patterns (Bretherton, 1987). Although Livesley, Schroeder, and Jackson (1990) regarded attachment as a prominent concern in dependent personality disorder, Hirschfeld, Klerman, and colleagues reported that interpersonal dependency comprised heightened reliance on others, deficient social self-confidence, and lack of autonomy (Hirschfeld et al., 1977; Hirschfeld, Klerman, Chodoff, Korchin, & Barrett, 1976). They considered heightened emotional reliance in particular to represent the intensity and fragility of attachments. Thus, coming from a different research and clinical tradition than Bowlby (1969, 1973) and contemporary attachment theory,

Hirschfeld, Klerman, Livesley, and their colleagues proposed a link between attachment and dependency. However, it is possible that the meanings of these concepts, though undoubtedly overlapping, may not be equivalent.

In certain respects, dependent personality disorder is one of the more difficult disorders to pin down and specify. To begin with, its chief clinical features—clinging and a pronounced need to be taken care of—lack a symptomatic counterpart that is identifiable in the way paranoid delusions, for example, represent a symptomatic exacerbation of the paranoid ideation that characterizes paranoid personality disorder. Second, although dependency is a feature that most clinicians can recognize, its associated features, such as diminished self-confidence, have not uniformly been noted to be part of a complex of features regularly associated with dependency. Moreover, it seems difficult to indicate a threshold level of dependency to denote when its presence is clinically prominent.

Millon (1969, 1996) called attention to a passive–dependent pattern in which patients accommodate to environmental requirements rather than acting on environmental demands as a preferred adaptational style. Passive accommodation is the predominant orientation in the passive–active polarity, and an orientation to others rather than self is the preferential adaptation in the self–other polarity. Consequently, seeking nurturance and protective support outweighs autonomous individuation as a motivational striving in dependent personality disorder. In the pleasure–pain polarity, enhancing pleasure and avoiding pain are approximately equivalent in valence, with neither dimension predominating. The self–other and passive–active polarities unfold in such a way that a dependent prototype materializes. This prototype is manifested in behavior by the accentuation of incompetence and helpless unassertiveness. Patients so disposed anxiously subordinate their own intentions in favor of compliance with the wishes or expectations of the people they depend on to ensure their well-being. They experience themselves and those around them in a simple-minded, uncritical manner, and their childlike and naive, unquestioning ways influence their attachment to supportive figures. Thus, patients with the prototypical dependent personality seek to establish near-total, inseparable bonds, disposing them to rely substantially on others.

Millon (1969, 1996) also differentiated five adult patterns of dependent personality disorder. Two of them emphasize qualities based on relative prominence of anxiously or compliantly submissive manifestations (the *disquieted* and *accommodating* subtypes, respectively). A third subtype is predominantly childlike (*immature*) in its clinical presentation, and two other subtypes show prominent anhedonia or anergia (the *ineffectual* subtype) and marked fusing or merging with the objects of their dependence (*selfless* subtype).

Millon (1996) considered several possible influences on the development of a predominantly dependent personality orientation. For example, anxious mothers might devote excessive attention to their offspring, leading to an overindulgent degree of concern. Young infants so exposed might thus be inclined to form a narrow range of attachment behaviors, possibly perpetuating a period of symbiotic dependency beyond a point when this might be expected to cease. Anxious mothers might perpetuate this protracted dependency because of their own needs for preserving close attachment and feelings of being threatened by their children's normal autonomy or independence.

Millon (1990) incorporated an evolutionary approach to understanding personality disorders. He characterized dependent personality disorder as representing a help-eliciting strategy for maximizing survival at a phylogenetic level as well as a behavior pattern for facilitating individual adaptation. Presumably, inherited dispositions and environmental events both influence overdeveloped help-seeking and clinging behaviors, on the one hand, and underdeveloped self-sufficiency behaviors, on the other. This configuration of overdeveloped and underdeveloped behavior patterns is manifested in the cognitive beliefs or schemas and affective–motivational systems forming the organization of attachment in dependent personality disorder.

Costa and Widiger's (1994) five-factor model denoted dependent personality as representing high levels of neuroticism and agreeableness and a low level of assertiveness. Cloninger's (1987) early characterization of passive–dependent personality emphasized low novelty seeking, high harm avoidance, and high reward dependence. He noted, however, that the resulting behavior pattern of deferential submissiveness overlaps with anxiety states in which introversion is also associated with prominent dependency and avoidant traits. Cloninger subsequently differentiated temperament and character dimensions as influences on personality development and its disturbances. In this modified formulation, Cloninger, Bayon, and Svrakic (1998) added low levels of self-directedness and self-transcendence and a high level of cooperativeness to the description of dependency. They also called attention to proneness to depression in dependent personality disorder.

Westen and Shedler's (1999a, 1999b) Q sort–derived classification scheme identified a dysphoric factor affecting the largest number of patients with Axis II disorders. This factor itself comprises five subfactors, one of which Westen and Shedler called *dysphoric: dependent–masochistic*, a factor comprising several features particularly characteristic of dependent personality disorder.

HISTRIONIC PERSONALITY DISORDER

Histrionic personality disorder, first known as *hysterical neurosis*, is a condition that came to light primarily through the pioneering efforts of Sigmund Freud and his early colleagues in psychoanalysis. Histrionic personality was the prototypical psychoneurosis in classical psychoanalysis. The fundamental concepts of psychoanalytic theory were formulated with histrionic (hysterical) patients in mind, including the first monograph in the field (Breuer & Freud, 1893–1895/1955). Freud's earliest reports of cases, such as those of Anna O. and Dora, presented important propositions such as conscious, preconscious, and unconscious experience; repression (and later, a broader concept of defense operations); and psychosexual stages as a model of development. Even the so-called "hydraulic model" evolved from Freud's thinking based on hysterical neurosis. However, this model—imported from the physical sciences and applied improperly (it now seems) to mental phenomena—was intended to explain hysterical symptoms as dammed-up energy representing drives (libido). Moreover, as a result of treating hysterical patients and the theoretical ideas this inspired, Freud formulated concepts such as resistance, transference, and analytic abstinence and neutrality. These became the foundation of the technical principles of psychoanalytic treatment.

Hysteria was not a newly discovered condition; it has been recognized in some fashion since antiquity. With Kraepelin (1923), however—contemporaneous with Freud—an understanding of hysteria took on a more clinically informed view. Kraepelin's influence established the descriptive characteristics of the disorder, drawing attention to such patients' excitability, lability of mood, and erotic or romantic preoccupations, among other features. The German phenomenological school of psychiatry elaborated on Kraepelin's description, emphasizing ingenuousness of perceived experience (Jaspers, 1948) and an exaggerated or self-aggrandizing manner to draw attention to themselves (Schneider, 1923/1950). Schneider also noted a hyperthymic temperament, which resembled Kraepelin's (1921) description but without the connotation now considered to reflect a disposition to bipolar mood dysregulation.

Freud's (Breuer & Freud, 1893–1895/1955) influence on the concept of hysteria represented a different tradition than those of Kraepelin and phenomenological psychiatry. Crediting Janet in part for influencing his view of unconscious processes and acknowledging Bernheim and Charcot for applying the hypnotic method to gain access to this sector of mental life (cited in Millon, 1996), Freud articulated a theory of hysterical neurosis as a compromise formation between drives and counterforces opposing their expression (Breuer & Freud, 1893–1895/1955). Freud commented on the prominent role of repressed erotic wishes and sometimes disturbed sexual functioning. W. Reich's (1933/1949) extension of the dramatic symptoms of hysterical illnesses (psychoneurosis) to incorporate a relatively asymptomatic hysterical character type was built on Abraham's (1921/1927c) and Freud's (1931/1961c) later thoughts about libidinal or psychosexual stages of development. W. Reich called attention to coquettish actions and appearance in hysterical patients and to their compliant suggestibility. He also noted such patients' sensitivity to disappointment accompanied by devaluation, an observation self psychology and object relations theory would much later consider to be important features of this and other disturbances.

Chodoff and Lyons (1958) extended W. Reich's (1933/1949) formulation of the hysterical character, particularly his observation of such patients' inclination to act provocatively in a seductive or pseudosexualized manner that escapes their awareness. Chodoff and Lyons noted that in their actual sexual behavior, patients with hysterical character are typically inhibited or even frigid or asexual. More to the point, the overt appearance of exhibitionistic or sexualizing behavior conceals a childlike dependency in which emotional outbreaks—often expressed as dramatic emotional lability or chaotic behavior—frequently conceal what is eventually revealed as their demand to be cared for. Their sexually provocative innuendos underlie an egocentric quality that calls attention to themselves. Further, their comprehension of their own affect states and motivations and those of others is notably shallow.

Shapiro (1965), an innovative theoretician from the psychoanalytic ego psychology tradition, is best known for his articulation of character styles, one of which was the hysterical character. He attempted to understand the ego and its functions, particularly how thinking, memory, and perception influenced personality. Thus, Shapiro's primary interest was the nuanced, stylistic description of disordered cognition–personality interactions in what was at the time called "neurotic character."

Shapiro (1965) emphasized various manifestations of repression in the hysterical personality style. He called attention to forgetting as the primary cognitive manifestation; hysterical individuals perceive reality in a diffuse, impressionistic way because they do not attend to, and therefore forget, details. This cognitive style creates a global, unarticulated grasp of events and people rather than a sharply defined one. Such patients are not inclined to concentrate carefully to reach decisions; rather, they are "hoping to be inspired" (Shapiro, 1965, p. 113) by a whim of the moment. Influenced by Rapaport (1951), who studied cognitive processes and personality, what Shapiro described was not an intuitive preference for cognitive processing, but rather an unresourceful but strongly ingrained style of thinking or problem solving. Because the richness of memories and of remembered experiences is transitory, a hysterical style is dominated more by immediate awareness than by measured and balanced reflection on experience. Shapiro believed that this form of thinking underlies histrionic patients' uncritical suggestibility, which takes the place of convictions or thoughtful understanding. Their judgment is therefore impressionistic, giving rise to labile and frequently undifferentiated affective expressions.

Kernberg (1996) suggested a clinical differentiation between a higher level form of hysterical personality that conforms to the ego psychological formulation of a phallic–oedipal level of personality organization and a more primitive form he described as an *infantile personality*, in which overt functioning at times resembles that of borderline personality organization. Indeed, there is considerable diagnostic overlap between histrionic and borderline disorders; comorbidity rates across studies range from 44% to 95% (Pfohl, 1995). Somatization disorder has also been linked to histrionic features (Lilienfeld, van Valkenburg, Larntz, & Akiskal, 1986). Kernberg thought that higher level hysterical personality disorder patients experience hypersexualized conflict in regard to specific persons who have come to represent restimulated oedipal objects. Nonconflictual areas of their lives may appear relatively stable; consequently, prominent disturbances of object relations do not occur in areas requiring capacities for intimacy, anxiety tolerance, or impulse control. This form contrasts with the more infantile form of hysterical personality, in which disinhibited hypersexuality and affective lability are more typically observed. Lazare (1971) also distinguished two levels, one corresponding to the phallic stage of development and the other to a less developmentally advanced oral stage level.

Despite its importance in psychoanalytic theories, histrionic personality disorder was studied with greater precision once confusing terms or concepts associated with this disorder—such as *hysteria* and *psychoneurosis*—fell into disuse. Consequently, the relatively uncommon symptomatic manifestations of hysteria or hysterical neurosis are more familiar to contemporary clinicians by their current designations as dissociative or conversion disorders on Axis I in the *DSM* (American Psychiatric Association, 1980, 1987, 1994, 2000). The prominent personality characteristics associated with hysterical reactions—first described by Freud (Breuer & Freud, 1893–1895/1955; Freud, 1908/1959a, 1931/1961c) and Abraham (1919/1953) but formalized by W. Reich (1933/1949) and Fenichel (1945) as asymptomatic hysterical character disorders—are now classified on Axis II as histrionic personality disorder. The primary features of histrionic personality have remained generally stable throughout most revisions of the *DSM* and the *International Classification of Diseases* (*ICD*; World Health Organization, 1992). Certain features have been deemphasized—such as outbursts of temper, vague or impressionistic speech, or manipulative behavior—only to be reintroduced at other times or assigned varying degrees of importance (Pfohl, 1995). For the most part, the cardinal features of histrionic (hysterical) personality disorder typically include a dramatic or exaggerated affective presentation characterized by shallow and labile emotional expressiveness, marked suggestibility or susceptibility to external influence, egocentrism accompanied by the need to be the center of attention, and provocative seductiveness or exaggerated vanity. Self-preoccupation, self-indulgence, and sometimes exploitative or manipulative actions are also associated characteristics.

D. F. Klein and Davis (1969) described an atypical form of depression they first called *hysteroid dysphoria*. This condition, which D. F. Klein (1974) subsequently called *endogenomorphic depression*, is characterized by labile and

154   DISORDERS OF THE SELF

shallow affect and romantic preoccupations associated with hypersensitivity to rejection. D. F. Klein and Davis demonstrated that hysteroid dysphoria was responsive to treatment with monoamine oxidase inhibitors. Stewart and Klein (1997) more recently noted a similarity between hysteroid dysphoria and borderline personality disorder.

Cloninger (1987) initially characterized histrionic personality disorder as showing a pattern of high novelty seeking and reward dependence accompanied by low harm avoidance. He noted a correspondence between this pattern and narcissistic, emotionally dependent, and impulsive–aggressive traits. Further, Cloninger, like others, commented on the similarity between histrionic and borderline patients insofar as they show a similar combination of traits, raising a question about the distinctiveness of these conditions. Cloninger speculated that quantitative temperament differences might differentiate borderline and histrionic personality disorders. However, in his later work using a modified temperament–character typology, he did not further address histrionic personality disorder.

Westen and Shedler's (1999a, 1999b) Q sort–derived typology identified a histrionic factor comprising items characteristic of both histrionic and borderline personality disorders. They considered this finding to illustrate the heterogeneity of borderline pathology, because such patients were identified on three of their Q-sort categories. Westen and Shedler observed that the quality of affect in the histrionic group was consonant with mood, whereas affect was ego dystonic in the other two categories (dysphoric: emotionally dysregulated and dysphoric: dependent–masochistic).

Millon's (1996) biopsychosocial–evolutionary model characterized histrionic patients as predominantly active and oriented toward others on the active–passive and self–other polarities, respectively. The histrionic prototype resembles dependent personality disorder in regard to patients' adaptive preference to seek out other people for the gratification of needs; however, histrionic patients differ insofar as they are disposed to an active orientation toward adapting to the world. This active orientation is characterized by their attention- and admiration-seeking interpersonal nature, whereas dependent personality disorder patients display a more passive accommodation style.

Millon (1996) distinguished six subtypes based on predominant features of the clinical presentation in histrionic personality disorder. Patients with a *theatrical* subtype have a predominant orientation to others that is based on making themselves appear as they believe others expect them to be. This orientation also captures such persons' chameleon-like ability to market themselves to appeal to what they believe other people want from them. It also represents a self-image not unlike the "as-if" character Deutsch (1942) described. Another subtype Millon delineated is a *vivacious* presentation, capturing the superficial, cheerful, and energetic nature some patients show in excitement seeking or excessive activity. Patients with both of these subtypes are distinctively superficial in virtually every aspect of their existence, seeking to minimize the serious side of life. Somewhat similar to these clinical manifestations are subtypes Millon designated *appeasing*, which emphasizes the approval-seeking quality of relationships with others, and *disingenuous*, which represents such patients' penchant for short-lived enthusiasms in stimulus-seeking behavior.

Millon (1996) described two subtypes that seem to characterize more destabilized presentations. The *infantile* subtype is characterized by a childish, immature manner of behavior and relating; he compared this subtype to the infantile personality type Kernberg (1975) emphasized as a primitively organized form of histrionic personality disorder. The *tempestuous* subtype emphasized the predominant appearance of labile affect in which impulsive acting out alternates with moody, depressive affect.

ANTISOCIAL PERSONALITY DISORDER

What is now designated in the *DSM* as antisocial personality disorder has been denoted in various ways at different times, in part to emphasize particular aspects of this condition. When the term *psychopathy* was the preferred designation, the highlighted personality characteristics were psychological aberrations (including heritable and developmental features) that secondarily produced the societal and interpersonal sequelae of this disturbance. Later, the term *sociopathy* came into common use, emphasizing the appreciable societal consequences of psychopathic behavior more as primary diagnostic features than as sequelae. A view such as Bursten's (1972) could be regarded as taking an intermediate position; Bursten considered sociopathy as manipulative but not necessarily criminal behavior that such patients justify by their contempt of others. Thus, sociopaths take advantage of societal structures to harm or deceive others in the service of elevating self-esteem.

The term *antisocial* has replaced both *psychopathic* and *sociopathic* since the second edition of the *DSM* was published in 1968; *dyssocial personality* is the preferred appellation in the *ICD*. There is also a provision in the fourth edition of the *DSM* (*DSM–IV*; American Psychiatric Association, 1994) for subthreshold antisocial behavior of sufficient concern to signal a need for careful attention or observation, designated by the two V codes representing appreciable behavior problems that do not unequivocally warrant a formal diagnosis for antisocial behavior of adults, and of children or adolescents. Confusion remains concerning the distinction between antisocial patients who have performed criminal acts and antisocial patients with no apparent criminal behavior. A history of criminality may denote a subtype of a broad antisocial personality; alternatively, it may represent the crucial defining feature of antisocial personality disorder, despite the fact that criminal behavior has never been considered a necessary condition for arriving at the diagnosis. Antisocial personality characteristics without criminality denote internal personality factors that may not have a clearly observable counterpart in behavior. The latter viewpoint is closer in spirit to the general definition of other personality disorders, emphasizing a relatively discrete and stable constellation of entrenched psychological signs. The fact that antisocial personality disorder has inevitable consequences for social–interpersonal relations is noncontributory for distinguishing between the disorder with and without criminality, because interpersonal problems occur in nearly all personality disorders.

Kraepelin (1918, p. 485) emphasized a constitutional basis in "psychopathic states," and he took care to distinguish the moral defects associated with this "insanity of degeneracy" from dementia praecox, because both illnesses typically follow a chronic, nonremitting (and therefore deteriorating) course. Kraepelin (1919) did note, however, that some patients could be considered "undeveloped cases of dementia praecox, as 'latent schizophrenia' according to Bleuler's terminology" (p. 258). Psychopathy occurs more frequently in men than in women, a stable finding across all studies of sex ratio in antisocial personality disorder. Using the Washington University diagnostic criteria (Feighner et al., 1972), Guze (1976) reported antisocial personality disorder in as many as 80% of incarcerated men and 65% of incarcerated women. Antisocial personality disorder is apparently less prevalent as a diagnosis with increasing age, possibly because such older patients' lifestyles are characterized more by a marginal existence on the fringes of society than by criminal behavior. Older patients typically show interpersonal problems and hostility but usually no longer present a significant threat to others; they also may deny symptoms or suffer memory disorders. Some die prematurely or are incarcerated for lengthy periods or for life. Millon (1996) traced the evolution of Kraepelin's thinking about psychopathic personalities and antisocial personality disorder to take into account varying degrees of criminal propensity (including manifestations of a calculating or manipulative amoral character, impulsive criminal acts, and a rootless or vagabond-like lifestyle).

Clinicians are frequently inclined to assign a diagnosis of antisocial personality disorder in prison populations and to underdiagnose this disorder in nonprison populations. Widiger and Corbitt (1995) pointed out that politicians or lawyers with antisocial personality characteristics who have no history of unemployment, defaulting on debts, or arrests probably would not satisfy criteria for the diagnosis, because their overt adaptation falls within normal limits. Widiger and Corbitt suggested that the diagnostic threshold would need to be lowered, therefore, if subtle impairment indicators were to be included. The comorbidity problem (particularly for narcissistic, borderline, and paranoid personality disorders on Axis II and substance abuse disorders on Axis I) is no less a concern with this disorder than with most other

Axis II disorders. Furthermore, clinicians cannot always be certain that sub-clinical or subtle features—such as a poor or marginal driving record, frequent job changes, propensity to feel boredom or externalize blame, "nerves of steel," or manipulativeness—are better represented as characteristics of psychopathy, other personality disorders, or no mental disorder at all.

There can be little doubt that antisocial personality disorder is among the most controversial diagnostic entities in the DSM (Hare, Hart, & Harpur, 1991; Millon, 1996; Widiger & Corbitt, 1995). It is also one of the most extensively investigated Axis II disorders. For this reason, my review in the sections that follow of its clinical characteristics and psychopathology is more extensive and wide ranging than for the other personality disorders discussed in previous chapters. The following sections discuss the descriptive personality features of antisocial personality disorder and its childhood antecedents, prognosis and course, etiology (according to learning theory, psychophysiological and neurobiological explanations, and family history and genetic perspectives), personality theory viewpoints, and psychoanalytic perspectives.

Descriptive Personality Features

Using the Psychopathy Checklist—Revised (PCL–R), Hare (1991) differentiated two factors in antisocial personality disorder. One is characterized by manipulation, superficial charm and affect, callous lying, and remorseless use of others. The second factor represents a chronically unstable and socially deviant lifestyle, including delinquency in children or adolescents and criminality in adults, parasitic use of others, and boredom leading to impulsive stimulation seeking. Cooke and Michie (2001) suggested a three-factor model including arrogant or deceitful interpersonal relationships, deficient affective experience, and impulsive or irresponsible behavior. The PCL–R is arguably the major assessment instrument in use for assessing antisocial personality disorder, though the Barratt Impulsivity Scale (Barratt & Patton, 1983) also measures important associated dimensions.

Cleckley (1941/1964) is frequently credited with providing one of the most comprehensive descriptions of psychopathy, emphasizing personality and cognitive dimensions of both overt and inferred behavior. His description is the foundation of the main personality pattern subtype identified in Hare's (1991) PCL–R model. Prominent personality characteristics are the absence of guilt or conscience, lack of remorse, incapacity to form intimate or lasting relationships, an engaging or charming manner, shallow or insincere affective experience, and lack of concern about or empathy for other people. Inability to learn from experience despite normal or above average intelligence is also commonly reported (Cleckley, 1941/1964). Cleckley also commented that psychopathy affects people in many walks of life. He noted that it may be masked by a relatively adaptive appearance (e.g., in politics or business) and thus is not confined exclusively to criminal offenders.

Cleckley (1941/1964) regarded psychopathy as a form of "semantic aphasia," based on the concept of syntactic aphasia in behavioral neurology (Head, 1926), describing psychopaths' inability to explain their subjective experiences and their purposive intentions despite otherwise normal behavior or appearances. Johns and Quay's (1962) comment that psychopaths "know the words but not the music" (p. 217) expresses a similar idea.[2] Widiger and Corbitt (1995) noted that the *DSM–IV* task force considered the personality features described by Cleckley, Millon (1996), and Hare (1991)—such as lack of empathy, inflated self-appraisal, and a glib or superficial manner—for use in the final version of the manual. However, these features were not included because of reliability problems in ascertaining the presence or absence of such traits in field trials studying antisocial personality disorder. Further, Widiger and Corbitt noted that adding personality features generated only minimal improvement in validity of the diagnosis, and their inclusion complicated the differential diagnosis of antisocial personality disorder and narcissistic personality disorder. Although these personality features were rejected for inclusion in the *DSM–IV*, they were nevertheless incorporated into the antisocial behavior section of V codes representing associated disorders worthy of clinical attention. Instead of including subtle and potentially unreliable items in the *DSM–IV*, the phrasing of the existing revised third edition (*DSM–III–R*; American Psychiatric Association, 1987) criteria was modified to emphasize general personality characteristics. However, fewer but more selective indications of specific behaviors were retained as examples to help anchor criterion ascertainment; these were included in the text revision edition of the *DSM–IV* (American Psychiatric Association, 2000). Hare and Hart (1995) nevertheless regarded as specious the reliability and comorbidity problems Widiger and Corbitt noted in their rationale for continuing to deemphasize classical psychopathy features of personality. Hare and Hart regarded both concerns to be no more problematic for antisocial personality disorder than for most other Axis II disorders.

Childhood Antecedents

The literature on delinquent youths is particularly important to consider because of the strong association between adolescent delinquency (conduct disorder) and antisocial personality disorder. McCord, McCord, and

---

[2]The musical *Assassins*, with a book by John Weidman and with music and lyrics by Stephen Sondheim (produced by the Roundabout Theater Company, New York, 2004), imagines the complex motivations and strivings of historical figures who attempted presidential assassinations. In a review, *The New York Times'* chief theater critic (Brantley, 2004) commented on "sly distortions" at certain points in the musical score to "approximate the skewed ways in which these characters *hear* everyday melodies. Listening, as sweet notes slide into dissonance, you may feel as if your own brain has slipped off the rails" (p. E-1). In another context, an analyst treating a patient with a vertical split (Goldberg, 2000), which I describe further in chapter 11, commented, "I could not imagine myself singing the words to his song, but I could hear myself whistling the tune" (p. 109).

Zola (1959) reported findings from a study of more than 600 delinquent and nondelinquent adolescents. In a prospective follow-up study using ratings of parental behavior obtained before delinquency onset, they found higher levels of neglect, fighting, and lax parental discipline in families of children who subsequently were delinquent. McCord and McCord (1964) and McCord (1982, 1991) emphasized family interactions, particularly parental conflict and aggression, rather than parental absence as the more important influence on subsequent criminality in adulthood. Another large-scale investigation of predictors of criminality was Glueck and Glueck's (1950) earlier follow-up study of family history antecedents in 1,000 cases. They reported disturbed family cohesion and discipline or supervision problems as important predictors of subsequent criminal behavior. Further, the families of delinquency-prone children experienced high rates of divorce or parental absence and of parental substance abuse and criminality. Moreover, the majority of delinquent children (but less than 10% of nondelinquent children) chose to socialize with other delinquent children.

One of the most influential epidemiological studies was reported in Robins's (1966) *Deviant Children Grown Up*, which demonstrated a continuity between conduct disorder in childhood and antisocial personality disorder in late adolescence and adulthood. Like Glueck and Glueck (1950), Robins reported that parents of such children showed a high degree of antisocial behavior themselves. She emphasized behavioral acts, which could be reliably measured, rather than personality characteristics such as those noted by Cleckley (1941/1964), which were difficult to assess. Robins's preference for behavioral factors was adopted in the third edition of the *DSM* (*DSM–III*; American Psychiatric Association, 1980) and its subsequent versions. However, critics faulted the *DSM* for emphasizing criminal behavior and for deemphasizing personality characteristics despite their uncertain interrater reliability (Hare et al., 1991; Millon, 1996; Rogers & Dion, 1991). Robins (1995) nevertheless suggested that the *DSM–IV* criteria, which are less specific than those of the *DSM–III* or the *DSM–III–R*, may correspond more closely to the "essence" (p. 138) of the disorder. Thus, some of the diagnostic criteria that are interpersonal in nature—represented perhaps more in the *ICD* (10th ed.; see World Health Organization, 1992) than in the *DSM–IV*—may contain elements of a personality pattern such as Cleckley's (1941/1964) classical description, Hare's (1991) Factor 1, Millon's (1996) personality prototype, and Kernberg's (1992) psychoanalytic description.

Prognosis and Course

Remission of antisocial personality disorder is relatively infrequent; more favorable outcomes have been found in patients who were least deviant at baseline assessment or who were older at follow-up (Black, 2001). Moffitt

(1993) differentiated a "life-course-persistent" subgroup, characterized by early onset and severe, chronic antisocial problems, from an "adolescence-limited" subgroup with conduct disorder in adolescence that was provoked by peer pressure. Patients in the latter subgroup generally remitted, which may be one explanation for the observation that most children with conduct disorder do not proceed to develop antisocial personality disorder, even though early-onset conduct disorder (before age 15) is nevertheless a risk factor. Black (2001) stressed the importance of early prevention efforts with at-risk conduct-disordered children that target such children and their parents whenever possible. He noted that children who are apprehended and punished for early offenses are less likely to progress to adult criminality than children who escape penalties, an observation that is consistent with Robins's (1966) finding that antisocial patients who served brief jail sentences earlier in their lives had better outcomes later in adulthood.

Etiology

I next consider various etiologies that have been discussed in the literature on antisocial personality disorder, derived from learning theory, neurobiology, and family history and genetic perspectives.

Learning Theory

Eysenck (1957) proposed a learning theory explanation of psychopathy, taking note of such patients' slow rate of conditioning. He argued that rapid buildup and slow dissipation of reactive inhibition resulted from high extraversion, a heritable temperament style that Eysenck hypothesized as interfering with the acquisition of social values and inhibitions. He thus considered psychopaths to be temperamentally undersocialized. Gray (1987) proposed the view that an imbalance exists between an overactive behavioral approach or activation system and an underactive inhibitory system. Consequently, motivation for rewards outweighs sensitivity to punishments. Gray postulated that antisocial personality disorder is likely to involve the septohippocampal circuit and noradrenergic and serotonergic neurotransmitters.

Diminished fearful inhibition has also been implicated as an important mechanism in antisocial personality (Cloninger, 1987; Hare, 1991; Lykken, 1995). As a result, a low level of anxiety is an important characteristic, appearing first in undersocialized children (Quay, 1987) and later in an adult (primary psychopathy) form. Such patients do not learn fear arousal and its temporal association with anticipated punishment as well as normal persons. As a result, response inhibition of antisocial behavior fails to occur, one explanation for antisocial patients' disinclination to learn or profit from experience and, consequently, their poor judgment and inability to delay gratification. Kilzieh and Cloninger's (1993) review of psychophysiological studies, however, noted inconclusive findings in studies of learning theory–based formulations of introversion–extraversion and arousal–inhibition mechanisms. Thus, it has not been clearly established whether poor avoidance learning and conditioning in antisocial personality disorder and psychopathy result from diminished responsiveness to punishment or from heightened sensitivity to reward.

Psychophysiological and Neurobiological Views

Electrophysiological studies in antisocial personality disorder patients or violent criminals have demonstrated slow wave form (low alpha frequency) electroencephalogram abnormalities (Venables, 1988) and inconsistent (reduced or enhanced P3 component) evoked potential responses (Kilzieh & Cloninger, 1993). Psychophysiological research has shown high pain thresholds, low sensitivity to anxiety, slow avoidance learning, and hyporeactivity to stimuli of high emotionality (Hare, 1965, 1978; Lykken, 1957; Patrick, Bradley, & Lang, 1993). Black (2001) suggested that antisocial personality disorder patients' chronically diminished autonomic reactivity may provoke risk-taking or thrill-seeking behavior in an attempt to reach an optimal level of arousal.

Recent literature also suggests appreciable involvement of the orbitofrontal cortical region in antisocial and violent behaviors (Damasio, 2000; Raine, Stoddard, Bihrle, & Buchsbaum, 1998; Volavka, 1999), an association that Blair and Cipolotti (2000) referred to as *neurologically acquired sociopathy*. Although there are fewer neuroimaging studies of antisocial personality disorder, one investigation of assaultive military personnel using positron emission tomography (Goyer, Andreason, Semple, & Clayton, 1994) and another of antisocial patients using magnetic resonance imaging (Raine, Buchsbaum, & LaCasse, 1997) demonstrated diminished glucose metabolic activity in the right temporal lobe and reduced prefrontal gray matter, respectively. Both of these regions may be involved in control of impulses and mood regulation.

Biederman et al. (1993) reported that because attention deficit disorder and conduct disorder frequently occur together in children, an attentional deficit may contribute to impulsivity and substance abuse, both of which are also prevalent in antisocial personality disorder. Siever and Davis's (1991) neurobiological model emphasizes a disturbance of impulse control as the integrating link in common among antisocial, borderline, and schizophrenia spectrum disorders. This model suggests the possibility that genetic and biological substrates underlying an impulsivity–aggression dimension of behavior and personality may provide a more satisfactory approach for classification than diagnosis-specific approaches, including the identification of subgroups of antisocial personality disorder and psychopathy. Siever and Davis's model also suggests neurobiological commonalities among antisocial personality disorder and several impulse control disorders, such as intermittent explosive disorder, kleptomania, pyromania, trichotillomania, eating disorders (particularly binge eating), and a broad range of compulsive or addictive behavior disorders such as compulsive shopping or gambling and sexual compulsivity. The relationship between impulsiveness as a personality trait and the range of impulse control disorders remains unclear, although it is a subject of active research interest. Furthermore, the interrelationships among antisocial personality disorder, impulse control disorders, and clinical disorders of attention suggest a complex pattern of interwoven etiologic pathways, adding as well to risk for aggression dyscontrol and substance abuse. Kraepelin (1918) astutely observed that "alcoholism in the parents easily stands first" (p. 517) among etiologic factors.

Schore (2003a) considered early abuse and neglect to be important influences on antisocial personality disorder, which he termed *developmentally acquired sociopathy*. His synthesis of attachment theory and neurobiology hypothesized that maternal neglect and hypoarousal dispose children to the disturbance of a specific parasympathetic influence on hypothalamic function at a critical period for establishing connections with the orbitofrontal cortex. Incorporating findings from studies by Blair (Blair, 1995; Blair, Morris, Frith, Perrett, & Dolan, 1999) and Raine (Raine, Lencz, Bihrle, LaCasse, & Colletti, 2000; Raine, Venables, & Mednick, 1997), Schore suggested that infant neglect and consequent hypoarousal of the autonomic nervous system induce overpruning of central–autonomic nervous system connections, accounting for psychopaths' affective dysregulation and underdeveloped inhibition of violence. He further hypothesized that the resulting underdeveloped orbitofrontal cortical system is insufficiently prepared to support neural networks that facilitate the interpretation of social stimuli and empathic learning or comprehension (Damasio, Tranel, & Damasio, 1990) in developmentally acquired sociopathy. Schore considered that such a deficit may also explain antisocial patients' predominant responsiveness to immediate stimuli and their "myopia for the future" (Bechara, Tranel, & Damasio, 2000, p. 2189).

Family History and Genetic Viewpoints

Cross-fostering studies that compared adoptees with their biological and adoptive parents demonstrated that sons' adult criminality was more frequently associated with biological parents' than with adoptive parents' criminality (Bohman, Cloninger, Sigvardsson, & von Knorring, 1982; Mednick, Gabrielli, & Hutchings, 1984; Moffitt, 1987). Caspi et al. (2002) demonstrated how a specific gene responsible for encoding an enzyme (monoamine oxidase A) involved in metabolizing neurotransmitters modified the effect of maltreatment in boys, which differentiated those with and without histories of maltreatment who subsequently manifested antisocial behavior as adults.

Cadoret, Troughton, Bagford, and Woodworth (1990) and Lyons, True, Eisen, and Goldberg (1995) demonstrated evidence of both heritable and shared environmental components in antisocial behavior. It can be difficult to disentangle the effects of genetic and social–environmental influences on factors that have been reported as predisposing for antisocial personality disorder, including low socioeconomic status in childhood (Rutter & Giller, 1983), maternal absence (Raine, Venables, et al., 1997), and paternal loss (Huttunen & Niskanen, 1978). Reports that obstetric and perinatal complications increase the risk for violence and criminal behavior raise a similar question (Mednick & Kandel, 1988; Raine, Brennan, & Mednick, 1994).

McCord (1982) questioned the existence of genetic transmission of criminal behavior, although she acknowledged that associated traits that predispose to criminality may be heritable. She also commented that genetic evidence for inherited potentialities should be regarded only as suggestive, because the impact of social or environmental influences often is not thoroughly considered.

Personality Theories

Millon's (1996) integrated biopsychosocial–evolutionary perspective identified the self–other and active–passive dimensions as particularly salient in antisocial personality disorder. In the self–other dimension, the self polarity, representing individuation, far outweighs the influence of a deficiency on the nurturant side of this polarity. However, orientation to others is indeed very likely deficient. In addition, activity supersedes passivity, and the pleasure–pain dimension is the least salient for understanding antisocial personality disorder. Millon commented that the active and self-oriented prototype characterizing antisocial personality (which he referred to as the *aggrandizing* personality pattern) contrasts with the passive and self-oriented prototype characterizing narcissistic personality disorder. Though they are different, these disorders are in certain respects not very far apart. Millon's characterization may help to explain why most observers of psychopathy and clinical antisocial personality disorder have commented that they are frequently accompanied by an exaggerated degree of narcissism.

Millon (1996) stressed that prototypical antisocial personality disorder (the person's active orientation to modifying the environment to get what they want, self-directed focus, and low differentiation between pleasure and pain) increases the likelihood that an antisocial lifestyle will include many of the behavioral manifestations Robins (1966) identified. Millon also described eight domains representing variants of the major personality dimensions of antisocial personality disorder. At a behavioral level, Millon distinguished *impulsive* and *irresponsible* types, denoting behavioral and interpersonal modes of action, respectively. At a phenomenological level, Millon identified three types characterized by (a) deviant thinking in an antisocial sense (but unrelated to formal thought disorder or psychosis), (b) an autonomous self-image (referring to a disinclination to see oneself as subject to traditional social rules), and (c) debased views of others' intentions (disposing to devaluation to counteract anticipated harm). He further identified two intrapsychic domains: a predominant propensity for projection that is typically acted out and an unruly (*disorganized*) personality structure that is lacking in well-developed internal controls. Millon also noted a biologically influenced type based on callous mood, irritability, and offensive coarseness.

As with all personality disorders, Millon (1996) conceptualized these behavioral, phenomenological, intrapsychic, and biological domains as interacting to create various configurations, which for antisocial personality disorder consist of the following subtypes: self-aggrandizement, sensitivity to being slighted or marginalized, exaggerated risk taking, ruthless aggressiveness, and a tendency to live at the fringes of society that gives rise to a nomadic existence not unlike Kraepelin's (1919) description of the drift into a vagrant lifestyle. Finally, Millon included nonpathological patterns, including one he called *normal antisocial* based on patterns that Oldham and Morris (1990) described. Such nonpathological manifestations may be found among fearless and adventuresome but risk-taking individuals; they may also encompass enterprising but confrontational individuals whose insistence on overly independent personal freedom pushes up against but manages to stay within the bounds of social conventions.

Cloninger, Svrakic, and Przybeck's (1993) temperament–character model identifies deficits in antisocial personality disorder in three temperament dimensions—reward dependence, harm avoidance, and persistence. Patients with antisocial personality disorder seem temperamentally activated only in the novelty-seeking dimension. A propensity for high novelty seeking consequently drives their desire to seek pleasure or excitement and governs most of their behavior, disposing them to impulsivity and intolerance for encumbrances such as regulations that get in their way. Antisocial personality disorder patients' low reward dependence makes them insensitive to social cues, their low harm avoidance causes minimal anticipatory anxiety or fear of danger, and their low persistence gives rise to their frequent disinclination to expend effort to reach goals and sometimes to mood lability. Antisocial personality disorder may represent an extreme form of a heritable pattern that Cloninger and Svrakic (1997) termed an "adventurous temperament." They considered this temperamental disposition also to be found in persons with alcoholism when character dimensions show immaturity, although the same temperamental disposition gives rise to exploration, imagination, or independent thinking when character is mature.

Cloninger and Svrakic (1997) noted that temperament, though an independent dimension of personality formation, nevertheless constrains character development. They reported that antisocial patients show low levels of all three of the character dimensions they described—self-direction, cooperativeness, and self-transcendence. Cloninger and Svrakic also regarded personality features of undisciplined irresponsibility, deficient empathy, hostile opportunism, and an underdeveloped sense of conscience or ideals to represent clinical manifestations of antisocial personality disorder, and they also linked them to substance abuse. Variations of these temperament and character dimensions also influence other forms of psychopathology (particularly borderline disorder), possibly accounting for some of its comorbidity with antisocial personality disorder. Finally, Cloninger, Svrakic, and Svrakic (1997) did not discount the potential influences of social learning and random environmental events—that is, luck—in explaining the variability of antisocial personality disorder's clinical manifestations.

Westen and Shedler's (1999b) Q sort–derived method for an empirical classification of personality disorders identified a factor they termed *antisocial–psychopathic disorder*. This factor consisted of items that would be easily recognizable from the standard personality descriptions by Cleckley (1941/1964), Hare (1991), and Millon (1996), including deceitfulness, tendency to take advantage of others, absence of remorse, hostility, impulsivity, and manipulativeness. An analysis of an adolescent sample they studied identified a similar factor including items such as frequent power struggles with adults, rebelliousness toward or defiance of authority figures, intense anger and oppositionality, and impulsivity (Westen & Chang, 2000).

Psychoanalytic Viewpoints

Psychoanalytic interest in psychopathy and antisocial personality disorder is generally limited compared with the attention devoted to neurotic and character disorders, probably because these patients' superego deficiencies and impulsivity make them poor candidates for psychoanalysis. Consequently, analysts have little experience with antisocial personality disorder. Josephs (1992) noted, however, that although the prognosis is poor for antisocial personality disorder with overt criminality, circumscribed change is possible in patients whose chief symptoms consist of exploitative or opportunistic behavior uncomplicated by substance abuse. Josephs's most optimistic prognosis was a functional rehabilitation in which overt or socially troublesome behavior is kept within tolerable bounds, sometimes with improved self-esteem or sublimated grandiosity. However, the fundamental characterological flaws (e.g., diminished empathic capacity or compassion) invariably remain unchanged. Josephs also considered such patients' capacity to experience and tolerate depression to be a favorable prognostic sign for psychotherapeutic treatment.

Freud (1915/1957c, 1916/1957d) made passing mention of criminal acts that resulted from pathological guilt. He described a guilt-ridden character as one manifestation of acting out, which he regarded as a transference displacement of thoughts or affects that could not be verbalized but were instead diverted into actions or behavior. He noted the uncharacteristically ego-alien nature of criminal acts, an observation that Goldberg (1999, 2000) also addressed in his expansion of Kohut's (1971) concept of the vertical split (described more fully in chap. 11). Freud did not comment further on criminality; however, Aichorn (1925/1983), W. Reich (1933/1949), and Eissler (1949) added to Freud's view. Aichorn treated delinquent adolescents and emphasized their superego deficits and their lack of internalization of parental values. He suggested a modification of technique whereby an analyst actively engages with delinquent patients by offering himself or herself as an ego ideal. Aichorn's approach, it should be noted, was a nonanalytic therapy (albeit one informed by psychoanalytic concepts) that modeled appropriate behavior and attitudes that were inherently deficient in such patients.[3]

Eissler (1949) commented on the unmet narcissistic demands of psychopathic patients, which precipitate aggression that is ultimately turned against society and its institutions. W. Reich (1933/1949) also took note of superego defects in a group of patients he termed "impulsive characters." Making use of the conflict model of classical drive theory, he emphasized how compromised superego development fails to inhibit instinctual urges, thus leading the individual to enact such impulses in society. W. Reich's formulation laid the groundwork for the predominant psychoanalytic view that criminality represented an externalized form of neurotic conflicts that might otherwise be expressed as symptoms or characterological manifestations.

Kernberg (1984) regarded antisocial personality disorder as a primitive form of character pathology, similar to prepsychotic disorders, dominated by splitting as a primary defense. He thus considered antisocial personality to be organized at a low level of ego and superego integration, similar to borderline, narcissistic, and inadequate or infantile personality organizations. Paris (1997) reviewed evidence linking antisocial and borderline personality disorders in view of the prevalence of impulsivity in both disorders. Apart from the greater prevalence among men of antisocial personality disorder and among women of borderline personality disorder, he suggested that these disorders may represent different clinical manifestations of a common underlying dimension.

Kernberg (1984) also regarded perversions, impulse-ridden conditions, and even hypomanic disorders as other manifestations of this level of psychological organization. Positive and negative self and object representations are poorly integrated in such patients, disposing them to impaired object constancy and compromised superego development. Kernberg emphasized the underdevelopment of the superego more than its becoming overwhelmed

---

[3]Kohut's (1971) view of narcissism and narcissistic transferences was influenced by Aichorn's (1925/1983) approach. Kohut interpreted Aichorn's recommendation as fostering a selfobject transference that would mobilize delinquent patients' hidden grandiosity or idealization, thus becoming part of the treatment and ultimately forming an ego ideal. Kohut's viewpoint is described in greater detail in chapter 8.

by guilt. He also noted that paranoia was typically unchecked and that instinctual impulses permeated many areas of antisocial patients' functioning.

Kernberg (1984/1989) considered antisocial personality disorder to be a subgroup of narcissistic personality disorder, representing a version he called *malignant narcissism* because paranoid and sadistic features are prominent alongside the superego pathology. However, Hart and Hare (1998), although they concurred with the association between psychopathy and narcissism, questioned whether the overlap was sufficiently prominent to justify viewing psychopathy as a subgroup of narcissism. Moreover, they also noted that the relationship between psychopathy and narcissism may not be any greater than their relationships with other personality disorders. Meloy (1988) and Stone (1993) also emphasized the close relationship between psychopathy and narcissism. Meloy particularly stressed the coexistence of detachment and overly aggressive intents to form intimate bonds, giving rise to the prominence of sadistic aggression accompanied by paranoid ideation rather than depression.

Impulsivity was one of the predominant features Frosch (1977) noted in antisocial–psychopathic characters, although he also observed that it was not unique to this disorder. He identified several distinguishing features of impulsive or acting out behaviors: They are not ego alien, there is minimal distortion of the motives giving rise to them, and there is pleasure in their expression. Frosch also differentiated between symptom impulse disorders (e.g., kleptomania, perversions, and explosive affect discharges like fire setting) and character impulse disorders, in which diffuse impulsivity, sometimes associated with nonspecific (soft) neurological signs, is embedded in the character pathology. Frosch did not discuss antisocial personality disorder as distinct from impulsive character, and thus he did not clearly indicate whether he thought it resembles a character impulse disorder more than a symptom impulse disorder. He did comment, however, that important features associated with psychopathic personality, such as absence of guilt and a diminished capacity for object relations, precluded conceptualizing such patients' disturbance as one primarily of impulsivity.

The predominant psychoanalytic view of antisocial personality disorder, therefore, is linked to impulse control. It has sometimes been referred to—although not formally so—as *impulsive personality*. Shapiro's (1965, 1981) examination of an impulsive character style emphasized how judgment, planning, and decision making are done quickly and without reflection. The person's ability to shift back and forth among possible courses of action is short circuited; therefore, the person does not consider alternative choices and consequences beyond those of the moment. Impulsive individuals thus lose sight of goals because they do "not have an interest in the object, but an interest in satisfaction" (Shapiro, 1965, p. 142). Their impulsivity also makes emotional attachments and career goals appear shallow; even social or political matters attract little interest.

Shapiro (1965) described a psychopathic variant of an impulsive style that is dominated by an underdeveloped sense of morals and a perfunctory experience of conscience. For this reason, he explained that such patients' glib insincerity and lying are related to their propensity for rapid, unreflective judgment. Impulsive patients are thus governed by immediate gratification of egocentric interest. What they do or say is based not on moral principles but rather on how well things might work out for them. Theirs is an orientation to reality based on "operating" and being on the lookout for opportunities. Consequently, they show little need to reflect or to ponder the implications of their actions, because their behavior is influenced only by what they want at any given moment and by the most expedient way to get it.

Many important psychoanalytic views, therefore, have called attention to antisocial personality disorder as a disturbance of impulse control. Such patients are considered to lack frustration tolerance and to be unable to delay gratification, and they are also deficient in anticipating the consequences of their actions. Aside from need states that are governed by intolerance for delay and its inevitable consequence of impulsive behavior, antisocial personality disorder is distinguished from a broader range of impulse control disorders by the prominence of mercenary motivations and opportunistic ways of manipulating people or situations. Other clinical manifestations that psychoanalytic observers emphasized are anger, envy, and narcissistic entitlement; lack of remorse, guilt, and sense of morality; and shallow object relations that are based not on affection or concern but rather on need lasting only as long as a need state exists. Such manifestations are typically considered to be derivatives of ego and superego deficits underlying antisocial personality disorder and psychopathic character pathology.

CONCLUSION

This chapter has reviewed the literature on dependent, histrionic, and antisocial personality disorders from the viewpoints of descriptive psychopathology and psychoanalytic theory. Dependent and, in particular, histrionic personality disorders have important precedents in psychoanalysis. Millon's (1996) biopsychosocial–evolutionary perspective and Bornstein's (1993) synthesis provide the most systematic integration of dependent personality disorder and includes psychoanalytic perspectives. Both of these disorders have benefited from important empirical studies concerning their validity, prevalence, and comorbidity using contemporary diagnostic criteria.

Antisocial personality disorder—which also is still known as *psychopathy* or *sociopathy* by many clinical investigators—is the most systematically studied of this group of disorders. A broad range of empirical studies have incorporated learning theory, psychophysiology and neurobiology, and family history and genetic approaches; there also are many studies of childhood antecedents, prognosis, and clinical course. This background will prepare the way for the self psychological approach to understanding these disorders presented in chapter 8.

8

A SELF PSYCHOLOGICAL VIEWPOINT: DEPENDENT, HISTRIONIC, AND ANTISOCIAL PERSONALITY DISORDERS

I will consider in this chapter the disorders I described in chapter 7, emphasizing how they represent patients' attempts to consolidate self-cohesion by securing alternative paths to repairing a weakened self. Thus, I will demonstrate from a self psychological viewpoint that dependent, histrionic, and antisocial personality disorders are all centered on an irreparable selfobject failure in one sector of the self. Almost invariably, it is mirroring that has been chronically injured; patients with these disorders attempt in different ways to secure self-cohesion through other selfobject functions. Dependent and antisocial personality disorder patients turn to idealizing or twinship selfobjects to secure selfobject responsiveness, with varying degrees of success. Even partial success finding an alternative route to strengthen self-cohesion may effect some degree of a functional rehabilitation of the self.

These disorders differ from the schizoid, schizotypal, and avoidant disorders discussed in chapter 4. The latter disorders are organized around attempting to secure mirroring selfobject responsiveness by struggling, usually unsuccessfully, with mirroring deficits. The outcome of this struggle typically is the prominent devitalization associated with withdrawing from needs for affirmation or recognition. Dependent and antisocial patients experience similar severely damaged mirroring deficiency, but some dependent and antisocial patients may be able to repair the self-cohesion deficit through idealization or twinship selfobject functions, whereas schizoid, schizotypal, and avoidant patients defensively withdraw because the possibility of idealizing or twinship selfobject responsiveness seems foreclosed for them. Dependent and antisocial personality disorder patients often fail to establish an alternative path, however, as I will describe in this chapter.

Histrionic personality disorder presents a more complex problem. I take the position that these patients do not show any real capacity to mobilize alternative pathways to repair the self when mirroring selfobject responsiveness has been closed off. That is, they do not attempt to seek idealizing or twinship selfobjects, at least not in an enduring or resourceful way. Rather, they doggedly pursue potential mirroring selfobjects, repeatedly trying to establish an alternative pathway in the same inefficacious way. Stated differently, histrionic personality disorder patients attempt to find an alternative pathway to repair the self, but they know only one way. Their pursuit of mirroring selfobjects leads nowhere, but this is a lesson they seem unable to learn. Like dependent and antisocial personality disorder patients, histrionic patients do not remain frozen or stymied as a result of their mirroring deficits; they do not withdraw into the depleted self states like most people with schizoid, schizotypal, and avoidant personality disorders. Nevertheless, these patients may be the least successful of all the ones discussed here in finding a workable alternative pathway.

If histrionic patients make the least resourceful and thus most unsuccessful attempts to establish an alternative pathway to secure self-cohesion, dependent personality disorder patients can be said to make the most successful attempt. Extreme dependency, their most characteristic feature, fosters turning to idealizing selfobjects to consolidate self-cohesion. Their success, however, depends on the availability and capacity of their idealized selfobjects to continue providing this kind of selfobject function. Antisocial personality disorder patients occupy an intermediate position between dependent patients—who sometimes succeed by sustaining an alternative pathway as long as their idealized selfobjects remain viable—and histrionic patients, who typically fail in this respect. Antisocial patients may attempt to bolster self-cohesion by making use of idealizing or twinship selfobjects. However, they may establish convincing appearances of an alternative path to repair self-esteem deficits, but the resulting selfobject functions frequently do not endure. For as long as they last, such attempts may enable antisocial patients to function better and perhaps provide the illusion that they have a greater capacity for empathy than may be the case.

The disorders discussed in this chapter, in addition to being different from the disorders predominantly of devitalization, also differ from the paranoid, obsessive–compulsive, and borderline disorders I described in chapter 6, for which the primary concern is forestalling fragmentation. This is not to say that fragmentation concerns do not occur at times for dependent, histrionic, and antisocial patients. However, fragmentation is usually secondary to their main difficulty, which is forging and then sustaining a compensatory structure through idealization or twinship to repair an irreparable deficit in the mirroring sector. These patients' personalities, therefore, are organized around striving to find a solution to compromised mirroring selfobject responsiveness. They attempt to circumvent a mirroring deficit to stabilize self-cohesion by seeking a different selfobject path. Kohut (1971, 1977) and M. Tolpin (1997) described such pathways as *compensatory structures*, referring to relatively stable adaptations that sustain the self when one selfobject pathway is substantially damaged.

Patients with dependent personality disorder may manage to establish a moderately successful compensatory structure. The measure of its success is the degree to which stable self-esteem is achieved and then internalized. However, sometimes such stability lasts only as long as idealizing or twinship selfobjects continue to function in this way, because it requires the continuing availability of the idealized or twinship selfobjects. The stabilization thus does not become internalized as a sufficiently robust structure of the self. It falls short of the kind of durable internalization by an alternative selfobject route that Kohut (1971, 1977) and M. Tolpin (1997) intended a compensatory structure to represent. Dependent personality disorder patients who do achieve some degree of reliably strengthened self-cohesion through a compensatory structure may therefore show a better functional adjustment, despite the continuing presence of a dependent lifestyle.

Patients with histrionic personality disorder fail to secure a stable compensatory structure. They seem unable to abandon their unresourceful attempts to repair an irreparably damaged path to secure self-cohesion. Patients with antisocial personality disorder present the appearance of having internalized viable compensatory structures; however, on closer analysis, their attempt to repair the self proves to be less genuinely robust or sustaining. What is merely an appearance of a stable compensatory structure is readily undone when sufficiently destabilizing external conditions expose its superficiality and marginal stability. Although Kohut (1971, 1977) considered defenses to represent failed consolidation of compensatory structures, a general indication of individuals' psychological health may be judged by the relative balance between defensive and compensatory structures. Consequently, patients with the three disorders I consider in this chapter may be striving to establish a compensatory structure, though in different degrees and with varying levels of success.

The concept of compensatory structures has not been particularly emphasized in other viewpoints in contemporary self psychology, such as intersubjectivity theory, motivational systems, or conceptualizations of the self influenced by developmental and infant observation studies. Accordingly, the discussion in this chapter concentrates on Kohut's (1971, 1977) and M. Tolpin's (1997) views of compensatory structures.

DEPENDENT PERSONALITY DISORDER

Dependency as a psychological concept is ubiquitous but elusive in most forms of psychoanalytic theory, including self psychology. Although the traditional psychodynamic link between orality and gratification provides an anchor for conceptualizing dependency in drive theory and ego psychology (Bornstein, 1993), one of the major thrusts of self psychology is its deemphasis of drives, particularly in Kohut's (1977, 1984) later writings. For example, Kohut (1981/1991) stated that the drive concept "led to the worst distortions of the perception of man that psychoanalysis is guilty of" (p. 529). Self psychology made use of the concept of dependency; however, it did not provide a definitive view on its prominence in certain kinds of patients or its etiologic roots. Consequently, self psychology, like most contemporary schools of psychoanalytic thinking, did not propose a conceptual view of dependent personality disorder.

However, self psychology clearly regarded pronounced dependency as a by-product of a deficient psychological structure. Siegel (1996), influenced by Kohut's (1971) emphasis on failure to acquire an internalized tension-regulating mechanism, noted that dependency served a protective function through dependent patients' seeking out of omnipotent idealized selfobjects. Idealization can thus function as a potentially viable alternative route for securing selfobject responsiveness when deficient or unresponsive mirroring has closed out the possibility of repairing chronic injuries to the self. In this way, idealization may promote the establishment of a compensatory structure if it can become internalized as a dependably calming structure of the self. Transitory experiences of idealization cannot strengthen self-cohesion to a sufficient degree, however.

In dependent personality disorder, dependency becomes the mainstay of a compensatory structure and can be important for achieving viable self-cohesion. Thus, dependency is not necessarily considered pejoratively as a symptom or characterological weakness but rather as a form of relating to a sustaining selfobject environment to make one's way in the world. Dependency, in this sense, stabilizes the self, though it is simultaneously a by-product of its success. Success, however, is a relative consideration, because compensatory structures may not entirely repair earlier injuries to an unmirrored self. Thus, for example, what is thought of as pathological (excessive) dependency is maladaptive, because it implies a brittle sense of the reliability of idealizing selfobjects. Dependency may thus fail to achieve a self-consolidating function should idealizing or twinship selfobjects fall short in providing a calming function that strengthens the self. Alternatively, dependent patients may in some way fail to internalize selfobject functions to solidify self-cohesion in the absence of their idealized selfobjects.

Thus, idealization or twinship takes the place of mirroring to secure and maintain dependent patients' self-cohesion. No longer prominently seeking affirmation of themselves, such patients typically turn to idealized selfobjects to experience the calming, tension-regulating gratification resulting from a compensatory structure built on idealization. Twinship selfobjects may provide a similar function through the conviction that such selfobjects are just like oneself. Both of these selfobject functions can invigorate the self by strengthening self-cohesion, compensating in this way for the depletion of deficient mirroring. Even with a relatively successful formation of a compensatory structure, dependent patients have an ongoing need for the comforting availability of idealizing or twinship selfobjects. Excessive dependency behavior and extreme sensitivity to rejection, however, indicate that a compensatory structure has failed to take root as an adequately internalized selfobject function. I suggest that a notable degree of dependency persists in both cases: It may exist in a contained, stable form if a compensatory structure is established, but in marked dependency, clinging and anxious, fretful concern about abandonment signal the degree of pathological dysfunction that defines a dependent personality disorder.

Kohut (1971) distinguished different degrees of idealization based on traumatic disruption of selfobject responsiveness. Early trauma disposes individuals to disruptions of tension regulation, and they may seek soothing through substance use or sexualization to calm tension states. Addictive behaviors may signal a faulty idealized selfobject function in which substances, relied on to soothe tension states, come to replace an internalized aspect of self experience. They serve the function of providing the assured calming that idealized selfobjects could not. Severe or chronic mirroring deficits may result in prominent vulnerabilities surrounding loss or unavailability of idealized selfobjects, which is particularly characteristic of dependent personality disorder because the concern about loss or separation is so pronounced. Disappointment in idealized selfobjects results when they cease to provide the level of responsiveness that dependent patients require. Their disillusionment precipitates a renewed search for new idealizing selfobjects to replace the self-regulating engagement they cannot manage without. It can be said that the function of selfobjects to strengthen or vitalize the self is transformed into the requirement that selfobjects take the place of an independent sense of self. Dependent patients' passive orientation to life (Millon, 1996) influences their characteristic acquiescence, which is built around an image of themselves as incapable of existing independently of their selfobjects.

Clinical Illustration of Dependent Personality Disorder

Ms. H. was a 23-year-old married Black woman who sought treatment at the recommendation of her employer. She had been contemplating undertaking treatment for several years, but it was not until her husband of 5 years spoke with Ms. H.'s boss about psychotherapy on her behalf that she felt confident enough to initiate treatment. Ms. H. and her husband worked in the same department of a manufacturing company, she as a receptionist and he in a sales position. In her previous job, Ms. H. had typically phoned her husband several times a day to complain about how mean her boss was to her. Her husband had secured the job Ms. H. currently held, and she saw her husband much of the time throughout the day. As she described it, "We're now together 24 hours a day."

After Ms. H. had been at her current job for 18 months, her supervisor announced that he would be leaving the company. Ms. H. felt, as she described it, that "I'll fall apart now; I don't know what I'm going to do." It was this event that precipitated her seeking psychotherapy and our first consultation. She was angry and felt deserted by her supervisor, whom she greatly admired, and she also was anxious because she did not know who would replace him or how her position might change. She telephoned me twice in the 4 days between our first and second appointments, not knowing how to manage her anxiety. I tried to provide some general reassurance, because I did not yet know enough about her clinical history or personality resources to understand what her telephone calls represented. I recognized, however, that she might have had the idea that she could contact me regularly as she felt the need to do so. I did not consider that the degree of anxiety this patient conveyed suggested an urgent clinical need, and I asked her to try to refrain from calling unless she felt there was an appreciable worsening of her mental status. She remained anxious but stable over the next few weeks, taking 3 days off to stay at home in the company of a close friend for support. Her internist prescribed diazepam, and she stayed in close contact with her husband and friends. After a month, Ms. H. terminated treatment, feeling less anxious but also frustrated at my attempt to limit contact with her to office visits spaced about 5 days apart. She was planning to seek a counselor through a local mental health agency, where she believed she could call or drop in as needed.

Ms. H.'s mother had divorced her father when Ms. H. was 7 years old. Ms. H. was angry with her mother for driving her father away, and she still did not understand why her parents divorced. She had continued to see her father following the divorce, though infrequently. Her relationship with him was cordial but distant, but she looked forward to his visits. Her father died when Ms. H. was 14 years old. Her mother remarried when Ms. H. was 17, but her mother divorced this second husband after only 10 months.

While an adolescent, Ms. H. greatly admired her elder brother and turned to him for advice and direction because she spurned her mother's advice as useless to her. The brother had a drinking problem, which Ms. H. downplayed until she could no longer ignore its seriousness. Throughout her adolescence, Ms. H. remained anxiously close to her mother while admiring her brother, whom she felt could do no wrong. Her attachment to her brother began before her father's death, and it became stronger—but not prominently so—after her father died. It was shortly after the brother's drinking problem became more evident about 5 years before she began treatment that she seemed to give up her idealization of him, feeling disappointment and anger because idealizing the brother had appeared to be sustaining for her. Ms. H. directed her anger and bitterness toward her mother, blaming her for driving away two husbands and for the brother's downfall.

Ms. H. seemed to feel lost as her compensatory idealization collapsed with her brother's deterioration. She blamed her mother, unable to realize that her bitterness toward her mother stemmed from having no real expectation that mirroring selfobject responsiveness was available from others. Consistent with deficient mirroring, this patient reported that she often felt bored and unsure about what she wanted for herself. Goals and ambitions seemed to follow instead of lead the decisions Ms. H. made or the direction her life assumed. She did well in high school but dropped out of college because the courses were "too easy" for her. She could not imagine ways she could have made her college life more engaging or interesting. She seemed either to turn to others for a purpose or to attach herself to familiar and comfortable situations around which she built her life.

When she had become unable to sustain her idealization of her brother 5 years previously, Ms. H. briefly consulted a psychotherapist in connection with an upsurge of angry bitterness toward her mother. She was surprised that her mother would not come with her; Ms. H. had simply assumed that her mother would also attend the sessions. Yet Ms. H. complained that her mother never let her make decisions for herself, that they communicated poorly, and that she felt that her mother misunderstood her. She also felt misunderstood when the therapist showed greater interest in the patient's relationship with her deceased father, at which point Ms. H. discontinued treatment.

Shortly thereafter, Ms. H. married a man she had been dating for 1 year "for no real reason—I wanted to break away from my mother and family." She had initially turned to her boyfriend as a protector she could admire and idealize, much as she had previously looked up to her brother. Several months after their marriage, her husband accepted a job in another city. While living in the other city, Ms. H. found herself uncomfortably distant from the edgy but close relationship with her mother and was perturbed by her husband's apparent unwillingness to appreciate how unhappy she felt. At her insistence, they moved back after being away for just 1 year. She gradually insinuated herself into her husband's workplace, thus perpetuating a level of close dependency despite feeling as psychologically alienated from him as she did from her mother.

Ms. H. seemed to look to her husband—as she had to her brother before him—to make all the troubles of her life disappear. Ms. H. was not happy in the marriage; she believed that her husband dismissed her problems as imaginary. Nonetheless, she had called him frequently when she was unhappy at her previous job, and she enjoyed working close by him in the same office. Ms. H. felt dependent on her mother and husband in spite of her dissatisfaction with both of these relationships, and she felt the need to have them close by or to know their whereabouts at all times. As an example of her near-clinging dependency, she would urge her husband and mother to return as quickly as possible whenever either one went out.

Ms. H. presented for treatment at a point of destabilized psychological equilibrium, and she did not remain in treatment long enough to confirm my suspicion that comorbid Axis I and Axis II disturbances were present. My impression was that her admired boss's anticipated move revived prominent dependency needs and intensified her clinging behaviors. The idealizing selfobject functions she had managed to secure from the boss now felt threatened. Ms. H. admired her boss's facility in making decisions and taking charge of difficult situations. She described his forceful determination glowingly, but she did not take her silent idealization to a level that posed a threat to her marriage. She thus seemed to re-create with her boss the psychological circumstances of her admiring idealization of her brother; she felt as dropped and deserted by her boss's relocation as she had by her brother's deterioration. Wherever the patient turned, she seemed unable to experience affirming, mirroring selfobject responsiveness, but she appeared to thrive on the idealizing selfobject functions provided in her relationships with her brother and boss.

I could not be certain how she had experienced her father's death at age 14, but I doubted that he had provided an admiring or echoing presence that might have constituted some degree of mirroring responsiveness. I also was unsure whether this patient earlier on attempted to forge an idealizing selfobject relationship with her father to provide a sense of calming reassurance. She did report recurring dreams of her father in a casket telling her that he was really alive. When she had this dream, Ms. H. would awaken her husband, asking him to stay awake with her so she would not be alone.

Ms. H. sought treatment at times in her life when existing idealizing selfobject functions threatened to unravel—5 years ago with her brother, and now with her boss. She had difficulty sustaining her precarious self-cohesion and was easily disappointed in the people she turned to as idealized selfobjects. She was crushed by the collapse of the temporarily stabilizing idealization of her brother when his deterioration was too disillusioning to sustain her brittle self-cohesion. She felt let down by her brother's alcoholism, which made it hard to continue admiring him and restimulated her disappointment and anger at her mother for failing her and her brother. Ms. H. had prematurely terminated treatment attempts on two occasions, first with a therapist whom she felt misunderstood her and then with me when she did not like hearing that she could not simply call or come by when she felt the need.

There was no indication that the idealized selfobjects she depended on to temporarily sustain a brittle self had firmly taken root to establish a more durable compensatory structure. She latched on to idealized selfobjects for as long as they remained available and held on to ambivalently perceived selfobjects who failed her in other ways. She seemed to lack a sense of who she was or what she wanted in her life—a frequent observation in people who not only have mirroring deficits but also seem to have little sense that affirmation of their talents and abilities is even possible, let alone expectable. Thus, she married her husband not because she had strong feelings for him but rather because he was there at a time when she felt desperate. She could not recover from having lost her idealized brother's sustaining availability, and she could not bear turning to her mother, who may have failed her as a mirroring selfobject. I suspected that she also sensed that her husband would indulge her dependency on him; consequently, she was comforted in knowing that he did not mind her relying on him for frequent contact when she felt needy. However, Ms. H. was not happy in her marriage, because she felt misunderstood and was not able to indicate to her husband a need she herself could barely comprehend.

Ms. H.'s feelings of chronic dissatisfaction with her mother suggested a quality of responsiveness that seemed too insubstantial to have established firmed-up self-cohesion based on mirroring. Ms. H. seemed to feel ignored by her mother, whom she felt to be preoccupied or unobservant. Ms. H. married a man whom she felt she could rely on, but also whom she hoped would protect her from her ambivalent relationship with her mother, whom she perceived as disappointing. Her ambivalence toward her husband suggested to me that being able to turn to him with anxious dependency was not the same thing as being able to admire a strong, vigorous idealized selfobject, but that it would have to do. As in her relationship with her mother, Ms. H.'s excessive and clinging dependency represented her best attempt to get by.

Ultimately, there was little evidence that Ms. H. had established a compensatory structure centering on idealization to stabilize and repair her brittle self-cohesion. Both dependent on and disappointed in her mother, Ms. H. had little hope of securing an idealized selfobject function with the mother. Her brother was unable to continue to provide this function either, when his own troubles had led to an escalating drinking problem. As her admiring relationship with the brother became unsustainable, Ms. H. impulsively married her husband in part to protect herself from lapsing into a dependent relationship with her chronically unsatisfying mother. Now disappointed in both her husband and her mother, Ms. H. had formed an idealizing selfobject relationship with her boss, and his leaving the company meant that another opportunity to establish a compensatory structure based on idealization was thwarted.

Kohut did not specifically address hysteria, nor did he differentiate between hysterical neurosis and hysterical or histrionic personality. Kohut (1996) did comment that hysterical personalities bring their dramatized clinical presentation to the developing transference in treatment, but he regarded such manifestations as masking a depression associated with empty, needy longings. He observed, for example, histrionic patients' inclination to "immediately fall in love with the therapist, they immediately are jealous of the therapist and his wife, or what have you. They threaten suicide" (Kohut, 1996, p. 116). Kohut, like most analysts and psychotherapists, considered such patients to be rare in contemporary clinical practice. He regarded hysterical patients as "pseudohysterics," because they characteristically conceal, even from themselves, a lonely depletion depression behind the noisy veneer they often present of romantic fantasies, frenetic activity, and sometimes self-overmedication or signs of substance abuse potential. Speaking about drive theory and ego psychology's emphasis on hysteria as a disturbance of the oedipal stage of libidinal development, Kohut (1996) wrote,

> The more you interpret the oedipal period, the worse they get because they are afraid those ideas [that they are in love with the analyst] will be taken away from them. Why? Because it is the continuous activity in the romantic conflict sphere of the oedipal background that gives them the sense of being alive. . . . They don't openly tell you that underneath they have a sense of emptiness, a sense of having something to fill in. . . . You must undercut the supposed oedipal issues by telling the patient you think that all this romantic falling in love probably covers a great sense of neediness . . . and then the patient will feel understood, and there will be a toning down of all the romantic and jealous and suicide threatening fireworks, and one can perhaps begin to go to work on the depressive sense of the self. (pp. 116–117)

Probably for Kohut, this description represented a self psychological version of the adage "Scratch a hysteric, and one finds a borderline"; what Kohut found, however, was a self disorder.

Thus, Kohut (1996) did not consider it essential that forbidden oedipal impulses be repressed to protect the ego. Rather, he regarded the oedipal wishes of hysteria as healthy manifestations of a prideful, vigorous self that require only to be responded to as such by the selfobject environment. Viewed in this way, oedipal impulses are strivings revealing what invigorates the self and not unacceptable urges to be eliminated. Kohut's interest was mainly to characterize the selfobject functions that sustain self-cohesion.

Kohut (1996, p. 116) regarded pseudohysterias as showing a "pseudo-oedipal involvement" that makes use of the drive upsurge of this developmental period to serve a function of intensifying the experience of a psychologically stimulated rather than a depressed or deadened self. He compared this with head banging or other forms of self-stimulation some deprived children engage in to feel psychologically vitalized. It also resembles adult manifestations of a depleted self, such as substance use; compulsive sexuality; or the exhilaration of normal activities that bring heightened pleasure, such as mountain climbing or intense athletic enterprises. Kohut also made the point that some children's experience of a chronically understimulating parental selfobject environment reflects their parents' unawareness of their developmental strivings for recognition. Histrionic patients have a vulnerable sense of self-esteem as a consequence of diminished, uninvolved engagement with their selfobject needs. Accordingly, they may exaggerate their experience of the oedipal phase and the fantasied longings it gives rise to in order to relieve the emptiness or joylessness of their existence.

Stated another way, Kohut's (1971, 1977) view of the oedipal phase resembled what could be thought of as the proud phallic narcissism of a young child with the language, motor, and conceptual skills to recognize in him- or herself a potential sense of mastery. Such a child desires only to show his or her mettle joyfully as an emerging man or woman in a playful display. That it is unrealistic or inflated is beside the point; the oedipal child looks to his or her parental selfobjects to acknowledge the normal grandiose impulse and to play along. An empathically responsive reaction by such selfobjects is to reflect through their own pride the sense of achievement the child is experiencing as a normal consequence of maturation. Kohut (1977) wrote,

> The parents will react to the sexual desires and to the competitive rivalry of the child by becoming sexually stimulated and counteraggressive, and, at the same time, they will react with joy and pride to the child's developmental achievement, to his vigor and assertiveness. (p. 230)

The oedipal child thus looks for the expectable glow of empathic joy from his or her oedipal selfobjects to affirm the budding robustness of the self. Kohut (1984) stated,

> The baby is born strong, not weak. . . . The human baby is born into a milieu of empathic–responsive selfobjects [that] can be properly taken as a baseline of normal psychological experience—the baby *is* strong—just as his being born into a milieu of oxygen can be properly taken as the baseline of his physiological functioning—the baby *is* healthy. (pp. 212–213)

Empathic failures by otherwise responsive parental selfobjects disappoint the oedipal child by undermining his or her normal needs for joyful pride. Their empathic breaches transform affectionate displays into fragmented sexual urges or turn healthy, playful assertion into destructive hostility. Both outcomes lead to conflict, anxiety, and the symptomatic or characterological disturbances of histrionic or obsessive–compulsive disorders. The crucial phenomenon Kohut (1977, 1984) emphasized was the fearfulness of children exposed to parental failures as oedipal selfobjects. He speculated that such parents misconstrue their children's needs because of their own overstimulation by and discomfort with their oedipal children's behavior or because of competitive retaliation. Such children's prideful self-cohesion thus begins to feel undermined, and they may experience their affectionate or assertive desires as being replaced by sexual or aggressive impulses, which come to represent disintegration products.

From the standpoint of how a parent's self-cohesion influences an oedipal child's self-cohesion, Kohut (1977) made the point in the following way, placing the oedipal phase requirements for parental selfobject empathic responsiveness in a similar context as the requirements of developmental periods preceding it:

> Parents who are not able to establish empathic contact with the developing self of the child will, in other words, tend to see the constituents of the child's oedipal aspirations in isolation—they will tend to see (even though generally only preconsciously) alarming sexuality and alarming hostility in the child instead of larger configurations of assertive affection and assertive competition—with the result that the child's oedipal conflicts will become intensified—just as a mother whose own self is poorly consolidated will react to the feces and the anal region and not to the total vigorous, proudly assertive anal-phase self of her child. (pp. 234–235)

Kohut (1977) believed that children who had more or less successfully established a firmed-up nuclear self could still be vulnerable to conflict later on during the oedipal stage. He did not consider the oedipal phase to be necessarily pathogenic, although he recognized that its incomplete or faulty resolution could produce overt psychopathology. But Kohut did not necessarily regard such disorders as structural neuroses in the traditional psychoanalytic sense. He instead viewed them as self disorders in which the self had become weakened or fragmented because the selfobjects of this developmental phase had failed to recognize and consequently to respond empathically to an oedipal child's expressions of affection or assertiveness. Parental empathic failures at this juncture lead therefore to disintegration products of a self undermined by a normal enough, joyful sense of competence associated with this phase of development. Such disintegration products represent a self that is overwhelmed by sexual or hostile–aggressive impulses.

I provide two illustrative examples. Both contain elements that might suggest a drive theory interpretation based on oedipal stage dynamics. Indeed, the first illustration—one of Freud's infrequent published case studies, Anna O.—was one of the earliest prototypical illustrations of the oedipal conflict in psychoanalysis. However, I will discuss the histrionic features from a self psychological viewpoint rather than from a drive theory perspective. The second example is from *The Psychology of the Self: A Casebook* (Goldberg,

1978). I present the illustration to show that what may seem to indicate a patient is turning to idealized selfobjects turns out, on closer scrutiny, to indicate that he or she is instead seeking mirroring responsiveness. These cases suggest how idealization may be the basis for patients' attempts to recover from chronic mirroring selfobject failures.

M. Tolpin (1993) reformulated one of the earliest and best known classic reports of hysteria in psychoanalysis, that of Anna O., who was a patient of Freud's colleague Josef Breuer. This patient fell ill around the time of her beloved father's terminal illness and death. Her hysterical illness consisted of falling into a somnolent state every afternoon that deepened after sunset into states of consciousness characterized by gaps in her train of thought; hallucinations of black snakes; and self-reports of darkness in her head, inability to think, becoming blind and deaf, and loss of the ability to think and speak in German (which gave way either to speaking English or a jargonlike mixture of several languages). Such states alternated with states of clear sensorium and lucid speech.

M. Tolpin (1993) reconsidered observations that Breuer recorded but did not include in *Studies in Hysteria* (Breuer & Freud, 1893–1895/1955). Anna O.'s tempestuous clinical course appeared to be in part provoked by her erotically tinged devotion to her father during his illness and by the transference formed with Breuer, who listened, as her father probably also did, with animated interest to Anna O.'s richly elaborated "private theatre . . . to embellish her monotonous life . . . to try to enliven herself " (M. Tolpin, 1993, pp. 12–13). Tolpin commented that whereas Freud viewed this as a product of repressed sexual urges, Breuer was more impressed by his patient's deprived *nourishment*—Breuer's word—and of her imagination and intelligence. M. Tolpin thought that Anna O.'s normal needs to be recognized and admired were thwarted by both parents, particularly her father, who strictly limited her education and imposed on her a restrictive lifestyle, despite his appreciation of his daughter's creative and intellectual gifts.

M. Tolpin's (1993) reconceptualization describes an example of a compensatory structure. M. Tolpin believed that Breuer's and her father's responsiveness to Anna O.'s thwarted needs did not remobilize the eroticization of an oedipal conflict but rather restarted and thus revitalized the stunted unmirrored self. Anna O. admired her father and—in treatment—Breuer; in her treatment with Breuer she thus came to life in a vivid psychological sense, making use of idealization as a compensatory structure. This structure enabled Breuer's patient to transform deficient mirroring into a degree of self-cohesion sufficient to sustain her career of humanitarian service and use of her creative imagination to write fiction and plays. Moreover, Anna O., encouraged and appreciated by a more stimulating involvement with her mother's extended family, discovered two women writers from another century whose work about women's rights deeply inspired her. She translated their writings and developed a passionate interest in women's rights. Thus,

Anna O. "could idealize, emulate, and metabolize those women into her own self protein, so to speak" (M. Tolpin, 1993, p. 22) to form the solid base of a compensatory structure built on idealization. Years after her illness, M. Tolpin wrote, this compensatory structure allowed Anna O. to reconstitute a self that had been disrupted first by her father's illness and later by interruptions in her treatment with Breuer.

The crucial point M. Tolpin (1993) made was that Anna O.'s thwarted mirroring needs could be restimulated with idealization as a compensatory structure. Idealized selfobject functions were sufficient to restore this patient's empathic responsiveness to allow her to pursue talents and goals instead of submerging them in fragmentations such as the hysterical conversion symptoms usually mentioned in reference to this case. To restore an unmirrored self that was unrevivable through mirroring, Anna O. may have managed to find a solution through idealization that could be sustained by an empathically responsive selfobject environment—a solution that would ultimately be cemented as an enduring, albeit vulnerable, compensatory structure out of which a modicum of self-cohesion could be constructed.

Although this reformulation of Anna O.'s illness and recovery provides a good example of a compensatory structure, I do not wish to suggest that such a successfully established compensatory structure is an expectable outcome of histrionic personality disorder. (Anna O. likely would not be considered today to have histrionic personality disorder as presently understood.) Most histrionic personality disorder patients are unsuccessful in their attempts to turn to idealized selfobjects to recover from a primary injury to the self in the mirroring sector.

Goldberg's (1978) case of a young woman with inhibited sexuality whose low-key appearance and dress subtly belied seductively calling attention to herself also would be regarded in classical drive theory as involving a hysterical personality. Aspects of this patient's eroticized transference corresponded with the sexualized attention seeking and coquettish manifestations of her other relationships, also seen in histrionic personality disorders. The focal issue in this extensive report of a 6-year analysis was that conflicts resulting from oedipal dynamics arose from a sense of injury and deprivation.

The patient's histrionic presentation was founded on her reliance on fantasies about fragile idealized selfobjects that easily collapsed when she was reexposed to a self state of chronic deficiency. For example, her fear of orgasm—she said she feared "my arms and legs will fly off. Oh, I hadn't meant to say that!" (Goldberg, 1978, p. 316)—was related to feeling out of control, which was juxtaposed with her frequent elaborate erotic daydreams about powerful, handsome men. Her feelings of being out of control related to her mother's selective disregard of the patient's developmental needs as a young girl after the mother became preoccupied with a new baby. The patient felt chronically ignored and psychologically dropped because she had not yet developed sufficient self-cohesion and a capacity for self-regulation. When she felt ignored as an adult, she turned with overcharged sexual stimulation to strong men to feel fortified.

The treating analyst regarded the crucial dynamic not as a focal oedipal struggle but rather as this patient's having been drawn into an intense self–selfobject relationship with her on-again, off-again self-absorbed mother who no longer needed her and then criticized her. The mother's chronic empathic failures effectively closed off the mirroring sector of the self as a viable means to internalize self-cohesion. The patient's preoccupation with idealized, omnipotent selfobjects in a sexualized form was the solution she found to secure self-cohesion. These desired selfobjects represented the calming safety that one so injured can merge with to secure protective soothing. In this case, however, this solution did not succeed in providing calming. It represented this patient's mirroring longings more than idealization to secure calming self-cohesion, because her solution was not internalized as a stable compensatory structure.

It is instructive to contrast this patient's fear of her arms and legs flying off during orgasm, representing disruption of self-cohesion, with M. Tolpin's (1997) comparison between pathological sexual excitement and "flying" in the sense of being transported by sexual stimulation. A sense of abandon represented by being transported could be possible when, as an outcome of normal development, selfobject needs are responded to in a calming, strengthening manner. In the *Casebook* example (Goldberg, 1978), the patient experienced herself as living the depleted existence of someone who seemed not to know what to do with intense needs that she could not easily stabilize. She attempted to repair injuries to a vulnerable self by her absorbing fantasies about eroticized, intriguing relationships, accompanied by the inhibited sexuality and attention-seeking features associated with histrionic personality disorder. In contrast to M. Tolpin's example of sexual excitement that is experienced when self-cohesion is firmed up, this patient's sexual excitement represented an experience of fragmentation. She could not easily regulate or calm herself because self-cohesion was destabilized.

Considered from a self psychological vantage point, these two cases demonstrate how histrionic personality disorder may be viewed as a condition that is organized around striving to establish an alternative pathway for securing cohesiveness of the self. Taking the form of a compensatory structure, such an alternative path is oriented toward idealization or twinship attempts to effect a recovery from a mirroring selfobject deficiency that is usually not repairable. The problem for histrionic patients is that they often fail to establish a viable compensatory structure. Consequently, they rarely achieve recovery from impaired self-cohesion.

Histrionic patients' orientation to the selfobjects they search for centers on a dramatic presentation of themselves. On close examination, their immature, grandstanding attention seeking usually reveals a deeper sense of desperation, longing, and emptiness that results from a mirroring disturbance in which their selfobject environment was unable to ensure affirmation of a budding, emerging sense of self. Superficial in articulating affect states, such patients display how a disturbed capacity for self-regulation disposes them to indiscriminately express tension states that they usually do not even recognize as inner tension. Thus, flitting here and there and everywhere becomes such persons' way of both reaching for and avoiding something they vaguely sense they need. They do not comprehend, however, that it is a well-internalized self-regulatory function they lack.

More often than not, such patients' mirroring deficit plays itself out in the form of coquettish, seductive hypersexuality, although it soon becomes evident that sexuality, whether mature or as a guise for being cared for in a childlike way, has little to do with the self-cohesion histrionic patients need. Their provocative behavior frequently leads others to think that they are conveying romantic intentions, but when others respond to such signals, histrionic patients act surprised or offended. They often fail to realize that although they intend their expressions to communicate to others that they are seeking idealization or twinship (soul mate) selfobject relationships, such expressions are easily misinterpreted by the objects of their flirtations, who may feel teased and angry. Indeed, mature love relationships do not commonly develop, because such patients lack sufficient psychological capacities to manage the deep affective involvement that goes beyond exaggerated, unrealistic illusions based on their pronounced mirroring needs. Thus, eroticization of relationships and dramatization of ongoing experiences, including those that occur in treatment, overlie a depleted, depressed core of an unmirrored self attempting to replace neediness and longing with "fireworks . . . that [give] them the sense of being alive" (Kohut, 1996, p. 117).

It could be argued that the shallow affects and difficulty regulating tension states found in histrionic personality disorder patients prevent them from establishing alternative pathways such as compensatory structures to repair self-cohesion deficits. Deficient mirroring exposes such patients to the usual consequences of devitalization and depletion; however, they experience affects superficially as they attempt to dispel unmirrored self states through their characteristic histrionic attention-seeking behavior. They may look up to others intensely and feel that they cannot manage without such exaggerated idealizations. They are prone to feeling unresponded to or disappointed, though they typically ward off disturbing affect states such as these through activity, flirtatious hypersexuality, or dramatizing affects. Consequently, because they repeatedly seek out admiring mirroring selfobjects— without understanding that they often get nowhere in this attempt—they do not usually develop a capacity to seek out selfobjects who can genuinely be idealized or who are enough like themselves to forge and thus stabilize self-cohesion.

Histrionic patients are likely to strive for mirroring responsiveness over and over, failing to comprehend that such efforts rarely succeed in sufficiently repairing their diminished self-cohesion. Their apparently limited capacity to recognize affect states beyond a general state of distress interferes with responding to their selfobject environment in ways other than making dramatic appeals to be admired. Consequently, histrionic patients appear incapable of establishing a genuine capacity for idealization. Instead, they seem to continually seek mirroring selfobject responsiveness that is unlikely to be forthcoming or sustainable.

Histrionic patients' dramatic clamoring for attention prevents them from escaping the emotional rut that characterizes their existence, and they remain weakened and vulnerable. Dysregulation states only restimulate the need for mirroring selfobject responsiveness. Thus, they remain stuck within their limited adaptive coping, and they are simultaneously distressed and perplexed that their efforts lead nowhere. Unlike dependent personality disorder, in which idealization or twinship may perhaps become the foundation of a stable compensatory structure, histrionic personality disorder patients most often fail to solidify an alternative route to secure self-cohesion. What may look like efforts to establish idealizing or twinship selfobject functions merely disguise these patients' real intent—to seek mirroring selfobject responsiveness—which most of the time seems doomed. Histrionic patients thus fail to get close enough to what they need to establish a stable compensatory structure as an alternative pathway to securing self-cohesion.

Clinical Illustration of Histrionic Personality Disorder

Ms. I., a 30-year-old married White woman with two children, was admitted to a medical service specializing in treating disorders with psychiatric sequelae. The program provided a modified inpatient psychiatric milieu that operated from an unlocked medical unit. Ms. I. complained of having felt vague abdominal pressures during the previous year, which she described as feeling like "someone was putting their hand there and pushing on it." Medical workups both before and during this hospitalization were negative, and the patient's internist and consulting gastroenterologist, feeling entertained by her but simultaneously annoyed, finally became impatient with her protestations and increasingly frequent office visits. They strongly suggested and then finally insisted that she attend this medical–psychiatric program, which she adamantly resisted doing for months, denying that her problem was psychological in nature. She had also refused to consult with a psychiatrist.

Her internist was an affable, fatherly man whose patients found him down-to-earth and approachable. As he got to know Ms. I. better, he realized that her relationships with her parents were problematic, a view she continually refused to accept, claiming she could not see how he got this idea. Rather than dismissing her as an annoying patient who drained his time, the internist was amused that Ms. I. could be so blindly oblivious to such a simple observation. Admittedly falling for her charming yet pathetic manner, he realized that he enjoyed talking with her and that she reminded him of Scarlett O'Hara in *Gone With the Wind*. He went along with her requests for more and more diagnostic studies, and he felt flattered by the appreciation she expressed during their talks; she repeatedly told him how much she looked up to him and his opinions. However, he also recognized that he was perpetuating her dependency on him, so he told her that he could no longer continue treating her unless she consented to the present hospitalization. The patient reluctantly agreed to his request, because it was the only way to keep him as her doctor. A psychiatric consultation ordered shortly after admission revealed no prominent Axis I condition. Ms. I. was prescribed a low dose of an anxiolytic compound, more to let her feel that she was getting some kind of treatment than because the consultant thought it was clinically warranted. The paragraphs that follow describe her hospital course; her behavior toward the treatment team, of which I was a member; and the milieu.

My diagnostic interviews with Ms. I. were characterized by difficulty in getting her to focus on the questions I asked. She acted in an overly friendly, almost chummy manner until she felt pushed in a direction she did not want to go. For example, when I asked Ms. I. about her father, she said that he was intellectual, quiet, and businesslike. She felt close to him, but she added that she did not feel that the relationship was affectionate. Her manner suggested a longing for something more in her relationship with her father, but it was difficult to get her to elaborate. Ms. I. would quickly say that I was putting words in her mouth about things she did not feel. She was skillful at being elusive, although she managed to say (or, I thought, to let slip out) that her father was not at home very much. After I tried to ask more about what she meant, Ms. I. acted confused by my questions, and she succeeded in throwing me off track. By the time the interview was over, I was not sure myself whether she had told me that she was referring to her father's absence now or while she was growing up in the parental home. I realized afterward that she easily slipped into feeling confused whenever she felt uncomfortable, blaming my questions as the cause of her confusion.

Ms. I. had been a homemaker since marrying 7 years previously, and she was formerly a salesperson in a department store. She had lived with her parents until she was married, except for a brief period when she had her own apartment—an idea her father "approved of" but which her mother did not. She returned to the parental home after having a car accident soon after she moved into the apartment so her mother could nurse her injuries. Ms. I. remained at her parents' home until she married 2 years later. She then resided one block from her parents' home in a house her parents bought for her and her husband, who was a salesman who had worked in her father's business for the past 3 years. Ms. I. stated that "the whole family works for my father," indicating that both of her brothers, in addition to her husband, were employed by her father.

Ms. I. said that her relationship with her mother was close, which she followed by saying that her mother was understanding of her "when she wants to be." The patient felt that as a result of her illnesses, her mother had learned to be concerned about her. My asking her to say more about this comment once again flustered Ms. I., who claimed that she did not understand what I was asking from her and that she felt she had told me so much about her family. She often experienced my interview questions as attacks or was confused by them. She would act petulant at such times, sometimes playfully so, and I sometimes wondered whether Ms. I. was acting flirtatiously. The inflections in her voice would increase, and she would suddenly draw blanks and then helplessly ask me to remind her what we were talking about. One effect of this interplay was to make me think twice about asking about anything, and I caught myself feeling angry at falling into her trap in spite of my resolve to avoid being taken in after I finally figured out what was going on. I felt like I was held hostage at one moment and then made into a villain the next, until finally—before I knew what was happening—I was drawn into having to rescue a damsel in distress.

I also soon discovered that Ms. I. would take nurses into her confidence about my questions that confused her, asking them for advice about what they thought she should say. Staff meetings revealed that this patient acted in a similar way with a dietician, who suggested dietary changes and attempted to make this patient aware of the links between her moods and her physical pain. Ms. I. vehemently rejected such ideas and was confused about what the dietician was trying to tell her. She insisted on alleviating her gastrointestinal distress without making any dietary changes.

This was the way it went, no matter what the topic or whom she spoke to. She told different stories to different people, and we had to resolve inconsistencies and fill in the many gaps she created (which she did masterfully, we all thought), taking our best guesses about what she actually had said. Indeed, one staff member commented that discussions of Ms. I. were more like a television quiz show than a treatment planning meeting. The entire staff was frustrated by her.

Ms. I. had engaged quickly with the treatment team staff, but she was not interested in other patients on the unit. She felt, I suspected, that other patients only distracted the staff from attending to her—not because she felt a sense of entitlement or that her problems were more interesting than anyone else's, but because she needed so much. Moreover, seeing other patients as distractions to begin with, she acted increasingly petulant and injured when other patients made disparaging comments in group psychotherapy about her self-indulgent manner. Ms. I. felt additionally injured when unit staff did not come to her defense.

Ms. I. managed to elicit maternal concern from some patients, whereas others found her vain, immature, and preoccupied with herself to an extent that she seemed indifferent to others. In various therapeutic groups and milieu community meetings, the patients who sensed her vulnerability seemed to want to protect her from critical and angry attacks by other patients who resented her childish, defenseless demeanor. Feeling herself to be too absorbed with her own problems to be of much use to other patients, she would occasionally make a comment (usually only when she felt she had to say something because other people had offered comments or suggestions), but what she had to say was characteristically trite or naive. Ms. I. behaved in a helpless, injured manner when her husband visited. Her father did not visit the unit, although her mother visited about twice each week. Her mother appeared stiff and uncomfortable in the hospital surroundings; she seemed eager to leave as soon as she could.

Ms. I. was skillful at being elusive, evidently to protect herself, but this need for self-protection was hard to empathize with, because the entire staff felt that she had undermined them and made them feel like failures. She came across as more defensive than paranoid, in part because she had a child-like, playful quality rather than an angry, accusatory tone. Nevertheless, she challenged our every effort to understand how she experienced the important people in her life. After several diagnostic interviews, I finally threw in the towel, feeling defeated and also ashamed that I had let her get the better of me when I had not even realized that the interviews had become a combat zone. Ms. I. seemed to engender similar reactions in most of the male staff and some female staff, almost all of whom spoke frequently about her "manipulativeness" and our need eventually to "confront" her—although initially we were not sure what it was we wanted to confront her about. We finally understood that her internist, initially charmed by and sympathetic toward her, eventually had felt impotent and wanted to be rid of her. The treatment team's "confrontation" represented little more than an ill-fated group accusation of the patient's manipulations—more out of frustration than anger—that likely repeated what the internist probably had done so that he would no longer continue feeling that he had failed. He, like us, felt frustrated more than angry with Ms. I. We could imagine why she needed to sidetrack everyone, but we also felt unable to stop her train. Ms. I. discharged herself, although she remained a patient of the admitting internist. We referred to our final staff conference on Ms. I. as her (and our) "postmortem."

Our frustration stemmed from being unable to successfully intervene to treat Ms. I.'s problem, despite being able to see it developing. We learned from the internist a few months later that his own frustration with Ms. I. reached a point at which he discharged her from his practice. Everyone involved in her treatment seemed thrown off course by her, though we still felt sympathetic and wanted to somehow protect this forlorn creature. These are not the usual sentiments felt by therapists who treat difficult manipulative patients (many of whom have borderline personality disorder). Splitting and projective identification are concepts therapists often use to understand patients who enact their psychological dynamics in ways that enrage or humiliate others. However frustrating histrionic patients may at times appear, therapists often see them as lost sheep whom they want to protect, because such patients go around in circles seeking mirroring responsiveness that hardly ever becomes metabolized as an internal structure. Patients like Ms. I. seem to need more and more; little apparently stays with them, and they come back for more of the same with no apparent end in sight. It is for this reason that histrionic personality disorder patients are frequently referred to as people constantly needing to be "fed."

It is possible that Ms. I. was ambivalently ignored as a child, leading her to size up whether people were on her side or whether they expected her to function more autonomously than she felt capable of. Thus, she sought ever-constant mirroring by eliciting signs of sensitive awareness of every feeling state. Ms. I. perceived almost anything else as an empathic breach, reacting as if others' incapacity to recognize her brittleness represented insensitivity and feeling confused or distressed. Her self-dramatizing, injured presentation seemed to divide the world into a sympathetic selfobject environment that attended to her need to be seen as vulnerable, on the one hand, and a punitive, rejecting selfobject environment that wanted her to grow up and assume responsibility for herself, on the other hand. She sought benevolent people to provide a calming function, but she had trouble comprehending why unsympathetic selfobjects could not see her distress.

This patient's self–selfobject experience of people as being either for her or against her illustrates my main point: Ms. I.'s self-cohesion was inflexibly centered on securing what inevitably turned out to be disappointing mirroring selfobject functions, nearly completely excluding any possibility of responding to or eliciting idealization or twinship selfobject functions. She looked up to people like her internist and one or two of the nurses and admired them for their sensitivity and insightfulness. However, what looked like idealization concealed Ms. I.'s deeper mirroring deficiency. An underlying depletion depression would likely have emerged had she not angrily rebuffed those she formerly respected once they no longer seemed on her side. Stated differently, this patient turned reflexively only to mirroring selfobjects to satisfy her needs for affect regulation, calming, and self-cohesion. Her reactions to events and people surrounding her were governed nearly totally by the degree to which others fulfilled an empathically responsive mirroring selfobject function. She seemed trapped into perpetually seeking mirroring, occasionally with some success but not to the extent she required to internalize or structuralize self experience.

There was no compelling evidence either from our observations or in Ms. I.'s history that she had much capacity to attempt to make use of idealization or twinship selfobject functions as compensatory structures to repair her self disorder and thus restore self-cohesion. This patient's dramatic, attention-seeking behavior, accompanied by superficial affect and compromised affect regulation, seemed to represent the failure of a compensatory structure to develop, disposing her to chronically undermined self-cohesion.

ANTISOCIAL PERSONALITY DISORDER

Kohut (1971) did not devote much attention to antisocial behavior or its underlying mechanisms, apart from noting that delinquent acts represent but one clinical manifestation of narcissistic behavior disorders; other manifestations include addictions and perversions. He regarded these narcissistic behavior disorders as symptomatic forms of the same core disturbance represented by narcissistic personality disorders. However, he did not address this matter in his later work, devoting most of his efforts to describing disorders of the self beyond narcissism. Goldberg (1995) expanded Kohut's ideas about perversions, which Goldberg (1999, 2000) further examined by characterizing certain other manifestations of narcissistic behavior disorders using the concept of the vertical split. I will describe the vertical split and the self disorders explained by this mechanism in chapter 11.

Antisocial personality disorder has attracted little attention from most psychoanalysts in recent decades, perhaps because such patients are rarely amenable to analytic treatment. Thus, the impetus treatment generates to stimulate theoretical thinking about antisocial personality disorder has been slow to develop. This is true of both self psychology and nearly all schools of psychoanalysis. Nevertheless, self psychological insights about the nature of the parent or caregiver selfobject environment, selfobject functions, and compensatory structures may facilitate an understanding of delinquent behavior.

Research interest in a neurobiological explanation for antisocial personality disorder undoubtedly will lead to a more complete understanding of its etiology. For example, family history of antisocial behavior and substance abuse, alone or in combination, may dispose individuals to neurobiological abnormalities, which in turn influence temperament and avoidance learning. These and related social learning deficits lead to impaired empathy, marked deficiency in interpersonal concern, and sometimes criminality. This approach to understanding antisocial personality disorder resembles in part the self psychological approach to schizotypal personality disorder I described in chapter 4. In both types of disorder, a familial predisposition, a neurobiological anomaly, or both compromises the development of a capacity for responsiveness to and from the selfobject environment. Though antisocial and schizotypal disorders may show such a deficit for different reasons, both disorders are susceptible to a biologically based predisposition interfering with developing empathy.

Kohut (1971) attributed antisocial acts to a partial breakthrough of repressed aspects of the grandiose self rather than to drive theory's viewpoint emphasizing superego defect and a weakened ego's control of drives. Imperviousness to customary social constraints underlies such patients' sense of entitlement, which is often accompanied by the braggadocio of boastful displays of greatness or power. This behavior signifies the mobilization of normally repressed archaic grandiose–exhibitionistic needs or strivings. As a result, delinquent or antisocial acting out may emerge in place of a secure sense of pride about one's accomplishments or abilities. The grandiosity of antisocial acting out signals a history of inadequate mirroring responsiveness in a selfobject environment that did not sufficiently affirm legitimate needs for admiration.

As I noted in chapter 7, Kohut's (1971) view on antisocial personality disorder was influenced by Aichorn's (1925/1983, 1936/1964) thinking about delinquency. Aichorn was well aware of the customary problem of sustaining a working alliance in the treatment of juvenile delinquents. He proposed an approach that actively fostered developing an emotional bond, which Kohut regarded as an idealizing transference, to restimulate concealed longings to admire a parent. Aichorn and Kohut thought that delinquent patients denied such longings, fearing that the awareness of affectionate, admiring feelings would indicate weakness or vulnerability. Kohut further thought that their idealizing yearnings were also defended out of fear of traumatic disillusionment should the objects of their idealization let them down. Consequently, their heightened grandiosity represented defensive self-protection from the disappointment and ensuing depression associated with the risk of idealization.

What Aichorn (1925/1983) suggested was that clinicians should initially accept rather than challenge delinquent patients' overt grandiose omnipotence and their contempt for values and ideals. His idea was that the strength of the bond that developed ultimately would allow a transformation of patients' grandiosity into an interest in idealized selfobjects previously concealed behind their defensive contempt of those they longed to admire. On the basis of this idea, Kohut (1971) developed the view that analytic treatment of narcissistic personality disorders was promoted by permitting a spontaneous therapeutic mobilization of an idealizing transference rather than by prematurely interpreting its meaning. Such premature interpretations potentially undermine a gradual emergence of ideals that delinquent patients long to admire. In this way, allowing idealization to develop could represent one viable pathway to repair injuries to the self.

What Kohut (1971) suggested was different than Aichorn's (1925/1983, 1936/1964) recommendation for conducting treatment of delinquents, however. Aichorn advised actively promoting a transference configuration presumed to be present albeit latent. Kohut recommended allowing idealization to emerge spontaneously, without active encouragement. Kohut may not have fully grasped at that early stage of his work just how important early, tentative revivals of patients' thwarted healthy strivings are in fostering emergent idealizing transferences. However, he did apparently appreciate (but did not emphasize in his writings) that such strivings reflected what he called the *leading edge* of development. Kohut saw leading edge strivings alongside the more easily recognized pathological indicators, which he referred to as the *trailing edge*.

In M. Tolpin's (2002) development of this early concept of Kohut's (using the term *forward edge* instead of *leading edge*), she noted that early tendrils of healthy strivings in normal development are driven underground when selfobject responsiveness is seriously misattuned. However, M. Tolpin observed that patients usually do not give up entirely the wish to revive such attempts. Patients frequently test potential selfobjects, including their analyst or therapist, to see whether they may restimulate a neglected aspect of their development. Unfortunately, such forward edge strivings are easily misinterpreted as manifestations of the trailing edge—that is, psychopathology—leaving patients feeling that legitimate desires are signs of their illness that must be suppressed. Aichorn's (1925/1983) recommendation to encourage the possibility of sustaining a therapeutic bond may also be reconsidered as a special case of a forward edge transference. He seemed to intuitively recognize that a latent idealization potentiality was revivable through the seemingly circuitous route of a therapist's accepting or even allying him- or herself with antisocial delinquents' defensive grandiosity.

In normal development, the grandiose–exhibitionistic self, dominated as it is by archaic omnipotence, requires that parents help their children modulate their sense of boundless power or greatness. Parents must simultaneously respond to their children's vigorous assertiveness, thus conveying their comprehension of normal mirroring needs; failure to do so conveys instead that young children's proud sense of their emerging accomplishments and naive greatness is unwelcome and unappreciated. As a result, rather than being tempered, such children's unbounded narcissistic or grandiose–exhibitionistic displays persist in an archaic form, apparently unresponsive to caregiver or environmental constraints. When this developmental process is compromised further by the underlying neurobiological anomalies that give rise to defective learning, impaired empathic capacity, and socialization deficits, it may ultimately develop into the form of psychopathology found in antisocial personality disorder.

The description of impaired empathic capacity in most investigations of antisocial personality disorder is not equivalent to the concept of unempathic selfobject responsiveness used in self psychology. As an example of the former, Blair (1995) observed that antisocial persons are less sensitive to others' affect states, which impedes accurate responding to social cues, and Blair, Jones, Clark, and Smith (1997) reported that psychopathic prisoners were more deficient at intuiting emotions from pictures than were prisoners not judged to be psychopathic. In contrast to this meaning of empathy,

Basch (1983) made the following observation from a self psychological framework:

> Some of the world's greatest scoundrels have been exquisitely and unerringly attuned to grasping the significance of the unconscious or unspoken affective communications of others and have used that knowledge to achieve base aims. Is this too empathy? Yes it is. (pp. 119–120)

Wolf (1988) provided a self psychological explanation of empathy in this example from everyday life: "The essence of a certain kind of salesmanship (or advertising) is exactly the salesman's empathic 'in tuneness' with the customer's needs and wishes" (p. 132).

Thus, empathic responsiveness is understood in self psychology as a well-developed capacity to comprehend others' need states. As such, there is no deficit in this capacity among antisocial personality disorder patients. Rather, the empathic deficit appears when parental selfobjects in childhood were chronically or severely misattuned to their children's selfobject needs. Such misattunements may dispose individuals to limited empathic capacity, and antisocial patients, like many other patients with self disorders, were so injured. However, they show no apparent limitation in their own capacity to empathically resonate with others.[1]

Although their capacity for sensitivity may not be impaired, antisocial patients run into problems when they make use of what they empathically grasp in a way that is consistent with the indifferent, unconcerned, or ruthless nature of their orientation to the people in their environment. From this vantage point, suggestions that an orbitofrontal cortical defect may impair empathy in antisocial personality disorder (Damasio, Tranel, & Damasio, 1990; Schore, 2003a) might refer more accurately to impairments in acting on the meanings of others' motivations rather than in accurately comprehending people's motives.

The availability of suitable idealized selfobjects in childhood normally strengthens the self by allowing young children to internalize parents' or caregivers' qualities of calming reassurance. This is a basis for the transmuting internalizations through which young children acquire psychological functions of self-regulation. The limited availability of caregivers as capable idealizing selfobjects interferes with establishing idealization as a basis for a workable compensatory structure as an alternative path for strengthening the self. A longing to turn in this way to idealizable selfobjects may nevertheless persist, regardless of how submerged it may be. Antisocial patients may recognize that their self-cohesion is not as robust as they make it appear to be. Silent, hidden yearnings for idealization may still be discernible, con-

---

[1]Shapiro (1965) made a similar observation about the paradox of narcissistic–impulsive personalities showing sensitive awareness about other persons, although their perceptiveness may not extend beyond sizing up what is needed to serve an exploitative or manipulative purpose. Shapiro considered this quality to be empathy, although he noted that it is an atypical use of the term, one that some observers might prefer to denote using a different term.

cealed though they may be behind antisocial patients' grandiosity and its manifestations, such as ruthless manipulativeness and invulnerability. For idealizing yearnings to be mobilized, patients' identification with the grandiosity of others would make use of silent idealizing longings to transform their unbridled grandiosity into a solution they can tolerate but which also buttresses self-esteem.

I describe the concept of vertical split in greater detail in chapter 11, but I mention it here to differentiate this unique configuration of personality from antisocial personality disorder. Kohut (1971) distinguished between two forms of experiencing the self: the *horizontal split*, in which mental phenomena are inaccessible to conscious experience (i.e., repressed), and the *vertical split*, in which mental phenomena are disavowed but not excluded from conscious awareness by repression. An example of the horizontal split is unawareness of one's motivations, as in the familiar idea of repressed thoughts or affects. People with a vertical split might engage in acts they know to be wrong and even undesirable but nevertheless still perform, though they do not know why they need to do so. Goldberg (1999) expanded the concept of the vertical split in narcissistic behavior disorders, emphasizing that patients often express disdain for their own behavior; for example, they may feel self-contempt about an addiction, perversion, or criminal misbehavior. Goldberg recognized that such acts—as well as a broader range of misbehaviors such as shoplifting, fraudulent behavior, and binge eating—bring relief, as criminal acts or risk-taking behaviors frequently do among antisocial personality disorder patients. Goldberg considered regularly repeated misbehavior as integral to antisocial personality disorder. The appearance of this misbehavior is dictated by opportunity. In contrast, misbehavior by patients with a vertical split that may take the form of criminal acts is more episodic. Its appearance is understood as serving a function of providing relief from dysphoric or anxious states. Further, antisocial patients' characteristic lack of remorse contrasts with the sometimes self-abhorrent reaction in patients with a vertical split.

Considering together these self psychological views of narcissistic behavior disorders, the vertical split, and delinquency, patients with antisocial personality disorder may be said to experience deficient idealized selfobject responsiveness that is superimposed on a disturbance in the mirroring sector of the self. Like dependent and histrionic personality disorders, antisocial personality disorder is characterized by compromised efforts to make use of idealization in establishing a compensatory structure. Where dependent patients readily rely on idealization as a primary mechanism for attempting to achieve self-cohesion (their success is often compromised by their overreliance on idealizing selfobjects), and histrionic patients may be too inflexibly wedded to seeking mirroring to be able to turn to idealizing selfobjects as a way to fortify the self, antisocial patients seem to occupy a middle ground.

Their middle ground represents a capacity to make use of idealization, particularly if it suits their needs to firm up self-cohesion, possibly by allying with selfobjects who they experience as powerful. However, basking in such idealized selfobjects' vigor may serve a purpose of sustaining their own grandiosity; it does not strengthen the self by staving off depression associated with diminished self-esteem. Antisocial patients' relative incapacity to experience depression makes it unnecessary to conceal depressive affects, because their fundamental neurobiological deficit precludes experiences of deeply felt affects. The appearance of idealization in antisocial personality disorder, therefore, is more an expression of admiration for others' strengths or values for exploitative purposes than it is a genuine strengthening of the self similar to a compensatory structure that helps stave off depletion or devitalization.

Like many other adaptive features of patients with antisocial personality disorder, the appearance of idealization is usually impermanent and superficial. Such persons' capacity for idealization may seem convincing, but clinicians must not be misled into believing that idealization is or may be harnessed to become a genuine compensatory structure. Rather, appearances of idealization in these patients are really pseudo-idealizations, because they are not internalized to provide a psychological structure or to bolster a weakened sector of the self. Their capacity to make use of selfobjects for idealization may operate only for as long as it is needed; its sustaining function for strengthening self-cohesion generally does not endure.

If traces of genuine, sustained idealization or twinship do appear, they are ephemeral and usually superficial. Occurrences of idealization may serve as a sustainable compensatory structure, but only in a limited way because of an inherently deficient capacity to internalize selfobject functions. However, a compensatory structure built up from idealization can occur, thus providing a functional albeit limited rehabilitation of the self. It is in this respect that I consider the capacity to establish a compensatory structure as a pathway to revitalize the self as a middle ground. In such relatively infrequent instances, it is important that the therapist carefully ascertain whether idealization genuinely exists as the basis for a compensatory structure, because it can easily be a deceptive impression of psychological adaptation or affective depth, as with nearly every other aspect of psychological functioning in antisocial personality disorder patients. To the extent that idealization is internalized to fortify the self as a workable compensatory structure, it may require lifelong bolstering to sustain its viability.

Clinical Illustration of Antisocial Personality Disorder

Mr. J. was a 20-year-old third-generation Japanese American man I saw in a court-ordered evaluation for violating a domestic violence order of protection. His mother sought the order to protect her daughters and herself from Mr. J.'s threats of aggression. During a recent argument about Mr. J.'s smoking marijuana in front of his younger siblings, he had pushed his mother against a wall. This action precipitated the protection order, but Mr. J. still visited his mother when he wanted to, although he had had no further outbursts of anger.

Mr. J. had frequently gotten into trouble as a boy. He was considered a smart aleck who was willful and who talked back to his parents, teachers, and authority figures. His parents had enrolled him in a military school toward the end of high school because, according to his father, he had received failing grades in regular schools for not turning in homework assignments, even when he completed them. His mother said that Mr. J. was uncontrollable, and it was her hope that a military school would teach him discipline. Mr. J. felt he was "thrown away by my family," commenting that his father visited him regularly but that his mother rarely came to see him.

Mr. J. ran away from the school, which led to an inpatient psychiatric hospitalization on an adolescent behavior disorders unit. His parents relented and let him finish high school locally, which he was proud of accomplishing on schedule. Mr. J. did what was needed to pass enough courses "on my own." He admitted feeling hurt and angry that although his mother attended the graduation, she declined an invitation to attend his graduation party. During that same year, his parents divorced. Mr. J. had shuttled back and forth for a few weeks or months at a time between living with his father, a friend, and a cousin; most recently, he had lived in his own apartment.

Mr. J. felt that his mother had not loved him for a long time and that she was stubborn and demanding, always reminding him of his misbehavior and irresponsibility. He believed that their relationship had been "destroyed," although he hinted that it was not beyond a point of repair. He felt closer to his father, because the father always came to his aid when he was in trouble. However, father and son had argued frequently in the past year, often because Mr. J., who worked erratically in his father's furniture store, was irresponsible about coming to work regularly and following supervisors' orders. Mr. J. complained that he did not like the work he was assigned to do, arrogantly proclaiming, "I can't work for anyone in my family. I just had to get away from my family." He had recently obtained a job in a convenience store; however, his father reported that Mr. J. was in danger of losing that job because of his undependability.

His mother reported having had problems with Mr. J. since he was 9 years old, when he was caught forging a check and shoplifting from stores. His irresponsibility about school homework assignments began at this time as well, and his mother related that the patient would become "violently" angry whenever he was confronted. There were no apparent episodes of violence or loss of control other than a short temper. She had not trusted him for many years, but she now was afraid of him because he once had threatened to kill her in the heat of an argument. She felt that her husband had always been too lax in disciplining Mr. J., and that Mr. J. would play one against the other to get his way. She also observed that Mr. J. was deceptive in his expressions of a sincere intention to change. She frequently felt disappointed that his behavior rarely matched his promises. She did not like his drinking and smoking marijuana around the other children.

His father reported that Mr. J. was often truant from school and was suspended in the 7th grade. He also was arrested as a juvenile for stealing a car at age 15. His father said that Mr. J. lied much of the time, stole money, and abused alcohol and marijuana. Nevertheless, his father also said, practically in the same breath, that he had noticed "many positive features over the past year," by which he meant that Mr. J. was able to care for himself better than in the past. However, caring for himself seemed to mean being canny in the father's eyes. For example, telling me how Mr. J. could look directly at him with a sincere expression while lying about whatever was at hand, the father added, I thought pridefully, "He's a politician; he's able to care for himself more." The father placed much of the responsibility for his son's problems on his ex-wife, whom he felt had been unaffectionate and inattentive to Mr. J. as he was growing up. He believed that his son "has to make his own mistakes," whereas he thought his ex-wife wanted to control Mr. J., as though he were still a boy.

On examination, I found no evidence of psychosis or mood disturbance. Mr. J. appeared seductively pleasant and engaging as he spoke about his problems, which he saw as related to finding his independence. He spoke angrily about his mother, whom he felt preferred his sisters to him, and he said that she refused to talk with him. He believed that she would not let him forget his past and that matters would never improve unless his mother would talk with him without a third party being present. Mr. J. spoke glowingly about his father, commenting on his father's business prowess and broad knowledge about many areas of practical life. He described his father as able to fix almost everything. Mr. J. did note that there had been tension between him and his father in the past year and that his father had been angry at Mr. J. and was not always "there for me when I need him like he used to be all the time." He felt his mother's declining his invitation to his high school graduation party was her way of demeaning his feeling "so proud that I did it on my own." Mr. J. said that the reason he moved out after living with his father was because his father was depressed about the divorce and "he wasn't fun to be around."

After agreeing to come for treatment, Mr. J. failed to show up for his first appointment and did not return a phone call. I informed the lawyer his father had retained to represent Mr. J., who reported this fact to the court. The lawyer also told me that Mr. J. had lost his job and that his driver's license had been suspended for nonappearance in traffic court. Mr. J. did not return phone calls to the lawyer, and he failed to appear in court as ordered.

Mr. J. had most of the earmarks of antisocial personality disorder, including both *Diagnostic and Statistical Manual of Mental Disorders* (4th ed.; American Psychiatric Association, 1994) criteria and positive Cleckley (1941/ 1964) and Hare (1991) psychopathy features. Despite Mr. J.'s comfortable middle-class family environment, with an intact family and no apparent social disadvantages, he nevertheless displayed at an early age telltale antisocial personality defects. These behavior patterns were initially overlooked but became progressively more problematic as Mr. J. experienced trouble with every societal institution he came into contact with—family, school, and work. He also showed the beginnings of a pattern of amoral behavior that included forgery, threats that led to a domestic violence protection order against him, violation of the conditions of a court order, suspension of his driver's license, and contempt of court.

Both Mr. J. and his father mentioned that the mother, although not overtly neglectful, had shied away from affection toward her son, seeming to treat him as unwelcome. The father had no memory of seeing her hug their son or of fussing over or playing with him beyond basic caretaking. His mother would not come in for an interview, although she agreed to speak with me by telephone, suggesting a tense and distant ambivalence similar to that showed by her attending her son's graduation but declining to attend the graduation party. I could not ascertain the mother's caregiving capacities very well because contact with this family was brief, limited mostly by the patient's premature withdrawal from treatment. Thus, I was unable to see what else might have emerged about his relationships with both parents.

Mr. J.'s father did not regard his ex-wife as an insensitive or rejecting mother toward her other children. She might have turned away from her son, sensing something different and perhaps frightening about him that prevented her from warming up to him. She did not ignore him or disregard his needs, but neither did she appear to enjoy him, even before he started getting into trouble. She was apparently warm and loving toward her daughters, making it seem less likely that her maternal capacity was impaired. This mother's emotional withdrawal from her son may have been due to some vague, imperceptible quality about Mr. J. as an infant; he may have been the kind of baby mothers sense is somehow different and to whom they respond with fearful hesitation rather than the sheer joy of a "love affair" with their baby. Whether this kind of "bad connection" reflected the faulty hardwiring of a neurobiological abnormality or a misattuned self–selfobject matrix, the affirming, buoying gleam in the mother's eye of the mirroring sector of the self seemed to have been interrupted or foreclosed. Inconstant mirroring may well have resulted from his mother's inability to find her son lovable. As a result, her affirmation of his buoyant self-esteem may also have been tentative or diminished in reaction to her fear of him, a child she might not have recognized psychologically as her own or felt that she could resonate with in the way a proud mother basks in a child who lights up her life.

Mr. J.'s father described himself as being absorbed in building his business and as living "like an ostrich" at home. He said that his wife often felt that money was not coming in as quickly as she wanted it and that she would withdraw sex as a punishment. Mr. J. seemed to have developed an admiring relationship with his father, partly because his father threw money at the problems Mr. J. was increasingly creating. He thus saw his father as being on his side, unlike his mother, who frequently criticized her son by reminding him of his misdeeds. Mr. J. felt that his father accepted and approved of him because the father himself needed a pal. His father may well have been insensitive to the insidious pattern that was developing in Mr. J.'s life. I would also not rule out the possibility that the father's own moral antenna was compromised, making it almost as difficult for him to distinguish right from wrong as it was for his son.

Mr. J.'s father seemed more unambivalently responsive to his son, which may have opened a door for a more felicitous selfobject responsiveness based on idealization. Mr. J. admired his father's accomplishments and all-knowing strength, but whether he admired his father in a genuinely idealizing fashion or whether he took advantage of his father's willingness to overlook his behavior and indulge his grandiosity was not entirely clear. As Mr. J. said, he appreciated that his father was always there for him, but Mr. J. also seemed to lose interest in his father when the father was depressed over the breakup of his marriage. Thus, for Mr. J., his father was "not fun," and Mr. J.'s capacity for gratitude being what it was, he moved on to greener pastures and—true to the spirit of the Cleckley–Hare psychopath—was indifferent to the person who had bailed him out every time he was in trouble. He may have attempted to establish a compensatory structure as long as he could experience his father as providing an available idealizable selfobject function. However, it also seemed that his capacity to internalize this idealizing selfobject responsiveness as a compensatory structure was too limited or unstable. Mr. J. could thus make use of this selfobject function to temporarily invigorate himself by looking up to his capable, successful father who could, as he said, fix anything.

CONCLUSION

In this chapter, I discussed dependent, histrionic, and antisocial personality disorders from a self psychological vantage point. The focal point for my consideration of these disorders is that there is one sector of the self—typically, mirroring—that has been irreparably damaged. Such patients face the problem of finding alternative pathways to repair the injuries to the self in order to restore a modicum of self-cohesion.

As a theoretical anchor for considering how alternative pathways may be forged, I centered the discussion in this chapter on Kohut's (1971, 1977) and M. Tolpin's (1997) concept of compensatory structures, or attempts to make use of idealizing or twinship selfobject functions to sufficiently strengthen compromised self-cohesion in the face of chronic or severe mirroring selfobject failures. I presented the view that dependent personality disorder patients potentially succeed best in establishing a compensatory structure, though its success ultimately is a function of these patients' capacity to internalize self-regulating functions of available idealized or twinship selfobjects. Histrionic personality disorder was described as the least successful of this group of disorders, because such patients' invariably futile search for mirroring selfobjects seems to impede what might otherwise represent a more resourceful attempt to secure self-cohesion through alternative selfobject pathways. I discussed antisocial personality disorder as representing a middle ground in patients' capacity to make use of idealized selfobjects, although these patients, too, typically fail to sufficiently internalize idealization or twinship as a reliable mental structure.

V

OTHER DISORDERS OF THE SELF (DEPRESSIVE PERSONALITY DISORDER, DISORDERS OF THE SELF AND SOMATIC REACTIVITY, AND DISAVOWAL AND THE VERTICAL SPLIT)

9

DEPRESSIVE PERSONALITY DISORDER

Subsyndromal forms of chronic depression represent a problematic entity in the diagnostic nomenclature. They have been referred to at various times as *depressive temperament* (Kraepelin, 1921), *depressive psychopathy* (Schneider, 1959), *depressive neurosis* (American Psychiatric Association, 1968), *depressive personality* (Chodoff, 1972; D. N. Klein, 1990), *endogenomorphic depression* (D. F. Klein, 1974), and *characterological depression* (Akiskal et al., 1980). The status of chronic but usually asymptomatic depressive personality as a discrete disorder remains unsettled. Depressive personality disorder was not granted an official designation in any of the editions of the *Diagnostic and Statistical Manual of Mental Disorders* (DSM; American Psychiatric Association, 1952, 1968, 1980, 1987, 1994) that provided criteria, although the broad concepts of depressive reaction and depressive neurosis did exist in the 1952 and 1968 versions, respectively. Criteria for depressive personality disorder were proposed for further study in an appendix of the fourth edition (*DSM–IV*; American Psychiatric Association, 1994).

There are many theoretical viewpoints concerning the pathogenesis of depression. However, it is often unclear whether certain theories were intended to pertain to syndromal (e.g., endogenous or melancholic) or subsyndromal (e.g., depressive personality) forms. Moreover, some theories of depression coexist with but are independent of the descriptive (Kraepelin,

1921) and German phenomenological (Jaspers, 1948; Schneider, 1950) traditions, which remain important influences on diagnostic nosologies. A renewed interest in Kraepelinian concepts during the past several decades has led to an emphasis on melancholic, hyperthymic, and cyclothymic temperaments as predominant influences on course and outcome in a broad range of depressive disorders.

I begin this chapter with a summary of issues pertaining to the differential diagnosis among forms of chronic, subsyndromal depression (including early-onset dysthymia), emphasizing a neo-Kraepelinian approach to the problem of depressive personality disorder. Following that, I will consider psychoanalytic viewpoints on neurotic depression and depressive character structure. Finally, I will present a self psychological conceptualization of chronic depression and depressive personality disorder and provide a case illustration.

DESCRIPTIVE PSYCHOPATHOLOGY AND THEORETICAL VIEWPOINTS

What is generally regarded as depressive personality disorder is probably closest in meaning to what was described as *neurotic depression* (depressive neurosis) in the second edition of the *DSM* (American Psychiatric Association, 1968); the general definition of this term was vague and nonspecific, whether or not syndromal features (now on Axis I) were present. This definition assumed psychoanalytic formulations of etiology and dynamics. Hirschfeld and Holzer (1994) regarded depressive personality disorder as an ego-syntonic condition characterized by extreme pessimism and negative beliefs about oneself and others. But even psychoanalytic perspectives concerning the etiology of depression spanned many theoretical positions, beginning with Freud's (1917/1957a) *Mourning and Melancholia* and extending to ego psychological, object relations, and interpersonal viewpoints (Arieti & Bemporad, 1978; Mendelson, 1974). Later in this chapter, I will present a more complete outline of several major psychoanalytic perspectives as a general theoretical background for presenting a self psychological viewpoint of depressive personality disorder.

Considering the problem from a different perspective, Shea and Hirschfeld (1996) proposed Watson and Tellegen's (1985) affective trait dimensions of high negative and low positive affectivity as a useful model for conceptualizing depressive personality. In Shea and Hirschfeld's model, negative affectivity (neuroticism) represents a generalized mood distress dimension, whereas positive affectivity (extraversion) represents a motivation–sensitive temperament dimension thought to be associated with depression. This model, which overlaps with other models of chronic depression, influenced the proposal for depressive personality disorder in an appendix of *DSM–*

IV. The intention was to identify a condition with specific criteria to be further studied to determine whether it might merit formal inclusion in subsequent editions. The criterion set for depressive personality disorder emphasizes cognitive–interpersonal attributes such as gloominess or joylessness, low self-esteem and self-depreciation, a pessimistic or worried nature, and guilt. Many of these features were identified by Schneider (1950) and modified by Akiskal (1983). They are typically phenomenological rather than endogenous (vegetative) features to maximize the clinical and theoretical differentiation between the proposed depressive personality disorder diagnostic entity and Axis I syndromal affective states.

As with most personality disorders, the problem of comorbidity presents complications for the proposed depressive personality disorder criteria. For example, depressive personality disorder frequently coexists with other personality disorders, particularly avoidant personality disorder (Phillips, Hirschfeld, Shea, & Gunderson, 1995). The relationship between depressive personality disorder and dysthymia also remains particularly uncertain; Hirschfeld and Holzer (1994) and D. N. Klein (1990) reported no more than moderate overlap between depressive personality disorder and either current or lifetime diagnosis of dysthymia, including early-onset dysthymia. Moreover, there remains a question concerning the relationships among syndromal (major) unipolar depression, so-called double depression (major depression and dysthymia), bipolar depression, and cyclothymia.

Definitions and Terminology

Kraepelin (1921) laid the groundwork for one of the earliest clinical descriptions of subsyndromal depression, which he called *depressive temperament*. He regarded chronic depression as a less severe condition on a continuum with what is now referred to as *unipolar* and *bipolar depression*. Kraepelin also noted that depressive temperament was present premorbidly in over 10% of manic–depressive (bipolar) patients. Kretschmer (1925) noted a similar relationship, and he called attention to combinations of melancholic and hypomanic states. Nevertheless, he considered such cycloid or cyclothymic conditions to represent extreme poles of a unitary illness.

Schneider (1923/1950), who was influential in the German school of phenomenological psychiatry, introduced the concept of chronic depression, which he termed *depressive psychopathy*. Schneider considered this condition to be continuous with normality; Kraepelin (1921), on the other hand, had regarded the same condition as a variant of melancholic or manic–depressive (bipolar) illness. Nevertheless, both Kraepelin's and Schneider's characterizations of mild chronic depression emphasized a presenting clinical picture dominated by a lifelong pattern of a brooding and pessimistic nature and an anhedonic, overly serious disposition. Both also noted such patients' characteristically introverted and self-doubting manner. Akiskal (1983) combined several of these features in his description of *subaffective dysthymia*, which is characterized by an indecisive, hypercritical, and petulant clinical presentation. Akiskal also included features of self-denigration and an overly ascetic, duty-bound hyperconscientiousness in his clinical description of subaffective dysthymia.

Conditions such as these and others, sometimes described as *mild depression, neurotic depression,* and *depressive personality disorder,* are important to study because of their early onset and chronic course. Klerman, Endicott, Spitzer, and Hirschfeld (1979) evaluated several definitions of neurotic depression, noting substantial overlap among them. They also commented on the imprecise clinical boundaries of these clinical concepts with other affective disorders. Klerman et al. concluded that *neurotic depression* was too vague a term for clinical diagnostic use. Moreover, in addition to problems of comorbidity, this disorder showed a highly variable course and response to treatment. European views seem to be more tolerant of the concept of neurotic depression, despite its exclusion in the 10th edition of the *International Classification of Diseases* (World Health Organization, 1992) after it had appeared in previous editions.

There also remains much terminological imprecision and conceptual uncertainty about the concepts of neurotic depression or minor depression (Angst, 1997) and their relation to dysthymia, depressive personality or temperament, and unipolar or bipolar depression (Akiskal, 1983; Huprich, 1998; D. F. Klein, 1974; Maj, 1997; Phillips & Gunderson, 1999; Phillips, Gunderson, Hirschfeld, & Smith, 1990; Stewart & Klein, 1997). Notwithstanding imprecise diagnostic definitions of neurotic depression and chronic depression, several satisfy contemporary diagnostic criteria for dysthymia. However, the relationship between dysthymia and the quality of depression consistent with an Axis II designation is not well understood (Kocsis & Frances, 1987).

Greater attention was also devoted to considering etiologically relevant factors based on family history, age of onset, clinical course, and response to treatment. One important early example of this approach was Winokur's (1972) distinction between *pure depressive disease* and *depression spectrum disease,* based partly on an aggregation of early-onset depression in women whose first-degree female relatives had depressive illnesses but whose male relatives tended to have alcoholism and antisocial personality disorder. This pattern suggested different phenotypic expressions forming a spectrum of a single (unitary) illness.

Attempts to more clearly define such disorders improved once the Axis I syndromal affective disorders and schizoaffective disorder gained greater conceptual and diagnostic precision. Important forerunners of the third edition of the *DSM* (American Psychiatric Association, 1980) and its successive iterations, such as the Feighner et al. (1972) criteria and the Research Diagnostic Criteria (Spitzer & Endicott, 1978), achieved greater specificity of syndromal depressive disorders. Distinctions between endogenous versus reactive, psychotic versus nonpsychotic, and primary versus secondary depression were once considered clinically and theoretically useful. However, differentiations such as these have been largely incorporated into the unipolar–bipolar distinction and milder but still symptomatic forms of affective disorder syndromes such as dysthymia and cyclothymia. Subtypes such as retarded, situational, and intermittent depression often implied milder forms of depression; however, uncertainty still remains concerning whether such forms represent valid subtypes.

Depressive personality disorder is a good illustration of the problem, because it is not clear whether this condition should be characterized as a discrete form of chronic depression or as a milder form of dysthymic disorder. Phillips et al. (1995) commented that the proposed *DSM–IV* criteria for depressive personality disorder appropriately represent important Axis II traitlike features, such as early onset and a persistent rather than episodic course. However, despite its inclusion in the *DSM–IV* for heuristic purposes, McLean and Woody (1995) regarded that decision as premature and without sufficient merit.

Differential Diagnosis

Phillips et al. (1990) reviewed arguments bearing on the relationship between depression and personality characteristics—for example, premorbid personality traits either predisposing to or influencing a depressive disorder—and postmorbid restitutional sequelae of depression such as resignation or timidity. They also considered comorbid personality disorders coexisting with depression. Their review argued for a discrete category of depressive personality disorder that differed from these depression–personality interrelationships. Phillips et al. considered depressive personality to be similar to other personality disorders in that it represents a chronic dysfunction of early onset and shows enduring traits that remain stable despite fluctuations in clinical status.

Phillips et al. (1995) later differentiated depressive personality disorder from dysthymia in that depressive personality disorder tends to be nonremitting and has an earlier onset than dysthymia. D. N. Klein (1990) demonstrated that depressive personality disorder showed acceptable reliability as well as convergent and discriminant validity as a distinct condition, despite its overlap with dysthymia. D. N. Klein also reported family history evidence for a trait-based symptomatic condition such as depressive personality disorder. This finding strengthened his suggestion that the depressive–affective spectrum should be extended to include this condition, because there appeared to be distinctive differences between depressive personality disorder and dysthymia. However, concerning its relation to Axis I, D. N. Klein, Taylor, Dickstein, and Harding (1988) reported an association between depressive personality disorder and syndromal depression and the presence of a family history of bipolar depression. D. N. Klein thus suggested that depressive personality may represent a clinically attenuated variant of major depression such as an early onset form of dysthymia.

Frances and Cooper (1981) stressed that depressive personality disorder appears to be less severe than dysthymia, although at that time, their differentiation as distinct illnesses had not yet been unequivocally established. The predominance of cognitive or subjectively affective symptoms in depressive personality disorder also distinguishes this disorder from the somatic symptoms that are more prominent in the clinical presentation of dysthymia. Moreover, other personality disorders frequently coexist in patients with major depressive syndromes, generally conferring a more unfavorable prognosis (Shea, Glass, Pilkonis, Watkins, & Docherty, 1987; Weissman, Prusoff, & Klerman, 1978). Kernberg (1984) also called attention to a predominantly masochistic character structure in depression.

Akiskal's (1983; Akiskal & Webb, 1983) contributions are particularly valuable for establishing a clinically anchored empirical basis for identifying subtypes of depressive phenomena. His conceptualizations of affective disorder syndromes have systematically emphasized delineating depressive and bipolar disorder subtypes. He further considered attenuated forms of these affective disturbances, and he contrasted their clinical courses and neurobiological relationships with primary syndromal disorders such as major depression and bipolar illness. He and his colleagues studied dysthymic and cyclothymic variants in particular, suggesting that they represent subsyndromal affective illnesses. Because these mood disorders frequently show chronic interpersonal or work dysfunctions or both, many clinicians regard them as compatible with a personality disorder diagnosis. However, Akiskal maintained that subsyndromal disorders are better understood as variants of a primary unipolar or bipolar mood disorder rather than as discrete disorders.

Akiskal and his colleagues (Akiskal, 1983; Akiskal & Webb, 1983) identified a spectrum of unipolar depressive conditions that included mild or subsyndromal forms. These low-grade depressive illnesses were often intermittent, but they were nevertheless chronic, and a subset showed an earlier onset than primary depressive disorders. Akiskal et al. (1980) proposed a classification of chronic depression based on family history, a biological marker (REM latency), treatment response, and age of onset. In some cases, an episodic major depressive illness was superimposed on a chronic depression (called *double depression*; Keller & Shapiro, 1982). These major depressive episodes resolved to a low-grade, subsyndromal state and not to a euthymic state.

Akiskal et al. (1980) described three patterns of chronic depression: (a) a residual of late-life primary unipolar depression, (b) depression secondary to nonaffective psychiatric or medical disorders (the primary–secondary distinction identified by Guze, Woodruff, & Clayton, 1971), and (c) early-onset characterological depression including both dysthymia and depressive personality disorder. Akiskal (1983; Akiskal & Webb, 1983) further subdivided the characterological subtype into two categories. The first category represents a "truly dysthymic" form of characterological depression—an antidepressant-responsive, subaffective variant of a primary affective illness. Akiskal regarded this subtype as belonging to a spectrum of disorders compatible with Kraepelin's and Kahlbaum's affective temperaments and Schneider's (1923/1950) description of depressive personality traits. Akiskal's second category of character-spectrum disorders, representing two thirds of an outpatient sample of characterological depressive patients, is a "truly characterological" form. This category resembles neither Kraepelin's (1921) depressive temperament nor the spectrum of primary (familial or genetic) affective disorders.

Akiskal (1997) later raised the question of whether some chronically depressed patients show a cyclothymic or bipolar diathesis rather than a unipolar diathesis based in part on their response to lithium or lithium augmentation therapy, family histories of bipolar illness, and a switch to hypomania either spontaneously or on pharmacological challenge. This more recent view of subsyndromal depression appears to have superseded his earlier view (Akiskal, 1983) of the two characterological depression subtypes, favoring in its place a unitary, continuum concept of depressive spectrum disorders. Consequently, a more pertinent distinction would be that between a spectrum of depressive illnesses and a spectrum of bipolar illnesses (soft bipolar spectrum). Akiskal thus considered characterological depression to be an antidepressant-nonresponsive form (even with vigorous antidepressant treatment, including a monoamine oxidase inhibitor when indicated). Such patients did not present with melancholic features during episodes of major depression, and they had normal REM latencies, in contrast with the shortened REM latencies and hypersomnia of subaffective dysthymic patients. They also displayed high rates of substance abuse and familial alcoholism and low rates of familial affective illness.

This more recent form of subsyndromal depression (Akiskal, 1997) resembled both Winokur's (1972, 1979) depression spectrum disease subtype and a psychoanalytic view of character pathology or depressive psychoneurosis. Although these patients demonstrated pronounced losses and disruptions in early development, Akiskal (1989) questioned whether such disadvantages were causative or contributory factors to the illness and suggested an alternative view to that of psychoanalysis, in which early developmental "friction" potentiated other events that might in turn trigger depressions. Thus, Judd and Akiskal (2000) wrote, "There are no natural boundaries between depression at the personality (temperament), dysthymic, major depressive, minor and residual SD [subsyndromal depressive] levels. They all appear to be part of a psychopathological continuum with the common denominator of a depressive trait" (p. 5).

Akiskal (1991, 1997) also commented that this character spectrum form of unipolar depression would probably become less common as newer antidepressant agents targeted for specific neurotransmitter receptor sites became available. Clinical experience with SSRI compounds during the past 2 decades has already demonstrated comparable if not superior efficacy compared with tricyclic antidepressant compounds. Akiskal recommended instituting aggressive pharmacological intervention, because even a partial antidepressant response is considered necessary to sustain what sometimes are relatively limited therapeutic gains achieved by psychological treatments alone. He also maintained that unsatisfactory responses to psychological interventions may wrongly motivate clinicians to modify such patients' diagnoses to reflect the intractable nature of character pathology. Akiskal considered this approach to be ill advised, in part because findings from 1-year (Judd & Akiskal, 2000) and 12-year (Judd et al., 1998) follow-up studies suggested that patients diagnosed with a particular depressive subtype often display features of another subtype later on. Thus, distinctions among Akiskal's (1983) originally proposed subtypes of characterological depression—subaffective dysthymia and character spectrum depression—seem to have shifted to a unitary concept of subsyndromal depression (Judd, Rapaport, & Paulus, 1994). Accordingly, entities like character spectrum depression or minor depression are being replaced by the view that depressive temperament predisposes individuals to a spectrum of depressive illnesses that may fluctuate longitudinally and for which pharmacological stabilization may be warranted in all or most of its clinical manifestations, and even prophylactically.

Akiskal (1986) also took note of a *hypomanic* or *cyclothymic temperament* (similar to Kraepelin's *hyperthymic temperament*), giving rise to a "soft" bipolar spectrum of affective illnesses in which antimanic mood stabilization is important either as a primary treatment or as a supplement to antidepressant therapy. Considering affective temperaments within a neurobiological framework not only may help to counteract patients' despair over a chronic, protracted, and debilitating condition but also may reduce clinicians' countertransferences to the discouraging impotence or therapeutic nihilism such patients readily evoke (Akiskal, 1989).

Akiskal (1983) pointed out that most forms of chronic depression represent admixtures in different degrees of subsyndromal and syndromal depression. In addition, early-onset dysthymia, the primary subsyndromal form, also appears to be a more pernicious subtype than late-onset dysythmia; it is associated with more frequent and severe affective illnesses, higher rates of lifetime major depressive episodes and anxiety disorders, and greater familial affective illness (D. N. Klein et al., 1988). D. N. Klein et al. (1995) reported evidence for a familial link between early-onset dysthymia and major depression, although dysthymia occurred more often in the first-degree relatives of dysthymic patients than in the relatives of major depressive patients. D. N. Klein et al. (1988) also reported familial associations with personality disorders for both early-onset dysthymia and major depression, though more so for the former group.

Akiskal and colleagues addressed the relationship of personality to affective disorders, including "minor" depression (Akiskal, 1991; Akiskal, Hirschfeld, & Yerevanian, 1983; Akiskal & Weise, 1992). They did not consider characterological predispositions as etiologic factors; rather, they regarded the temperamental predisposition to affective dysregulation as a genetically transmitted precursor. Temperamentally based mood dysregulation in interaction with other risk factors may predispose individuals to depression caused by life stressors. Alternatively, affective temperament predispositions may produce interpersonal or relationship disturbances that maintain the chronicity of the underlying depressive condition by interfering with social–interpersonal supports that might otherwise facilitate recovery. In this way, Akiskal (1989) viewed personality manifestations not as causative factors but as sequelae that either chronically persist or that modify the clinical presentation during an episode of illness. He thus considered it important to distinguish between personality changes following recovery from an episode of affective illness and long-term personality changes that result from recurrent episodes.

Mild or intermittent affective disturbances associated with unstable life histories, sometimes accompanied by substance abuse, also call attention to characterological features of the depressive personality. Such disturbances have often been considered as neurotic, borderline, or antisocial disorders. In Akiskal's (1986) view, certain of these disturbances, when typified by subtle hypomanic periods that were easily obscured by the generally tempestuous nature of these patients' lives, were better conceptualized as mild bipolar illnesses such as the Bipolar II type. Such subsyndromal affective disorders resembled bipolar disorders insofar as both conditions had similar family histories of bipolar illness, age of onset, shortened REM latency, pharmacological mania in response to tricyclic antidepressant therapy, and a favorable response to antimanic agents. The pattern suggested a spectrum of phenotypic clinical presentations that Akiskal regarded as having a bipolar genetic diathesis.

Davis and Akiskal (1986) and Akiskal et al. (1985) also considered the affective component of borderline personality disorder as a fundamental biological disturbance. They suggested that borderline personality might be more closely related to one or more forms of affective disorder than to personality disorder. Moreover, Akiskal and his colleagues did not regard subsyndromal depression, particularly a character spectrum subtype, to be overrepresented in borderline personality disorder to a degree greater than that observed clinically in a full range of affective disorders. Akiskal et al. (1985) noted that borderline personality disorder showed appreciable overlap with a number of psychiatric illnesses, more so with affective disorders than with schizophrenia.

Akiskal's (1983, 1991, 1997; Judd et al., 1994) contributions are particularly valuable for establishing a clinically anchored empirical basis for identifying subtypes of depressive phenomena. His views relied on Kraepelin's (1921) concept of a depressive temperament, which Kraepelin introduced to denote a common substrate for depression. Kraepelin also identified a hyperthymic temperament that underlay manic and hypomanic states and probably also mild, subclinical states of hyperarousal. Hyperthymic temperament usually disposes to soft bipolar clinical presentations. Akiskal (1986, 1989) has also investigated views that both temperaments may coexist or that a cyclothymic temperament may account for clinical presentations of both subsyndromal depression and subsyndromal hypomania, occurring in brief alternating sequences. A cyclothymic temperament may also characterize mild subclinical mood dysregulation anomalies in which neither affective pole reaches even a clinically subacute level. But neither are such patients typically euthymic. Thus, mild affective lability rather than euthymia constitutes the primary disturbance.

Contrary to some beliefs about the treatment of personality disorders before the introduction of the explicit criteria of the third edition of the DSM, there is good evidence for a favorable response to pharmacotherapy in many cases of chronic depression (Kocsis, 1997; Kocsis & Frances, 1987). However, there is less evidence regarding differential treatment responsiveness between patients with depressive personality disorder and those with dysthymia, including subaffective dysthymia. The typically protracted course and often limited results of psychotherapy in most forms of chronic depression add to the uncertainty in differentiating between these conditions on the basis of response to treatment. It is also unclear whether response to treatment helps to ascertain whether particular forms of chronic depression, including depressive personality disorder, represent variants of Axis I affective disorder or whether they represent Axis II personality disorders.

Moreover, it remains possible that a depressive temperament may signal long-term adaptational life adjustments that have coalesced to form a distinct entity such as that designated as depressive personality disorder. According to this view, depressive personality disorder may represent what Akiskal et al. (1983) called *postdepressive phenomena*, which also may be aggravated by noncompliance with pharmacotherapy maintenance treatment, insufficient dosage or unattempted augmentation strategies that may produce only a partial antidepressant response, premature termination related to intolerance or mismanagement of side effects, withdrawal from treatment, or other consequences of poor compliance (e.g., use of alcohol or other substances as replacements for active drug therapy).

Theoretical Approaches

Extending beyond the descriptive psychopathology of depression, many theoretical systems in psychology and psychiatry have contributed important perspectives, notably classical learning theory, cognitive–behavioral expansions on learning theory, interpersonal psychologies, and trait theories. Without reviewing this extensive literature, I note only that such theoretical viewpoints emphasized a broad, general concept of depression, devoting little attention to clinical characteristics or subtypes, including what might be construed as depressive personality disorder.

One form of subsyndromal chronic depression that was identified by response to treatment is a condition that D. F. Klein (1974) called *endogenomorphic depression*, which he originally referred to as *hysteroid dysphoria* (D. F. Klein & Davis, 1969). Rejection sensitivity and diminished self-esteem figure prominently in D. F. Klein and Davis's (1969) formulation of this form of intermittent atypical depression. It is characterized by hyperphagia and hypersomnia during the depressive phase and histrionic–narcissistic personality traits during euthymic interepisodic periods. Despite its psychological precipitants and strong personality disorder features, D. F. Klein and Davis regarded hysteroid dysphoria predominantly as a dysregulated neurotransmitter (phenylethylamine) deficit, noting its favorable response to monoamine oxidase inhibitor therapy and its poor response to tricyclic antidepressant therapy.

Cloninger, Bayon, and Svrakic (1998) proposed a melancholic configuration derived from their Temperament and Character Inventory. This configuration was typified by low levels of three character dimensions: cooperativeness, self-directedness, and self-transcendence. They reported this pattern to be prevalent in patients with unipolar depression and dysthymia (using Akiskal's [1983] criteria), although they noted that the melancholic pattern was also found in other personality disorders. Cloninger et al. considered that the melancholic type represented a dimensional model of Kraepelin's general view of temperaments. It predisposed to a broad range of subsyndromal states or antecedents of personality disorders, in addition to Axis I syndromes and Axis II personality disorders.

Westen and Shedler (1999a) identified a dysphoric factor on the Shedler–Westen Assessment Procedure, their inventory of personality disorders. This dysphoric factor, which they found in one fifth of their sample, comprised five subtypes—avoidant, high functioning, emotionally dysregulated, dependent, and hostile–externalizing. They suggested that these subtypes indicated multiple distress triggers (e.g., abandonment) and different styles for regulating painful affect states (e.g., self-mutilation or desperate seeking of attachments). Westen and Shedler's (1999a, 1999b) model, which might be described as a dimensional–categorical hybrid, also suggested that the dysphoric factor was found in many patients more typically represented by other types of personality disorders. Westen and Shedler (1999b) commented that "Axis II may have overfocused on the ways such patients are socially dysfunctional and underfocused on the ways in which they are in pain" (p. 281).

Millon's (1996) conceptualization of depressive personality disorder emphasized the pleasure–pain and active–passive polarities, in which hypersensitivity to psychological distress and passive hopelessness are the predominant influences on psychological adaptation. Thus, such patients are inclined to react to the unhappiness and gloom pervading their lives as inevitable and unavoidable. In consideration of the personality prototypes Millon described, patients with depressive personality disorder display prominent features of a melancholic temperament (the biopsychological level), and they appear overtly forlorn or disconsolate (behavioral level). Such patients act interpersonally in ways that fail to self-protectively conceal their needs and demands. At an internal phenomenological level of experience, their experience may be characterized by pessimistic ideation and devalued self-esteem. They also feel forsaken and thus prone to devitalization. Further aspects of the internal (intrapsychic) world of the depressive prototype are a prevailing sense of inner depletion and a degree of self-denial suggesting that "in a sense, they have adopted a mechanism of 'playing dead' as a means of remaining alive" (Millon, 1996, p. 302). Millon noted that deficient parental involvement leads to patients with this disorder giving up on themselves and others. Among all of the conceptualizations of depressive personality disorder, it is Millon's that comes closest phenomenologically to Kohut's (1977, 1984) and M. Tolpin and Kohut's (1980) descriptions of self disorders.

PSYCHOANALYTIC VIEWPOINTS

Throughout much of the past century, psychodynamic viewpoints represented a dominant influence on formulations of depressive neurosis or depressive personality. It deserves mention that psychoanalytic theories have not generally differentiated depressive neurosis from depressive personality; thus, explanations of depression generally pertain to both conditions. Depressive phenomena did not occupy Freud's attention until relatively late in his early theoretical writing (Arlow & Brenner, 1964). Freud (Breuer & Freud, 1893–1895/1955) originally considered depression to be a somatic process—a form of anxiety neurosis (neurasthenia) that was linked to hypochondriasis.

It was not until *Mourning and Melancholia* that Freud (1917/1957a) began to consider a psychological basis for depression. In this work he presented his formulation about melancholia as a conflicted hostile wish resulting from object loss or loss of object love. Unlike mourning, melancholic depression was associated with a loss of self-regard, a loss that was experienced as impoverishing the ego. Prior to psychoanalysis' later emphasis on the structural theory, the concept of ego was not well delineated; it was probably thought of more or less as a precursor of the self (Goldberg, 1975; Zetzel & Meissner, 1973). A lost object was presumed to be incorporated in this self-ego, and indeed, Freud seemed to regard the introjection of a lost object as regression associated with the transformation of withdrawn object libido into narcissistic libido (Freud, 1914/1957b). The ego thus became the cathected object, which is what Freud (1917/1957a) meant by his often-quoted comment that "The shadow of the object fell upon the ego" (p. 249).

Freud also considered Abraham's (1924) view emphasizing the primary importance of the oral stage of libidinal development in melancholia. He recognized that certain similarities with the anal fixation of obsessive–compulsive neurosis—particularly repressed hostile wishes—could explain ambivalent affects in respect to a lost object in depression. Although the libido theory declined in importance as the structural theory became the predominant basis for explaining mental life, Rado (1928), Fenichel (1945), and Arieti and Bemporad (1978) nevertheless commented on the importance of oral stage dynamics in depression. They emphasized the importance of clinging dependence related to maternal affectional needs and early attachment difficulties.

Rado (1928) extended the psychoanalytic theory of the pathogenesis of depression, emphasizing the importance of aggression surrounding conflict between superego and ego. This formulation de-emphasized self-esteem loss and ego helplessness in favor of ambivalence and guilt as mental forces potentiating depression. Identification was considered the principal mechanism to explain how aggression originally directed against a lost object became turned against the self. Thus, Rado explained how hostile wishes directed toward a lost, introjected love object are turned against the self (retroflexion of rage) and transformed into guilt, which is then experienced as depression. Through intropunitive self-reproach, affection and narcissistic gratifications were restored, a position with which Fenichel (1945) concurred.

With the emergence of psychoanalytic ego psychology, Bibring's (1953) model shifted theoretical interest away from oral stage needs to the helplessness of the ego to provide a sense of well-being (balanced narcissism). Although he agreed that oral needs are important, Bibring had a broader view of oral stage dynamics that led him to emphasize diminished self-esteem and regression to states of helplessness. In his view, helplessness could arise from frustrations at any of the psychosexual stages, and he focused particular attention on the experience of depression as an ego state. Bibring's view stressed conflict within the ego itself more than conflict between ego and superego. Conflict thus represented a disparity between one's narcissistic longings and the ego's awareness of its powerlessness to recover after one feels unloved or unappreciated. In this regard, Bibring did not consider depressive reactions as necessarily representing object-directed hostility turned defensively against the self.

Although Jacobson (1964, 1971) also regarded loss of self-esteem and helplessness as important considerations in depression, her view was largely centered on how self and object representations were acquired in development. She attempted to explain influences on self-esteem, taking note of the ego ideal and related concepts of idealization and depreciation as important elements in depression. Thus, pronounced disappointment in love objects could produce devaluation, interfering with the development of normal self-esteem and separation of self and object representations. As a result, the ego ideal as a component of the superego would not develop properly. Jacobson in this way emphasized what she considered to be an unstable or poorly integrated ego–superego regulatory relationship in which unstable idealizations accompanied devaluation of love objects. There would follow vulnerability to disappointment and dependent helplessness, ultimately potentiating depression.

Jacobson (1964, 1971) also speculated about the psychological dynamics of managing aggression and the vacillation between depreciation and self-inflation occurring in various mixed affective states, including cyclothymia and manic depression. However, psychoanalytic theorists generally did not devote particular attention to differentiating between neurotic and psychotic depression or between depressive and manic–depressive (bipolar) illnesses. Distinctions among forms of depression were based largely on severity of reality distortions (Fenichel, 1945; Rado, 1928). Jacobson, however, emphasized ego regression rather than libidinal (oral stage) regression, a view that Zetzel (1960) and Searles (1965) considered unresolved and perhaps as representing an overambitious theoretical leap.

Rubinfine (1968) stressed narcissistic disillusionment as a factor in feelings of helplessness, and Zetzel (1965) also regarded diminished self-esteem and the incapacity to renounce omnipotence as critical factors in the development of the depressive character structure. Blatt (1974) postulated two depressive types that differed in the psychodynamic configurations giving rise to them. One form, the *anaclitic* type, based on the importance of the mother–child bond, was organized around vulnerability to threatened loss and potential withdrawal of affection. Blatt's second form, the *introjective* type, was organized around a punitive superego, thus more closely resembling the hostility–guilt formulation Rado (1928) and Fenichel (1945) described.

Originating with Melanie Klein's (1930, 1935) introduction of the concept of the depressive position, a British object relations perspective began to take shape. In M. Klein's formulation, the perception of maternal objects as whole rather than part objects was considered to represent an important achievement of early development. Spillius (1988) and Bronstein (2001), more recent theorists who have followed M. Klein's views and further developed them, accepted her distinction between paranoid–schizoid and depressive positions. However, they regarded them less as phases of development than as prototypes of relatedness based on internal fantasies of early mother–infant object relations. M. Klein's viewpoint of a position incorporated object relationships, fantasies, sources of anxiety, and defenses. According to

M. Klein, the depressive position is the basis for ambivalence, a point in the development of object relations that is characterized by a capacity to both love and hate the mother. It makes guilt surrounding hostility possible, compared with the persecutory anxiety surrounding sadistic, destructive impulses characterizing the earlier paranoid–schizoid position.

Achieving a depressive position would therefore represent the diminished significance of projected rage in favor of a better developed sense of internal and external reality of both infant and mother. M. Klein (1930, 1935) explained chronic depression as the inability to avoid the anxiety associated with destroying love objects. Consequently, aggression is repressed, producing unabated self-persecution. Introjecting hostility thus served the purpose of attempting reparation by protecting the good maternal object from the infant's aggression. M. Klein's views, although different from those of Freud (1917/1957a), Abraham (1924), and Rado (1928) in several important respects, were also similar to theirs insofar as she emphasized the importance of introjected anger at love objects and of attempts to recover from intropunitive states. It is unclear from her writings how broadly she intended her views to apply to type or severity of depressive conditions, though she seemed clearly to have in mind major depression or psychotic depression. It is less certain whether her concept extended to a condition such as depressive personality or even dysthymia.

Although M. Klein's view (1930, 1935) has been considered controversial at times and is certainly different from classical psychoanalytic ego psychology, her work influenced a generation of important object relations theorists, including Fairbairn (1944) and Guntrip (1969). As object relations theories developed beyond M. Klein's views, other theoretical positions emerged relating object loss to depression. Sandler and Joffe (1969), for example, emphasized the loss of a sense of well-being more than object loss as an important influence on the helpless, resigned quality of depression. Consequently, they regarded attempts to maintain an ideal state of well-being as a central regulatory principle, superordinate to the pleasure and reality principles of drive theory.

Bowlby (1969, 1973), whose work is justifiably credited with originating contemporary interest in infant attachment and its applications to psychoanalysis, identified the importance of patterns of attachment between infant and mother (Goodman, 2002). He described how qualities of maternal involvement dispose to grief and mourning and recognized the importance of prolonged unavailability of maternal caretaking. Bowlby's view was based not on a drive theory formulation of psychological development, but rather on qualities of the interaction bond (attachment) that mothers established with their infants (Goodman, 2002). Bowlby thus identified several patterns of insecure attachment drawn from his impressions that what appeared at first to be reactions of distress or protest subsequently turned into apparent mourning reactions. These reactions resulted in states of despair and sometimes of detachment in the face of prolonged separations from the mother.

Bowlby's (1969, 1973) views contrasted with those of most psychoanalytic observers, whose focus centered on oral stage deprivations. Consequently, his views were in large part rejected by the major psychoanalytic movements of his time–ego psychology and object relations theory. His emphasis on childhood mourning and a depression-like state resembled Bibring's (1953) and Zetzel's (1960) descriptions, but it was at odds with ego psychology's view that mourning was less fully formed in children and therefore more limited or short lived.

More recently, Kernberg (1984) described a depressive–masochistic personality type in which patients' motivations concerning others are centered on provoking rejection or maltreatment. Relationships of this nature precipitate depressive reactions in such patients and frequently induce guilt in the people with whom they are intimately involved. The masochistic nature of such patients' personality structure underlies the often-observed relationship between depression and self-defeating or masochistic personality dynamics, a relationship the *DSM–IV* proposal intended to represent. Though it is a view of uncertain status, it is nonetheless notable that in the context of chronic depression, Kernberg attempted to extend a psychoanalytic perspective to the pathogenesis of depressive personality.

The psychoanalytic literature is also neutral regarding depressive personality disorder or temperament as a discrete entity that may potentiate unfavorable life situations or interpersonal difficulties. Furthermore, although psychoanalytic viewpoints may identify factors precipitating episodes of affective illness, they do not attempt to explain different clinical presentations of depression. In concluding this section on psychoanalytic viewpoints about depression and before discussing Kohut's contributions, it is instructive to point out that Chodoff's (1972) cautious integrative attempt to extract some essential similarities among psychoanalytic perspectives did find some consistency among a wide range of theorists. Despite the variety of theoretical viewpoints, Chodoff commented that several psychoanalytic writers ascribed varying degrees of etiologic importance to oral stage needs or strivings. In more recent self psychological formulations, oral needs and the consequences of their frustration—collectively termed *oral aggression*—are frequently considered not as much as resulting from drive states as occurring in the context of maternal ministrations that provide calming, attachment, or affect-regulating functions.

Another notable point concerning Chodoff's (1972) article is that it appeared at a point in time that coincided with accelerating interest in specifying critical features of depression and delineating reliable and valid subtypes of depressive disorders. This effort also coincided with the appearance of diagnostic criteria aimed at reducing the heterogeneity of schizophrenia in order to bring the broad American definition of schizophrenia into greater alignment with international definitions. As a consequence, some cases of what would formerly have been considered schizophrenia were now being reclassified as affective disorders. This led to greater attention to diagnostic criteria of a broad range of unipolar and bipolar affective disorders, some of which were represented in Feighner et al.'s (1972) criteria and the Research Diagnostic Criteria (Spitzer, Endicott, & Robins, 1978). In anticipation of the substantial revision represented by the third edition of the *DSM* (American Psychiatric Association, 1980), there seemed to have occurred a greater division between theorists whose primary focus emphasized clinical description and validity of subtypes of depression and theorists whose main focus remained with characterizing dynamics of depressive phenomena. The degree of detail I provided in my discussion of descriptive psychopathology, particularly concerning differential diagnosis, should not be construed as representing a view that is disparate from that of psychoanalytic theories of depression. Rather, I prefer to think of these areas as representing different traditions that at present seem diverse but that ultimately will require integration in order to achieve greater coherence.

A SELF PSYCHOLOGICAL VIEWPOINT

It may seem surprising that narcissism was the prototypical self disorder, given how depressive personality disorder is so prominently characterized by major clinical indications of a self disorder—feelings of lethargy, anhedonia, and diminished enthusiasm to summon the requisite energy needed to meet work and other life responsibilities. Thus, not even as ubiquitous a phenomenon as depression was formulated as a particular self disorder, whereas perversions, addictions, and delinquency initially received attention as narcissistic behavior disorders. Because selfobject functions also were not considered to be diagnosis specific, depression was generally understood as a common symptom of a self disorder.

Individuals may experience depressive lack of zest or ennui either briefly in response to injuries or slights or chronically when mirroring, idealizing, or twinship selfobjects are insufficiently responsive to sustain self-cohesion. Regarded in this way, empathic selfobject failures lead to vulnerable self-cohesion that may become manifested clinically in various forms of depressive reactions. Depression as a predominant (and often exclusive) clinical disturbance may therefore be a manifestation of a self organization that has become undermined. The particular form a depressive reaction takes is not crucial for recognizing self-esteem injuries. Rather, the types of selfobject failures and their origins are more important considerations for understanding what is provocative about precipitating events, however muted or subtle the clinical presentation may be. Self psychology's emphasis on selfobject functions and vulnerability to empathic failures can provide a framework for understanding how the resulting depressive phenomena may reflect compromised self-cohesion. The self may be depleted because it is unmirrored, lacks available idealizable selfobjects to sustain its ambitions or goals, or is without the twinship selfobject experience of being allied with another to ensure communion in depth that may become sustaining. Life events that produce disappointment in others or demoralization about oneself may be superimposed on an already depression-prone existence in which hopelessness and diminished fulfillment are constant companions.

A self psychological viewpoint does not negate explanations that stress patients' introjected anger (guilt) or ambivalence surrounding loss or abandonment. However, a self psychological understanding of depressive personality disorder emphasizes the prominence of self states dominated by depletion or devitalization, signaling insufficiently fortified self-cohesion. Kohut (1977) and M. Tolpin (1978) called this phenomenon *depletion depression*. One reason why self psychology does not emphasize aggression, object loss, or guilt as important triggering events is because such explanations often seem alien to patients. It is not necessarily the case that such formulations are invalid; rather, they are beside the point. In their place, a self psychological approach frames interpretations around understanding how patients' injuries re-expose them to fragile self-cohesion. As a result, they lack the energy to struggle on with a sense of purpose or enthusiasm.

Thus, chronically depressed patients frequently find themselves devitalized or disappointed by the misattuned responsiveness of others rather than as a consequence of their anger or guilt. Interpretations framed around aggression, guilt, or object loss emphasize an experience-distant level of understanding. Though they may be reasonably accurate as far as they go, such interpretations nonetheless represent misdirected therapeutic intentions that may repeat rather than repair misattunements of patients' selfobject environment. Such interpretations may miss the point that chronically depressed patients typically are left with little more than a profound sense of emptiness when they feel overwhelmed by a selfobject world that has left them cold.

Patients with chronic depressive personality disorder are thus particularly prone to a degree of depletion that nearly totally pervades their lives, which are characterized by a pronounced sense of emptiness that is experienced as though the world had turned its back on them. For this reason, the main emphasis of a self psychological viewpoint of depressive personality centers on a sense of the self as depleted by the unavailability of affectively enlivening selfobjects, whether through insufficient mirroring, idealization, or twinship as primary structures or as compensatory structures. Such patients preserve only a shell of an existence, one that is lacking in zest or purpose. They cannot muster the optimism that an enlivening selfobject surround can be revived. Thus enfeebled, a persistent affect state of low-grade depression comes to represent the loss of vitality of the self.

Depressive personality disorder patients are chronically gloomy, pessimistic, and beaten down, and they feel themselves to be disappointments to others and to themselves. Unfortunately, they also inevitably wear down their selfobject surround with their ever-present misery. Such patients make others—including their psychotherapists—feel perpetually burdened in spite of the others' sympathetic tolerance. Thus, the people in their lives often need to keep their distance, because it is difficult to tolerate relationships for long with patients who have an unabating joyless, defeated demeanor. The clinical manifestations of chronic depressive personality disorder thus invite the very reactions from people that brought on and maintain the disorder in the first place. Such secondary reactions to the consequences of this kind of disturbance exacerbate the condition. The probability that needed selfobjects will psychologically withdraw compounds the already considerable strain such patients experience in securing ongoing selfobject responsiveness. This is an important point to emphasize in treatment because psychotherapists are also vulnerable to this form of countertransference disengagement, a point well noted by Akiskal (1989).

The stresses of life become filtered through these patients' characteristic predisposition to respond affectively to injuries to a weakened, devitalized self. Any external precipitant may revive the sense of a selfobject world that does not protect such patients from the injuries provoked by setbacks in life. M. Tolpin and Kohut (1980) emphasized the rupture of the self–selfobject unit in which selfobjects psychologically "vanish." Children who are exposed to parental empathic breaches of sufficient magnitude undergo the loss of a buoyant, energetic, and proud self. They are left "underpowered . . . the child and his world fall apart or become empty and devitalized" (p. 430).

These patients' devalued self-esteem, pessimistic inability to imagine feeling worthwhile or lovable, and chronic devitalization are features that Millon (1996) emphasized in his phenomenological characterization of the depressive prototype, which resembles Kohut's (1977, 1984) and M. Tolpin and Kohut's (1980) description of self disorders. The confluence of these viewpoints, originating from different though overlapping traditions, is captured in a singularly important characteristic of depressive personality disorder. Millon's observation that depressive personality disorder patients play dead in order to stay alive is remarkably close to M. Tolpin and Kohut's description of the same phenomenon: Such patients "feel unreal, shadowy, ghost-like, empty; their human surroundings, their possessions, their world, become dead, devoid of substantiality" (p. 430).

Regulation of affective experience to sustain self-cohesion is also at the center of the intersubjectivity viewpoint (Socarides & Stolorow, 1984–1985; Stolorow, Brandchaft, & Atwood, 1987), which considers a capacity for affective regulation to be a crucial outcome of empathic selfobject attunement. A capacity for tolerating disappointments and depressive affect states is regarded as integrative if an empathic selfobject environment accurately appreciates how distressing such self states can be. This kind of reliable, accurately attuned selfobject presence can help absorb the intensity of depressive affects, thus creating a degree of calm integration of painful affective experiences. In its absence, Socarides and Stolorow (1984–1985) observed two outcomes of parental empathic failures in development that may dispose individuals to chronic depression. In one outcome, the child with an affectively unattuned mother who does not help the child to manage or understand depressive affects may blame himself or herself for these affects in order to preserve a needed selfobject. This kind of child eventually experiences a predominant sense of self-denigration and hopelessness. A second potential outcome occurs when a child whose depressive affects are not recognized or responded to comes to dissociate these affects, leading to chronic emptiness.

Intersubjectivity theory has added to self psychology's emphasis on mothers' empathy with moment-to-moment need states of their infants. Its particular focus rests with empathy as serving an affective regulatory function. Other followers of self psychology also have called attention to the mutual regulation and influence of the mother–infant dyad (Beebe & Lachmann, 1988, 2002). They have emphasized how mothers' empathic responsiveness to signs of distress in their infants (e.g., affect states brought on by disruptions of maternal care, including prolonged separations and disappointments) promotes soothing in both their infants and in themselves as they see their infants calm down. This kind of mutual affective regulation ultimately enables infants (and later on, young children) to acquire a sufficient degree of internal regulation for soothing or calming themselves.

As language and conceptual skills emerge, attaching words or symbols to affect states provides a way for children to identify what they feel. Caregiver–child misattunements, however, may interfere with this process when caregivers do not help their children make sense of the affects they experience. One manifestation of such intersubjectively influenced disconnections may be depressive states, particularly if misattunements are frequent. Chronic depression may thus represent unarticulated affects of disappointment or, sometimes, despair when chronic empathic failures dominate caregiver–infant dyadic (intersubjective) interactions (Socarides & Stolorow, 1984–1985). Attachment theorists of a self psychological and intersubjectivity persuasion have also noted a tendency of individuals to react to disruptions of self-regulation with depression. According to this view, depression results from empathic breaches of the mutually regulating influences of attachment systems throughout life (Lichtenberg, 1983; Shane, Shane, & Gales, 1998).

CLINICAL ILLUSTRATION OF
DEPRESSIVE PERSONALITY DISORDER

Although there are abundant clinical reports of the treatment of depression, including its chronic forms with early onset, there is a far more limited literature on projective assessment of such disorders. In particular, little attention has been paid in the assessment field to disorders such as those discussed in this chapter. Thus, with few exceptions (Huprich, 1998, 2005), personality assessment has not systematically addressed conditions such as dysthymia or subsyndromal variants like depressive personality disorder or temperament. For this reason, I have selected for this chapter a clinical illustration of the projective personality assessment of a patient with chronic depression but without a history of major depression or bipolarity to describe a self psychological approach to what might be clinically considered to be a depressive personality disorder.

Mr. K. was a 40-year-old married White accountant with a history of subclinical dysphoria since early adolescence. He had been considered shy and unassertive as an adolescent and during his college years, and he first sought treatment while in college for his chronic subjective unhappiness and difficulty motivating himself. Mr. K. reported a "pall of gloom" that he experienced most of the time, which he believed had existed for as long as he could remember. He ignored this affect state, thinking it was a "normal part of the human condition everyone had," and he just did his work regardless of the cloud he always felt enveloping him. Mr. K. did not seem to experience exacerbations of this persistent affect state, although periods of difficulty motivating himself for work and brief periods of keeping a distance from his family had occurred at various times over the years, prompting him occasionally to consult a psychiatrist. Since college, Mr. K. had had two brief periods of psychotherapy combined with trials of antidepressant medications that may have been too brief or of too low a dose to have achieved therapeutic efficacy. I saw this patient for psychological testing on referral from a psychiatrist he had consulted who was considering psychoanalysis as the treatment of choice.

I administered the Rorschach (Comprehensive System; Exner, 2003), Thematic Apperception Test (TAT; H. A. Murray, 1943), and Human Figure Drawings (Handler, 1996) to Mr. K. (Silverstein, 1999). At the outset of the evaluation, after completing his drawing of a person, he commented, "It's better than I thought I could do; it surprised me." His surprise was not so much at being pleased with himself as it was at not failing when he expected to, perhaps capturing his Weltanschauung of feeling defeated almost before he began anything. After registering his initial note of surprise, he proceeded to describe his drawing as "sad, distraught, just standing still doing nothing." He went on to say (describing the figure in the drawing) that there was also "some positive in him, but it isn't available . . . he just doesn't see it." The glimmer of hopefulness quickly gave way to his elaborating that "his negative feelings pervade, it seems so dominant in him. His whole life he's been rewarded in a negative manner. There were never positive feelings of accomplishment." Asked to imagine the figure's future, Mr. K. first said that it was questionable, there's no progression. He's backsliding, the growth has stopped. There's a general malaise; it overshadows a lot of things. There's a lack of earning power; standing still in one's development. He refrains from getting involved. He's reluctant to make decisions and move ahead.

When asked to say what he saw the figure in the drawing doing, Mr. K. said, "Just nothingness—doing nothing. Vacillation."

His characterization depicted a predominant self state of an anhedonic sense of joylessness and a feeling of failure to move forward, despite fleeting hopeful moments that seemed too unconvincing for him to trust. His verbalizations depicted the self state of a person with an ingrained sense of failure, dragged down by defeat that has left him psychologically immobile and with little sense of relief. That there was a hint of hopefulness probably had enabled him at times to seek a remedy for the despair he often experienced.

Mr. K. elaborated his drawing of a person of the opposite sex differently. He depicted a woman who wanted to develop further than she had but who was at the same time complacent in her life and not interested in striving for much more than she had accomplished. Although this drawing represented his seeing other people as also having achieved less than they might have, Mr. K. reserved his pervasive sense of devitalization for himself, noting in a spontaneous comment comparing the two drawings, "While she's gone up, I've gone down."

Rorschach findings revealed no indicators of serious disturbance, depression, or adaptive (coping) deficits related to depression. This protocol indicated that there were sufficient psychological resources for managing most stressors and a generally stable capacity for tolerating frustration, persevering against obstacles, and maintaining self-control. My analysis also suggested, however, that Mr. K. was inclined to narrow his way of viewing people and situations by favoring a logical, objectified approach to events occurring around him (Lambda = 1.14). Consequently, he could be particularly intolerant of ambiguous situations, downplaying subtleties in favor of seeking uncomplicated solutions to problems. This patient vacillated between expressive and ideational approaches to psychological experiences (EB = 4:3.5), often unpredictably, though not at the expense of avoiding affective experience (Afr = .67), which was typically expressed in a reserved or restrained manner (FC:CF+C = 3:2). Although he appeared introspective and self-concerned, Mr. K. seemed more dissatisfied with or even vulnerable in his existence (3r+(2)/R = .57; MOR = 2 ; An+Xy = 4; FD = 2). Inclined toward passivity, acting deferentially, and accommodating himself to other people (a:p = 3:7), Mr. K. could simultaneously appear aloof.

Probing more closely, I inferred that his malaise, constricting anergia, and indecisiveness overlay a depleted self searching for something that would allow him to feel more securely anchored. He seemed to feel diminished and beaten down ("butchered," as he said on two Rorschach cards), but also to be searching for a more sure-footed direction from which he could derive a sense of feeling vitalized. For example, his first Rorschach percept on Card III was that of a bow tie, which he described as formal looking, suggesting "sophistication, being grown up, maturation." He followed this response with one of cartoonlike, formally dressed waiters lifting a dome off a dish they were serving. His third response described a dead rooster that had been butchered in preparation for cooking. His final response was of a cross-sectional view of the brain. In describing the rooster response, Mr. K. mentioned that it was the same color as the bow tie he saw previously. However, he added that the bow tie did not have the feeling of being dead like his rooster response did; the bow tie "has a more up feeling," but nevertheless it was "like a clown." A comment made parenthetically about his response of the brain was, "We're working on my brain here. I know the symbolism; I'm trying to get help."

Through this sequence of responses, Mr. K. seemed to express his wish to have attained a successful station in life, but the feeling that he could not progress beyond what was presumably a cartoonlike or clownlike self-image was probably closer to the image suggested by the percept of the beaten-down, dead rooster. The image of a brain, with its connotation of intellect, seemed to provoke a spontaneous association about getting help, perhaps representing a desire for an idealizing selfobject that might enable him to feel stronger. It echoed another Rorschach response of an owl (Card I), which he said looked wise and also reminded him of a nursery rhyme. Thus, wisdom, like Mr. K.'s response of a brain on Card III, may represent the sought-after invigoration of a depleted self he both desired and trivialized as the stuff of nursery rhymes. Further, his initial response to Card I was of a bat that seemed frightening; however, he went on to say, "If you really think about it, it's an insect eater and a help to the environment." But he reported another bat on Card V, this time "with diminutive wings that just aren't developed . . . these gizmos coming down are wings which are usually big and beautiful, but they're not unfolded yet, they're not developed." Thus, a selfobject environment that could be helpful could turn out to be fragile and not yet able to help because it was underdeveloped.

On Cards IX and X of his Rorschach protocol, Mr. K. described three other responses as cartoonlike images. One of these responses, "a cartoon character of a fat old mouse or rat, not intimidating; it's drawn to be softened for children" had been preceded by a response of "Darth Vader opposing another figure . . . maniacal and villainous." Thus, a formidable figure was transformed into a "benign, not intimidating . . . softened" image, which Mr. K. called "whimsical." This response suggested that something that seemed dangerous or villainous was not to be taken seriously, as if all the huffing and puffing of the powerful, imposing Darth Vader imagery was little more than fanciful whimsy. It was similar to the final cartoon character Mr. K. described, Pecos Pete (Card X), "the fall guy for the roadrunner's antics." A self psychological view would emphasize this sequence of responses and the elaborations they evoked as reflecting Mr. K.'s predominant experience of himself as being weakened. He felt himself to be immobilized and to be an impotent laughingstock. Looking beyond the self-depreciating imagery of several of his responses, it was possible to discern nevertheless a longing to experience selfobjects as strengthening.

Mr. K. thus sought a form of selfobject experience that would provide either mirroring or idealizing to repair injuries to self-esteem. Imagery such as that suggested by his Darth Vader percept may represent the kind of assured, idealized selfobject function this man sought to help him slay his dragons, so to speak. It simultaneously reflected Mr. K.'s disappointment that idealized selfobjects could not help him out of his dilemma; thus, strengthening of self-cohesion was all the more tenuous. He expressed little confidence that the revitalizing selfobject experience he needed would ever be more than a fanciful illusion that had been softened to prevent him from feeling belittled or intimidated. Nevertheless, the longing did not disappear, however driven underground or unrealistic a hope it seemed to him. Typically, patients with prominently devitalized self states such as that presented by Mr. K. do not necessarily abandon their search for invigorating selfobject experience. Their search continues to remain important for attempting to repair injured self-cohesion.

Mr. K.'s last response to Card IX, following the Darth Vader–cartoon rat sequence and preceding the cartoonish Pecos Pete response on Card X, was

> sort of a vague cup, a reward cup. It's not really quite formed, there's some sort of rising thing . . . a loving cup someone might have won for a sporting event. It looks like a chalice . . . invokes some sort of promise.

This was not the only time Mr. K. had spoken about rewards; earlier, his elaboration of a figure drawing had described how the figure could not grow because "negative rewards" blocked a sense of accomplishment. Later, on Card 1 of the TAT, Mr. K. told a story about a boy who was too tired or lacking in energy to practice the violin because "he just never got any reward" for his efforts to become accomplished. His story told of parents who cajoled and prodded the boy to practice, not seeming to notice his desire to be rewarded. The promise of a reward expressed in Mr. K.'s Rorschach response of the chalice acknowledging an accomplishment seemed also to represent a kind of selfobject responsiveness that he felt deeply missing in his life. Here and elsewhere in his projective test responses, Mr. K. seemed to be conveying the empty depression of someone whose needs for recognition had been unresponded to or ignored.

In a similar way, most of Mr. K.'s TAT stories were pervaded by affects of tired exhaustion blocking his efforts and joyless persevering in life. For example, no one appeared to rescue the boy of Card 1 from his unhappy feelings of failed accomplishment stemming from absent rewards. He told a story of a saddened woman on Card 3BM who "brushes herself off and life goes on" after discovering her house was vandalized. Thus, Mr. K. appeared in a veiled way to yearn for something other than a selfobject existence that left him having to brush himself off in some way and then joylessly carry on. He seemed alone with his unhappiness, probably unable to convey what he was experiencing or what he was looking for in others.

Mr. K.'s story in response to TAT Card 6BM described a mother and her grown son who is "not quite a man; he's old enough to be a man, but he isn't." He proceeded to describe how the mother supported the man "but it's not verbalized." At the same time, she did not stand up to the man's father if she thought the father was wrong. In Mr. K.'s story, the man never felt he had "credibility; he never knew his father was irrational, so he couldn't find out he was right." The man ended up dependent on his mother—"he just hasn't learned those skills." Mr. K. seemed to be relating not only the fact that his needs to feel affirmed or recognized had been ignored, but also the result of such unresponsive mirroring—an incapacity to feel sufficiently strengthened to hold himself up to the world with vigor and confidence.

Lacking the possibility for establishing a compensatory structure to reconstitute a depleted self through idealization or twinship selfobjects, Mr. K. seemed to characteristically experience himself as diminished and empty. His was a chronically uninvigorated depletion depression that left him feeling insignificant and just managing to get by in life. He managed this, however, at a cost of the pervasive anhedonia of a joyless existence. His experience of himself was as someone who had endured a lifetime of undermined self-esteem that foreclosed feeling proud or enthusiastic.

These test findings suggested an ingrained depression of long standing, subacute but persistent, in which Mr. K. experienced his life as being stuck in time and going nowhere. This psychological testing consultation hinted at what had not worked in previous treatment attempts—that is, at which of Mr. K.'s selfobject needs were triggered and how prior treatment efforts had exposed this patient to further injury or disappointment. The point of a consultation such as this is not to prescribe a form of treatment; rather, its benefit derives from highlighting what to watch for to avert another potential impasse in subsequent treatment. This consultation helped to clarify the meaning of this patient's former withdrawals from treatment as representing his disappointment in unempathic attunement rather than as representing depressive anergia or resistance. Failure to address this dynamic need in treatment might reexpose Mr. K. to the injuries that may have undermined previous treatment efforts. I also note that a dynamic understanding such as this is independent of and thus neutral in respect to this patient's clinically prominent depressive anergia, which is the basis for the diagnostic impression of depressive personality.

These results also highlight the forward edge transference (M. Tolpin, 2002) that may need to be recognized and engaged in his treatment. What Mr. K. tried to convey was what he needed from treatment—an idealizing selfobject function he could hold on to while he recovered from his predominant self state of being "not quite a man" whose "diminutive wings just aren't developed." Mr. K. may thus have been expressing a need for understanding more of the forward edge than of the trailing edge of his development; the disappointments and failures he already knew all too well. His projective test imagery brought into view what M. Tolpin thought of as budding tendrils of the forward edge transference; examples are the promise represented by the chalice of Card X and the expressed hope that he might be able to talk about his injuries instead of submerging the possibility of their being understood as another lost hope "that isn't verbalized" and regarding which he could do little more than brush himself off and plod on with his self still injured instead of repaired.

CONCLUSION

Affective disorders appear to have fairly specific biological origins such as serotonergic neurotransmitter pathways or the depressive, hyperthymic, or cyclothymic temperamental predispositions that Kraepelin described. Investigators have described various specific forms of depressive reactions—for example, major (unipolar) depression and bipolar depression—and various forms of chronic depressions such as dysthymia, depressive personality disorder, and cyclothymia. It is not presently known whether chronic depression represents one or more discrete disorders or whether it represents an attenuated form of a primary Axis I disorder. Consequently, the status of depressive personality disorder as a valid Axis II entity remains unclear.

This chapter has reviewed literature concerning depressive personality disorder from multiple standpoints, including descriptive psychopathology, contemporary personality disorder theory and research, and psychoanalytic theory before describing how self psychology may add to its understanding. The power of psychological theories lies not as much in their relevance for explaining forms of depression or its prognosis as in their ability to explain why personality factors perpetuate a life dominated by chronic depression. However, it is probably misguided to consider that specific personality configurations alone could potentiate conditions such as depressive personality disorder or subsyndromal depression. More likely, complex biological–personality–developmental interactions underlie hardwired affective (depressive) syndromes and depressive personality disorder. Thus, depressogenic biological vulnerability factors and psychological precipitating factors are viewed as jointly triggering the onset or exacerbation of depressive reactions, independent of severity or chronicity.

A self psychology viewpoint on depressive personality disorder emphasizes how the unavailability of affectively enlivening selfobjects perpetuates an enfeebled self characterized by the usual indications of self disorders—

diminished zest or enthusiasm, chronic boredom, and lack of goals. The role of depletion of the self can be a focus for understanding the experience of psychological life in patients for whom the organization of personality is consistent with that represented by descriptions of a depressive personality disorder pattern.

Whether or not depressive personality disorder or temperament represents a diagnostic entity with clinical course, family history, and neurobiologic features that would differentiate it from dysthymia (D. N. Klein, 1990) or other variants of sybsyndromal depression (Akiskal, 1989, 1997), there may be good reasons to continue to isolate this type of chronic depression for further study. The marked prominence of low-grade dysphoric mood affecting most or all areas of functioning in life dominates projective assessment findings, as shown in this case illustration. Although a pattern like this may not differentiate an early onset form of chronic depression from dysthymia, a self psychological viewpoint may nonetheless provide an important perspective on the quality of depletion or devitalization such patients experience.

10

DISORDERS OF THE SELF AND
SOMATIC REACTIVITY

An ample body of literature has demonstrated that psychological influences on somatic functions substantially affect illness onset, course, recovery, and duration of remission. Different traditions in psychology, including psychoanalytic theory, have developed views on psychological factors in illness, some of which have not stood the test of time. The focus of psychosomatic medicine (or as it is often now called, *behavioral medicine*) has widened from specifying psychological precipitants of discrete disorders, such as gastrointestinal diseases, headache, essential hypertension, and chronic pain, to examining broad aspects of health, such as psychological risk factors, prevention, compliance with maintenance treatment or health habits, and relapse prevention.

In this chapter, I will consider concepts of psychoanalytic self psychology that have bearing on illness onset and course. I will attempt to demonstrate how compromised self-cohesion and selfobject failures may influence somatic reactions and the course of somatic disorders by provoking or exacerbating illness episodes. To frame the self psychological explanation that follows later in this chapter, I begin with a discussion of aggravating and minimizing psychological factors.

SOMATIC REACTIVITY: AGGRAVATING (PROVOCATIVE) AND MINIMIZING PSYCHOLOGICAL FACTORS

One way to conceptualize personality factors related to illness onset and recovery is to consider psychological events as either aggravating or minimizing somatic reactivity. Aggravating factors produce excessive somatic distress relative to physical pathology (exclusive of factitious disorders, malingering, and Munchausen syndrome). Perturbations of psychological states such as anxiety, anger, or depression, as well as self states such as devitalization, fragmentation, or narcissistic rage, are examples of aggravating factors. Such mental states may both precipitate episodes of physical illness and affect the course and prognosis of an organic disease. Stressful events, premorbid personality factors, a relatively distinct Axis II disorder, and a history of trauma also may operate as factors that affect illness onset and recovery. Preoccupation with bodily integrity and overconcern about somatic function are also influenced by personality dispositions and are frequently accompanied by impaired social or work functioning. Somatic complaints often exceed the degree of distress that is justified by organic pathology. Psychological states also may influence disorders in which physical pathology has been ruled out or is presumed to be absent, such as hypochondriasis, somatization disorder (Briquet's syndrome), conversion disorder, and body dysmorphic disorder.

The customary presumption about somatoform disorders entails both absence of organic pathology and presence of discernible psychological factors (exclusive of somatic delusions) as precipitants. The prevalence of heightened somatic reactivity patterns is largely unknown in patients with Axis I disorders and with medical problems secondary to Axis I disorders or their treatments (e.g., hyperglycemia or renal complications).[1] It also is not known whether specific personality types or disorders influence hypo- or hypersensitivity of somatic reactivity. Somatic sensitivity may also represent exaggerated interest in body function or health such as that seen in fashion models, dancers, athletes, and natural remedies enthusiasts who may not be psychiatrically ill.

Minimizing somatic complaints (hyporeactivity) is a different psychological adaptation to bodily processes. It includes ignoring signs of somatic illness, appearing uninterested in obtaining relief, remaining unconvinced that treatments will be effective, and stoically tolerating or becoming habituated to pain that most people would find difficult to endure. Some patients who minimize somatic concerns do not seek treatment. They may mini-

---

[1] I exclude from consideration in this context psychiatric sequelae of medical disorders such as the dementias or the schizophrenia-like symptoms associated with Wilson's disease, a hereditary disorder of copper metabolism that is reversible with penicillamine therapy, sometimes combined with other anticopper agents. In disorders such as these, and also with psychiatric side effects of various medications, mental disturbances are secondary to the primary medical condition. Such mental symptoms sometimes respond to appropriate medical treatments, such as titrating or discontinuing medications that provoke side effect profiles dominated by cognitive or affective symptoms.

mize experiencing symptoms to the degree that they barely register their presence. For example, schizophrenics often show diminished responsiveness to somatosensory stimuli and insensitivity to pain (Arieti, 1945; Bleuler, 1950; Dworkin, 1994).

Further, *alexithymia* has been described as a personality or behavior pattern in psychosomatic patients that involves an incapacity to recognize affect states and that impoverishes how such patients experience and express emotion states (Krystal, 1998; J. McDougall, 1974; Nemiah & Sifneos, 1970). Alexithymic patients may experience somatic reactions as a substitute for affects they cannot identify, let alone comprehend, and their diminished, undifferentiated affective experience leaves them unable to signal distress about these somatic reactions. Schore's (2003b) review of recent findings on alexithymia suggested that this pattern reflects nondominant cerebral hemisphere dysfunction in which hyporesponsivity of orbitofrontal circuits compromises recognition and interpretation of affective signals.

Explanations for these patterns of minimizing somatic symptoms remain elusive. Variations in threshold levels of psychophysiological responsiveness probably contribute to somatic reactivity (Ax, 1953; Sternbach, 1966). Further, time-limited somatic stress responses are well-known occurrences in both normality and psychopathology (Grinker, 1953; Selye, 1956). Constitutional, genetic, and temperamental factors also may contribute to somatic responsivity patterns. Much remains to be learned about the specific influences of these factors and, more important still, their interactions.

PERSONALITY FACTORS IN SOMATIC DYSFUNCTION

Early views on psychological factors affecting physical conditions originated in psychoanalysis, which emphasized dammed-up or undischarged libidinal energy, a view Freud did not revisit after proposing his revised theory of anxiety (Alexander, 1950; M. Klein, 1935; Rosenfeld, 1964). Psychoanalytic interest in organic illness included a broad range of psychological manifestations, such as somatic compliance in respect to conversion symptoms, psychosomatic (psychophysiological) disorders, and hypochondriasis. An organ specificity view such as Alexander's (1950), which emphasized specific intrapsychic conflicts in particular illnesses, is largely considered unsubstantiated as a satisfactory causative explanation. A more likely hypothesis would be that generalized or nonspecific psychological factors of various types contribute to physiological disturbances, some of which may be constitutionally determined (Lipowski, 1968; Lowy, 1975).

In a general statement concerning psychological factors affecting physical conditions, the revised third edition of the *Diagnostic and Statistical Manual of Mental Disorders* (DSM–III–R; American Psychiatric Association, 1987) "accepts the tradition of referring to certain factors as 'psychological,' although it is by no means easy to define what this term means" (p. 333). Classifications of psychological factors affecting medical illnesses and somatoform disorders shifted in the fourth edition (DSM–IV; American Psychiatric Association, 1994) to emphasize the influence of these disorders on the course, treatment, precipitation or exacerbation, and health risks of medical conditions. For example, the DSM–IV noted that "psychological or behavioral factors play a potential role in the presentation or treatment of almost every general medical condition . . . [and] may affect the course of almost every major category of disease" (p. 676). The DSM–IV also has recognized that both Axis I and Axis II disorders affect general medical conditions and that "a personality trait or a maladaptive coping style significantly affects the course or treatment of a general medical condition. Personality traits can be subthreshold for an Axis II disorder" (p. 676).

Such cautious statements appropriately recognize the relevance of psychological events in somatic dysfunction and simultaneously acknowledge the inherent difficulties in determining their clinical importance. Thus, DSM–IV leaves open for clinical judgment considerations of personality and psychological events insofar as these influence the temporal relationship between environmental events and physical illness, recovery, and complications of treatment (including iatrogenic factors). It also highlights the importance of exercising care in establishing whether a relationship actually exists. Careful judgment is thus required to establish a diagnosis of any of the somatoform disorders, particularly hypochondriasis and pain disorder. Such determinations are usually aided by ascertaining the presence or absence of demonstrable organic evidence, often with the aid of the superior resolution afforded by modern imaging methods.

Medical professionals frequently recognize nonspecific personality factors as influencing somatic disturbances; they may call such patients "crocks" or "thick chart patients" (Lipsitt, 1970). However, the influences of discrete Axis II personality disorders on somatic disturbances are not well understood. Millon (1969, 1996) considered somatic dysfunctions as coping strategies, and somatoform reactions were cited in several personality styles in his biopsychosocial model. In Millon's view, somatic dysfunctions in certain personality types represent conflict between acquiescent dependency and assertive independence.

Byrne, Steinberg, and Schwartz (1968) studied the health characteristics and use of medical consultations in a nonpatient student sample in relation to the repression–sensitization personality dimension they proposed. Their findings indicated that "sensitizers" of emotional experience generally reported more somatic complaints than "repressors" and that male sensitizers in particular sought medical attention more frequently than male repressors. There was no repression–sensitization personality difference among women who sought medical help. Barsky (1979, 1983) proposed a concept similar to sensitization, which he termed *amplification*, to denote heightened perceptual experience of and affective focusing on physical symptoms. He distinguished amplification from minimization, and he regarded amplification as a personality trait characteristic of a *somatizing personality*, a condition of long standing dominated by marked absorption with or fear of disease. He included in this description hypochondriacal concerns and chronic pain complaints, among other vaguely delineated reaction patterns to physical illness.

Barsky (1979, 1983) emphasized intrapsychic and interpersonal aspects of somatization, noting particularly the influence of depression, even in patients with an absence of subjective depression. This so-called "masked" depression (Lopez-Ibor, 1972) or depressive equivalent (Lowy, 1975) is a phenomenon perhaps best represented by a comment attributed to the eminent British psychiatrist Henry Maudsley: "The sorrow which has no vent in tears may make other organs weep." Barsky also emphasized three predominant personality traits in somatizing personalities: masochistic self-sacrificing; interpersonal dependency; and aggression, either in the form of blaming others when feeling deprived or wronged or in an indirect (passive–aggressive) form.

Other somatizing personality styles exist—for example, a minimizing style, characterized by stoicism or denial, and a passive–avoidant style. Schore (2003b), influenced by recent literature on the adult sequelae of trauma, called attention to affective more than cognitive aspects of somatic dissociation, emphasizing the importance of autonomic hyporesponsivity. Lowy (1975) also acknowledged the influence of personality characteristics besides depression in somatizing patients, but he did not characterize a particular personality pattern. He acknowledged the prevalence of traits that Ruesch (1948) called *infantile personality* and that Marty and de M'Uzan (1963) described as concrete operational thinking (*pensée operatoire*), which was later included in Nemiah and Sifneos's (1970) alexithymia concept.

Alexithymia is a particularly interesting concept related to somatization and psychological experience. It influences how patients experience and express emotional phenomena; they seem unable to identify or differentiate their own affect states, and their capacity to express affects using language is compromised. As a result, emotions are vague, poorly articulated experiences. The words alexithymic patients use to describe their feeling states are obscure and empty of meaning. Alexithymic patients also reveal impoverishment or concreteness of thought processes in which a capacity for symbolic thought and imagination are diminished. Lumley, Stettner, and Wehmer (1996) regarded alexithymia as a disorder of affect dysregulation, and Sifneos (1991) observed that such patients "give the impression of being different, alien beings, having come from an entirely different world, living in the midst of a society which is dominated by feelings. They are like living computers totally devoid of feelings" (p. 119).

Nemiah and Sifneos (1970) identified alexithymia as a prominent clinical feature of psychosomatic patients. Krystal (1998) and J. McDougall (1974) also noted that such patients seem detached from people and appear to be loners, and Krystal (1978) observed that they showed an impaired capacity for taking care of themselves. They may appear emotionally numbed—presumably to avoid pain—and they may also be contemptuous of others' expressions of sentiment or emotionality. In addition to its occurrence in somatizing patients, alexithymia has been reported in trauma patients (Van der Kolk, 1993), Holocaust survivors (Niederland, 1968), substance abusers (Finn, Martin, & Pihl, 1987; G. J. Taylor, Parker, & Bagby, 1990), and pathological gamblers (Lumley & Roby, 1995). Sifneos (1991) suggested that traumatic experiences in infancy before the acquisition of language capabilities may produce alexithymia by interfering with young children's learning to use words to express affect states. Krystal (1998) commented on the protective function of psychosomatic illnesses against recognizing narcissistic defects. Further, associations with familial correlates of dysfunctional affective expressiveness have been reported (Berenbaum & James, 1994; Lumley, Mader, Gramzow, & Papineau, 1996).

SELF PSYCHOLOGY AND SOMATIZATION

Somatization reactions and disorders of organic dysfunction did not occupy a prominent role in psychoanalytic theory. Alexander's (1950) writings on psychosomatic illnesses were among the earliest psychoanalytic formulations, but his view of conflict-specific illnesses has not been uncritically accepted. In general, patients with somatoform disorders or hypochondriacal reactions are rarely considered optimal candidates for analytic treatment unless there coexists appreciable anxiety, depression, or other overt psychological distress. Conversion and dissociative disorder patients are also infrequently seen by analysts, despite these conditions' importance as clinical syndromes that led to several of the earliest and most fundamental principles of psychoanalysis. Even alexithymia has not attracted widespread interest beyond the notable exception of J. McDougall's (1974, 1989) and Sifneos's (1991) writings, perhaps because alexithymic patients also are considered poor or marginal candidates for analytic treatment. Little more than modest interest exists in somatization disorders or organic illness among contemporary psychoanalysts who claim orientations in the object relations, interpersonal, or intersubjective schools. The same may be said of self psychology as well.

Kohut wrote about somatic dysfunctions only in passing and nearly always in a broad context of psychophysiological reactions expressing disguised self states. Kohut (1971) did comment parenthetically in a footnote that he had observed how some patients with narcissistic pathology showed hypersensitivity to drafts and cold temperatures as part of a general difficulty regulating skin temperature for keeping warm. He speculated that shame reactions resulting from narcissistic injuries might influence vasoconstriction of the skin and mucous membranes; however, his observation that such patients tended to rely on others for providing warmth may be a more psychologically pertinent comment about such patients' self disorders.

Self psychology has shown relatively limited interest in somatization disorders, although these conditions may nevertheless represent disturbances of self and affect regulation. Somatization reactions point to an internal sense of destabilized self-cohesion; they signify disruptive affect states that cannot be sufficiently modulated. The psychological experience of being affectively overwhelmed may thus represent a self state similar to fragmentation in which such patients express vulnerable or weakened self-cohesion as somatic disturbances. In this way, somatization reactions seem to short-circuit psychological experiences of distress, such as feeling flooded by dysregulated affects. Kohut's (1971) view was that selfobject deficits centering on failure to internalize self-soothing capacities may take the form of somatic reactions as a substitute for consolidating psychological intactness (self-cohesion), much as addictions or perversions are considered attempts to subdue painful affect states that cannot otherwise be relieved or calmed.

According to this way of viewing somatization reactions—as expressions of self states that become too difficult to tolerate—somatic hyper- or hyporeactivity may represent a breakdown of self-cohesion. Treating somatization reactions or somatic preoccupations requires helping patients recognize the psychological experience of selfobject failures and potential fragmentation. In treatment, this recognition would be accomplished by gradually introducing this idea and replacing somatic concerns with a language for patients to describe—and eventually recognize and tolerate—how internal experiences of affect states become alienated from their awareness. As J. McDougall (1974) observed, concerns about illness and somatic functions estrange patients from the process by which people become aware of affect states, which is the same process that becomes engaged in nearly all forms of psychotherapeutic endeavor.

Thus, in treating somatic disorders, the links between bodily phenomena and psychological events or feeling states need to be restored. Brickman (1992) proposed that treatment of somatizing patients requires establishing what he called a *desomatizing selfobject transference*, which he described as the formation of a selfobject relationship through which affective links are created via ongoing experiences. By allowing a preparatory period to permit a selfobject bond to coalesce, therapists help patients come to tolerate linkages with affects that were formerly defensively sequestered. Once this selfobject transference becomes established, psychotherapeutic work can unfold in a customary way, in which psychological experience—rather than bodily preoccupations—is at the forefront of treatment.

Rickles (1986) commented on the inability to regulate affective experience in patients with alexithymia and related somatization disturbances involving disconnections between bodily processes and psychological experience. He compared the treatment of such disorders to a similar problem found in patients with self disorders who rely on chemical substances to manage or contain affect. Citing how disavowal interferes with symbolic experiences of psychological events, Rickles regarded splitting off self or affective experiences as a mechanism that may lead to alexithymia. In this respect, he considered alexithymic or psychosomatic phenomena as a type of self disorder.

Because disavowal impoverishes self experience and patients' capacity to establish selfobject relationships with people, their access to symbolic functions consequently is limited. Rickles (1986) commented that misguided attempts to prematurely interpret psychological experiences are rarely therapeutically efficacious; they are experienced instead as narcissistic injuries. As a result, the body seems to function as though it were itself a selfobject that has become split off from experience. Bodily dysfunctions or illnesses thus substitute for psychological experience. Whereas other patients with self disorders experience selfobject failures of mirroring or idealization with depression or anger (representing feeling slighted, depleted, or undermined), patients with somatizing forms of self disorders may fail to notice events impinging on their psychological lives. They instead note and respond psychologically to bodily functions or illnesses as letting them down or failing them.

Intersubjectivity theorists in self psychology also have not specifically addressed somatic disorders, although their emphasis on the importance of affect as an organizer of psychological experience may readily be extended to this group of disorders (Socarides & Stolorow, 1984–1985; Stolorow & Atwood, 1992). According to an intersubjectivity view, one consequence of children's experiences of unrecognized affective experience by their caregivers is the expectation that having affects is unwelcome or threatening. Like Rickles (1986), Stolorow and his colleagues (Socarides & Stolorow, 1984–1985; Stolorow & Atwood, 1992) noted how affective experience becomes walled off, adding that isolating affective experience protects the selfobject or intersubjective surround. Such children thus do not acquire symbols for integrating their emotional experiences with words, even as language and cognitive abilities become increasingly available. Furthermore, they are not helped by caregivers to understand or verbalize what they feel at any given moment. Caregivers who thus deflect integrating affective areas of experience foster their children's diminished symbolization capacities. Such caregivers compromise their children's articulation of what they feel and how they differentiate emotion states. Children so impoverished lack ways to find words to talk about their affects, which becomes fertile soil for alexithymia and psychosomatic or somatization disturbances.

Bollas (1989) proposed a similar idea, although it was not identified with self psychology, in his description of what he called a *normotic personality*, which is dominated by a marked disinclination to access subjective experience. Such individuals, who are not necessarily without affects, are unable to introspect about their psychological experiences, particularly painful experiences, and they seem to appear deceptively untroubled or "normal." Bollas thought that some psychosomatic patients had a normotic disposition resembling alexithymia. He speculated that the parents of such persons avoided responding to their children's affective experiences, experiences Bollas regarded as the core of the self. Thus, during play activities, their parents were disinclined to teach them to elaborate on emotion states or to engage with them in playful imagination, ultimately discouraging them from using language to articulate feeling states. Such children's imaginative inner lives were consequently ignored because fantasy and affect were left unacknowledged.

Studies of mother–infant interactions have produced findings with implications for understanding the somatization of mental experience. This observational literature demonstrates that the interactive influence of the mother–infant dyadic system is more influential than internal (intrapsychic) experiences of early development for regulating drives and for organizing mental representations of the self and object world. Beebe and Lachmann (1994, 2002) described responsive matching interactions between infants and mothers, such as echoing or imitation in vocal interactions, that suggested synchronization of mother–infant affect states. They regarded such interactions as promoting attunement between mother and infant for strengthening the infant's sense of the self. Beebe and Lachmann also considered faulty matches between infants and mothers a basis for asynchronous mutual affect regulation, producing what they called *misregulated* affect states. Ongoing experiences of mother–infant misattunements produce misregulation that does not benefit from self-righting when reparative attempts occur, as self-righting almost always does in normal development when an attuned, synchronous mother–infant dyad is predominant. Thus, misregulation without repair may be responsible for chronic affective dysregulation, which over time develops into overt psychopathology, including somatization disorders or alexithymia.

Expansions of self psychological theory, such as intersubjectivity theory and related views of mutual affect regulation derived from mother–infant observations, offer novel ways of thinking about disturbances in regulating disrupted affective states. Related views about self-regulation and development have also been proposed from areas such as developmental psychopathology (Fonagy, Gergely, Jurist, & Target, 2002) and object relations theory (Bion, 1962). Their emphasis on affect as an organizer of the self and self experience is consistent with the ideas proposed by Brickman (1992) and Rickles (1986), who made use of self psychological concepts to reconsider disturbances of somatization. If mutual influence as a crucial component of regulating affects has been interrupted or is otherwise flawed, somatic states of distress may become disconnected from the affective states linked with them. Such disconnections may take the form of a minimization of affect states such as alexithymia; alternatively, mutual affect dysregulation may be manifested as somatic hyperarousal. It is not generally understood why affect misattunement or dysregulation operates as a minimizing factor for some people, disposing them to somatic hyporeactivity such as alexithymia, and as an aggravating factor for others, disposing them to heightened somatic distress.

CLINICAL ILLUSTRATION OF SOMATIC DYSFUNCTION

Mr. L. was a 25-year-old single White man who was employed as an announcer for a Hungarian–American radio station run by his father. At about age 12, when puberty began, Mr. L. had experienced brief periods of extreme physical discomfort, about which he could say only, "I'd be jumpy." He stated that the feeling was one of pressure or tension, mostly in the chest, lasting a few minutes several times throughout the day. Two years later, he developed a convulsive disorder characterized by loss of consciousness (without aura) and thrashing about, sometimes with drooling and biting of the tongue. According to descriptions by observers, he displayed head bobbing and squatting on his knees but no tonic–clonic movements. Frequency of occurrence was unknown, because most of these episodes were nocturnal. At the time of treatment, he no longer had convulsive episodes during the daytime, and he described his seizures or seizure equivalents as being weaker and less disturbing to him. He had been examined at a major university medical center, and he also had consulted the Mayo Clinic for an evaluation. All neurological examinations, including electroencephalograms and related brain wave studies, were within normal limits.

According to the neurologist who had followed his care for 4 years, all of the previous consultations noted a prominent psychosomatic component, which Mr. L. was reluctant to consider. The neurologist noted no fundamental change in seizure status, which was partially controlled by anticonvulsant medications, during the past 4 years. Mr. L. was currently being reevaluated in the hospital concerning his response to anticonvulsants and his inability to consider the possibility that his condition was aggravated by psychological factors. Another consulting neurological opinion confirmed the impression that Mr. L.'s reactions did not represent true convulsive episodes. Hypoglycemia had been ruled out as a possible contributing factor. Family history was noncontributory. Mr. L. had had an automobile accident at age 21 in which he sprained his neck, but otherwise his medical history and a physical examination were unremarkable.

Mr. L. had made what sounded to me like a histrionic suicide attempt at age 20 after his girlfriend had left him, which the family physician treated with emotional support at home because the family refused to consider a psychiatric hospitalization. Two years before my evaluation, Mr. L. had also become "hysterical" (his term) after an argument with his brother while his parents were out of town attending to business. He described this reaction as a brief period of intense crying and screaming because the brother did not do something. A psychiatric consultation reported no psychotic process or overt disturbance warranting psychotropic medication.

Neuropsychological testing revealed above average intelligence and grossly intact cognitive–perceptual skills. Marginally lower memory ability was detected relative to intelligence, but memory was still considered within normal limits. Findings of a projective psychological testing evaluation revealed a tightly guarded, constricted personality; the presence of obsessive–compulsive and narcissistic defenses; and conflict over keeping hostility controlled. Sensitivity to criticism or slights was also noted, together with an inclination to be oppositional, sometimes accompanied by cynical sarcasm.

Mr. L. described his mother as a stern, no-nonsense hard worker who always kept herself busy. He was the third child of four, and he felt that his mother encouraged him and his younger brother to be more independent than his older sisters. He thought of himself as a favored child because he was the oldest son, but he felt that that ended when he was older and his parents began demanding more from him. Mr. L.'s father was apparently a formidable, domineering figure in the home, a man who "controls everything and everybody." His father owned several businesses, and many people in the Hungarian–American community relied on him for jobs and for favors based on his influence. Mr. L. recalled that as a child, in order to talk to his father, he had to wait in line with other people who wanted favors from his father. The patient worried about not succeeding as an adult, and thus he stayed within the businesses of his family's orbit. Mr. L. thought his father was more controlling and less encouraging of his independence when he was growing up than his mother had been. Mr. L. commented, "The appellate court was my mother, but the Supreme Court was my father."

Mr. L. had attended a private high school where he earned average grades, feeling little motivation to study. His parents were demanding and criticized him for not working harder. He was somewhat overweight and not interested in sports, and because his parents were immigrants and he did not fit a typical suburban stereotype, Mr. L. was beaten or spit on by other boys. Although he felt like an outcast and was not happy at the school, his parents did not want him to transfer, thinking that he had to withstand his mistreatment and learn to adjust. He himself did not want to leave for fear that the community in his family's orbit would think he could not succeed at this rigorous and prestigious school. He was happier at the college he attended, however. Mr. L. had worked for his father since graduating from college and had lived in his own apartment until he was evicted recently because his seizures frightened his neighbors. Mr. L. had moved back to his parents' home 3 months earlier.

I saw Mr. L. in weekly psychotherapy for 3 months. He was anxious about knowing what to talk about, and there were extended periods of silence when he wanted me to ask him questions to help him along. He was somber and serious in overall mood, feeling more comfortable talking about physical symptoms, such as a strain in his back or how his tongue hurt from a seizure and made it hard for him to talk. Slowly and reluctantly, Mr. L. talked about events happening in his life, such as having to arrange a banquet for his father, which he did not want to do. He noted that he was required to make a speech in Hungarian at the banquet, which he afterward thought he had botched. Even my simple comment that botching the speech must have made him feel bad was met by his minimizing its emotional meaning before again falling silent. Whenever I would attempt to focus on affect states or emotional reactions, Mr. L. would minimize their relevance, saying my observations were trivial.

Mr. L. began to arrive late for sessions after four or five weeks, complaining more about biting his tongue, and he wondered whether he would have anything to talk about. He once asked to leave a session early because his tongue was hurting. Mr. L. mentioned that it was becoming harder to talk on the radio because of the tongue biting. He worried whether he would be able to run the family businesses after his father retired and whether the sponsors would continue to support the radio station if his father were not supervising it. When I attempted to explore his concerns, he was silent at first and then would abruptly change the subject (e.g., to how he would like to marry the girlfriend who had rejected him) with no apparent awareness of what he was doing.

He disallowed my suggestion that his former girlfriend's rejection and his fear of being rejected by the local Hungarian community were connected in any way. Mr. L. would say that he did not understand what I meant, sometimes fixating on minor details of the remarks I made. Usually speaking in a deliberate manner and barely concealing his contempt, he often said that I was wrong about him and that I misunderstood his intentions. His rejection of nearly everything I said seemed to represent doing to me what he experienced everyone in his surround as doing to him. When I pointed out that his father also misunderstood him, he became silent, but by his gestures I thought he was considering what I had said. After a minute or two of silence, he mentioned that he was looking forward to buying a condominium because he hoped the distance from his father would improve their relationship.

A few weeks later, Mr. L. said that he was enraged that his father had threatened to withdraw the loan he had offered Mr. L. to buy an apartment because Mr. L. had failed to deliver on some requests the father made concerning the businesses. He appeared tense as he seemed to realize that he could not easily deny his anger. He again fell silent for a while, took out a cigarette and offered me one, and then abruptly changed the subject, talking about how solitary he had been feeling lately. He told me that he had asked a girl he once knew "if we might become more close," but that she was not interested. I suggested to him that he wished for closeness or companionship (because he had just asked a girl to become close and offered me a cigarette). He politely but cynically disagreed, although I thought his politeness was a sign of his warming up.

The treatment continued in this way for another month with little further movement. He continued to feel that I misunderstood him and that what I thought about him was wrong. He remained affectively stiff and remote. He was frustrated that his seizures continued and that his doctors had no better treatment to offer him. He could not see how talking about what happened in his life or the connections I tried to point out could lead anywhere or help to relieve his seizures. After 3 months, Mr. L. decided to terminate treatment.

This patient's treatment course demonstrated a rigidly inaccessible affect life. Emotions were kept out of his awareness most of the time and were shunned with contemptuous disdain when I commented on them. Mr. L. would divert his attention to practical matters, showing little or no comprehension that he closed down an entire sector of his experience—what events and people meant to him. This young man could talk about the frustration of living with a largely untreatable seizure disorder that defied explanation by several neurologists and that may have led to his being evicted from his apartment, but without sounding obviously frustrated. He could talk about the uncontrollable tongue biting and how it interfered with his work as a radio announcer, yet his words of desperation did not seem deeply felt. I did not doubt that he felt frustrated, but it was difficult to empathize with his desperation when his words sounded so far removed from what he probably actually experienced. What I apprehended much of the time was his cold and distanced reserve. Talking about himself and his life seemed to perturb him as much as living with a seizure disorder did.

Amplifying his somatic experiences and minimizing their affective undercurrents did not preclude Mr. L.'s being able to occasionally talk about being enraged or wanting to experience intimacy with a woman. He felt rather acutely the burden of assuming responsibility for the family businesses and his uncertainty about succeeding, never losing sight of the fact that his critical, overcontrolling father was watching his every move. Mr. L. had words to indicate what mattered in his life, but he seemed alienated from the lived affective experiences themselves. He was intelligent enough to comprehend my interpretations about events and their temporal connections with affect states, most of which were straightforward and not particularly complex. However, Mr. L. closed himself off to becoming aware of such connections, possibly because they might lead to affects he could not integrate. When I suggested connections to him, his characteristic silence or change of subject seemed to reflect his sealing over their affective meanings. It was difficult for him to feel closeness, and it was equally difficult for him to talk about his desires. He was uncomfortable accepting supportive understanding, despite his occasional tentative responsive gestures from which he quickly retreated.

I inferred that Mr. L. had been repeatedly left to his own devices to tolerate distressing affects without the benefit of caregivers whose ingrained old world values may have interfered with helping him understand what he was feeling; I speculated that his stern, hardened mother, who asked her son to tough it out at a school where he felt demeaned, failed to respond empathically to the hurt such a young boy must have endured. I also saw how a critical, demanding father who wanted his son to do his bidding and not defy his will could produce humiliation and rage. It was not difficult to imagine what it must have been like for Mr. L. as a young boy to patiently wait his turn in line to make some contact with his father. His interior life was effectively foreclosed as he shut down any way for others to become affectively close to him and to respond in kind. He dared not risk getting close to experiencing the injuries to a still-vulnerable, weakly consolidated self. The disconnections between the meanings of events and any feelings about such experiences prevented Mr. L. from comprehending his internal emotional life. It is also understandable that he probably was unable to develop an internal self-regulatory capacity.

Discerning how dysregulated affects threaten to destabilize self-cohesion is at the center of a self psychological view of somatic disturbances, in which somatic symptoms operate much like ingrained personality deficits. So regarded, self disorders and the somatic reactions they may perpetuate can be maladaptive in the way that many personality disorders are. I suggest that selfobject failures to help individuals regulate their affect states may influence somatic reactivity phenomena by aggravating their intensity or minimizing cognitive–affective reactions to them. Mr. L. appeared to show both of these somatic reactivity patterns. He showed an exacerbation of somatic distress when affect (self) states were mobilized that he could not modulate. He also was unable to experience the powerful affective reactions that clearly were so destabilizing. I make no attempt to explain why Mr. L. experienced what seemed to be an atypical (psychogenic) seizure pattern; caution is certainly in order in suggesting a link between his markedly constricted personality, a crippling self disorder, and a seizure disorder that was becoming increasingly immobilizing. Though right (nondominant) cerebral hemisphere dysfunction has been reported in both conversion seizures (Devinsky, Mesad, & Alper, 2001) and in emotional reactions to bodily stimuli (Devinsky, 2000), the clinical picture represented by Mr. L.'s history and illness course leaves many questions unanswered. It seems clear that Mr. L.'s capacity for tolerating disruptive affective states was profoundly diminished and that he suffered from a seriously compromised capacity to sustain self-cohesion. However, it is difficult to speculate about the role of neurophysiological events as influences on this man's atypical seizure pattern, his suboptimal response to anticonvulsant therapy, and the perpetuation of his self and affect dysregulation disorder.

Mr. L. seemed burdened by selfobject failures that undermined self-cohesion. An associated affect dysregulation disturbance may have aggravated his seizure disorder. Simultaneously, poorly consolidated self-cohesion may have impaired his capacity to symbolize affect states. This patient's somatic hyperreactivity pattern may thus function as a signpost denoting the severity of the self disorder associated with or underlying his illness. It may also highlight how a somatic reactivity pattern may operate as an ingrained, enduring maladaptation to life such as that seen in personality disorders.

CONCLUSION

This chapter considered somatic disorders from a self psychological viewpoint, emphasizing how self-cohesion deficits may either aggravate or minimize somatic reactivity. Dysfunction that is associated with somatic hypo- and hyperreactivity includes disorders such as exacerbations of episodes of physical illnesses, somatic overconcern, hypochondriasis, and somatization disorder; these disorders were described in this chapter as attempts to manage disruptive affect states. Such patients are thought to show weakened self-cohesion preventing them from internalizing a capacity to calm or soothe disorganizing affect states. Patients with a somatic hyperreactivity pattern may show aggravated somatic reactions because they become overwhelmed by affective stimulation, sometimes to a functionally immobilizing degree. They may report histories suggestive of unempathic selfobject responsiveness that fails to recognize the presence or intensity of affect states. They seem left to their own devices to manage affect states they cannot understand or regulate; affective distress therefore remains insufficiently modulated and cannot easily be relieved.

A second broad group of somatic reactivity patterns is characterized by minimizing awareness or concern about somatic signals (somatic hyporeactivity). Represented by inattention to somatic functions, neglect of self-care, or alexithymia, this pattern is also thought to be indicative of self-cohesion deficits. This disturbance is centered on selfobject failures characterized by unrecognized and thus unassisted regulation of intense affects. Patients with a minimizing or hyporeactive pattern have found a solution in disregarding potentially distressing affect states by turning away or shutting them out.

I do not suggest that either the hyperreactive (aggravated) or the hyporeactive (minimizing) somatic reactivity pattern directly produces somatic illness or exacerbates somatic distress. My emphasis in this chapter has been on describing these two broad patterns and suggesting a self psychological approach for understanding them. Aggravating and minimizing patterns of somatic reactivity are chronic, and they represent ingrained, habitual behavior patterns in respect to somatic functions. As a result, they share a similarity with the kinds of ingrained behavior patterns considered to represent personality disorder.

11

DISAVOWAL: THE VERTICAL SPLIT

Among the more valuable and durable contributions psychoanalysis has introduced, the concept of defense is fundamental to all of its various perspectives and major schools. Moreover, the concept of defense also has had broad acceptance outside psychoanalytic theory itself. *Repression* was for all intents and purposes synonymous with *defense* in Freud's earliest formulations of the concept. Among the defense mechanisms, repression and denial concern expunging mental phenomena from conscious awareness—such as memories, affects, and motives (wishes)—in both normality and psychopathology. I will describe in this chapter another mechanism related to expunging mental phenomena—*disavowal*, a defense that operates differently than repression and denial because it isolates or sequesters mental contents rather than eliminates them from conscious awareness. Kohut (1971) differentiated disavowal from repression, and Goldberg (1999) further elaborated the concept of disavowal in his discussion of a phenomenon that Kohut referred to as the *vertical split*. In this chapter, I will discuss the vertical split as a way personality is organized; it may be thought to operate like a personality disorder.

Disavowal is an aspect of conscious awareness in which people know about and acknowledge particular actions, though they do not "know" that side of themselves experiencing such disavowed states—that is, an aspect of their experience is cut off from behavior. They do not know what propels the behavior, yet they understand that it is necessary and vital. Disavowal is not synonymous with the idea that affects may become isolated or walled off from thoughts. Further, reality is not distorted; thus, disavowed actions are not psychotic-like, and people are not unaware that the actions occur in reality. Rather, the meaning of that reality seems strangely unfamiliar (Basch, 1983–1984).

Kohut's interest in disavowal originated with his interest in narcissism (Kohut, 1966, 1971). Specifically, he gave as examples grandiose attitudes or behavior coexisting alongside a depressive core, in which people recognize that both self states are present but seem to feel, metaphorically, as if they are not the same person experiencing both self states (Kohut, 1996). Kohut contrasted disavowed grandiosity (the vertical split)—of which a person is aware but from which he or she feels alienated—with the repressed grandiosity (the horizontal split) of which a person is unaware that operates defensively to conceal uncertainty or weakness. Kohut did not, however, further develop the concept of the vertical split. One of his close colleagues, Arnold Goldberg, further delineated its clinical characteristics and extended its scope to include a range of disturbances beyond grandiosity. For example, Goldberg (1999, 2000) considered certain manifestations of narcissistic behavior disorders—such as shoplifting, cross-dressing, some forms of infidelity, and binge eating—as representing disavowed self states when they are uncharacteristic of a person's typical behavior and when they are usually concealed from most people. Such patients are aware of, though simultaneously puzzled by, their unquestioned need for the so-called misbehavior. Goldberg also formulated an approach to its treatment based on an understanding of the vertical split as a self disorder. Though neither Kohut nor Goldberg regarded the vertical split as a distinct personality disorder, the vertical split in some respects resembles an essential feature of a personality disorder—it involves a stable, ingrained configuration of aberrant personality and behavior.

In this chapter, I will first discuss disavowal and repression in psychoanalytic theory. I then discuss the distinction between disavowal and disorders of dissociation. The remainder of the chapter will consider Kohut's (1971) and Goldberg's (1999, 2000) views of the vertical split, including implications for its treatment and a discussion of the relationship between this phenomenon and concepts of personality disorders.

DISAVOWAL AND REPRESSION

Comparing disavowal and repression necessitates a brief review of the relationship between the concept of repression and the topographic point of view in psychoanalytic metapsychology. Freud's (Breuer & Freud, 1893–1895/1955) earliest theory of mental functions was derived from his theory of mental life, as he understood it at that time, as being divided into sectors of conscious, unconscious, and preconscious experience. The topographic point of view followed closely from Freud's earlier discovery that splitting of mental phenomena characterized the symptoms he and Breuer observed and attempted to treat, particularly in hysteria. Influenced by his work with Charcot on hypnosis and by Janet's and Breuer's thinking about hysteria, Freud considered hysteria to be a condition in which two states were kept apart or dissociated from one another, representing a splitting of conscious experience or awareness (see Boring, 1950).

Philosophers such as Leibniz and physiologists like Helmholtz had already distinguished between experiences that were conscious and those that were not. With Freud's emphasis on unconscious experience as a motivational influence on mental life—particularly its abnormalities, which he considered to be the psychoneuroses—Freud proposed the idea of repression to explain why unconscious phenomena remained outside of conscious awareness. As he gradually recognized that repression was but one among several such mechanisms, Freud (1915/1957c) later formulated a broader view of defense as a counterforce in opposition to drives. Thus, Freud limited repression to explanations about unconscious mental contents that were excluded (forgotten) from conscious experience. This was the idea of a repression barrier, and it constituted an early notion of a division or splitting of aspects of psychological experience.

Kohut (1971), in his early exposition of a psychology of the self, acknowledged Freud's (1927/1961b) concept of a repression barrier, in which "the patient suffers from a sort of ignorance" (p. 155), and thus, mental contents become inaccessible. Kohut referred to this phenomenon as the *horizontal split*. He also described another division of mental contents, which he termed the *vertical split*, to denote aspects of experience that were accessible to conscious awareness but were simultaneously disavowed or walled off.[1] He considered the vertical split to represent a modification of a split Freud (1927/1961b, 1940/1964) had identified within the ego to explain fetishism, in which distorted ideas about the fetish were separated from the ego's perception of reality (Rubovits-Seitz, 1999). Kohut was describing an aspect of self experience that was not kept out of conscious awareness by the motivated forgetting of repression (or *ignorance*, as in the quotation from Freud). Because disavowed mental content contradicted one's predominant self-image, it was kept apart from, but not out of, conscious awareness.

DISAVOWAL AND DISSOCIATION

The second distinction I will discuss is that between disavowal and dissociation. Disorders of dissociation are usually Axis I syndromes, some of

---

[1]The significance of the terms *horizontal* and *vertical* to designate these mental phenomena was a directional metaphor Kohut (1971) used to denote that conscious and unconscious experience could be represented schematically by a horizontal line (the repression barrier) dividing them; in contrast, a vertical line represented schematically mental contents that were experienced side by side.

which occur infrequently, such as dissociative identity disorder and dissociative fugue (formerly known as *multiple personality disorder* and *psychogenic fugue states*, respectively). Others, such as depersonalization disorder, occur more frequently. Moreover, depersonalization and derealization phenomena occur often in other Axis I disorders. No Axis II personality disorder is particularly comorbid with disorders of dissociation, nor has it been suggested that any of the personality disorders form a continuum with dissociation that would be similar to the spectrum concept proposed as a possible link between disorders such as schizoid or schizotypal personality disorder and schizophrenia or between depressive personality and major depression. Dissociative disorders represent a direct connection with disturbances characterized by some form of separation or splitting of mental phenomena. A theoretically neutral nosologic system such as the *Diagnostic and Statistical Manual of Mental Disorders* (4th ed., text revision; American Psychiatric Association, 2000) has described dissociation as "a disruption in the usually integrated functions of consciousness, memory, identity, or perception" (p. 519). Thus, dissociative disorders do entail an alteration of cognition.

Disavowal, however, does not appear to involve a distortion of cognitive processes. It appears to be a phenomenon of mental life in which sectors of experience are kept out of awareness. Goldberg (1999) also considered dysphoric affects to be relatively more accessible in patients with dissociation than in patients for whom disavowal was prominent, which is another feature differentiating dissociative disorders from patients with a vertical split.

Repression and dissociation thus serve defensive functions as they are viewed in psychoanalysis, including self psychology. Their function is to keep mental contents outside of conscious experience. Kohut (1968, 1971) expanded the range of split-off mental contents to include aspects of self experience that are not unconscious but that often represent contradictory self states. Such self states are not repressed or dissociated from conscious awareness because of intrapsychic conflict. Rather, such disavowed self states coexist in conscious awareness, thus creating a vertical split in the experience of the self. Goldberg (1999) observed that "parallel, divided personalities often seem able to live with one another" (p. 11).

THE VERTICAL SPLIT:
CLINICAL–THEORETICAL CONSIDERATIONS

Goldberg's (1999) concept of the vertical split was broader than Kohut's (1971) original view; it emerged from Goldberg's (1995) earlier study of perversions (such as cross-dressing in otherwise conventional-appearing persons) as a prototypical example. He thus expanded the forms of psychopathology that could be explained by the concept of vertical split beyond Kohut's original idea of split-off grandiosity. Goldberg's broadened view regarded infidelity as a more prototypical form when it occurs to manage unexperienced painful affect states. Thus, Goldberg thought that the narcissistic behavior disorders—encompassing addiction and some of its variants (including promiscuity, eating disorders, and substance use disorders), perversions, and delinquency—also resulted from a vertical split in the experience of the self. Goldberg particularly stressed not only that the offending experience or misbehavior represented by the vertical split was in conscious awareness but that in addition, patients frequently abhorred this aspect of themselves. A good illustration of a vertical split was described in a work of classic fiction, Robert Louis Stevenson's *The Strange Case of Dr. Jekyll and Mr. Hyde* (1886/ 2003).

Goldberg (1999) differentiated such patients' harsh judgments about themselves from intropunitiveness or superego pathology and antisocial personality. He emphasized that behavior that is maintained by a vertical split is usually thought by such patients to be an aspect of self experience to be disowned and shunned. Some examples might include a financially well-off person who shoplifts or a person who, although satisfied in his or her marriage, engages in furtive affairs. Secret activities such as binge eating and cross-dressing are still other examples, although such behaviors may overlap with impulse disorders.

Goldberg (1999) emphasized a distinction between the vertical split and the concept of splitting in object relations theories. Both views of splitting denote sectors of personality or experience that are in conflict with one another. Object relations views of splitting usually characterize a defensively walled-off phenomenon closer to repression. In contrast, a vertical split remains in awareness or is readily accessible to conscious experience. Although the split-off sectors exist side by side despite being in opposition to one another, in some people they may coexist without overt distress. Other people with a vertical split may dislike the offending aspect of their experience. For example, to use the example of binge eating, some patients cannot wait to binge, and others hate their impulse to binge.

Shapiro (1981) observed a similar clinical phenomenon, which he described as actions that are motivated by conflict and schism in the personality but that cannot be explained on that basis alone. Apart from unconscious motivations such as guilt, he seemed to stop short of considering other dynamic factors to explain, for example, why a successful businessman would forge checks, noting that even among successful businessmen who experience guilt, not all forge checks. Shapiro observed that an action such as forging checks is both "in character" and simultaneously alien. For instance, referring to the example of the businessman, Shapiro said, "He does not seem to completely recognize himself in this behavior; he may experience his own behavior as strange or peculiar, as something he does not entirely want or even intend to do" (p. 22). A self psychological view of the same phenomenon would very likely consider this behavior to be consistent with the dynamic of a vertical split.

Origins in Development

Goldberg's (1999) view of the vertical split traces its origin to painful affect states that are disavowed. Disavowal leading to a vertical split is thought to arise in childhood from interactions with parents or caregivers who are unavailable to help their children identify affect states. Such children are left to endure unverbalized affect states on their own. Their caregivers may themselves be unaware of their own affects; consequently, they are uncomfortable with managing their children's affect states (Socarides & Stolorow, 1984–1985). Failure to soothe or help regulate their children's affective reactions, particularly disturbing affect states, leads such children to resort to regulating heightened and sometimes intolerable affects by disavowing their existence in the form of engaging in an activity that brings relief (Basch, 1988; Goldberg, 1999).

An action such as a narcissistic behavior disorder serves a stabilizing or self-regulatory function in an attempt to achieve some degree of cohesiveness of the self. The split-off sectors of affective experience so created develop in adolescence or adulthood into the misbehaviors of the vertical split. They are comprehensible in the same way that self disorders are understood as seeking to achieve a repair of the self in the face of empathic selfobject failures. Underlying the misbehaviors that bring relief, there typically exist unarticulated affect states that are not experienced—usually depression, but sometimes anxiety or anger. The quality of the depression that emerges in treatment is usually characterized by emptiness, lack of zest, or purposelessness. In this way, as Goldberg (1999) noted, "the child has disappeared, has found a solution" (p. 36) in the split-off misbehavior. Caregivers who cannot tolerate their children's intense affective experiences thus turn a blind eye; it "is somehow registered and appreciated by the parent who implicitly prefers a misbehavior that can be ignored to a depression that cannot be" (Goldberg, 1999, p. 36). Treating a vertical split may be expected to expose such concealed affects, not because they are repressed but because they are hidden from view by the action of the split.

Treatment Considerations

The unverbalized meanings of the selfobject functions sustaining each side of a vertical split are important to understand in treatment. The therapeutic work involves promoting integration of both sides of the split, often going back and forth between these sides while empathically understanding the need for both sides to sustain self-cohesion. Goldberg (1999) noted that "every patient with a vertical split needs the recognition of each side. Unfortunately, therapists tend to pick one sector and therefore implicitly support the split" (p. 119). Thus, addressing one or the other side alone typically serves to maintain the split by ignoring or silencing the other selfobject connection. Goldberg also advised taking care to avoid a situation in which "seeing things exactly as the patient does makes blind men of us both" (p. 162). He addressed special problems in treating the vertical split, particularly the importance of clinicians' recognizing in themselves a "'touch' of the same deviance" and "temporarily [suspending] a judgmental stand . . . by not taking sides" (p. 171), to recognize and make use of in treatment a parallel split within themselves. Recognition of a parallel split promotes an understanding of what may underlie their patients' splits. Attempting to suppress offending misbehavior or being overly tolerant of it may lead to enactments occurring outside a clinician's awareness such as boundary lapses or moralistic distancing from the misbehavior. Reactions such as these undermine a therapeutic understanding of patients with a vertical split.

Once a split has been engaged, a crucial part of the work of treatment is exposing the frequently underlying depression that led to and maintains the vertical split represented by the misbehavior. Its clinical understanding would follow the customary self psychological approach to the selfobject transferences based on the emergence of phase-specific selfobject needs. As selfobject needs and empathic breaches become clearer, the underlying depression and its precipitants may come to feel more psychologically authentic than the misbehavior patients enact through the vertical split.

Goldberg (1999) emphasized the importance of clinicians' taking care to avoid assuming moralistic positions or overly rapid judgments about what may be right or wrong, which patients do not need clinicians to reinforce or educate them about, because they already know this about their "misbehavior" and frequently consider it to be wrong or despicable, although necessary or compelling. Thus, Goldberg concluded,

> Some patients might need some misbehavior to be tolerated and some to be condemned. . . . It is not enough to condemn or condone a behavior, nor is it enough to comment on the behavior from afar. . . . One must somehow move to the middle, to know what it is and what it is like and yet not need to do it. (p. 110)

Stated another way, one of the analysts in Goldberg's casebook who treated a case of a vertical split remarked that "I could not imagine myself singing the words to his song, but I could hear myself whistling the tune" (Goldberg, 2000, p. 109).

CLINICAL ILLUSTRATION OF THE VERTICAL SPLIT

Goldberg (2000), in collaboration with several colleagues, published a volume of cases demonstrating various forms of the vertical split and their treatment in psychoanalysis or psychotherapy. This casebook was a companion volume to his theoretical exposition of the vertical split (Goldberg, 1999).

Because good clinical examples of the vertical split are available elsewhere, I will present in this section a case of psychodiagnostic testing to demonstrate how this clinical phenomenon may appear in an assessment of personality using projective tests (Silverstein, 1999).

The patient, Ms. M., was a 26-year-old single White woman who sought treatment in connection with a deepening romantic involvement with a coworker at the bank where she had worked for the past year. Ms. M. was engaged to be married to a man she had been dating for 7 years. She seemed confused by her behavior, not knowing why she had become involved with her coworker or why she continued her involvement with him. She felt that the affair could go nowhere, but she could not resist the excitement she felt with him, despite the fact that he was not interested in a committed relationship. She would occasionally see him in clubs with other women, and this made her feel anxious and angry, even though she knew he dated other women. Ms. M. was judgmental about herself and troubled by her inability to do what she considered to be the right thing by terminating the affair. She observed that this man was kind to her and that she was attracted by the similarity of their interests, the compatibility of their personalities, and the excitement of their erotic relationship. She was emotionally drawn both to him and to her fiancé, with whom she continued to have a satisfying sexual relationship. However, she felt with her coworker "like I'm 16 again. . . . We're like kids in the playground who tease each other." In contrast, Ms. M. appreciated her long-time boyfriend's steadiness and reliability, though she also reported a growing sense of blandness about him that irritated her. She felt she wanted to do more stimulating things with her life while she was young, and she found herself increasingly slowed down by limitations associated with her fiancé's pain from a chronic back injury, which sapped his energy.

Ms. M. described the difference between these men as though she herself were two different people, feeling invigorated by a sense of abandon with her coworker and feeling a comfortable sense of stability through her fiancé's dependability. She experienced guilt about the affair, but what was equally apparent was the anticipatory regret were she to give it up. As she described her feeling, Ms. M. appeared tearful but did not seem entirely aware of tears welling up or the depth of the sadness she seemed to experience. She quickly changed the subject to talk about the frenetic activity of making wedding arrangements. Over a period of 4 months in psychotherapy, there was no indication of a self-destructive pattern of sabotaging her wedding arrangements or jeopardizing her relationship with her fiancé. Ms. M. also related a recent fantasy in which she would starve herself to become ill so that her fiancé would understand why they should break off their engagement, thus leaving her free to run off with the other man.

Ms. M. lived with her parents and two brothers, and she spoke by telephone with her fiancé daily, spending weekends and some weekdays with him. Ms. M. said that he was easygoing, made no demands on her, and did not ask her to account for her time when she was out at night either with friends or with the other man. Ms. M.'s father actively abused alcohol until she was 9 years old. He was not prone to angry outbursts or abusive behavior at home, and she remembered him sleeping a great deal before he became sober. Her father was still quiet, and Ms. M. saw him as depressed, even though he was more involved with family activities than he had been when he was drinking. She felt she hardly knew her father before he was sober, but she now felt closer to him and enjoyed him more than she did as a child, despite their limited conversations. Ms. M. described a generally warm but not particularly close relationship with her mother, noting that they sometimes fought because they were too much alike in temperament. She saw her parents' life together as sad, in part because her father was afraid of driving and preferred to stay at home; she felt that her father's inactivity left her mother shortchanged, living a dutiful but joyless life.

The findings of the Comprehensive System (Exner, 2003) structural summary of Ms. M.'s Rorschach were generally unremarkable, pointing to mild but chronic overload resulting from difficulty coping with the demands she experienced in her life. Tension and irritability were noted, accompanied by limited tolerance for frustration and by impulsivity. She showed a diminished openness to experience and an avoidant style, viewing her life through a narrow frame of reference. This personality style likely would have disposed Ms. M. to be intolerant of uncertainty and ambiguity, preferring clearly defined and well-structured situations with simple solutions. She was as a result inclined to make hasty and sometimes careless decisions that might not be well thought through, despite unimpaired reality testing. Ms. M. would be considered affectively reserved or controlled, and she showed indications of passivity.

More than these findings, which might be typical of many outpatients with a variety of presenting complaints, an inspection of thematic content and the sequence of associations in several of her Rorschach responses illuminated the function of the vertical split in the organization of this woman's psychological experience. It hinted at reasons why this structure of personality may have come about. Ms. M.'s Rorschach began normally enough with responses on Card I of a bug and a bat; however, the inquiries about these percepts revealed that she saw them together in a single response rather than as separate or discrete objects. She proceeded to explain how they were related or why they were together: The bug was a "little tiny" animal that did not know the bat was coming, and then the bat swooped down and ate the bug. Thus, what seemed at first glance to be a fairly typical sequence of responses suggested instead that objects usually kept separated were actually combined, not in a way that would indicate that their perceptual boundaries were distorted or merged, but rather as a way of expressing something Ms. M. apprehended about a predator and its prey.

On Card II, she continued to reveal how segmented her experiences could be. Ms. M. first saw two people playing pat-a-cake, which she clarified as little girls having fun. She then saw a butterfly, commenting on inquiry first about how colorful it was and how it was free to fly where it wanted to go. She then added as an aside that butterflies start out as ugly caterpillars before they become beautiful insects. After the butterfly response, Ms. M. reported two people playing pat-a-cake, which she clarified on inquiry as different people than those of her earlier percept, this time "holding hands and coming closer to each other." When asked on inquiry how she saw them coming closer, Ms. M. said it reminded her of two lovers who had not seen each other in a long while. She gave no indication that she was revising her earlier response of two little girls playing pat-a-cake, nor did she make a reference to seeing something similar or different than the earlier response on this card. Thus, it seemed clear that she was intending these responses as two separate percepts. Both responses, although similar in the activity reported, were also quite different insofar as the people in the first response were children and the people in the second response were in a more intimate relationship. There was nothing about these responses that suggested dissociation, though her awareness of different sides of her experience remained unintegrated. It is cautiously suggestive of the way Ms. M. spoke about herself and her coworker boyfriend—as lovers and also like children in a playground. Again, although this must remain at best a speculative inference, what was particularly striking about these responses was that she made no comment about the first pat-a-cake response when she delivered the second response, as if she were oblivious to but not unaware of having already given a similar response.

The psychological phenomenon I am calling attention to is neither forgetting (repression) nor dissociation; it is instead Ms. M.'s way of apprehending her psychological world in which aspects of reality are both remembered and experienced but are kept apart from each other. This patient did not seem to be aware of one side when another aspect of her awareness was in the foreground. Considering Ms. M.'s responses on Card II together with her responses on Card I (the bug and the bat), it was becoming more apparent that this patient was responsive to disparate aspects of her experience of events in ways that kept the disparate sides apart while still remaining aware of both sides. Thus, children and lovers or predator and prey were not merged, confabulated, or dissociated, but they were kept apart from each other as if a wall of glass separated one image from the other. With this interpretation in mind, I noted also that Ms. M.'s response of a butterfly on Card II contained the idea that butterflies are transformed caterpillars. That is, the same organism is at different times two disparate forms of the same organism. Moreover, like children in a playground who grow up to become intimate lovers, "ugly" caterpillars become "beautiful" butterflies. Like her butterfly, Ms. M. seemed to be expressing a wish to be free to have what she wanted. It suggested a function that the vertical split may serve—to go back and forth between the two sides.

On several other cards, Ms. M. continued to produce several responses suggesting unusual incongruities, sometimes playfully and sometimes with an indifferent concern about how objects fit together or made sense. For example, on Card IV she described Bigfoot with a snake hat over its head. She elaborated this odd image as if the snake were something just thrown over Bigfoot's head as "an accessory, maybe Bigfoot's a king, he looks like he's royalty, maybe he's the leader of his tribe." On Card V, Ms. M. reported a bat and then added, "But then it has rabbit legs hanging out the end of it." She also gave two responses of dinosaurs, one of which was flying, about which she wondered, "It would be weird seeing a huge flying dinosaur; imagine being in a plane and seeing that." Indeed! I could well imagine how she could be amused and then troubled by experiences that freely came over her. Furthermore, as with her earlier responses, Ms. M. seemed to feel no particular need to explain or justify such incongruities. Only when she was asked to explain how she saw such incompatible images would she describe a way to make sense of what she saw. Thus, this patient could see a predominant object that would become her main response, and then she would see other features that she did not bother to keep apart from the dominant images she saw.

What can be said about the kind of thinking such responses may indicate? Perhaps Ms. M. was careless or lazy, perhaps uncritical or uncensored; certainly, at the very least, her perception and thinking could be quite idiosyncratic. Her sometimes playful manner notwithstanding, the possibility of a thought disorder could not be ignored—Rorschach Comprehensive System (Exner, 2003) variables reflecting reality or thinking distortions included a $WSum6$ index of 24, which was considerably elevated, and a $WA\%$ of .75, which was low, and 4 of her 11 human contents responses were of unreal or mythical figures. Several of her responses received formal scores for disordered thinking, including some of the examples I have cited, but this was not necessarily the casual, indifferent quality of thinking or perception seen conventionally on the Rorschach as disordered thinking nor, for that matter, as impaired judgment or reality testing. Ms. M. was not psychotic, nor did she show a pervasive pattern of poor judgment. Though her capacity for logical thinking might be questioned, intrusive or worrisome thoughts associated with unmet needs also appeared to constitute prominent aspects of the quality of Ms. M.'s thinking.

I do not wish to create the impression that I am disregarding an important (and one of the more reliable) Rorschach signs in this case. However, I also wish to highlight another point of view about interpreting this idiosyncratic way of organizing experience that does not necessarily require considering it as subjugating reality to fantasy. Stated another way, concluding from the incongruous or fabulized combinations contained in Ms. M.'s Rorschach protocol only that logical thinking is compromised may be analogous to attempting to treat the misbehavior of a vertical split by fostering such a patient's desire to be able to cease that activity. In contrast, understanding the meaning of Ms. M.'s idiosyncratic response combinations may be the Rorschach counterpart of Goldberg's (1999, 2000) admonition that clinicians should comprehend the need states compelling both sides of a vertical split—that is, metaphorically, to whistle their tune and hear the words without having to sing the lyric.

All of these and several other responses provided a picture of Ms. M.'s way of organizing her world. Apart from the possibility of thought disorder, this patient's casual manner of organizing or editing (censoring) perceptual elements reflected her experience of her life. She would see something, then see something else, and then casually put the two images together side by side without concern for how things go together. It seemed clear that her idiosyncratic style was familiar to her and that she was untroubled by it. Ms. M. seemed comfortable with experiencing disparate images that would not normally be integrated. She was aware of disparities and simultaneously unconcerned about them, which may be why she could feel distress about her affair as if it were conducted by a different person while still realizing that it was she who felt that way and that it was she who also felt invigorated in her relationship with her coworker. She became adept at experiencing her psychological world in just such a way. As with her incongruous Rorschach responses, although Ms. M. had the capacity to recognize that being engaged and having an affair did not go together, she could sometimes be indifferent about this and at other times guilty. However, her sense of guilt was not the intropunitive guilt of intrapsychic conflict.

This case illustration describes what a vertical split may look like on an instrument such as the Rorschach. Thus, aside from and as well as representing a reality distortion, responses such as Ms. M.'s may provide further understanding about the kind of disavowal that characterizes a vertical split. Although her response style might be considered as being too loose or as having strayed too far from the task for some tastes, Rorschach examiners have no special answer to the dilemma of differentiating imaginative flights of fancy from loose associations beyond assigning scores and codes to denote thinking anomalies. It is understood that elevations of such scores do not necessarily correspond to disorders of thinking and that in the final analysis, it is the use of clinical judgment that ultimately decides the matter. Notwithstanding these allowances, many of Ms. M.'s responses and verbalizations pushed the limits of tolerance for logical thinking, even on an instrument that can invite regression as readily as the Rorschach can. But there was no evidence of serious psychopathology suggesting a psychotic process or thought disorder in either her history or her clinical presentation over 4 months of treatment, at which point I referred her for psychoanalysis.

It remains my impression that the fanciful and at times idiosyncratic thinking seen throughout Ms. M.'s Rorschach protocol was more likely to indicate a rich capacity for disinhibited associative thinking, in which at times she attempted to keep intrusive ideas and affect states separate and disavowed, consistent with the concept of a vertical split. I am not suggesting, however, that such a Rorschach presentation is a diagnostic indicator of a vertical split, because only careful empirical investigation would be able to substantiate such a conclusion.

THE VERTICAL SPLIT IN RELATION TO PERSONALITY DISORDERS

Like most personality disorders, a vertical split is of long standing, relatively ingrained, and episodic when its manifestations become intensified. I do not suggest that the vertical split be designated as a personality disorder, either as a categorical entity or based on dimensional trait features, despite its conformity with most criteria for defining personality disorders. There may also be other psychoanalytic and theoretical explanations for this phenomenon besides that of self psychology. It is nevertheless a condition that has not been formally studied; thus, little is known about its diagnostic overlap with other disorders, the reliability of assigning the diagnosis, and its population prevalence. Nor can it be said that the vertical split cannot be better characterized using existing Axis I or Axis II diagnoses.

One reason for discussing the vertical split is to call further attention to this personality pattern for further study, highlighting its chief characteristics in a context both of Axis II personality disorders and a self psychological approach to personality disorders. My primary purpose is to note that it is a condition affecting psychological functioning that operates in many crucial respects like a personality disorder, regardless of any potential recognition it may or may not be accorded as a nosological entity.

CONCLUSION

This chapter has addressed disavowal, which self psychology refers to as the *vertical split*. Based largely on Goldberg's (1999, 2000) further development of Kohut's (1971) concept of a vertical split, I have discussed how forms of misbehavior such as narcissistic behavior disorders represent split-off self states that when accurately understood usually represent unarticulated manifestations of depression. A vertical split requires understanding of both sides to integrate its disparate elements and to explore the reasons why such a split seems necessary for maintaining patients' self-cohesion. I also have discussed potential relationships between a vertical split and personality disorders.

AFTERWORD

Discovering the essential characteristics of disorders of personality and attempting to classify such disorders in the most parsimonious way are endeavors that belong together. They are united by traditions of careful observation and description, reliable measurement, and empirical investigation, and they are integrated under a broad umbrella of theoretical coherence. Naturally, findings are not always interpreted in the same ways; thus, controversy is no less present in the contemporary study of personality disorders than it is in any other field.

Sometimes, however, to achieve a unity of purpose about a method of studying phenomena, a field of study needs to selectively narrow its scope. Viewpoints are accepted if they conform to current scientific and clinical standards for providing useful data. Other viewpoints are excluded if they either have outlived their theoretical usefulness or have failed to provide a reliable method for study that is capable of being proved incorrect by philosophy of science standards. Concerning the field of contemporary studies of personality disorders, psychoanalysis may be a case in point.

In the past 30 or more years, psychoanalysis as a clinical method and body of theory has had a sharply delimited influence on current directions in personality disorder research. Beginning with the multiaxial classification system of the third edition of the *Diagnostic and Statistical Manual of Mental Disorders* (DSM; American Psychiatric Association, 1980), the declining influence of psychoanalysis on contemporary personality disorder theory and research has also extended to formal diagnostic nosologies represented by subsequent versions of the DSM and the *International Classification of Diseases* (World Health Organization, 1992). Psychoanalysis has not yet reached the point of being excluded, but it may well be on its way. I reach this conclusion because although there have been advances in psychoanalysis in the past 3 decades, few have substantively contributed to the study of personality disorders.

Consequently, these fields of study have grown farther apart during the past 3 decades than they ever were before (Silverstein, 2005). During this same period, personality disorder research, inextricably linked with classification and nosology, has benefited from advances in instrumentation and measurement, psychiatric epidemiology, and neurobiology far more than it has benefited from the insights of psychoanalysis. Perhaps prophetically, but surely as perceptively as always, Grinker (1965) once remarked (although about a different subject),

> I, and many others, have faith that out of psychoanalytic theory could come fruitful and testable hypotheses instead of the worn-out hackneyed reiterations and reformulations and the stultifying stereotypes stated as positive facts, based only on inferences. . . . I hope that what is fruitful can be extracted by serious scientists who can doubt as well as speculate, who can critically observe and experiment as well as infer. (p. 124)

Psychoanalysis—probably more than ever, and perhaps also more in respect to the study of personality and its disorders than other fields—straddles the fence between legitimate inquiry and respectability, on the one hand, and bad science (certainly on philosophy of science grounds) on the other hand. For some, it is clear where psychoanalysis belongs; such people exist on either side of the fence. For others, there is uncertainty. Still others are convinced of its value, usually because they somehow benefited from its strangely unreliable method; they are discomfited by the awareness, embedded in the fabric of their Weltanschauung, that so deeply enriching an enterprise is miles away from an acceptable standard for verifying its propositions.

I am writing from the perspective of someone in this last group. I do not suggest that by extending Kohut's (1971) self psychology to personality disorders I have stated a compelling case for its inclusion rather than its exclusion as a valid area for further study. I offer no hint of a testable method to examine its propositions that is any less unreliable than other psychoanalytic methods. I have attempted only to demonstrate both theoretically and clinically how a viewpoint first articulated by Kohut—and developed further by his close colleagues and by subsequent advances in self psychology—might explain personality disorders as they are presently characterized.

This is an explanation that has not previously been considered in a systematic way. Kohut himself was not as concerned about diagnosis-specific differentiations as he was with investigating a broad range of psychopathological disturbances that might benefit from a self psychologically informed explanation. I have made no argument in this book that a self psychological formulation is superior to any other explanatory attempt. I trust that I have concentrated my efforts on extending a self psychological perspective to this group of disorders. Toward this effort, I have also attempted to remain aware of but neutral concerning important nosologic concerns in the field, most notably that pertaining to a categorical or dimensional classification scheme.

I have also considered a self psychological approach as an explanation for other disturbances that are not conventionally considered to be personality aberrations or that have demonstrated equivocal validity as discrete entities. For example, it remains uncertain whether depressive personality and somatic reactivity patterns may be better explained as personality disorders or as other types of clinical disorders. These disturbances conform in principle to the main requirement of the definition of a personality disorder: a long-standing, ingrained maladaptation of living producing demonstrable impairment in several areas of functioning. Other such conditions are also recognized, with varying degrees of confidence concerning their validity. I have not considered here disturbances that at other points in time have been viewed as personality disorders (e.g., passive–aggressive and masochistic or self-defeating personalities).

In light of the reasons why psychoanalysis and the study of personality disorders have parted ways, what then is the justification for following the path I have chosen in this volume? My answer is that the conceptual and clinical phenomena that self psychology emphasizes seem to identify certain aspects of disorders of personality that are not well explained by descriptions that presently exist. To make this point clear, I have chosen detailed cases rather than selective clinical vignettes to show how self psychology's clinical and developmental insights are discerned to their best advantage when the clinical illustrations are examined in broad perspective rather than in cross-section. I cannot know whether a better method for their study will ever arise from within self psychology or any other clinical approach, despite the relatively recent availability of mother–infant observation literature and developmental–clinical studies of attachment that offer some promise for this purpose. I mainly wish to keep in focus a viewpoint for explaining personality disorders that runs the risk of being overlooked as research endeavors emphasize different directions.

Partly for theoretical reasons and partly for heuristic purposes, I have tentatively proposed a conceptual schema for applying self psychological concepts to characterize personality disorders as they are now denoted on Axis II. This approach to rethinking personality disorders in consideration of self psychological concepts could be considered as a framework to highlight how these disorders represent attempts to preserve or restore self-cohesion. Thus, I have denoted devitalization, the forestalling of fragmentation, and alternative paths to securing self-cohesion as superordinate concepts to frame self psychological ideas such as mirroring, idealizing, and twinship selfobject functions; disintegration products; and compensatory structures. This framework focuses on developmental life tasks people struggle with when self-cohesion has been compromised; it represents various solutions to restoring self-esteem (Kohut, 1977). Stated another way, withdrawing into a devitalized or depleted self, forestalling fragmentation, and attempting to find alternative pathways to repair injuries to the self may be adaptations patients with personality disorders forge to secure whatever degree of self-cohesion might be possible for them. Often they are unsuccessful, but sometimes people may achieve partially workable adaptations (e.g., if a compensatory structure can be established or if a vulnerability to fragmentation can be managed despite the toll it may exact on general functioning). It is, after all, the relative failure of such adaptations as resolutions that gives rise to the various clinical disturbances or maladaptations of Axis II, whether they are called *disorders of the self* or *personality disorders*.

I do not think I began with as explicit an idea as developmental or life tasks when I devised a plan for recharacterizing the personality disorders of Axis II. However, such a recharacterization became increasingly evident as I continued thinking about these personality (self) disorders. Only now have I been able to formulate this viewpoint, mindful of the importance of including if not a terminology then at least a language (Schafer, 1976) to specify what to look for. At least this much would be necessary for an approach such as the one I have proposed in this volume. I intend for it to be treated as a beginning but serious attempt to add a self psychological understanding to the field of personality disorders in consideration of the issues of greatest concern for its scientific study. In so doing, I call attention to self psychological processes that are at least partially distinguishable from one another. It is premature to claim that these phenomena can be reliably differentiated, though undoubtedly they overlap. Framing the broad conceptual outline of these self psychological concepts in a way that makes clinical sense is a preliminary step toward developing a method to study self psychological phenomena. For this reason, therefore, I also think of the framework I presented in this book as one that may be modified and refined as need be, attentive both to the conceptual integrity of self psychology's ideas and to the need to devise a plausible method to bring them into an acceptable level of scientific clinical discourse.

Thus, I do not necessarily consider my recharacterization as a final self psychological explanation of personality disorders, but I do consider it as a reasonable way to think about these disorders. I also want to reiterate that my recharacterization of Axis II personality disorders is not meant to replace the cluster groupings (odd/eccentric, disorganized, and fearful) that presently exist in the fourth edition of the DSM (American Psychiatric Association, 1994). These clusters were identified because they were considered to hold some value in subgrouping Axis II disorders, although their empirical validity has been questioned in recent years. I make no comment about that point; however, I note that the groupings I have proposed on the basis of self psychological principles are offered with the intention of representing an alternative or parallel classification.

One important current direction in personality disorders research suggests continua that include syndromal disorders, personality aberrations, and normal variants. Influenced by Kraepelin (1923) and many before him, the idea that temperaments operate as predispositions to a wide range of mental states has informed Akiskal's (1989, 1997) work most closely, but also the views of Cloninger and colleagues (Cloninger, 1987; Cloninger, Svrakic, & Przybeck, 1993) and of Siever and Davis (1991). Clarifying boundaries between Axis II disorders and their respective Axis I syndromal counterparts using concepts that are not disorders themselves may enable better classification schemata and, perhaps more important, may open up exciting areas of inquiry that not so long ago could only be guessed might be possible to study. I speak here of integrating theories of personality pathology with neurobiology (with its advances in imaging techniques to study brain morphology and to map neural networks and neurotransmitter systems), genetics (with its advances in studying linkages and molecular mechanisms), and psychometrics (with its greater sophistication in areas such as test theory, item response theory, and multivariate analysis). If psychoanalysis (including self psychology) were in a better position to specify its main concepts in a more explicit, operationalized manner—without undermining the depth and accuracy of its more important concepts—it too might benefit from the potential links with other sciences it has always craved. But there has been notable progress since Freud's *Project for a Scientific Psychology* (Freud, 1895/1966) such as recent theoretical innovations that have attempted to forge such alliances (Gedo, 1991; Levin, 1991; Schore, 2003a, 2003b; Solms & Turnbull, 2002).

These attempts—and there are others as well—have exploited advances in several areas of inquiry to gain a better understanding of fields like personality disorders and self psychology, fields that are limited by their appeal to clinical observation for their basic data. Such alliances are particularly valuable because they are not confined to examining psychopathology and its variables alone. Thus, for example, personality theory and the theoretical–clinical study of personality disorders may now more comfortably address questions concerning how their concepts may be informed by advances in basic and clinical research in genetics and neurobiology. Consequently, one may speak of spectrum concepts of schizophrenia, depression, or psychopathy, for example, with greater confidence now that genetically related disorders with different phenotypic expressions may resemble one another more closely than previously thought. Further, the interest in and active search for endophenotypes (Gottesman & Shields, 1973) to better understand clinical phenotypes is very likely an important advance in how clinical thinking is proceeding.

At another level of understanding, it is important to identify variables that are particularly germane to disorders of interest and also to measure them and their critical components with maximal precision. For example, with reference to schizophrenia, Cromwell (1975) wrote that it may be more important for understanding prognosis to gain a better knowledge of laboratory measures at a molecular level (such as reaction time performance) or selected variables such as premorbid social adjustment than to rely on clinical data. This point of view is not far from one Meehl (1973) would surely have advised pursuing; Meehl once said that if one could ask a patient only one question in order to reach a diagnosis, the most informative question should pertain to whether the patient had a schizophrenic first-degree relative. Cromwell also observed that "the time has come to accept the fact that what is clinically relevant may not be etiologically relevant" (p. 615). He wrote that in 1975; Holzman (1996, 2003) said as much more recently. But just as Holzman eschewed overarching theories as frequently misguided and sometimes logically indefensible, he also noted that the sweep of broad theories is cautiously important to impart meaning to the more precise and therefore privileged facts of scientific findings. Holzman (1996) also noted, writing about personality disorders, that

> the vagueness of these syndromes is even more striking than that of the Axis I disorders. . . . It appears that the strategies adopted for the study of diseases will not work for the study of these personality exaggerations. . . . The dimensions to be studied are how a person comes to grips with reality constraints, what the quality of thinking is, how problems are solved, how information is stored, how affect is modulated. We thus deal here not with disease states but with action styles. . . . We shall not advance further in our understanding of these so-called disorders unless we understand that laws of persons rather than of diseases must be studied. . . . Correlates must designate more than relationships or covariations. They must point to critical organizing features, to neural networks, and back again to models of total functioning. (p. 597)

Bold new schemes for formulating personality and its organization have been proposed and studied, such as Millon's (1990, 1991, 1996) recent evolutionary model, which he has masterfully integrated with his biopsychosocial perspective, and Schore's (2003a, 2003b) similarly masterful integration of a wide-ranging body of theory and empirical findings spanning diverse areas of neurobiology, attachment theory, and self psychology. Westen and Shedler (1999a, 1999b) have applied psychometric analysis to clinical phenomena in one of the most sophisticated uses of this method of analysis to date. Even a thoughtful excursion into realms of philosophy and spirituality in relation to personality (Cloninger, 2004) was recently proposed by one of the foremost investigators in the field of personality disorders. Though these mainly are theoretical organizations of a large body of knowledge, such integrations— which are among the most respected and important formulations in their fields—take good advantage of empirical findings to reach a level of theoretical breadth that can guide personality theory and research. That Axis II has benefited from and undoubtedly will continue to be affected by incremental advances and broad integrations is reflected by the very existence of this series under Theodore Millon's editorship, which he has aptly entitled *Personality-Guided Psychology.*

As well as presenting a self psychological formulation of a number of personality disorders, I have also attempted to place this viewpoint in the context of current progress in the field of personality disorders research and theory. It is not common to find discussions of psychoanalytic subjects together with as different a tradition as that of descriptive psychopathology. I have intentionally favored driving home this context throughout this book. I have not been exhaustive in surveying these fields, though I sought to include some of the more important developments preceding and following the period of Kohut's (1971) most productive work. Though I have argued for the merits of considering a self psychological approach to understanding disorders of personality, I have also tried to avoid the misguided argument that a self psychological approach represents an integration of knowledge superior to other psychoanalytic theories or that the self psychological viewpoint is the most preferable explanation of clinical disorders of personality. Thus, all of the examinations of disorders in this book have considered a self psychological explanation either alongside or, in a few rare instances, in direct relationship with select theories of personality, descriptive psychopathology, and accrued knowledge from contemporary personality disorders theory and research.

That said, it has been an ongoing effort to balance Kohut's (1971) self psychology with other psychoanalytic views and even with other self psychological viewpoints while also looking over my own shoulder to consider theoretical viewpoints and findings in the personality disorders research area. Though it sometimes has been a complex balancing act, it has also been a necessary one. As I observed in the Introduction, although psychoanalysis historically had a guiding influence on thinking about personality disorders, this has not been the case during the past 35 years. It is not so much that their paths diverged as that they developed in different directions while remaining relatively unaware of or unconcerned about where the other was heading (Silverstein, 2005). For the most part, I have not tried to bring these different voices together; I have instead made an effort to present these various views side by side without attempting, as Goldberg (1998) observed while commenting about a related area, "to diminish differences or to integrate disparate ideas into some sort of uniformity" (p. 254). Goldberg also noted that disparate views may become "reabsorbed in one another or evolved in a totally new form," emphasizing the importance of suspending judgment about what cannot yet be seen while "it is to be hoped that we shall all continue to look" (p. 254). Resisting this temptation proved more difficult than searching for commonalities or discrepancies. I believe that allowing the tension to simply emerge as disparate fields develop, though they may sometimes branch apart, was preferable to seeking what would have diverted me from what I consider a more suitable focus at this juncture—examining potential contributions of self psychology, mindful of personality disorders theory and research.

I have also suggested that there exists tension even within the field of self psychology. There are those, for example, who embraced its revolutionary freedom from what Grinker (1965, p. 124) called certain "stultifying stereotypes." Many believed that Kohut's (1971) integration of his ideas with the existing body of psychoanalytic theory, particularly Freud's ideas, was a profoundly forward-looking step. Nevertheless, one sometimes hears words to the effect that Kohut opened a door to a previously closed room but did not go far enough inside the room. Teicholz's (1999) recent reconsideration of Kohut's contributions in a context both of ego psychology and of postmodern schools such as relational psychoanalysis offers a particularly notable examination of this issue. So, too, are Goldberg's (1998) and Shane and Shane's (1993) reflections.

Even within mainstream psychoanalysis, Brenner (2002), long a noted proponent of classical drive theory and ego psychology, recently questioned the primacy of a central tenet of the structural theory or tripartite model of id, ego, and superego. He proposed a formidable challenge to this time-honored bulwark of psychoanalysis, arguing for abandoning the structural theory in favor of adopting an organizing framework built around conflict and compromise formation. This may be as radical a formulation within psychoanalytic theory as Kohut's (1977, 1984, 1996) suggestion that the self supersedes the ego as a determinant of mental life and psychic functioning. I note Brenner's reformulation here not because it stands alone as a major reformulation in psychoanalysis but because it seems to hold particular relevance for many of the psychoanalytic views about personality (character) disorders noted throughout this book.

Other far-reaching psychoanalytic frameworks, particularly relational psychoanalytic approaches, may also hold such promise. Despite their current popularity, it is not yet clear what such views will add to psychoanalytic theory and technique or how they will influence thinking about personality disorders. The same may be said concerning the newly emerging field of attachment theory, an area of inquiry that although very much the province of developmental theory, has also been claimed as a viewpoint that is far too important to be ignored by psychoanalysis. Thus, integrative attempts have been forged between attachment theory and research with psychoanalytic object relations theory (Goodman, 2002) and self psychology (Beebe & Lachmann, 2002; Lichtenberg, 1983; Shane, Shane, & Gales, 1998), to mention only a few. This is an interface that shows much promise for contributing to an expanded way of thinking about personality disorders.

I thus emphasize the complexity of some of the multilayered theoretical and clinical research traditions into which I seek to position the psychology of the self. I have attempted to examine its contributions concerning the self and self-cohesion to add an important point of view for thinking about personality disorders. I have suggested a schema for organizing some of the main premises of self psychology. It can be informative only in a heuristic sense insofar as it provides a way of integrating self psychology's ideas with progress in broader fields of the study of personality disorders. If it succeeds in so doing, I am hopeful that the schema I propose in this volume will enjoy subsequent modification and refinement.

REFERENCES

Abraham, K. (1924). A short study of the development of the libido, viewed in the light of mental disorders. In *Selected papers on psycho-analysis* (pp. 418–502). London: Hogarth Press.

Abraham, K. (1927a). The first pregenital stage of the libido. In *Selected papers on psycho-analysis* (pp. 248–279). London: Hogarth Press. (Original work published 1916)

Abraham, K. (1927b). Notes on the psycho-analytic investigation and treatment of manic–depressive insanity and allied conditions. In *Selected papers on psycho-analysis* (pp. 137–156). London: Hogarth Press. (Original work published 1911)

Abraham, K. (1927c). Psycho-analytic studies on character-formation. In *Selected papers on psycho-analysis* (pp. 370–417). London: Hogarth Press. (Original work published 1921)

Abraham, K. (1953). A particular form of neurotic resistance against the psycho-analytic method. In *Selected papers on psycho-analysis* (pp. 303–311). New York: Basic Books. (Original work published 1919)

Adler, G. (1989). Uses and limitations of Kohut's self psychology in the treatment of borderline patients. *Journal of the American Psychoanalytic Association, 37,* 761–785.

Aichorn, A. (1964). The narcissistic transference of the "juvenile imposter." In O. Fleischmann, P. Kramer, & H. Ross (Eds.), *Delinquency and child guidance: Selected papers by August Aichorn* (pp. 174–191). New York: International Universities Press. (Original work published 1936)

Aichorn, A. (1983). *Wayward youth.* Chicago: Northwestern University Press. (Original work published 1925)

Akiskal, H. (1983). Dysthymic disorder: Psychopathology of proposed chronic depressive subtypes. *American Journal of Psychiatry, 140,* 11–20.

Akiskal, H. S. (1986). The clinical significance of the "soft" bipolar spectrum. *Psychiatric Annals, 16,* 667–671.

Akiskal, H. S. (1989). New insights into the nature and heterogeneity of mood disorders. *Journal of Clinical Psychiatry, 50*(Suppl.), 6–10.

Akiskal, H. S. (1991). Chronic depression. *Bulletin of the Menninger Clinic, 55,* 156–171.

Akiskal, H. S. (1997). Overview of chronic depressions and their clinical management. In H. S. Akiskal & G. B. Cassano (Eds.), *Dysthymia and the spectrum of chronic depressions* (pp. 1–34). New York: Guilford Press.

Akiskal, H. S., Chen, S. E., Davis, G. C., Puzantian, V. R., Kashgarian, M., & Bolinger, J. M. (1985). Borderline: An adjective in search of a noun. *Journal of Clinical Psychiatry, 46,* 41–48.

Akiskal, H. S., Djenderedjian, A. H., Rosenthal, R. H., & Khani, M. K. (1977). Cyclothymic disorder: Validating criteria for inclusion in the bipolar affective group. *American Journal of Psychiatry, 134,* 1227–1233.

Akiskal, H. S., Hirschfeld, R. M., & Yerevanian, B. I. (1983). The relationship of personality to affective disorders. *Archives of General Psychiatry, 40,* 801–810.

Akiskal, H. S., Rosenthal, T. L., Haykal, R. F., Lemmi, H., Rosenthal, R. H., & Scott-Strauss, A. (1980). Characterological depressions: Clinical and sleep EEG findings separating "subaffective dysthymias" from "character-spectrum" disorders. *Archives of General Psychiatry, 37,* 777–783.

Akiskal, H. S., & Webb, W. L. (1983). Affective disorders: I. Recent advances in clinical conceptualization. *Hospital and Community Psychiatry, 34,* 695–702.

Akiskal, H. S., & Weise, R. E. (1992). The clinical spectrum of so-called "minor" depression. *American Journal of Psychotherapy, 46,* 9–22.

Alexander, F. (1950). *Psychosomatic medicine: Its principles and applications.* New York: Norton.

American Psychiatric Association. (1952). *Diagnostic and statistical manual of mental disorders.* Washington, DC: Author.

American Psychiatric Association. (1968). *Diagnostic and statistical manual of mental disorders* (2nd ed.). Washington, DC: Author.

American Psychiatric Association. (1980). *Diagnostic and statistical manual of mental disorders* (3rd ed.). Washington, DC: Author.

American Psychiatric Association. (1987). *Diagnostic and statistical manual of mental disorders* (3rd ed., rev.). Washington, DC: Author.

American Psychiatric Association. (1994). *Diagnostic and statistical manual of mental disorders* (4th ed.). Washington, DC: Author.

American Psychiatric Association. (2000). *Diagnostic and statistical manual of mental disorders* (4th ed., text revision). Washington, DC: Author.

Andreas-Salome, L. (1921). The dual orientation of narcissism. *Psychoanalytic Quarterly, 31,* 1–30.

Andreasen, N. C. (1982). Negative symptoms in schizophrenia: Definitions and reliability. *Archives of General Psychiatry, 39,* 784–788.

Angst, J. (1997). Minor and recurrent brief depression. In H. S. Akiskal & G. B. Cassano (Eds.), *Dysthymia and the spectrum of chronic depressions* (pp. 183–190). New York: Guilford Press.

Arieti, S. (1945). Primitive habits and perceptual alternations in the terminal stage of schizophrenia. *Archives of Neurology and Psychiatry, 53,* 378–384.

Arieti, S. (1974). *Interpretation of schizophrenia.* New York: Basic Books.

Arieti, S., & Bemporad, J. R. (1978). *Severe and mild depression: The psychotherapeutic approach.* New York: Basic Books.

Arlow, J. A., & Brenner, C. (1964). *Psychoanalytic concepts and the structural theory.* New York: International Universities Press.

Aron, L. (1996). *A meeting of minds: Mutuality in psychoanalysis.* Hillsdale, NJ: Analytic Press.

Ax, A. F. (1953). The physiological differentiation between fear and anger in humans. *Psychosomatic Medicine, 15*, 433–442.

Bacal, H. A. (1985). Optimal responsiveness and the therapeutic process. In A. Goldberg (Ed.), *Progress in self psychology* (pp. 202–226). New York: Guilford Press.

Bacal, H. A. (1989). Winnicott and self psychology: Remarkable reflections. In D. W. Detrick & S. P. Detrick (Eds.), *Self psychology: Comparisons and contrasts* (pp. 259–275). Hillsdale, NJ: Analytic Press.

Bacal, H. A., & Herzog, B. (2003). Specificity theory and optimal responsiveness: An outline. *Psychoanalytic Psychology, 20*, 635–648.

Bacal, H. A., & Newman, K. (1990). *Theories of object relations: Bridges to self psychology*. New York: Columbia University Press.

Balint, M. (1968). *The basic fault*. London: Tavistock.

Barratt, E. S., & Patton, J. H. (1983). Impulsivity: Cognitive, behavioral, and psychophysiological correlates. In M. Zuckerman (Ed.), *Biological bases of sensation seeking, impulsivity and anxiety* (pp. 17–116). Mahwah, NJ: Erlbaum.

Barsky, A. J. (1979). Patients who amplify bodily sensations. *Annals of Internal Medicine, 91*, 63–70.

Barsky, A. J. (1983). Overview: Hypochondriasis, bodily complaints, and somatic styles. *American Journal of Psychiatry, 140*, 273–283.

Basch, M. F. (1983). Empathic understanding: A review of the concept and some theoretical considerations. *Journal of the American Psychoanalytic Association, 31*, 101–126.

Basch, M. F. (1983–1984). The perception of reality and the disavowal of meaning. *Annual of Psychoanalysis, 11*, 125–154.

Basch, M. F. (1988). *Understanding psychotherapy*. New York: Basic Books.

Battaglia, M., Przybeck, T. R., Bellodi, L., & Cloninger, C. R. (1996). Temperament dimensions explain the comorbidity of psychiatric disorders. *Comprehensive Psychiatry, 37*, 292–298.

Baudry, F. D. (1983). The evolution of the concept of character in Freud's writings. *Journal of the American Psychoanalytic Association, 31*, 3–31.

Bechara, A., Tranel, D., & Damasio, H. (2000). Characterization of the decision-making deficit of patients with ventromedial prefrontal cortex lesions. *Brain, 123*, 2189–2202.

Beck, A. T., & Freeman, A. (1990). *Cognitive therapy of personality disorders*. New York: Guilford Press.

Beebe, B., & Lachmann, F. M. (1988). Mother–infant mutual influence and precursors of psychic structure. In A. Goldberg (Ed.), *Progress in self psychology: Vol. 3. Frontiers in self psychology* (pp. 3–25). Hillsdale, NJ: Analytic Press.

Beebe, B., & Lachmann, F. M. (1994). Representation and internalization in infancy: Three principles of salience. *Psychoanalytic Psychology, 11*, 127–165.

Beebe, B., & Lachmann, F. M. (2002). *Infant research and adult treatment: Co-constructing interactions*. Hillsdale, NJ: Analytic Press.

Berenbaum, H., & James, T. (1994). Correlates and retrospectively reported antecedents of alexithymia. *Psychosomatic Medicine, 56*, 353–359.

Bernstein, D. P., Useda, D., & Siever, L. J. (1995). Paranoid personality disorder. In W. J. Livesley (Ed.), *The DSM–IV personality disorders* (pp. 45–57). New York: Guilford Press.

Bibring, E. (1953). The mechanism of depression. In P. Greenacre (Ed.), *Affective disorders: Psychoanalytic contributions to their study* (pp. 13–48). New York: International Universities Press.

Biederman, J., Faraone, S. V., Spencer, T., Wilens, T., Norman, D., Lapey, K. A., et al. (1993). Patterns of psychiatric comorbidity, cognition, and psychosocial functioning in adults with attention deficit hyperactivity disorder. *American Journal of Psychiatry, 150*, 1792–1798.

Bion, W. R. (1962). *Learning from experience.* London: Heinemann.

Black, D. W. (2001). Antisocial personality disorder: The forgotten patients of psychiatry. *Primary Psychiatry, 8*, 30–81.

Blair, R. J. R. (1995). A cognitive developmental approach to morality: Investigating the psychopath. *Cognition, 57*, 1–29.

Blair, R. J. R., & Cipolotti, L. (2000). Impaired social response reversal: A case of acquired sociopathy. *Brain, 123*, 1122–1141.

Blair, R. J. R., Jones, L., Clark, F., & Smith, M. (1997). The psychopathic individual: A lack of responsiveness to distress cues? *Psychophysiology, 34*, 192–198.

Blair, R. J. R., Morris, J. S., Frith, C. C., Perrett, D. I., & Dolan, R. J. (1999). Dissociable neural responses to facial expressions of sadness and anger. *Brain, 122*, 883–893.

Blashfield, R. K., & McElroy, R. (1995). Confusions in terminology used for classificatory models. In W. J. Livesley (Ed.), *The DSM–IV personality disorders* (pp. 407–416). New York: Guilford Press.

Blatt, S. J. (1974). Levels of object representation in anaclitic and introjective depression. *Psychoanalytic Study of the Child, 29*, 107–157.

Bleuler, E. (1950). *Dementia praecox or the group of schizophrenias* (J. Zinkin, Trans.). New York: International Universities Press. (Original work published 1911)

Bohman, M., Cloninger, C. R., Sigvardsson, S., & von Knorring, A. L. (1982). Predisposition to petty criminality in Swedish adoptees: I. Genetic and environmental heterogeneity. *Archives of General Psychiatry, 39*, 1233–1241.

Bollas, C. (1989). Normotic illness. In B. L. Smith & M. G. Fromm (Eds.), *The facilitating environment: Clinical applications of Winnicott's theory* (pp. 317–344). Madison, CT: International Universities Press.

Boring, E. G. (1950). *A history of experimental psychology* (2nd ed.). New York: Appleton-Century-Crofts.

Bornstein, R. F. (1993). *The dependent personality.* New York: Guilford Press.

Bornstein, R. F. (2005). Psychodynamic theory and personality disorders. In S. Strack (Ed.), *Handbook of personology and psychopathology* (pp. 164–180). Hoboken, NJ: Wiley.

Bowlby, J. (1969). *Attachment and loss: Vol. 1. Attachment.* New York: Basic Books.

Bowlby, J. (1973). *Attachment and loss: Vol. 2. Separation: Anxiety and anger.* New York: Basic Books.

Braff, D. L. (1986). Impaired speed of information processing in nonmedicated schizotypal patients. *Schizophrenia Bulletin, 7,* 499–508.

Brandchaft, B., & Stolorow, R. (1984). The borderline concept: Pathological character or iatrogenic myth? In J. Lichtenberg, M. Bornstein, & D. Silver (Eds.), *Empathy II* (pp. 333–357). Hillsdale, NJ: Analytic Press.

Brandchaft, B., & Stolorow, R. D. (1988). The difficult patient: An intersubjective perspective. In N. Slavinska-Holy (Ed.), *Borderline and narcissistic patients in therapy* (pp. 243–266). Madison, CT: International Universities Press.

Brantley, B. (2004, April 23). A demon gallery of glory hounds. *New York Times,* p. E-1.

Brenner, C. (2002). Conflict, compromise formation, and structural theory. *Psychoanalytic Quarterly, 71,* 397–417.

Bretherton, I. (1987). New perspectives on attachment relations: Security, communication, and internal working models. In J. D. Osofsky (Ed.), *Handbook of infant development* (2nd ed., pp. 1061–1100). Oxford, England: Wiley.

Breuer, J., & Freud, S. (1955). Studies on hysteria. In J. Strachey (Ed. & Trans.), *Standard edition* (Vol. 2). London: Hogarth Press. (Original work published 1893–1895)

Brickman, B. (1992). The desomatizing selfobject transference: A case report. In A. Goldberg (Ed.), *Progress in self psychology: Vol. 8. New therapeutic visions* (pp. 93–108). Hillsdale, NJ: Analytic Press.

Bronstein, C. (2001). *Kleinian theory: A contemporary perspective.* London: Whurr.

Bursten, B. (1972). The manipulative personality. *Archives of General Psychiatry, 26,* 318–321.

Bursten, B. (1973). Some narcissistic personality types. *International Journal of Psychoanalysis, 54,* 287–300.

Byrne, D., Steinberg, M. A., & Schwartz, M. S. (1968). Relationship between repression–sensitization and physical illness. *Journal of Abnormal Psychology, 73,* 154–155.

Cadoret, R. J., Troughton, E., Bagford, J., & Woodworth, G. (1990). Genetic and environmental factors in adoptee antisocial personality. *European Archives of Psychiatry and Neurological Sciences, 239,* 231–240.

Carpenter, W. T., Jr., Heinrichs, D. W., & Wagman, A. M. I. (1985). On the heterogeneity of schizophrenia. In M. Alpert (Ed.), *Controversies in schizophrenia: Changes and constancies: Proceedings of the 74th Annual Meeting of the American Psychopathological Association, New York City, March 1–3, 1984* (pp. 25–37). New York: Guilford Press.

Caspi, A., McClay, J., Moffitt, T. E., Mill, J., Martin, J., Craig, I. W., et al. (2002, August 2). Role of genotype in the cycle of violence in maltreated children. *Science, 297,* 851–854.

Chapman, L. J., Chapman, J. P., & Raulin, M. L. (1976). Scales for physical and social anhedonia. *Journal of Abnormal Psychology, 87,* 374–407.

Chodoff, P. (1972). The depressive personality. *Archives of General Psychiatry, 27,* 666–677.

Chodoff, P., & Lyons, H. (1958). Hysteria, the hysterical personality and "hysterical" conversion. *American Journal of Psychiatry, 114,* 734–740.

Clark, L. A. (1993). *Manual for the Schedule for Nonadaptive and Adaptive Personality (SNAP).* Minneapolis: University of Minnesota Press.

Clark, L. A. (1999). Dimensional approaches to personality disorder assessment and diagnosis. In C. R. Cloninger (Ed.), *Personality and psychopathology* (pp. 219–244). Washington, DC: American Psychiatric Press.

Cleckley, H. (1964). *The mask of sanity.* St. Louis, MO: Mosby. (Original work published 1941)

Cloninger, C. R. (1987). A systematic method for clinical description and classification of personality variants. *Archives of General Psychiatry, 44,* 573–588.

Cloninger, C. R. (2004). *Feeling good: The science of well-being.* New York: Oxford University Press.

Cloninger, C. R., Bayon, C., & Svrakic, D. M. (1998). Measurement of temperament and character in mood disorders: A model of fundamental states as personality types. *Journal of Affective Disorders, 51,* 21–32.

Cloninger, C. R., Przybeck, T. R., Svrakic, D. M., & Wetzel, R. D. (1994). *The Temperament and Character Inventory (TCI): A guide to its development and use.* St. Louis, MO: Center for Psychobiology of Personality.

Cloninger, C. R., & Svrakic, D. M. (1997). Integrative psychobiological approach to psychiatric assessment and treatment. *Psychiatry: Interpersonal and Biological Processes, 60,* 120–141.

Cloninger, C. R., Svrakic, D. M., & Przybeck, T. R. (1993). A psychobiological model of temperament and character. *Archives of General Psychiatry, 50,* 975–990.

Cloninger, C. R., Svrakic, N. M., & Svrakic, D. M. (1997). Role of personality self-organization in development of mental order and disorder. *Development and Psychopathology, 9,* 881–906.

Cooke, D. J., & Michie, C. (2001). Refining the construct of psychopathy: Towards a hierarchical model. *Psychological Assessment, 13,* 171–188.

Costa, P. T., Jr., & McCrae, R. R. (1992). *The NEO–PI–R manual.* Odessa, FL: Psychological Assessment Resources.

Costa, P. T., Jr., & Widiger, T. A. (Eds.). (1994). *Personality disorders and the five-factor model of personality.* Washington, DC: American Psychological Association.

Cromwell, R. L. (1975). Assessment of schizophrenia. In M. R. Rosenzweig & L. W. Porter (Eds.), *Annual review of psychology* (Vol. 26, pp. 593–619). Palo Alto, CA: Annual Reviews.

Crow, T. J. (1980). Molecular pathology of schizophrenia: More than one disease process? *British Medical Journal, 280,* 1–9.

Damasio, A. R. (2000). A neural basis for sociopathy. *Archives of General Psychiatry, 57,* 128–129.

Damasio, A. R., Tranel, D., & Damasio, H. (1990). Individuals with sociopathic behavior caused by frontal damage fail to respond autonomically to social stimuli. *Behavioral Brain Research, 41,* 81–94.

Davis, G. C., & Akiskal, H. S. (1986). Descriptive, biological, and theoretical aspects of borderline personality disorder. *Hospital and Community Psychiatry, 37,* 685–692.

Davis, R. D., & Millon, T. (1993). The five-factor model for personality disorders: Apt or misguided? *Psychological Inquiry, 4,* 104–109.

Deutsch, H. (1942). Some forms of emotional disturbance and their relationship to schizophrenia. *Psychoanalytic Quarterly, 11,* 301–321.

Devinsky, O. (2000). Right cerebral hemisphere dominance for a sense of corporeal and emotional self. *Epilepsy and Behavior, 1,* 60–73.

Devinsky, O., Mesad, S., & Alper, K. (2001). Nondominant hemisphere lesions and conversion nonepileptic seizures. *Journal of Neuropsychiatry and Clinical Neuroscience, 13,* 367–373.

Dworkin, R. H. (1994). Pain insensitivity in schizophrenia: A neglected phenomenon and some implications. *Schizophrenia Bulletin, 20,* 235–248.

Ebb, F., & Fosse, B. (1976). *Chicago: A musical vaudeville.* New York: Samuel French.

Eissler, K. R. (1949). *Searchlights on delinquency: Essays in honor of August Aichorn.* New York: International Universities Press.

Endicott, J., & Spitzer, R. L. (1978). A diagnostic interview: The Schedule for Affective Disorders and Schizophrenia. *Archives of General Psychiatry, 35,* 837–844.

Erikson, E. H. (1950). Growth and crises of the "healthy personality." In M. J. E. Senn (Ed.), *Symposium on the healthy personality* (pp. 91–146). Oxford, England: Josiah Macy, Jr. Foundation.

Exner, J. E., Jr. (2003). *The Rorschach: A comprehensive system: Vol. 1. Basic foundations* (4th ed.). New York: Wiley.

Eysenck, H. J. (1957). *The dynamics of anxiety and hysteria: An experimental application of modern learning theory to psychiatry.* Oxford, England: Praeger.

Eysenck, H. J. (1987). The definition of personality disorders and the criteria appropriate to their definition. *Journal of Personality Disorders, 1,* 211–219.

Fairbairn, R. (1944). Endopsychic structure considered in terms of object-relationships. *International Journal of Psychoanalysis, 25,* 70–93.

Fairbairn, R. (1954). Observations on the nature of hysterical states. *British Journal of Medical Psychology, 27,* 116–125.

Federn, P. (1953). *Ego psychology and the psychoses.* Oxford, England: Basic Books.

Feighner, J. P., Robins, E., Guze, S. B., Woodruff, R. A., Winokur, G., & Munoz, R. (1972). Diagnostic criteria for use in psychiatric research. *Archives of General Psychiatry, 26,* 57–63.

Fenichel, O. (1945). *The psychoanalytic theory of neurosis.* New York: Norton.

Finn, P. R., Martin, J., & Pihl, R. O. (1987). Alexithymia in males at high genetic risk for alcoholism. *Psychotherapy and Psychosomatics, 47,* 18–21.

First, M., Gibbon, M., Spitzer, R. L., Williams, J. B. W., & Benjamin, L. S. (1997). *User's guide for the Structured Clinical Interview for the* DSM–IV *Axis II Personality Disorders.* Washington, DC: American Psychiatric Press.

Fish, B. (1977). Neurobiologic antecedents of schizophrenia in children: Evidence for an inherited, congenital neurointegrative deficit. *Archives of General Psychiatry, 34,* 1297–1313.

Fiske, D. W. (1949). Consistency of the factorial structures of personality ratings from different sources. *Journal of Abnormal and Social Psychology, 44,* 329–344.

Fonagy, P., Gergely, G., Jurist, E. L., & Target, M. (2002). *Affect regulation, mentalization, and the development of the self.* New York: Other Press.

Fonagy, P., Steele, M., Steele, H., Leigh, T., Kennedy, R., Mattoon, G., et al. (1996). The relation of attachment status, psychiatric classification, and response to psychotherapy. *Journal of Consulting and Clinical Psychology, 64,* 22–31.

Fosshage, J. L. (1992). The selfobject concept: A further discussion of three authors. In A. Goldberg (Ed.), *Progress in self psychology: Vol. 8. New therapeutic visions* (pp. 229–239). Hillsdale, NJ: Analytic Press.

Frances, A., & Cooper, A. M. (1981). Descriptive and dynamic psychiatry: A perspective on *DSM–III. American Journal of Psychiatry, 138,* 1198–1202.

Frances, A. J., Pincus, H. A., Widiger, T. A., Davis, W. W., & First, M. B. (1990). *DSM–IV:* Work in progress. *American Journal of Psychiatry, 147,* 1439–1448.

Freud, S. (1955). Notes upon a case of obsessional neurosis. In J. Strachey (Ed. & Trans.), *Standard edition* (Vol. 10, pp. 153–249). London: Hogarth Press. (Original work published 1909)

Freud, S. (1957a). Mourning and melancholia. In J. Strachey (Ed. & Trans.), *Standard edition* (Vol. 14, pp. 243–258). London: Hogarth Press. (Original work published 1917)

Freud, S. (1957b). On narcissism: An introduction. In J. Strachey (Ed. & Trans.), *Standard edition* (Vol. 14, pp. 73–102). London: Hogarth Press. (Original work published 1914)

Freud, S. (1957c). Repression. In J. Strachey (Ed. & Trans.), *Standard edition* (Vol. 14, pp. 146–158). London: Hogarth Press. (Original work published 1915)

Freud, S. (1957d). Some character types met with in psychoanalytic work. In J. Strachey (Ed. & Trans.), *Standard edition* (Vol. 14, pp. 311–333). London: Hogarth Press. (Original work published 1916)

Freud, S. (1957e). A special type of object choice made by men. In J. Strachey (Ed. & Trans.), *Standard edition* (Vol. 11, pp. 165–175). London: Hogarth Press. (Original work published 1910)

Freud, S. (1958). Psycho-analytic notes upon an autobiographical account of a case of paranoia (dementia paranoides). In J. Strachey (Ed. & Trans.), *Standard edition* (Vol. 12, pp. 3–82). London: Hogarth Press. (Original work published 1911)

Freud, S. (1959a). Character and anal erotism. In J. Strachey (Ed. & Trans.), *Standard edition* (Vol. 9, pp. 169–175). London: Hogarth Press. (Original work published 1908)

Freud, S. (1959b). Inhibitions, symptoms and anxiety. In J. Strachey (Ed. & Trans.), *Standard edition* (Vol. 20, pp. 87–175). London: Hogarth Press. (Original work published 1926)

Freud, S. (1961a). The ego and the id. In J. Strachey (Ed. & Trans.), *Standard edition* (Vol. 19, pp. 12–66). London: Hogarth Press. (Original work published 1923)

Freud, S. (1961b). Fetishism. In J. Strachey (Ed. & Trans.), *Standard edition* (Vol. 21, pp. 149–158). London: Hogarth Press. (Original work published 1927)

Freud, S. (1961c). Libidinal types. In J. Strachey (Ed. & Trans.), *Standard edition* (Vol. 21, pp. 215–220). London: Hogarth Press. (Original work published 1931)

Freud, S. (1961d). Neurosis and psychosis. In J. Strachey (Ed. & Trans.), *Standard edition* (Vol. 19, pp. 148–153). London: Hogarth Press. (Original work published 1924)

Freud, S. (1964). Splitting of the ego in the process of defence. In J. Strachey (Ed. & Trans.), *Standard edition* (Vol. 23, pp. 275–278). London: Hogarth Press. (Original work published 1940)

Freud, S. (1966). Project for a scientific psychology. In J. Strachey (Ed. & Trans.), *Standard edition* (Vol. 1, pp. 283–343). London: Hogarth Press. (Original work published 1895)

Fromm, E. (1947). *Man for himself.* New York: Holt, Rinehart & Winston.

Fromm-Reichmann, F. (1950). *Principles of intensive psychotherapy.* Chicago: University of Chicago Press.

Frosch, J. (1977). The relation between acting out and disorders of impulse control. *Psychiatry: Journal for the Study of Interpersonal Processes, 40,* 295–314.

Frosch, J. (1988). Psychotic character versus borderline. *International Journal of Psychoanalysis, 69,* 347–357.

Gabbard, G. O. (1994). *Psychodynamic psychiatry in clinical practice.* Washington, DC: American Psychiatric Press.

Gedo, J. E. (1991). *The biology of clinical encounters: Psychoanalysis as a science of mind.* Hillsdale, NJ: Analytic Press.

Giovacchini, P. L. (1979). The many sides of helplessness: The borderline patient. In J. Leboit & A. Caponi (Eds.), *Advances in psychotherapy of the borderline patient* (pp. 123–157). Northvale, NJ: Jason Aronson.

Glueck, S., & Glueck, E. (1950). *Unraveling juvenile delinquency.* Cambridge, MA: Harvard University Press.

Goldberg, A. (1975). The evolution of psychoanalytic concepts of depression. In E. J. Anthony & T. Benedek (Eds.), *Depression and human existence* (pp. 125–142). Boston: Little, Brown.

Goldberg, A. (1978). *The psychology of the self: A casebook*. New York: International Universities Press.

Goldberg, A. (1995). *The problem of perversion: The view from self psychology*. New Haven: Yale University Press.

Goldberg, A. (1998). Self psychology since Kohut. *Psychoanalytic Quarterly, 67*, 240–255.

Goldberg, A. (1999). *Being of two minds: The vertical split in psychoanalysis and psychotherapy*. Hillsdale, NJ: Analytic Press.

Goldberg, A. (Ed.). (2000). *Errant selves: A casebook of misbehavior*. Hillsdale, NJ: Analytic Press.

Goodman, G. (2002). *The internal world and attachment*. Hillsdale, NJ: Analytic Press.

Gottesman, I. I., & Shields, J. (1973). Genetic theorizing and schizophrenia. *British Journal of Psychiatry, 122*, 15–30.

Goyer, P. F., Andreason, P. J., Semple, W. E., & Clayton, A. H. (1994). Positron-emission tomography and personality disorders. *Neuropsychopharmacology, 10*, 21–28.

Gray, J. A. (1987). Perspectives on anxiety and impulsivity: A commentary. *Journal of Research in Personality, 21*, 493–510.

Greenacre, P. (1971). Notes on the influence and contribution of ego psychology to the practice of psychoanalysis. In J. B. McDevitt & C. F. Settlage (Eds.), *Separation–individuation* (pp. 171–200). New York: International Universities Press.

Grinker, R. R. (1953). *Psychosomatic research*. New York: Norton.

Grinker, R. R., Sr. (1965). Identity or regression in American psychoanalysis? *Archives of General Psychiatry, 12*, 113–125.

Grinker, R. R., Sr., Werble, B., & Drye, R. C. (1968). *The borderline syndrome: A behavioral study of ego–functions*. New York: Basic Books.

Gunderson, J. G. (1977). Characteristics of borderlines. In P. Hartocollis (Ed.), *Borderline personality disorders* (pp. 173–192). New York: International Universities Press.

Gunderson, J. G., & Phillips, K. A. (1991). Borderline personality disorder and depression: A current overview of the interface. *American Journal of Psychiatry, 148*, 967–975.

Gunderson, J. G., Ronningstam, E., & Smith, L. E. (1995). Narcissistic personality disorder. In W. J. Livesley (Ed.), *The DSM–IV personality disorders* (pp. 201–212). New York: Guilford Press.

Gunderson, J. G., Zanarini, M. C., & Kisiel, C. L. (1995). Borderline personality disorder. In W. J. Livesley (Ed.), *The DSM–IV personality disorders* (pp. 141–157). New York: Guilford Press.

Guntrip, H. (1969). *Schizoid phenomena, object relations, and the self*. New York: International Universities Press.

Guntrip, H. (1971). *Psychoanalytic theory, therapy, and the self*. New York: Basic Books.

Guze, S. B. (1976). *Criminality and psychiatric disorders*. Oxford, England: Oxford University Press.

Guze, S. B., Woodruff, R. A., & Clayton, P. J. (1971). Secondary affective disorder: A study of 95 cases. *Psychological Medicine, 1*, 426–428.

Handler, L. (1996). The clinical use of figure drawings. In C. S. Newmark (Ed.), *Major psychological assessment instruments* (2nd ed., pp. 206–293). Boston: Allyn & Bacon.

Hare, R. D. (1965). Temporal gradient of fear arousal in psychopaths. *Journal of Abnormal Psychology, 70*, 442.

Hare, R. D. (1978). Electrodermal and cardiovascular correlates of psychopathy. In R. D. Hare & D. Schalling (Eds.), *Psychopathic behavior approaches to research* (pp. 87–110). New York: Wiley.

Hare, R. D. (1991). *The Hare Psychopathy Checklist—Revised.* Toronto: Multihealth Systems.

Hare, R. D., & Hart, S. D. (1995). Commentary on antisocial personality disorder: The *DSM–IV* field trial. In W. J. Livesley (Ed.), *The* DSM–IV *personality disorders* (pp. 127–134). New York: Guilford Press.

Hare, R. D., Hart, S. D., & Harpur, T. J. (1991). Psychopathy and the proposed *DSM–IV* criteria for antisocial personality disorder. *Journal of Abnormal Psychology, 100*, 391–398.

Hart, S. D., & Hare, R. D. (1998). Association between psychopathy and narcissism: Theoretical views and empirical evidence. In E. F. Ronningstam (Ed.), *Disorders of narcissism: Diagnostic, clinical, and empirical implications* (pp. 415–436). Washington, DC: American Psychiatric Association.

Hartmann, H. (1939). *Ego psychology and the problem of adaptation.* New York: International Universities Press.

Hartmann, H. (1964). *Essays on ego psychology.* New York: International Universities Press.

Hartmann, H., Kris, E., & Loewenstein, R. M. (1946). Comments on the formation of psychic structure. *Psychoanalytic Study of the Child, 2*, 11–38.

Head, H. (1926). *Aphasia and kindred disorders of speech.* Oxford, England: Oxford University Press.

Hempel, C. G. (1965). *Aspects of scientific explanation.* New York: Free Press.

Hirschfeld, R. M. A., & Holzer, C. E. (1994). Depressive personality disorder: Clinical implications. *Journal of Clinical Psychiatry, 55*(Suppl.), 10–17.

Hirschfeld, R. M. A., Klerman, G. L., Chodoff, P., Korchin, S. J., & Barrett, J. (1976). Dependency—self-esteem—clinical depression. *Journal of the American Academy of Psychoanalysis, 4*, 373–388.

Hirschfeld, R. M. A., Klerman, G. L., Gough, H. G., Barrett, J., Korchin, S. J., & Chodoff, P. (1977). A measure of interpersonal dependency. *Journal of Personality Assessment, 41*, 610–618.

Hirschfeld, R. M. A., Shea, M. T., & Weise, R. (1995). Dependent personality disorders. In J. W. Livesley (Ed.), *The* DSM–IV *personality disorders* (pp. 239–256). New York: Guilford Press.

Hoch, P. H., & Polatin, P. (1949). Pseudoneurotic forms of schizophrenia. *Psychiatric Quarterly, 23*, 248–276.

Hoffman, I. Z. (1992). Some practical implications of a social–constructivist view of the psychoanalytic situation. *Psychoanalytic Dialogues, 2*, 287–304.

Holzman, P. S. (1996). Reflections on the developing science of psychopathology. In S. Matthyse, D. L. Levy, J. Kagan, & F. M. Benes (Eds.), *Psychopathology: The evolving science of mental disorder* (pp. 583–605). New York: Cambridge University Press.

Holzman, P. S. (2003). Less is truly more: Psychopathology research in the 21st century. In M. F. Lenzenweger & J. M. Hooley (Eds.), *Principles of experimental psychopathology: Essays in honor of Brendan A. Maher* (pp. 175–193). Washington, DC: American Psychological Association.

Horney, K. (1945). *Our inner conflicts.* New York: Norton.

Huprich, S. K. (1998). Depressive personality disorder: Theoretical issues, clinical findings, and future research questions. *Clinical Psychology Review, 18*, 477–500.

Huprich, S. K. (2005). Rorschach assessment of depressive personality disorder. In S. K. Huprich (Ed.), *Rorschach assessment of the personality disorders* (pp. 371–393). Mahwah, NJ: Erlbaum.

Huttunen, M. O., & Niskanen, P. (1978). Prenatal loss of father and psychiatric disorders. *Archives of General Psychiatry, 35*, 429–431.

Jackson, J. H. (1887). Remarks on evolution and dissolution of the nervous system. *Journal of Mental Science, 33*, 25–48.

Jacobson, E. (1953). Contribution to the metapsychology of cyclothymic depression. In P. Greenacre (Ed.), *Affective disorders: Psychoanalytic contributions to their study* (pp. 49–83). New York: International Universities Press.

Jacobson, E. (1964). *The self and the object world.* New York: International Universities Press.

Jacobson, E. (1967). *Psychotic conflict and reality.* New York: International Universities Press.

Jacobson, E. (1971). *Depression: Comparative studies of normal, neurotic, and psychotic conditions.* New York: International Universities Press.

Jang, K. L., & Vernon, P. A. (2001). Genetics. In W. J. Livesley (Ed.), *Handbook of personality disorders: Theory, research, and treatment* (pp. 177–195). New York: Guilford Press.

Jaspers, K. (1948). *General psychopathology.* London: Oxford.

Johns, J. H., & Quay, H. C. (1962). The effect of social reward on verbal conditioning in psychopathic and neurotic military offenders. *Journal of Consulting Psychology, 36*, 217–220.

Josephs, L. (1992). *Character and self-experience.* New York: Columbia University Press.

Judd, L. L., & Akiskal, H. S. (2000). Delineating the longitudinal structure of depressive illness: Beyond clinical subtypes and duration thresholds. *Pharmacopsychiatry, 33*, 3–7.

Judd, L. L., Akiskal, H. S., Maser, J. D., Zeller, P. J., Endicott, J., Coryell, W., et al. (1998). A prospective 12-year study of subsyndromal and syndromal depressive symptoms in unipolar major depressive disorders. *Archives of General Psychiatry, 55,* 694–700.

Judd, L. L., Rapaport, M. H., & Paulus, M. P. (1994). Subsyndromal symptomatic depression (SSD): A new mood disorder? *Journal of Clinical Psychiatry, 55,* 18S–28S.

Kalus, O., Bernstein, D. P., & Siever, L. J. (1995). Schizoid personality disorder. In W. J. Livesley (Ed.), *The DSM–IV personality disorders* (pp. 58–70). New York: Guilford Press.

Karasu, T. B. (1994). A developmental metatheory of psychopathology. *American Journal of Psychotherapy, 48,* 581–599.

Keller, M. B., & Shapiro, R. W. (1982). "Double depression": Superimposition of acute depressive episodes on chronic depressive disorders. *American Journal of Psychiatry, 139,* 438–442.

Kendler, K. S., Masterson, C. C., & Davis, K. L. (1985). Psychiatric illness in first-degree relatives of patients with paranoid psychosis, schizophrenia and medical illness. *British Journal of Psychiatry, 147,* 524–531.

Kernberg, O. F. (1967). Borderline personality organization. *Journal of the American Psychoanalytic Association, 15,* 641–685.

Kernberg, O. F. (1975). *Borderline conditions and pathological narcissism.* New York: Jason Aronson.

Kernberg, O. F. (1984). *Severe personality disorders: Psychotherapeutic strategies.* New Haven, CT: Yale University Press.

Kernberg, O. F. (1989). The narcissistic personality disorder and the differential diagnosis of antisocial behavior. *Psychiatric Clinics of North America, 12,* 553–570.

Kernberg, O. F. (1992). *Aggression in personality disorders and perversions.* New Haven, CT: Yale University Press.

Kernberg, O. F. (1996). A psychoanalytic theory of personality disorders. In J. F. Clarkin & M. Lenzenweger (Eds.), *Major theories of personality disorders* (pp. 106–140). New York: Guilford Press.

Kety, S. S., Rosenthal, D., Wender, P. H., & Schulsinger, F. (1968). Mental illness in the biological and adoptive families of adopted schizophrenics. In D. Rosenthal & S. S. Kety (Eds.), *Transmission of schizophrenia* (pp. 345–362). Oxford: Pergamon Press.

Kilzieh, N., & Cloninger, R. (1993, Spring). Psychophysiological antecedents of personality. *Journal of Personality Disorders* (Suppl. 1), 100–117.

Klein, D. F. (1974). Endogenomorphic depression. *Archives of General Psychiatry, 31,* 447–454.

Klein, D. F. (1977). Psychopharmacological treatment and delineation of borderline disorders. In P. Hartocollis (Ed.), *Borderline personality disorders* (pp. 365–383). New York: International Universities Press.

Klein, D. F., & Davis, J. (1969). *The diagnosis and drug treatment of psychiatric disorders*. Baltimore: Williams & Wilkins.

Klein, D. N. (1990). Depressive personality: Reliability, validity, and relation to dysthymia. *Journal of Abnormal Psychology, 99*, 412–421.

Klein, D. N., Riso, L. P., Donaldson, S. K., Schwartz, J. E., Anderson, R. L., Ouimette, P. C., et al. (1995). Family study of early-onset dysthymia. *Archives of General Psychiatry, 52*, 487–496.

Klein, D. N., Taylor, E. B., Dickstein, S., & Harding, K. (1988). The early–late onset distinction in *DSM–III* dysthymia. *Journal of Affective Disorders, 14*, 25–33.

Klein, M. (1930). The importance of symbol formation in the development of the ego. *International Journal of Psychoanalysis, 11*, 24–39.

Klein, M. (1935). A contribution to the psychogenesis of manic–depressive states. *International Journal of Psychoanalysis, 16*, 145–174.

Klerman, G. L., Endicott, J., Spitzer, R., & Hirschfeld, R. M. (1979). Neurotic depressions: A systematic analysis of multiple criteria and meanings. *American Journal of Psychiatry, 136*, 57–61.

Knight, R. P. (1953). Borderline states. *Bulletin of the Menninger Clinic, 17*, 1–12.

Kocsis, J. H. (1997). Chronic depression: The efficacy of pharmacotherapy. In H. S. Akiskal & G. B. Cassano (Eds.), *Dysthymia and the spectrum of chronic depressions* (pp. 66–74). New York: Guilford Press.

Kocsis, J. H., & Frances, A. J. (1987). A critical discussion of *DSM–III* dysthymic disorder. *American Journal of Psychiatry, 144*, 1534–1542.

Kohut, H. (1959). Introspection, empathy, and psychoanalysis: An examination of the relationship between mode of observation and theory. *Journal of the American Psychoanalytic Association, 7*, 459–483.

Kohut, H. (1966). Forms and transformations of narcissism. *Journal of the American Psychoanalytic Association, 14*, 243–272.

Kohut, H. (1968). The psychoanalytic treatment of narcissistic personality disorders. *Psychoanalytic Study of the Child, 23*, 86–113.

Kohut, H. (1971). *The analysis of the self: A systematic approach to the psychoanalytic treatment of narcissistic personality disorders*. New York: International Universities Press.

Kohut, H. (1972). Thoughts on narcissism and narcissistic rage. *Psychoanalytic Study of the Child, 27*, 350–400.

Kohut, H. (1977). *The restoration of the self*. New York: International Universities Press.

Kohut, H. (1980). Summarizing reflections. In A. Goldberg (Ed.), *Advances in self psychology* (pp. 473–554). Madison, CT: International Universities Press.

Kohut, H. (1984). *How does analysis cure?* (A. Goldberg & P. Stepansky, Eds.). Chicago: University of Chicago Press.

Kohut, H. (1991). On empathy. In P. H. Ornstein (Ed.), *The search for the self: Selected writings of Heinz Kohut: 1978–1981* (Vol. 4, pp. 525–535). New York: International Universities Press. (Original work published 1981)

Kohut, H. (1996). *The Chicago Institute lectures* (P. Tolpin & M. Tolpin, Eds.). Hillsdale, NJ: Analytic Press.

Kohut, H., & Wolf, E. (1978). The disorders of the self and their treatment: An outline. *International Journal of Psychoanalysis, 59,* 413–425.

Kolb, L. C. (1968). *Noyes' modern clinical psychiatry* (7th ed.). Philadelphia: W. B. Saunders.

Kraepelin, E. (1919). *Dementia praecox and paraphrenia* (R. M. Barclay, Trans.). Huntington, NY: Krieger.

Kraepelin, E. (1921). *Manic–depressive insanity and paranoia* (R. M. Barclay, Trans.). Edinburgh, Scotland: E. S. Livingstone.

Kraepelin, E. (1923). *Clinical psychiatry: A text-book for students and physicians* (Rev. ed.; A. R. Diefendorf, Ed. & Trans.). New York: Macmillan.

Kretschmer, E. (1925). *Physique and character.* New York: Harcourt Brace.

Krystal, H. (1975). Affect tolerance. *Annual of Psychoanalysis, 3,* 179–219.

Krystal, H. (1978). Trauma and affects. *Psychoanalytic Study of the Child, 33,* 81–116.

Krystal, H. (1998). Affect regulation and narcissism: Trauma, alexithymia, and psychosomatic illness in narcissistic patients. In E. F. Ronningstam (Ed.), *Disorders of narcissism* (pp. 299–325). Washington, DC: American Psychiatric Press.

Langfeldt, G. (1971). Schizophrenia: Diagnosis and prognosis. In R. Cancro (Ed.), *The schizophrenic syndrome: An annual review* (pp. 689–704). New York: Brunner/Mazel.

Lax, R. F. (1989). Introduction. In R. F. Lax (Ed.), *Essential papers on character neurosis and treatment* (pp. 1–20). New York: New York University Press.

Lazare, A. (1971). The hysterical character in psychoanalytic theory. *Archives of General Psychiatry, 25,* 131–137.

Lazare, A., Klerman, G. L., & Armor, D. (1970). Oral, obsessive and hysterical personality patterns: Replication of factor analysis in an independent sample. *Journal of Psychiatric Research, 7,* 275–290.

Leary, T. (1957). *Interpersonal diagnosis of personality.* New York: Ronald.

Levin, F. M. (1991). *Mapping the mind: The intersection of psychoanalysis and neuroscience.* Hillsdale, NJ: Analytic Press.

Lichtenberg, J. D. (1983). *Psychoanalysis and infant research.* Hillsdale, NJ: Analytic Press.

Lichtenberg, J. D. (1989). *Psychoanalysis and motivation.* Hillsdale, NJ: Analytic Press.

Lichtenberg, J. D., Lachmann, F. M., & Fosshage, J. L. (1992). *Self and motivational systems: Toward a theory of psychoanalytic technique.* Hillsdale, NJ: Analytic Press.

Liebert, R. S. (1988). The concept of character: A historical review. In R. A. Glick & D. I. Meyers (Eds.), *Masochism: Current psychoanalytic perspectives* (pp. 27–42). Hillsdale, NJ: Analytic Press.

Lilienfeld, S. O., van Valkenburg, C., Larntz, K., & Akiskal, H. S. (1986). The relationship of histrionic personality disorder to antisocial personality and somatization disorders. *American Journal of Psychiatry, 143,* 718–722.

Lipowski, Z. J. (1968). Review of consultation psychiatry and psychosomatic medicine: III. Theoretical issues. *Psychosomatic Medicine, 30*, 395–422.

Lipsitt, D. R. (1970). Medical and psychological characteristics of "crocks." *Psychiatry in Medicine, 1*, 15–25.

Livesley, W. J. (1987). Theoretical and empirical issues in the selection of criteria to diagnose personality disorders. *Journal of Personality Disorders, 1*, 88–94.

Livesley, W. J. (1995). Past achievements and future directions. In W. J. Livesley (Ed.), *The* DSM–IV *personality disorders* (pp. 497–505). New York: Guilford Press.

Livesley, W. J., Schroeder, M. L., & Jackson, D. N. (1990). Dependent personality disorder and attachment problems. *Journal of Personality Disorders, 4*, 131–140.

Livesley, W. J., & West, M. (1986). The *DSM–III* distinction between schizoid and avoidant personality disorders. *Canadian Journal of Psychiatry, 31*, 59–62.

Lopez-Ibor, J. J. (1972). Masked depressions. *British Journal of Psychiatry, 120*, 245–258.

Loranger, A. W. (1999). *International Personality Disorder Examination manual: DSM–IV module.* Washington, DC: American Psychiatric Press.

Lowy, F. H. (1975). Management of the persistent somatizer. *International Journal of Psychiatry in Medicine, 6*, 227–239.

Lumley, M. A., Mader, C., Gramzow, J., & Papineau, K. (1996). Family factors related to alexithymia characteristics. *Psychosomatic Medicine, 58*, 211–216.

Lumley, M. A., & Roby, K. R. (1995). Alexithymia and pathological gambling. *Psychotherapy and Psychosomatics, 63*, 201–206.

Lumley, M. A., Stettner, L., & Wehmer, F. (1996). How are alexithymia and physical illness linked? A review and critique of pathways. *Journal of Psychosomatic Research, 41*, 505–518.

Lykken, D. T. (1957). A study of anxiety in the sociopathic personality. *Journal of Abnormal and Social Psychology, 55*, 6–10.

Lykken, D. T. (1995). *The antisocial personalities.* Mahwah, NJ: Erlbaum.

Lyons, M. J., True, W. R., Eisen, S. A., & Goldberg, J. (1995). Differential heritability of adult and juvenile antisocial traits. *Archives of General Psychiatry, 52*, 906–915.

Mahler, M. S. (1968). *On human symbiosis and vicissitudes of individuation: Vol. 1. Infantile psychosis.* New York: International Universities Press.

Mahler, M. S., Pine, F., & Bergman, A. (1975). *The psychological birth of the human infant.* New York: Basic Books.

Main, M., & Goldwyn, R. (1994). *Adult attachment scoring and classification systems* (6th ed.). Unpublished manuscript, University College, London.

Maj, M. (1997). A critical reappraisal of the concept of neurotic depression. In H. S. Akiskal & G. B. Cassano (Eds.), *Dysthymia and the spectrum of chronic depressions* (pp. 130–147). New York: Guilford Press.

Marty, P., & de M'Uzan, M. (1963). La pensée operatoire [Operational thought]. *Revue Psychoanalitique, 27*(Suppl.), 345–356.

Masterson, J. F. (1988). *The search for the real self: Unmasking the personality disorders of our age*. New York: Free Press.

Mattia, J. I., & Zimmerman, M. (2001). Epidemiology. In W. J. Livesley (Ed.), *Handbook of personality disorders: Theory, research, and treatment* (pp. 107–123). New York: Guilford Press.

McAdams, D. P. (1992). The five-factor model in personality: A critical appraisal. *Journal of Personality, 60*, 329–361.

McCord, J. (1982). A longitudinal view of the relationship between paternal absence and crime. In J. Gunn & D. P. Farrington (Eds.), *Abnormal offenders, delinquency and the criminal justice system* (pp. 113–128). Chichester, England: Wiley.

McCord, J. (1991). Family relationships, juvenile delinquency, and adult criminality. *Criminology, 29*, 397–417.

McCord, W., & McCord, J. (1964). *The psychopath: An essay on the criminal mind*. Oxford, England: Van Nostrand.

McCord, W., McCord, J., & Zola, I. K. (1959). *Origins of crime: A new evaluation of the Cambridge–Somerville Youth Study*. New York: Columbia University Press.

McDougall, J. (1974). The psychosoma and psychoanalytic process. *International Review of Psychoanalysis, 1*, 437–459.

McDougall, J. (1989). *Theaters of the body: A psychoanalytic approach to psychosomatic illness*. New York: Norton.

McDougall, W. (1932). *Introduction to social psychology*. New York: Scribners. (Original work published 1908)

McGlashan, T. H. (1983). The "we-self" in borderline patients: Manifestations of the symbiotic self-object in psychotherapy. *Psychiatry, 46*, 351–361.

McLean, P., & Woody, S. (1995). Commentary on depressive personality disorder: A false start. In W. J. Livesley (Ed.), *The DSM–IV personality disorders* (pp. 303–311). New York: Guilford Press.

Mednick, S. A., Gabrielli, W. F., & Hutchings, B. (1984, May 25). Genetic influences in criminal convictions: Evidence from an adoption cohort. *Science, 224*, 891–894.

Mednick, S. A., & Kandel, E. S. (1988). Congenital determinants of violence. *Bulletin of the American Academy of Psychiatry and the Law, 16*, 101–109.

Meehl, P. E. (1954). *Clinical versus statistical prediction: A theoretical analysis and a review of the evidence*. Minneapolis: University of Minnesota Press.

Meehl, P. E. (1962). Schizotaxia, schizotypy, schizophrenia. *American Psychologist, 17*, 827–838.

Meehl, P. E. (1973). Why I do not attend case conferences. In *Psychodiagnosis: Selected papers* (pp. 225–302). Minneapolis: University of Minnesota Press.

Meissner, W. W. (1978). Theoretical assumptions of concepts of the borderline personality. *Journal of the American Psychoanalytic Association, 26*, 559–598.

Meloy, J. R. (1988). *The psychopathic mind*. Northvale, NJ: Jason Aronson.

Mendelson, M. (1974). *Psychoanalytic concepts of depression* (2nd ed.). New York: Spectrum.

Menninger, K. (1930). *The human mind*. New York: Knopf.

Miller, J. (1985). How Kohut actually worked. In A. Goldberg (Ed.), *Progress in self psychology* (Vol. 1, pp. 12–30). New York: Guilford Press.

Millon, T. (1969). *Modern psychopathology: A biosocial approach to maladaptive learning and functioning*. Philadelphia: W. B. Saunders.

Millon, T. (1990). *Toward a new personology: An evolutionary model*. New York: Wiley.

Millon, T. (1991). Classification in psychopathology: Rationale, alternatives, and standards. *Journal of Abnormal Psychology, 100*, 245–261.

Millon, T. (1996). *Disorders of personality: DSM–IV and beyond* (2nd ed.). New York: Wiley.

Millon, T. (2000). Sociocultural conceptions of the borderline personality. *Psychiatric Clinics of North America, 23*, 123–136.

Millon, T., Davis, R., & Millon, C. (1994). *Manual for the Millon Clinical Multiaxial Inventory—III*. Minneapolis, MN: National Computer Systems.

Millon, T., & Martinez, A. (1995). Avoidant personality disorder. In W. J. Livesley (Ed.), *The DSM–IV personality disorders* (pp. 218–233). New York: Guilford Press.

Mitchell, S. (1988). *Relational concepts in psychoanalysis*. Cambridge, MA: Harvard University Press.

Modell, A. (1963). Primitive object relationships and the predisposition to schizophrenia. *International Journal of Psychoanalysis, 44*, 282–292.

Moffitt, T. E. (1987). Parental mental disorder and offspring criminal behavior: An adoption study. *Psychiatry: Journal for the Study of Interpersonal Processes, 50*, 346–360.

Moffitt, T. E. (1993). Adolescence-limited and life-course-persistent antisocial behavior: A developmental taxonomy. *Psychological Review, 100*, 674–701.

Murray, H. A. (1943). *Thematic Apperception Test: Manual*. Cambridge, MA: Harvard University Press.

Murray, R. M., O'Callaghan, E., Castle, D. J., & Lewis, S. W. (1992). A neurodevelopmental approach to the classification of schizophrenia. *Schizophrenia Bulletin, 18*, 319–332.

Nemiah, J., & Sifneos, P. (1970). Affect and fantasy in patients with psychosomatic disorders. In O. Hill (Ed.), *Modern trends in psychosomatic medicine* (Vol. 2, pp. 175–189). London: Butterworth.

Niederland, W. G. (1968). Clinical observations of the "survivor syndrome." *International Journal of Psychoanalysis, 49*, 313–315.

Ogden, T. (1994). *Subjects of analysis*. Northvale, NJ: Jason Aronson.

Oldham, J. M., & Morris, L. B. (1990). *The personality self-portrait*. New York: Bantam.

O'Neill, E. (1941). The great god Brown. In *Nine plays by Eugene O'Neill* (pp. 307–377). New York: Modern Library. (Original work published 1926)

Ornstein, P. H. (1978). The evolution of Heinz Kohut's psychoanalytic psychology of the self. In P. H. Ornstein (Ed.), *The search for the self: Selected writings of Heinz Kohut: 1950–1978* (Vol. 1, pp. 1–106). New York: International Universities Press.

Paris, J. (1995). Commentary on narcissistic personality disorder. In W. J. Livesley (Ed.), *The DSM–IV personality disorders* (pp. 213–217). New York: Guilford Press.

Paris, J. (1997). The dynamics of psychotherapy under Medicare. *Canadian Psychiatric Association Journal, 22*, 137–139.

Patrick, C. J., Bradley, M. M., & Lang, P. J. (1993). Emotion in the criminal psychopath: Startle reflex modulation. *Journal of Abnormal Psychology, 102*, 82–92.

Pfohl, B. (1995). Histrionic personality disorder. In W. J. Livesley (Ed.), *The DSM–IV personality disorders* (pp. 173–192). New York: Guilford Press.

Pfohl, B., & Blum, N. (1995). Obsessive–compulsive personality disorder. In W. J. Livesley (Ed.), *The DSM–IV personality disorders* (pp. 261–276). New York: Guilford Press.

Phillips, K. A., & Gunderson, J. G. (1999). Depressive personality disorder: Fact or fiction? *Journal of Personality Disorders, 13*, 128–134.

Phillips, K. A., Gunderson, J. G., Hirschfeld, R. M. A., & Smith, L. E. (1990). A review of the depressive personality. *American Journal of Psychiatry, 147*, 830–837.

Phillips, K. A., Hirschfeld, R. M. A., Shea, M. T., & Gunderson, J. G. (1995). Depressive personality disorder. In W. J. Livesley (Ed.), *The DSM–IV personality disorders* (pp. 287–302). New York: Guilford Press.

Pine, F. (1988). The four psychologies of psychoanalysis and their place in clinical work. *Journal of the American Psychoanalytic Association, 36*, 571–596.

Pollak, J. M. (1987). Relationship of obsessive–compulsive personality to obsessive–compulsive disorder: A review of the literature. *Journal of Psychology, 121*, 137–148.

Pollak, J. M. (1995). Commentary on obsessive–compulsive personality disorder. In W. J. Livesley (Ed.), *The DSM–IV personality disorders* (pp. 277–283). New York: Guilford Press.

Quay, H. C. (1987). Patterns of delinquent behavior. In H. C. Quay (Ed.), *Handbook of juvenile delinquency* (pp. 118–138). New York: Wiley.

Rado, S. (1928). The problem of melancholia. *International Journal of Psychoanalysis, 9*, 297–313.

Rado, S. (1956). *Psychoanalysis of behavior: Collected papers.* New York: Grune & Stratton.

Rado, S. (1959). Obsessive behavior. In S. Arieti (Ed.), *American handbook of psychiatry* (Vol. 1, pp. 269–274). New York: Basic Books.

Rado, S. (1969). *Adaptational psychodynamics.* New York: Science House.

Raine, A., Brennan, P., & Mednick, S. A. (1994). Birth complications combined with early maternal rejection at age 1 year predispose to violent crime at age 18 years. *Archives of General Psychiatry, 51*, 984–988.

Raine, A., Buchsbaum, M., & LaCasse, L. (1997). Brain abnormalities in murderers indicated by positron emission tomography. *Biological Psychiatry, 42,* 495–508.

Raine, A., Lencz, T., Bihrle, S., LaCasse, L., & Colletti, P. (2000). Reduced prefrontal gray matter volume and reduced autonomic activity in antisocial personality disorder. *Archives of General Psychiatry, 57,* 119–127.

Raine, A., Stoddard, J., Bihrle, S., & Buchsbaum, M. (1998). Prefrontal glucose deficits in murderers lacking psychosocial deprivation. *Neuropsychiatry, Neuropsychology, and Behavioral Neurology, 1,* 1–7.

Raine, A., Venables, P. H., & Mednick, S. A. (1997). Low resting heart rate at age 3 years predisposes to aggression at age 11 years: Evidence from the Mauritius Child Health Project. *Journal of the American Academy of Child and Adolescent Psychiatry, 36,* 1457–1464.

Rapaport, D. (1951). *Organization and pathology of thought.* New York: Columbia University Press.

Reich, A. (1960). Pathologic forms of self-esteem regulation. *Psychoanalytic Study of the Child, 15,* 215–232.

Reich, W. (1949). *Character analysis* (3rd ed., T. P. Wolfe, Trans.). New York: Orgone Institute Press. (Original work published 1933)

Rickles, W. H. (1986). Self psychology and somatization: An integration with alexithymia. In A. Goldberg (Ed.), *Progress in self psychology* (Vol. 2, pp. 212–226). New York: Guilford Press.

Ritzler, B., & Rosenbaum, G. (1974). Proprioception in schizophrenics and normals: Effects of stimulus intensity and interstimulus interval. *Journal of Abnormal Psychology, 83,* 106–111.

Robins, L. (1995). Commentary on antisocial personality disorder. In W. J. Livesley (Ed.), *The DSM–IV personality disorders* (pp. 135–140). New York: Guilford Press.

Robins, L. N. (1966). *Deviant children grown up: A sociological and psychiatric study of sociopathic personality.* Oxford, England: Williams & Wilkins.

Rogers, R., & Dion, K. (1991). Rethinking the *DSM–III–R* diagnosis of antisocial personality disorder. *Bulletin of the American Academy of Psychiatry and Law, 19,* 21–31.

Rosenfeld, H. (1964). On the psychopathology of narcissism. *International Journal of Psychoanalysis, 45,* 332–337.

Rubinfine, D. L. (1968). Notes on a theory of depression. *Psychoanalytic Quarterly, 37,* 400–417.

Rubovits-Seitz, P. F. D. (1999). *Kohut's Freudian vision.* Hillsdale, NJ: Analytic Press.

Ruesch, J. (1948). The infantile personality—the core problem of psychosomatic medicine. *Psychosomatic Medicine, 10,* 134–144.

Rutter, M. (1987). Temperament, personality and personality disorder. *British Journal of Psychiatry, 150,* 443–458.

Rutter, M., & Giller, H. (1983). *Juvenile delinquency: Trends and perspectives.* Harmondsworth, England: Penguin.

Salzman, L. (1985). Psychotherapeutic management of obsessive–compulsive patients. *American Journal of Psychotherapy, 39,* 323–330.

Sandler, J., & Joffe, W. G. (1969). Towards a basic psychoanalytic model. *International Journal of Psychoanalysis, 50,* 79–90.

Schachtel, E. G. (1959). *Metamorphosis: On the development of affect, perception, attention, and memory.* New York: Basic Books.

Schachtel, E. G. (1966). *Experiential foundations of Rorschach's test.* New York: Basic Books.

Schafer, R. (1976). *A new language for psychoanalysis.* New Haven, CT: Yale University Press.

Schmideberg, M. (1959). The borderline patient. In S. Arieti (Ed.), *American handbook of psychiatry* (Vol. 1, pp. 398–416). New York: Basic Books.

Schneider, K. (1950). *Psychopathic personalities.* London: Cassell. (Original work published 1923)

Schneider, K. (1959). *Clinical psychopathology* (M. W. Hamilton, Trans.). New York: Grune & Stratton.

Schore, A. N. (2003a). *Affect dysregulation and disorders of the self.* New York: Norton.

Schore, A. N. (2003b). *Affect regulation and the repair of the self.* New York: Norton.

Searles, H. (1965). *Collected papers on schizophrenia and related subjects.* New York: International Universities Press.

Selye, H. (1956). *The stress of life.* New York: McGraw-Hill.

Shane, M., & Shane, E. (1993). Self psychology after Kohut: One theory or many? *Journal of the American Psychoanalytic Association, 41,* 777–797.

Shane, M., Shane, E., & Gales, M. (1998). *Intimate attachments: Towards a new self psychology.* New York: Guilford Press.

Shapiro, D. (1965). *Neurotic styles.* New York: Basic Books.

Shapiro, D. (1981). *Autonomy and rigid character.* New York: Basic Books.

Shea, M. T. (1995). Interrelationships among categories of personality disorders. In W. J. Livesley (Ed.), *The DSM–IV personality disorders* (pp. 497–505). New York: Guilford Press.

Shea, M. T., Glass, D. R., Pilkonis, P. A., Watkins, J., & Docherty, J. P. (1987). Frequency and implications of personality disorders in a sample of depressed outpatients. *Journal of Personality Disorders, 1,* 27–42.

Shea, M. T., & Hirschfeld, R. M. A. (1996). Chronic mood disorder and depressive personality. *Psychiatric Clinics of North America, 19,* 103–120.

Siegel, A. M. (1996). *Heinz Kohut and the psychology of the self.* London: Routledge.

Siever, L. J., Coccaro, E. F., Zemishlany, Z., Silverman, J., Klar, H., Losonczy, M. F., et al. (1987). Psychobiology of personality disorders: Pharmacologic implications. *Psychopharmacology Bulletin, 23,* 333–336.

Siever, L. J., & Davis, K. L. (1991). A psychobiological perspective on the personality disorders. *American Journal of Psychiatry, 148,* 1647–1658.

Sifneos, P. E. (1991). Affect, emotional conflict, and deficit: An overview. *Psychotherapy and Psychosomatics, 56,* 116–122.

Silverstein, M. L. (1999). *Self psychology and diagnostic assessment: Identifying selfobject functions through psychological testing.* Mahwah, NJ: Erlbaum.

Silverstein, M. L. (2001). Self-object functions, self states, and intimate forms of musical composition: Influences from literary texts on the art song. In A. Goldberg (Ed.), *Progress in self psychology: Vol. 17. The narcissistic patient revisited* (pp. 197–219). Hillsdale, NJ: Analytic Press.

Silverstein, M. L. (2005). Self psychological foundations of personality disorders. In S. Strack (Ed.), *Handbook of personology and psychopathology* (pp. 181–197). New York: Wiley.

Socarides, D. D., & Stolorow, R. D. (1984–1985). Affects and selfobjects. *Annual of Psychoanalysis, 12–13,* 105–119.

Solms, M., & Turnbull, O. (2002). *The brain and the inner world: An introduction to the neuroscience of subjective experience.* New York: Other Press.

Spillius, E. B. (1988). *Melanie Klein today: Developments in theory and practice: Vol. 1. Mainly theory.* London: Routledge.

Spitz, R. (1965). *The first year of life.* New York: International Universities Press.

Spitzer, R. L., & Endicott, J. (1978). *Schedule for Affective Disorders and Schizophrenia (SADS).* New York: New York State Psychiatric Institute, Biometrics Institute.

Spitzer, R. L., Endicott, J., & Gibbon, M. (1979). Crossing the border into borderline personality and borderline schizophrenia. *Archives of General Psychiatry, 36,* 17–24.

Spitzer, R. L., Endicott, J., & Robins, E. (1978). *Research Diagnostic Criteria (RDC) for a selected group of functional disorders* (3rd ed.). New York: New York Psychiatric Institute.

Stephens, J. H. (1978). Long-term prognosis and follow-up in schizophrenia. *Schizophrenia Bulletin, 4,* 25–37.

Stern, A. (1938). Psychoanalytic investigation of and therapy in the borderline group of neuroses. *Psychoanalytic Quarterly, 7,* 467–489.

Stern, D. N. (1985). *The interpersonal world of the infant.* New York: Basic Books.

Sternbach, R. A. (1966). *Principles of psychophysiology: An introductory text and readings.* Oxford, England: Academic Press.

Stevenson, R. L. (2003). *The strange case of Dr. Jekyll and Mr. Hyde: An authoritative text, backgrounds and contexts, performance adaptations, criticism* (K. Linehan, Ed.). New York: Norton. (Original work published 1886)

Stewart, J. W., & Klein, D. F. (1997). Chronic (and hysteroid) dysphorias. In H. S. Akiskal & G. B. Cassano (Eds.), *Dysthymia and the spectrum of chronic depressions* (pp. 174–182). New York: Guilford Press.

Stolorow, R. D., & Atwood, G. E. (1992). *Contexts of being.* Hillsdale, NJ: Analytic Press.

Stolorow, R., Brandchaft, B., & Atwood, G. (1987). *Psychoanalytic treatment: An intersubjective approach.* Hillsdale, NJ: Analytic Press.

Stone, M. H. (1993). *Abnormalities of personality*. New York: Norton.

Strauss, J. S., Klorman, R., & Kokes, R. F. (1977). Premorbid adjustment in schizophrenia: The implications of findings for understanding, research, and application. *Schizophrenia Bulletin, 3*, 240–244.

Sullivan, H. S. (1947). *Conceptions of modern psychiatry*. New York: Norton.

Summers, F. (1994). *Object relations theories and psychopathology*. Hillsdale, NJ: Analytic Press.

Taylor, G. J., Parker, J. D. A., & Bagby, R. M. (1990). A preliminary investigation of alexithymia in men with psychoactive substance dependence. *American Journal of Psychiatry, 147*, 1228–1230.

Taylor, S. (1995). Commentary on borderline personality disorder. In W. J. Livesley (Ed.), *The* DSM–IV *personality disorders* (pp. 165–172). New York: Guilford Press.

Teicholz, J. G. (1999). *Kohut, Loewald, and the postmoderns: A comparative study of self and relationship*. Hillsdale, NJ: Analytic Press.

Terman, D. M. (1988). Optimum frustration: Structuralization and the therapeutic process. In A. Goldberg (Ed.), *Progress in self psychology: Vol. 4. Learning from Kohut* (pp. 113–125). Hillsdale, NJ: Analytic Press.

Thelen, E., & Smith, L. B. (1994). *A dynamic systems approach to the development of cognition and actions*. Cambridge, MA: MIT Press.

Tolpin, M. (1971). On the beginnings of a cohesive self: An application of the concept of transmuting internalization to the study of the transitional object and signal anxiety. *Psychoanalytic Study of the Child, 26*, 316–352.

Tolpin, M. (1978). Self-objects and oedipal objects—A crucial developmental distinction. *Psychoanalytic Study of the Child, 33*, 167–184.

Tolpin, M. (1980). Discussion of "Psychoanalytic developmental theories of the self" by Morton Shane and Estelle Shane. In A. Goldberg (Ed.), *Advances in self psychology* (pp. 47–68). New York: International Universities Press.

Tolpin, M. (1986). The self and its selfobjects—a different baby. In A. Goldberg (Ed.), *Progress in self psychology* (Vol. 11, pp. 115–128). New York: International Universities Press.

Tolpin, M. (1993). The unmirrored self, compensatory structure, and cure: The exemplary case of Anna O. In B. Magid (Ed.), *Freud's case studies: Self psychological perspectives* (pp. 9–29). Hillsdale, NJ: Analytic Press.

Tolpin, M. (1997). The development of sexuality and the self. *Annual of Psychoanalysis, 25*, 173–187.

Tolpin, M. (2002). Doing psychoanalysis of normal development: Forward edge transferences. In A. Goldberg (Ed.), *Progress in self psychology: Vol. 18. Postmodern self psychology* (pp. 167–190). Hillsdale, NJ: Analytic Press.

Tolpin, M., & Kohut, H. (1980). The disorders of the self: The psychopathology of the first year of life. In S. Greenspan & G. H. Pollock (Eds.), *The course of life: Psychoanalytic contributions toward understanding personality development: Vol. 1. Infancy and early childhood* (pp. 425–458). Washington, DC: National Institute of Mental Health.

Tolpin, P. (1980). The borderline personality: Its makeup and analyzability. In A. Goldberg (Ed.), *Advances in self psychology* (pp. 299–316). Madison, CT: International Universities Press.

Tolpin, P. (1983). A change in the self: The development and transformation of an idealizing transference. *International Journal of Psychoanalysis, 64*, 461–483.

Tomkins, S. (1963). *Affect, imagery and consciousness* (Vol. 2). New York: Springer.

Torgerson, S. (1995). Commentary on paranoid, schizoid, and schizotypal personality disorders. In W. J. Livesley (Ed.), *The DSM–IV personality disorders* (pp. 91–102). New York: Guilford Press.

Trop, J. L. (1994). Self psychology and intersubjectivity theory. In R. D. Stolorow, G. E. Atwood, & B. Brandchaft (Eds.), *The intersubjective perspective* (pp. 77–91). Northvale, NJ: Jason Aronson.

Vaillant, G. E. (1964). Prospective prediction of schizophrenic remission. *Archives of General Psychiatry, 11*, 509–518.

Van der Kolk, B. A. (1993). Biological considerations about emotions, trauma, memory and the brain. In S. A. Ablon, D. Brown, & E. J. Khantzian (Eds.), *Human feelings: Explorations in affect development and meaning* (pp. 221–258). Hillsdale, NJ: Analytic Press.

Venables, P. H. (1988). Psychophysiology and crime: Theory and data. In M. A. Sarnoff & T. E. Moffitt (Eds.), *Biological contributions to crime causation* (pp. 3–13). Dordrecht, the Netherlands: Martinus Nijhoff.

Volavka, J. (1999). The neurobiology of violence: An update. *Journal of Neuropsychiatry and Clinical Neurosciences, 11*, 307–314.

Wallerstein, R. S. (1983). Self psychology and "classical" psychoanalytic psychology: The nature of their relationship. In A. Goldberg (Ed.), *The future of psychoanalysis* (pp. 19–63). New York: International Universities Press.

Watson, D., & Tellegen, A. (1985). Toward a consensual structure of mood. *Psychological Bulletin, 98*, 219–235.

Weissman, M. M., Prusoff, B. A., & Klerman, G. L. (1978). Personality and the prediction of long-term outcome of depression. *American Journal of Psychiatry, 135*, 797–800.

Westen, D., & Chang, C. (2000). Personality pathology in adolescence: A review. In L. T. Flaherty & A. H. Esman (Eds.), *Adolescent psychiatry: Developmental and clinical studies* (pp. 61–100). Hillsdale, NJ: Analytic Press.

Westen, D., & Cohen, R. P. (1993). The self in borderline personality disorder: A psychodynamic perspective. In Z. V. Segal & S. J. Blatt (Eds.), *The self in emotional distress: Cognitive and psychodynamic perspectives* (pp. 334–368). New York: Guilford Press.

Westen, D., & Shedler, J. (1999a). Revising and assessing Axis II, Part I: Developing a clinically and empirically valid assessment method. *American Journal of Psychiatry, 156*, 258–272.

Westen, D., & Shedler, J. (1999b). Revising and assessing Axis II, Part II: Toward an empirically based and clinically useful classification of personality disorders. *American Journal of Psychiatry, 156*, 273–285.

Westen, D., & Shedler, J. (2000). A prototype matching approach to the diagnosis of personality disorders. *Journal of Personality Disorders, 14,* 109–126.

Widiger, T. A. (1992). Categorical vs. dimensional classification: Implications from and for research. *Journal of Personality Disorders, 6,* 287–300.

Widiger, T. A. (1993). The *DSM–III–R* categorical personality disorder diagnoses: A critique and an alternative. *Psychological Inquiry, 4,* 75–90.

Widiger, T. A., & Corbitt, E. M. (1995). Antisocial personality disorder. In W. J. Livesley (Ed.), *The DSM–IV personality disorders* (pp. 103–126). New York: Guilford Press.

Widiger, T. A., Mangine, S., Corbitt, E. M., Ellis, C. G., & Thomas, G. V. (1995). *Personality Disorder Interview—IV: A semistructured interview for the assessment of personality disorders.* Odessa, FL: Psychological Assessment Resources.

Williams, T. (2004). *A streetcar named Desire.* New York: New Directions. (Original work published 1947)

Wing, J. K., Cooper, J. E., & Sartorius, N. (1974). *The measurement and classification of psychiatric symptoms.* London: Cambridge University Press.

Winnicott, D. W. (1965). *The maturational process and the facilitating environment.* London: Hogarth Press.

Winnicott, D. W. (1971). *Playing and reality.* London: Routledge.

Winokur, G. (1972). Depression spectrum disease: Description and family study. *Comprehensive Psychiatry, 13,* 3–8.

Winokur, G. (1979). Unipolar depression: Is it divisible into autonomous subtypes? *Archives of General Psychiatry, 36,* 47–52.

Wolf, E. S. (1988). *Treating the self: Elements of clinical self psychology.* New York: Guilford Press.

Wolf, E. S. (1994). Varieties of disorders of the self. *British Journal of Psychotherapy, 11,* 198–208.

World Health Organization. (1992). *The ICD–10 classification of mental and behavioural disorders: Diagnostic criteria for research.* Geneva: Author.

Zanarini, M. C. (1993). Borderline personality disorder as an impulse spectrum disorder. In J. Paris (Ed.), *Borderline personality disorder: Etiology and treatment* (pp. 67–85). Washington, DC: American Psychiatric Press.

Zanarini, M. C., Gunderson, J. G., Frankenburg, F. R., & Chauncey, D. L. (1989). The revised Diagnostic Interview for Borderlines: Discriminating BPD from other Axis II disorders. *Journal of Personality Disorders, 3,* 10–18.

Zetzel, E. R. (1960). Introduction to symposium on depressive illness. *International Journal of Psychoanalysis, 41,* 476–480.

Zetzel, E. (1965). Depression and the incapacity to bear it. In M. Schur (Ed.), *Drives, affects, behavior* (Vol. 2, pp. 243–274). New York: International Universities Press.

Zetzel, E., & Meissner, W. W. (1973). *Basic concepts of psychoanalytic psychiatry.* New York: Basic Books.

Zilboorg, G. (1941). Ambulatory schizophrenia. *Psychiatry, 4,* 149–155.

AUTHOR INDEX

Abraham, K., 19, 68, 99, 103, 104, 147, 152, 154, 217, 219
Adler, G., 135
Aichorn, A., 167, 167n, 193, 194
Akiskal, H., 107, 109, 110, 154, 207, 208, 210, 211, 212, 213, 214, 215, 223, 231, 267
Alexander, F., 235, 238
Alper, K., 246
American Psychiatric Association, 3, 6, 13, 28, 32, 62, 63, 97, 146, 154, 156, 159, 160, 200, 205, 206, 208, 221, 235, 236, 252, 263, 266
Andreasen, N. C., 64
Andreasen, P. J., 162
Andreas-Salome, L., 31
Angst, J., 208
Arieti, S., 68, 206, 217, 235
Arlow, J. A., 216
Armor, D., 106, 147
Aron, L., 23, 104
Atwood, G. E., 23, 47, 48, 75, 78, 117, 223, 240
Ax, A. F., 235

Bacal, H. A., 24, 35, 36, 37, 40, 45
Bagby, R. M., 238
Bagford, J., 163
Balint, M., 36
Barratt, E. S., 158
Barrett, J., 149
Barsky, A. J., 236, 237
Basch, M. F., 195, 254
Battaglia, M., 66
Baudry, F. D., 20, 27, 103, 104
Bayon, C., 18, 151, 215
Bechara, A., 163
Beck, A. T., 29
Beebe, B., 23, 48, 77, 89, 224, 241, 270
Bellodi, L., 66
Bemporad, J. R., 206, 217
Benjamin, L. S., 14
Berenbaum, H., 238
Bergman, A., 31, 148
Bernstein, D. P., 63, 99
Bibring, E., 217, 220

Biederman, J., 162
Bihrle, S., 162, 163
Bion, W. R., 241
Black, D. W., 160, 161, 162
Blair, R. J. R., 162, 163, 194
Blashfield, R. K., 17
Blatt, S. J., 218
Bleuler, E., 13, 25, 62, 64, 70, 107, 235
Blum, N., 107
Bohman, M., 163
Bollas, C., 240
Boring, E. G., 251
Bornstein, R. F., 19, 147, 174
Bowlby, J., 149, 219, 220
Bradley, M. M., 162
Braff, D. L., 63
Brandchaft, B., 23, 47, 78, 117, 134, 135, 223
Brantley, B., 159n
Brennan, P., 164
Brenner, C., 216
Bretherton, I., 149
Breuer, J., 152, 154, 183, 216, 250
Brickman, B., 239, 241
Bronstein, C., 218
Buchsbaum, M., 162
Bursten, B., 29, 156
Byrne, D., 236

Cadoret, R. J., 163
Carpenter, W. T., Jr., 64
Caspi, A., 163
Castle, D. J., 67
Chang, C., 166
Chapman, J. P., 67
Chapman, L. J., 67
Chauncey, D. L., 14
Chodoff, P., 149, 153, 205, 220
Cipolotti, L., 162
Clark, F., 194
Clark, L. A., 13, 15
Clayton, A. H., 162
Clayton, P. J., 210
Cleckley, H., 158, 160, 166, 200
Cloninger, C. R., 14, 15, 16, 18, 66, 72, 102, 106, 111, 112, 151, 155, 161, 162, 163, 165, 166, 215, 267, 268

Cohen, R. P., 136
Colletti, P., 163
Cooke, D. J., 158
Cooper, A. M., 210
Cooper, J. E., 13
Corbitt, E. M., 14, 157, 158, 159
Costa, P. T., Jr., 15, 16, 29, 151
Cromwell, R. L., 267, 268
Crow, T. J., 64

Damasio, A. R., 162, 163, 195
Damasio, H., 163, 195
Davis, G. C., 213
Davis, J., 154, 215
Davis, K. L., 12, 15, 70, 72, 99, 110, 162, 267
Davis, R., 13
Davis, R. D., 16, 17
Davis, W. W., 16
de M'Uzan, M., 237
Deutsch, H., 108, 109, 136, 155
Devinsky, O., 246
Dickstein, S., 209
Dion, K., 160
Djenderedjian, A. H., 110
Docherty, J. P., 210
Dolan, R. J., 163
Drye, R. C., 99, 136
Dworkin, R. H., 235

Ebb, F., 74n
Eisen, S. A., 163
Eissler, K. R., 167
Ellis, C. G., 14
Endicott, J., 13, 17, 63, 69, 208, 221
Erikson, E. H., 104
Exner, J. E., Jr., 84, 123, 225, 257, 259
Eysenck, H. J., 16, 161

Fairbairn, R., 35, 36, 65, 147, 219
Federn, P., 68, 69
Feighner, J. P., 13, 62, 157, 208, 221
Fenichel, O., 20, 31, 38, 99, 103, 147, 154, 217, 218
Finn, P. R., 238
First, M., 13, 16
Fish, B., 67
Fiske, D. W., 16
Fonagy, P., 77, 241
Fosse, B., 74n
Fosshage, J. L., 23, 117
Frances, A., 16, 210

Frankenburg, F. R., 14
Freeman, A., 29
Freud, S., 19, 20, 30, 38, 68, 69, 99, 102, 103, 104, 147, 152, 154, 166, 183, 206, 216, 217, 219, 250, 251, 267
Frith, C. C., 163
Fromm, E., 104
Fromm-Reichmann, F., 68
Frosch, J., 107, 108, 168

Gabbard, G. O., 104
Gabrielli, W. F., 163
Gales, M., 23, 47, 224, 270
Gedo, J. E., 267
Gergely, G., 241
Gibbon, M., 13, 69
Giller, H., 164
Giovacchini, P. L., 135
Glass, D. R., 210
Glueck, E., 160
Glueck, S., 160
Goldberg, A., 6, 24, 50, 133, 159n, 166, 183, 184, 185, 192, 196, 216, 249, 250, 252, 253, 254, 255, 260, 261, 269, 270
Goldberg, J., 163
Goldwyn, R., 88
Goodman, G., 219, 270
Gottesman, I. I., 267
Goyer, P. F., 162
Gramzow, J., 238
Gray, J. A., 161
Greenacre, P., 126
Grinker, R. R., Sr., 99, 108, 109, 136, 235, 264, 270
Gunderson, J. G., 14, 28, 109, 110, 207, 208
Guntrip, H., 36, 65, 66, 77, 219
Guze, S. B., 157, 210

Handler, L., 225
Harding, K., 209
Hare, R. D., 14, 158, 159, 160, 161, 162, 166, 168, 200
Harpur, T. J., 158
Hart, S. D., 158, 159, 168
Hartmann, H., 20, 31, 103, 148
Head, H., 159
Hempel, C. G., 18
Heinrichs, D. W., 64
Herzog, B., 24
Hirschfeld, R. M., 147, 149, 206, 207, 208, 213

Hoch, P. H., 107
Hoffman, I. Z., 23
Holzer, C. E., 206, 207
Holzman, P. S., 268
Horney, K., 71, 148
Huprich, S. K., 208, 225
Hutchings, B., 163
Huttunen, M. O., 164

Jackson, D. N., 149
Jackson, J. H., 64
Jacobson, E., 31, 34, 69, 109, 217, 218
James, T., 238
Jang, K. L., 16
Jaspers, K., 25, 152, 206
Joffe, W. G., 219
Johns, J. H., 159
Jones, L., 194
Josephs, L., 66, 105, 166
Judd, L. L., 211, 212, 213
Jurist, E. L., 241

Kalus, O., 63
Kandel, E. S., 164
Karasu, T. B., 112
Keller, M. B., 210
Kendler, K. S., 99
Kernberg, O. F., 16, 24, 27, 32, 33, 34, 35,
    46, 65, 99, 108, 109, 134, 135, 136,
    153, 156, 160, 167, 210, 220
Kety, S. S., 62, 67, 99
Khani, M. K., 110
Kilzieh, N., 16, 161, 162
Kisiel, C. L., 110
Klein, D. F., 110, 154, 155, 205, 208, 215
Klein, D. N., 205, 207, 209, 212, 231
Klein, M., 35, 46, 64, 65, 69, 100, 101, 109,
    134, 135, 218, 219, 235
Klerman, G. L., 106, 147, 149, 208, 210
Klorman, R., 62
Knight, R. P., 62, 107, 109
Kohut, H., 3, 4, 5, 6, 21, 22, 23, 24, 27, 32,
    34, 35, 36, 37, 38, 39, 40, 41, 42,
    44, 45, 46, 50, 73, 81, 83, 88, 115,
    116, 116n, 117, 118, 119, 120, 126,
    127, 131, 133, 134, 136, 145, 167,
    167n, 173, 174, 175, 180, 181, 182,
    186, 192, 193, 196, 201, 222, 223,
    238, 239, 249, 250, 251, 251n, 252,
    261, 264, 265, 269, 270
Kokes, R. F., 62
Kolb, L. C., 98

Korchin, S. J., 149
Kraepelin, E., 13, 25, 62, 64, 98, 107, 147,
    152, 157, 163, 165, 205, 206, 207,
    211, 214, 266
Kretschmer, E., 70, 71, 72, 107, 207
Kris, E., 148
Krystal, H., 81, 235, 237, 238

LaCasse, L., 162, 163
Lachmann, F. M., 23, 48, 77, 89, 117, 224,
    241, 270
Lang, P. J., 162
Langfeldt, G., 62
Larntz, K., 154
Lax, R. F., 20, 103
Lazare, A., 106, 147, 154
Leary, T., 29
Lencz, T., 163
Levin, F. M., 267
Lewis, S. W., 67
Lichtenberg, J. D., 23, 47, 49, 77, 81, 94, 117,
    224, 270
Liebert, R. S., 104
Lilienfeld, S. O., 154
Lipowski, Z. J., 235
Lipsitt, D. R., 236
Livesley, W. J., 12, 17, 70, 149
Loewenstein, R. M., 148
Lopez-Ibor, J. J., 237
Loranger, A. W., 14
Lowy, F. H., 235, 237
Lumley, M. A., 237, 238
Lykken, D. T., 161, 162
Lyons, H., 153
Lyons, M. J., 163

Mader, C., 238
Mahler, M. S., 31, 32, 148, 149
Main, M., 88
Maj, M., 208
Mangine, S., 14
Martin, J., 238
Martinez, A., 70
Marty, P., 237
Masterson, C. C., 99
Masterson, J. F., 136
Mattia, J. I., 28
McAdams, D. P., 16
McCord, J., 159, 160, 164
McCord, W., 159, 160
McCrae, R. R., 16
McDougall, J., 235, 237, 238, 239

McDougall, W., 15
McElroy, R., 17
McGlashan, T. H., 136
McLean, P., 209
Mednick, S. A., 163, 164
Meehl, P. E., 67, 268
Meissner, W. W., 136, 216
Meloy, J. R., 168
Mendelson, M., 206
Menninger, K., 71, 72
Mesad, S., 246
Michie, C., 158
Miller, J., 46
Millon, C., 13
Millon, T., 13, 15, 16, 17, 18, 19, 29, 30, 61,
        66, 67, 68, 69, 70, 71, 72, 79, 94,
        98, 101, 103, 105, 106, 107, 108,
        111, 121, 150, 151, 152, 155, 156,
        157, 158, 159, 160, 164, 166, 169,
        175, 216, 223, 236, 268
Mitchell, S., 23, 104
Modell, A., 108
Moffitt, T. E., 160, 163
Morris, J. S., 163
Morris, L. B., 106, 165
Murray, H. A., 87, 122, 225
Murray, R. M., 67

Nemiah, J., 235, 237
Newman, K., 24, 36, 37, 40
Niederland, W. G., 238
Niskanen, P., 164

O'Callaghan, E., 67
Ogden, T., 47
Oldham, J. M., 106, 165
O'Neill, E., 116n
Ornstein, P. H., 38

Papineau, K., 238
Paris, J., 28, 167
Parker, J. D. A., 238
Patrick, C. J., 162
Patton, J. H., 158
Paulus, M. P., 212
Perrett, D. I., 163
Pfohl, B., 107, 154
Phillips, K. A., 110, 207, 208, 209
Pihl, R. O., 238
Pilkonis, P. A., 210
Pincus, H. A., 16
Pine, F., 21, 31, 148

Polatin, P., 107
Pollak, J. M., 106, 107
Prusoff, B. A., 210
Przybeck, T. R., 14, 66, 102, 165, 267

Quay, H. C., 159, 161

Rado, S., 68, 71, 104, 105, 217, 218, 219
Raine, A., 162, 163, 164
Rapaport, D., 153
Rapaport, M. H., 212
Raulin, M. L., 67
Reich, A., 31, 34
Reich, W., 19, 20, 31, 64, 71, 99, 103, 104,
        152, 153, 154, 167
Rickles, W. H., 239, 240, 241
Ritzler, B., 67
Robins, E., 13, 63, 221
Robins, L., 160, 161, 164,
Roby, K. R., 238
Rogers, R., 160
Ronningstam, E., 28
Rosenbaum, G., 67
Rosenfeld, H., 31, 235
Rosenthal, D., 62, 99
Rosenthal, R. H., 110
Rubinfine, D. L., 218
Rubovits-Seitz, P. F. D., 127, 251
Ruesch, J., 237
Rutter, M., 14, 164

Salzman, L., 105
Sandler, J., 219
Sartorius, N., 13
Schachtel, E. G., 124, 147
Schafer, R., 266
Schmideberg, M., 107, 108
Schneider, K., 13, 25, 62, 70, 103, 107, 152,
        205, 206, 207, 211
Schore, A. N., 18, 72, 110, 163, 195, 235,
        237, 267, 268
Schroeder, M. L., 149
Schulsinger, F., 62, 99
Schwartz, M. S., 236
Searles, H., 68, 218
Selye, H., 235
Semple, W. E., 162
Shane, E., 23, 47, 50, 224, 270
Shane, M., 23, 47, 49, 50, 224, 270
Shapiro, D., 99, 100, 103, 105, 120, 131, 147,
        153, 168, 169, 195n, 253
Shapiro, R. W., 210

Shea, M. T., 15, 147, 206, 207, 210
Shedler, J., 14, 17, 18, 66, 69, 72, 102, 106, 112, 151, 155, 166, 215, 268
Shields, J., 267
Siegel, A. M., 174
Siever, L. J., 12, 15, 63, 70, 72, 99, 110, 162, 267
Sifneos, P., 235, 237, 238
Sigvardsson, S., 163
Silverstein, M. L., 74n, 256, 264, 269
Smith, L. B., 47, 49
Smith, L. E., 28, 208
Smith, M., 194
Socarides, D. D., 48, 81, 223, 224, 240, 254
Solms, M., 267
Spillius, E. B., 218
Spitz, R., 31
Spitzer, R. L., 13, 14, 17, 63, 69, 208, 221
Steinberg, M. A., 236
Stephens, J. H., 62, 99
Stern, A., 107
Stern, D. N., 23, 32, 48
Sternbach, R. A., 235
Stettner, L., 237
Stevenson, R. L., 253
Stewart, J. W., 155, 208
Stoddard, J., 162
Stolorow, R., 23, 47, 48, 49, 75, 78, 81, 117, 134, 135, 223, 224, 240, 254
Stone, M. H., 121, 168
Strauss, J. S., 62
Sullivan, H. S., 68, 148
Summers, F., 36, 37, 48
Svrakic, D. M., 14, 18, 102, 111, 151, 165, 166, 215, 267
Svrakic, N. M., 111, 166

Target, M., 241
Taylor, E. B., 209, 212
Taylor, G. J., 238
Taylor, S., 110
Teicholz, J. G., 32, 270
Tellegen, A., 206
Terman, D. M., 45
Thelen, E., 47, 49
Thomas, G. V., 14
Tolpin, M., 24, 32, 41, 42, 46, 78, 81, 83, 118, 126, 145, 173, 174, 183, 184, 185, 194, 202, 216, 222, 223, 229
Tolpin, P., 134
Tomkins, S., 47
Torgerson, S., 63

Tranel, D., 163, 195
Trop, J. L., 118
Troughton, E., 163
True, W. R., 163
Turnbull, O., 267

Useda, D., 99

Vaillant, G. E., 62, 99
Van der Kolk, B. A., 238
van Valkenburg, C., 154
Venables, P. H., 162, 164
Vernon, P. A., 16
Volavka, J., 162
von Knorring, A. L., 163

Wagman, A. M. I., 64
Wallerstein, R. S., 50
Watkins, J., 210
Watson, D., 206
Webb, W. L., 210, 211
Wehmer, F., 237
Weise, R. E., 147, 213
Weissman, M. M., 210
Wender, P. H., 62, 99
Werble, B., 99, 136
West, M., 70
Westen, D., 14, 17, 18, 66, 69, 72, 102, 106, 112, 136, 151, 155, 166, 215, 268
Wetzel, R. D., 14
Widiger, T. A., 14, 15, 16, 17, 29, 151, 157, 158, 159
Williams, J. B. W., 14
Williams, T., 146
Wing, J. K., 13
Winnicott, D. W., 35, 36, 65, 77, 149
Winokur, G., 208, 211
Wolf, E., 23, 24, 42, 83, 115, 131, 133, 195
Woodruff, R. A., 210
Woodworth, G., 163
Woody, S., 209
World Health Organization, 5, 13, 66, 154, 160, 208, 263

Yerevanian, B. I., 213

Zanarini, M. C., 14, 110
Zetzel, E., 216, 218, 220
Zilboorg, G., 107
Zimmerman, M., 28
Zola, I. K., 160

SUBJECT INDEX

Abandonment, fear of, 146
Abraham, K., 19, 68, 99, 103–104, 147, 152, 154, 217, 219
Acting out, 166, 193
Adler, G., 135
Affective disorders, 63, 109–110, 221
Affect regulation, 117–118, 121, 223–224, 241
Affects, as primary organizers of experience, 48
Age, and antisocial personality disorder, 157
Aggression, 65, 126, 134–135, 217; projected, 120–121
Aichorn, A., 167–167n, 193–194
Akiskal, H., 110, 207–208, 210–214, 223, 267
Alexander, F., 235, 238
Alexithymia, 235, 237–240
Alienation, 71
Alter ego transference, 39, 41–42
Amplification, and somatic dysfunction, 236–237
Anal character, 104
Anal stage, 103–104
Anankastic personality, 103
Andreas-Salome, L., 31
Anhedonia (pleasure deficiency), 67
Anna O. (case study), 182–184
Antisocial (term), 156
Antisocial personality disorder, 110, 145, 169–170, 172–173, 202
    clinical illustration, 197–201
    descriptive psychopathology, 156–161
    etiology, 161–164
    personality theories and, 164–166
    self psychological view, 192–197
Antisocial–psychopathic disorder, 166
Apparatuses of secondary autonomy, 104
Arieti, S., 68, 217
"As if" personality, 108–109, 155
Assassins (musical), 159n
Assortative mating, 82
Attachment anxiety, 121
Attachment theory, 23, 149–150, 219–220, 224, 270
Attuned responsiveness, 39, 117–118

Atwood, G. E., 75
Autistic personality, 64
Autocentric perspective, 147
Avoidance, 70–71, 88
Avoidant personality disorder, 61, 63, 69, 73–75, 101–102, 147, 171–172, 207
    clinical illustration, 89–94
    descriptive psychopathology, 70–72
    self psychological view, 87–89

Bacal, H. A., 35–36, 40, 45
Balint, M., 36
Barratt Impulsivity Scale, 158
Barsky, A. J., 236–237
Basch, M. F., 195
Baudry, F. D., 20, 103–104
Bayon, C., 151, 215
Beck, A. T., 29
Beebe, B., 89, 241
Behavioral medicine, 233
Bemporad, J. R., 217
Bergman, A., 31
Bernstein, D. P., 63, 99
Bibring, E., 217, 220
Biederman, J., 162
Big Five (five-factor model), 15–18
Biopsychosocial–evolutionary model, 155–156, 164, 169, 268
Bipolar depression, 207
Black, D. W., 161–162
Blair, R. J. R., 162–163, 194
Blashfield, R. K., 17
Blatt, S. J., 218
Bleuler, E., 13, 25, 62, 64, 70
Bollas, C., 240–241
Borderline (term), 107–108
Borderline personality disorder, 62, 69, 97–98, 115–118, 147, 154–155, 167, 213
    clinical illustration, 136–141
    descriptive psychopathology, 107–113
    self psychological view, 133–136
Borderline personality organization, 109
Bornstein, R. F., 19
Bowlby, J., 149, 219–220
Brandchaft, B., 134–135

Brenner, C., 270
Breuer, Josef, 183–184, 251
Brickman, B., 239, 241
Brittleness, 98, 142
Bronstein, C., 218
Bursten, B., 29, 156
Byrne, D., 236

Cadoret, R. J., 163–164
Caspi, A., 163
Chapman, J. P., 67
Chapman, L. J., 67
Character, 14, 19
Character disorder, 19, 64
Characterological depression, 205
Character pathology, 103–104, 167
Charcot, René, 152, 251
Chicago (musical), 74n
Chodoff, P., 153, 220–221
Chronic depression, 205–206
Cipolotti, L., 162
Clark, L. A., 15
Classification issues, 12, 15–18. *See also*
    Comorbidity problem
Cleckley, H., 158–160, 166, 200
Clinical illustrations: antisocial personality
    disorder, 197–201
    avoidant personality disorder, 89–94
    borderline personality disorder, 136–
    141
    dependent personality disorder, 176–
    179
    depressive personality disorder, 224–230
    histrionic personality disorder, 187–192
    narcissistic personality disorder, 50–57
    obsessive–compulsive personality disor-
    der, 128–133
    paranoid personality disorder, 122–125
    schizoid personality disorder, 79–82
    schizotypal personality disorder, 84–87
    somatic dysfunction, 242–247
    vertical split, 255–261
Cloninger, C. R., 14–16, 18, 66, 72, 102, 106,
    111–112, 151, 155, 215, 267
    and antisocial personality disorder, 161–
    162, 165–166
Coconstruct, 48
Comorbidity problem, 13, 15–18, 44, 69–70,
    99, 107, 146n, 154, 157–158, 207
Compensatory structures, 145, 173–174,
    183–187, 265–266
Conduct disorder, 159–160

Conflict, 104–106, 127
Conflict models, 18–24, 167
Constriction, 105, 120
Cooke, D. J., 158
Cooper, A. M., 210
Corbitt, E. M., 157, 159
Costa, P. T., Jr., 29, 151
Criminality, 156–158, 159n. *See also* Delin-
    quency
Cromwell, R. L., 267–268
Cyclothymia, 207
Cyclothymic temperament, 214

Davis, G. C., 213
Davis, J., 154–155, 215
Davis, K. L., 15, 72, 99, 110, 162–163, 267
Davis, R. D., 16–17
Defense, 249, 251
Deficit models, 18–24
Deficit states, and self-cohesion, 22
Deficit syndrome, 64
Delinquency, 159–160, 193, 196
Delusional disorder, 99
De M'Uzan, M., 237
Denial, 249
Dependency, 146, 149, 174–175
Dependent personality disorder, 145, 155–
    156, 169, 172–173, 202
    clinical illustration, 176–179
    descriptive psychopathology, 145–151
    self psychological view, 174–175
Depersonalization, schizoid, 65
Depersonalization disorder, 252
Depletion, 42–43, 73–75, 94, 222, 231
Depletion anxiety, 118
Depletion depression, 118, 222
Depression, 151, 207–209, 237, 254–255
    differential diagnosis, 209–214, 218
    psychoanalytic views, 216–221
    theoretical perspectives, 214–215
Depression spectrum disease, 208
Depressive–masochistic personality type, 220
Depressive neurosis, 205
Depressive personality disorder, 74–75, 205–
    206, 220, 230
    clinical illustration, 224–230
    descriptive pathology, 206–214
    self psychological view, 221–224, 230–
    231
Depressive position, 101, 218–219
Depressive prototype, 223
Depressive psychopathy, 205, 207

Depressive spectrum disorders, 211–212
Depressive temperament, 205, 207
Desomatizing selfobject transference, 239
Deutsch, H., 108–109, 155
Developmental life tasks, and self-cohesion, 265–266
Developmentally acquired sociopathy, 163
Developmental psychopathology, and somatization, 241
Devitalization, 73–75, 222, 265–266
Diagnostic criteria and assessment, 12–14
Diagnostic Interview for Borderlines, 14
Disappointment, sensitivity to, 153
Disavowal, 249–252, 254
Disintegration anxiety, 118
Disintegration products, 22, 43, 46, 115, 117, 182, 265–266
Dissociation, 251–252
Dissolution, sense of, 115
Distancing, 73, 120, 223
Double depression, 207, 210
Drive theory, 3, 28, 37–38, 45–46, 64, 68, 99, 103–104, 126, 147, 167, 174, 180
DSM (Diagnostic and Statistical Manual of Mental Disorders), 3–4, 32, 146, 154, 205
DSM–II, 206
DSM–III, 13, 16, 62–63, 160, 208, 221, 263
DSM–III–R, 159, 235–236
DSM–IV, 6–7, 24, 28, 63, 97, 156, 159–160, 200, 205, 236, 252, 266
    and depressive personality disorder, 206–207, 209, 220
DSM–IV–TR, 159
Dyads, bidirectional influence of, 48
Dysphoric factor, 215
Dyssocial personality, 156
Dysthymia, 207–212, 214, 231

Ego (term), 36
Ego concept, 216–217
Ego ideal, 30–31, 167
Ego psychology, 3, 28, 37–38, 104, 113, 148, 153, 174, 180, 217
Ego weakness, 109
Eissler, K. R., 167
Empathic deficits, 75–76, 181–182, 185, 194–195, 221–222
Empathic listening, 37
Empathy, 37, 39, 195n
Endicott, J., 17, 69, 208
Endogenomorphic depression, 154, 205, 215

Envy, 98
Erikson, E. H., 104
Explosive personality, 111
Eysenck, H. J., 16, 161

Fairbairn, R., 35–36, 65, 147, 219
Family cohesion, and delinquency, 159–160
Family history: and antisocial personality disorder, 163–164
    and depressive personality disorder, 208–210, 212–213
Family system, impaired, 82–83
Fanatic character, 102
Federn, P., 68–69
Feighner, J. P., 13, 62, 208, 221
Fenichel, O., 20, 31, 38, 103, 147, 154, 217–218
First, M. B., 16
Fish, B., 67
Fiske, D. W., 16
Fonagy, P., 77
Forward edge, in development, 194
Forward edge transference, 46, 126
Fosshage, J. L., 23, 117–118
Fragmentation of the self, 42–43, 98, 115–116, 120, 141, 239, 265–266
Fragmentation-prone disorders, 173
Frances, A. J., 16, 210
Freeman, A., 29
Freud, S., 19–20, 68–69, 99, 104, 147, 166, 216, 219, 235
    and hysterical neurosis, 151–154
    Mourning and Melancholia, 206, 216–217
    and narcissism, 27, 30–31; and obsessional/compulsive neurosis, 102–103
    and oedipal conflict, 182–184
    Project for a Scientific Psychology, 267
    and repression, 250–251
Fromm, E., 104
Fromm-Reichmann, F., 68
Frosch, J., 108, 168
Frustration, and self-cohesion, 45–46

Gabbard, G. O., 104
Gales, M., 47
Genetic factors, 75, 163–164, 267
Gibbon, M., 69
Giovacchini, P. L., 135
"Glue" metaphor, 116n
Goldberg, A., 6–7, 50, 166–167, 182–185, 192, 196, 269–270

and vertical split, 249–250, 252–255, 260–261
Grandiose–exhibitionistic self, 39–40
Grandiosity, 28, 38, 43, 76
Gray, J. A., 161
Greenacre, P., 126
Grinker, R. R., 99, 108–109, 264, 270
Guilt, 105, 166–167
Gunderson, J. G., 28–29, 110
Guntrip, H., 36, 65–66, 77, 219
Guze, S. B., 157

Hare, R. D., 158–160, 166, 168, 200
Harmony of the self, 38
Hart, S. D., 168
Hartmann, H., 20, 31, 103–104
Helplessness, 217–218
Hirschfeld, R. M., 149–150, 206–208
Histrionic factor, 155
Histrionic personality disorder, 110–111, 145, 169, 172–173, 202
    clinical illustration, 187–192
    descriptive psychopathology, 151–156
    self psychological view, 180–187
Holzer, C. E., 206–207
Holzman, P. S., 268
Horizontal split, 196, 250–251, 251n
Horney, K., 71, 148
Human Figure Drawings, 225–226
Hydraulic model, 152
Hyperalertness, 116, 119–120, 141–142
Hyperscanning, 100
Hypersensitivity, 146–147
Hypersexuality, 186
Hyperthymic temperament, 212, 214
Hypervigilance, 71–72, 100, 119
Hypomanic temperament, 212
Hysteria (term), 154
Hysterical character, 152–153
Hysterical neurosis, 151–153
Hysterical personality, 153–154
Hysteroid dysphoria, 154–155, 215

ICD (International Classification of Diseases), 5, 13, 66, 102–103, 154, 156, 160, 208, 263
Idealization, 39–42, 44–46, 172, 174–175, 183–184, 193–197, 265–266
Identity diffusion, 109–110
Impulse control disorders, 162–163, 168–169
Impulsive personality, 168
Infant. See Mother–infant interactions

Infantile personality, 154, 237
Information variance, 17–18
Instability, chronic, 110, 116, 142
Integration, of vertical split, 254–255
Integrative viewpoint, 47
Internalization, 45
International Personality Disorder Examination, 14
Intersubjective contexts, 47–48, 75
Intersubjectivity theory, 4, 23, 47–49, 75
    and avoidant personality disorder, 89, 94
    and borderline personality disorder, 134–135
    and depressive personality disorder, 224
    and fragmentation-prone disorders, 117–118
    and obsessive–compulsive personality disorder, 127–128
    and paranoid personality disorder, 121
    and schizoid personality disorder, 78
    and schizotypal personality disorder, 83–84
    and somatization, 240
Invariant organizing principles, 48
Isolation, 64, 71, 78, 88

Jackson, J. Hughlings, 64
Jacobson, E., 31, 34, 69, 109, 217–218
Janet, Edouard, 152, 251
Jang, K. L., 16
Jaspers, K., 25
Joffe, W. G., 219
Johns, J. H., 159
Josephs, L., 66, 105, 166
Judd, L. L., 211

Kalus, O., 63
Karasu, T. B., 112
Kendler, K. S., 99
Kernberg, O. F., 16, 24, 65, 99, 210, 220
    and antisocial personality disorder, 160, 167–168
    and borderline personality disorder, 108–109, 134–136
    and histrionic personality disorder, 153–154, 156
    and narcissistic personality disorder, 27, 32–35, 46
Kety, S. S., 62
Kilzieh, N., 16, 161–162
Klein, D. F., 154–155, 215

Klein, D. N., 207, 209–210, 212–213
Klein, M., 35, 46, 64–65, 69, 100–101, 109, 134–135, 218–219
Klerman, G. L., 149–150, 208
Knight, R. P., 107, 109
Kohut, Heinz, 3, 21, 23, 32, 58, 115, 117–118, 216, 269–270
    and antisocial personality disorder, 192–193
    and borderline personality disorder, 133–135
    and compensatory structures, 173–174, 201–202
    and dependent personality disorder, 174–175
    and depression, 222–223
    and histrionic personality disorder, 180–182
    and narcissistic personality disorder, 21, 27, 34–35, 44–47, 83, 167n
    and obsessive–compulsive personality disorder, 126–127
    and paranoid personality disorder, 118–120
    Restoration of the Self, 22
    and the self, 37–39, 73–74, 116n, 127, 136
    and self-cohesion, 36, 50, 127
    and selfobject functions, 39–42, 48, 88, 116
    and self psychology, 4–5, 21–24, 50, 264
    and somatic dysfunction, 238–239
    and vertical split, 6–7, 34, 167, 196, 249–251, 251n, 252, 261
"Kohut's baby," 32
Kolb, L. C., 98
Kraepelin, E., 13, 25, 62, 64, 98, 102, 107, 147, 152, 266
    and antisocial personality disorder, 157, 163, 165
    and depression, 207, 211, 214
Kretschmer, E., 70–72, 103, 107, 207
Krystal, H., 237–238

Lachmann, F. M., 89, 117–118, 241
Lax, R. F., 103
Lazare, A., 154
Leading edge
    in development, 194
    in treatment, 45–46
Learning theory, 161–162
Leary, T., 29

Lichtenberg, J. D., 47, 49, 94, 117–118
Liebert, R. S., 104
Livesley, W. J., 17, 149–150
Lost object, 216–217
Lowy, F. H., 237
Lumley, M. A., 237
Lyons, H., 153
Lyons, M. J., 163–164

Mahler, M., 31–32, 148–149
"Mahler's baby," 32
Marty, P., 237
Masked depression, 237
Masterson, J. F., 136
Maudsley, Henry, 237
McAdams, D. P., 16
McCord, J., 159–160
McCord, W., 159–160
McDougall, J., 237–239
McDougall, W., 15
McElroy, R., 17
McGlashan, T. H., 136
McLean, P., 209
Meehl, P. E., 67, 268
Meissner, W. W., 136
Melancholic pattern, 215
Meloy, J. R., 168
Menninger, K., 71–72
Mild depression, 208
Millon, T., 15–19, 29–30, 61, 66–67, 69–72, 79, 94, 98, 121, 236, 268
    and antisocial personality disorder, 157, 159–160, 164–166
    and borderline personality disorder, 107–108, 111
    and dependent personality disorder, 150–151
    and depressive personality disorder, 216, 223
    and histrionic personality disorder, 155–156
    and obsessive–compulsive personality disorder, 105–106
    and paranoid personality disorder, 101–102
Millon Clinical Multiaxial Inventory, 13
Mirroring, 35–36, 39–40, 42–46, 265–266
Mirroring deficits, 73–79, 88–89, 145, 171–172, 185–186
Mirror transference, 39
Misregulated affect states, 241
Modell, A., 108

Moffitt, T. E., 160–161
Morris, L. B., 106, 165
Mother, "good enough," 35
Mother–infant dyad, 48, 148, 224
Mother–infant interactions, 23, 32, 48, 77, 89, 241
Motivational systems, 23, 47, 49–50
Murray, R. M., 67

Narcissism, 27, 167n; malignant, 168
Narcissistic behavior disorders, 22, 37, 83, 133, 192, 196, 253–254, 261
Narcissistic personality disorder, 21, 27–28, 31–32, 37, 44–47, 70, 83, 101
   and antisocial personality disorder, 164, 168, 192–193
   and borderline personality disorder, 110, 133
   clinical illustration, 50–57
   descriptive psychopathology, 28–30
   psychoanalytic views, 30–36
   self psychological view, 37–50
Negative symptom syndrome, 64
Nemiah, J., 237
Neurobiology, 162–163, 192, 267
Neurologically acquired sociopathy, 162
Neurotic character, 153
Neurotic depression, 206, 208
Newman, K., 36, 40
Nonlinear dynamic systems theory, 47, 49
Normal personality (term), 14
Normotic personality, 240–241

Object (term), 37–38
Object relations theories, 147, 241, 253, 270
   and borderline personality disorder, 109, 113
   and depression, 218–219
   and narcissistic personality disorder, 35–36
   and paranoid personality disorder, 100–101
   and schizoid personality disorder, 64–66
Obsessive–compulsive disorder (Axis I), 107
Obsessive–compulsive personality disorder, 97–98, 101, 103, 115–118, 181
   clinical illustration, 128–133
   descriptive psychopathology, 102–107
   self psychological view, 126–128
Oedipal complex, 23
Oedipal conflict, 182–184

Oedipal stage, 180–182
Ogden, T., 47
Oldham, J. M., 106, 165
O'Neill, E., 116n
One-person psychology, 23, 48
Oral aggression, 220
Oral stage, 147, 217
Ornstein, P. H., 38

Pandevelopmental regression, 67
Paranoia, 99
Paranoid personality disorder, 97–98, 115–118, 133
   clinical illustration, 122–125
   descriptive psychopathology, 98–102
   self psychological view, 118–121
Paranoid–schizoid position, 65, 100–101
Paranoid style, 99–100
Paris, J., 28, 167
Part object, 100
Passive–dependent pattern, 150
Passive–detached prototype, 66–67
Persistence, 102
Personality Disorder Interview, 14
Personality disorder research, 11–25, 263–271
Personality factors, in somatic dysfunction, 235–238
Personality theories, and antisocial personality disorder, 164–166
Phallic narcissism, 31
Pharmacotherapy, and depressive personality disorder, 212, 214
Phenomenological psychiatry, 152, 206–207
Phillips, K. A., 110, 209
Phobic disorder, 70
Pine, F., 21, 31
Pollak, J. M., 106
Postdepressive phenomena, 214
Preemergent phase disorders of the self, 83, 133
Preformed inclinations, 79
Present State Examination, 13
Prison populations, and antisocial personality disorder, 157
Projective identification, 109
Proprioception, 67
Przybeck, T. R., 14, 102, 165–166
Pseudohysterias, 180–181
Pseudosublimatory potential, 33
Psychoanalysis, and personality disorders, 3–4, 18–24, 263–271

antisocial personality disorder, 166–169, 192

dependent personality disorder, 147–149

depressive personality disorder, 220

histrionic personality disorder, 151–153

obsessive–compulsive personality disorder, 103–106

schizophrenia, 68–69

Psychobiological model, 66

Psychometrics, 267

Psychoneurosis (term), 154

Psychopathology, and normal personality, 14–15

Psychopathy, 156, 158–159, 169–170

Psychopathy Checklist, 14

Psychopathy Checklist—Revised, 158

Psychophysiology, 162–163

Psychotic character, 99, 108

Quay, H. C., 159

Rado, S., 67–68, 71, 104–105, 217–219

Rage, narcissistic, 34, 43, 46, 121, 133–134

Rapaport, D., 153

Rat Man, 20, 103

Reich, A., 34

Reich, W., 19–20, 30–31, 64, 71, 99, 103–104, 152–154, 167

Rejection, 88–89

Relational psychoanalysis, 4

Repetitive dimension, 83–84, 118

Repression, 153, 249–252

Repression barrier, 251

Research Diagnostic Criteria, 63, 208, 221

Rickles, W. H., 239–241

Ritual, and obsessive–compulsive personality disorder, 105

Robins, L., 161, 164; *Deviant Children Grown Up*, 160

Ronningstam, E., 28–29

Rorschach test, 84–86, 123–125, 225–228, 257–261

Rosenthal, D., 62

Rubinfine, D. L., 218

Rubovits-Seitz, P. F. D., 127

Ruesch, J., 237

Rutter, M., 14

Sadistic personality disorder, 101

Sandler, J., 219

Schachtel, E. G., 124, 147

Schedule for Affective Disorders and Schizophrenia, 13

Schedule for Nonadaptive and Adaptive Personality, 13

Schizoid factor, 66

Schizoid personality disorder, 61, 69–70, 73–75, 85, 120, 133, 171–172

clinical illustration, 79–82

descriptive psychopathology, 62–67

self psychological view, 75–79

Schizoid problem, 77

Schizophrenia, 62–64, 67–70, 99, 107, 267–268

defining, 13, 16–17, 220–221

nuclear syndrome, 62–63

paranoid, 99

parental, 82–83

process/poor-prognosis form, 62

Schizophrenia spectrum, 62, 67, 99

Schizotypal (term), 67

Schizotypal disorders, 61

Schizotypal personality disorder, 63, 73–75, 85, 99, 110, 171–172

clinical illustration, 84–87

descriptive psychopathology, 67–70

self psychological view, 82–84, 192

Schmideberg, M., 107–108

Schneider, K., 13, 25, 62, 70, 103, 107, 152, 207, 211

Schore, A. N., 18, 72, 110, 163, 235, 237, 268

Schreber, Judge, Freud's analysis of, 99

Schulsinger, F., 62

Searles, H., 68, 218

Self, 21, 37–39, 74

action, 67

false, 36, 66, 77

fragmentation of, 42–43, 98, 115–116, 120, 141, 239, 265–266

true, 36, 66

Self-cohesion, 32, 38, 40–41, 45, 50, 76, 94, 116, 127, 239, 265–266. *See also* Fragmentation of the self

Self-depreciation, 38–39, 43, 146

Self-esteem, diminished, 217–218

Selfobject, 21, 36–38, 44

Selfobject dimension, 83–84, 118

Selfobject environment, impoverished, 76–77, 82, 116, 119

Selfobject functions, 21, 35, 39–42. *See also* Idealization; Mirroring; Twinship

Selfobject transferences, 46, 58

Self-pity, 147
Self psychology, 3–4; as deficit model, 20–24
    and intersubjectivity, 48–49
    later developments, 23–24
    and personality disorders, 264–266
    traditional/classical, 4–5
Self-regulation, and motivational systems, 49
Self-reporting, 13
Self-righting, 49
Self-selfobject functions, 21
Self-selfobject unit, 35, 223
Self-with-other consolidation, 50
Semantic aphasia, 159
Sensitization, and somatic dysfunction, 236–237
Shame, 43
Shane, E., 47, 50, 270
Shane, M., 47, 49–50, 270
Shapiro, D., 99–100, 105, 120, 131, 147–148, 153, 168–169, 195n, 253
Shea, M. T., 15, 206
Shedler, J., 17–18, 66, 69, 72, 102, 106, 112–113, 151, 155, 166, 215, 268
Siegel, A. M., 174
Siever, L. J., 15, 63, 72, 99, 110, 162–163, 267
Sifneos, P., 237–238
Smith, L. B., 47, 49
Smith, L. E., 28–29
Socarides, D. D., 224
Social inhibition, 70
Social–interpersonal theory, 148
Sociopathy, 156, 169–170
Soft bipolar spectrum, 211–212
Somatic dysfunction: clinical illustration, 242–247; personality factors in, 235–238
Somatic hyperreactivity, 247
Somatic hyporeactivity, 247
Somatic reactivity, 234–235
Somatization disorder, 154; self psychology view, 238–242
Somatizing personality, 237
Spillius, E. B., 218
Spitz, R., 31
Spitzer, R. L., 17, 69, 208
Splitting, 64–65, 109, 167, 253. *See also* Vertical split
Spontaneity, diminished, 100
Stage theory of development, 148–149
Stephens, J. H., 99

Stern, A., 107
Stern, D. N., 32
Stevenson, R. L., *Strange Case of Dr. Jekyll and Mr. Hyde*, 253
Stewart, J. W., 155
Stolorow, R., 47–49, 75, 134–135, 224
Stone, M. H., 121, 168
Structured Clinical Interview for the DSM–IV Axis II Personality Disorders, 13
Subaffective dysthymia, 208
Subjective object, 35
Suggestibility, 153
Sullivan, H. S., 68, 148
Summers, F., 36
Svrakic, D. M., 14, 102, 111, 151, 165–166, 215
Svrakic, N. M., 111, 166
SWAP–200 (Shedler–Westen Assessment Procedure), 14, 17, 215
Symptomatic regression, 110

TAT (Thematic Apperception Test), 87, 122–123, 225, 228–229
Taylor, E. B., 209–210, 212–213
TCI (Temperament and Character Inventory), 14, 215
Teicholz, J. G., 32, 270
Tellegen, A., 206
Temperament, 14–15, 267
Temperament–character model, 165–166
Terman, D. M., 45
Terminal personality, 69
Thelen, E., 47, 49
Therapeutic bond, 193–194
Tolpin, M., 32, 41, 46, 118, 126, 173–174, 183–185, 194, 201–202, 216, 222–223
Tolpin, P., 134
Tomkins, S., 47
Torgerson, S., 63
Trailing edge: in development, 194; in treatment, 45–46
Transmuting internalization, 41, 45, 116
Trop, J. L., 118
Twinship, 39, 41–42, 46, 78, 175, 265–266
Twinship transference, 39
Two-person psychology, 23

Unipolar depression, 207
Unreality, sense of, 223

Vaillant, G. E., 99

Vernon, P. A., 16
Vertical split, 34, 36, 167, 192, 196, 249–250, 251n, 252–255, 261
    clinical illustration, 255–261

Wallerstein, R. S., 50
Watson, D., 206
Wender, P. H., 62
We-self, 136
Westen, D., 17–18, 66, 69, 72, 102, 106, 112–113, 136, 151, 155, 166, 215, 268
Widiger, T. A., 15–17, 29, 151, 157, 159

Williams, Tennessee, *A Streetcar Named Desire*, 146
Wilson's disease, 234n
Winnicott, D. W., 35–36, 65–66, 77, 149
Winokur, G., 208, 211
Withdrawal, 77–78
Withholding, 71
Wolf, E., 42, 83, 115, 133, 195
Woody, S., 209

Zanarini, M. C., 110
Zetzel, E., 218, 220
Zola, I. K., 160

ABOUT THE AUTHOR

Marshall L. Silverstein received his PhD in clinical psychology in 1974 from Wayne State University, Detroit, Michigan. He is currently professor of psychology at Long Island University, C. W. Post Campus, Brookville, New York. He was previously senior psychologist at Michael Reese Medical Center, Chicago, Illinois, and director of training in psychology at the Illinois State Psychiatric Institute, Chicago. A diplomate of the American Board of Professional Psychology in clinical psychology, Dr. Silverstein also was affiliated with the Department of Psychiatry, University of Chicago, Chicago, Illinois, and the School of Education and Social Policy, Northwestern University, Evanston, Illinois. He conducts research on neuropsychological dysfunction and premorbid functioning in relation to the course and outcome of schizophrenia and affective disorders. Other areas of research and clinical interest are cognition–personality interactions and psychoanalytic self psychology. Dr. Silverstein is the author of *Self Psychology and Diagnostic Assessment: Identifying Selfobject Functions Through Psychological Testing* as well as 70 research and clinical articles.